China Briefing

Asia Society

The Asia Society is a nonprofit, nonpartisan public education organization dedicated to increasing American understanding of Asia and broadening the dialogue between Americans and Asians. Through its programs in contemporary affairs, the fine and performing arts, and elementary and secondary education, the Society reaches audiences across the United States and works closely with colleagues in Asia.

The views expressed in this publication are those of the individual contributors.

CHINA BRIEFING

The Contradictions of Change

William A. Joseph, Editor

Published in Cooperation with the Asia Society
Karen S. Fein, Series Editor

An East Gate Book

M.E. Sharpe
Armonk, New York
London, England

An East Gate Book

Library of Congress ISSN: 0740-8005
ISBN 1-56324-887-5 (c)
ISBN 1-56324-888-3 (p)

BM (c) 10 9 8 7 6 5 4 3 2 1
BM (p) 10 9 8 7 6 5 4 3

Contents

Tables and Figures vii
Preface ix
Map xi

Introduction: The Contradictions of Change
William A. Joseph 1

Racing Against Time: Institutional Decay and Renewal in China
Minxin Pei 11

China's Economic Progress: Is It Sustainable?
Penelope B. Prime 51

Gender Equality in China: Two Steps Forward, One Step Back
Nancy E. Riley 79

China's Popular Culture in the 1990s
Jianying Zha 109

Hong Kong on the Eve of Reunification with China
Suzanne Pepper 151

Taiwan in the 1990s: Moving Ahead or Back to the Future?
Cal Clark 195

The United States and China: Managing a Stormy Relationship
Steven I. Levine 223

Chronology
Nancy R. Hearst 249

Glossary 297
Suggestions for Further Reading 313
About the Contributors 317
Index 319

Tables and Figures

Tables

Table 1.1	Total Government Revenue in China, 1978–1993	22
Table 1.2	Share of the Budget: Selected Central Government Expenditures in China, 1978–1994	23
Table 1.3	Increases in Social Group Purchase of Consumer Goods, 1983–1992	27
Table 1.4	Rising Crime Rate and Declining Case Resolution Rate in China, 1985–1990	33
Table 2.1	Indicators of China's National Economy	52
Table 2.2	Comparative Infrastructure Indicators, 1992	64
Table 3.1	Indicators of Gender Equality in Selected Countries	90
Table 6.1	Indicators of Taiwan's Economic Development	198
Table 6.2	Indicators of Taiwan's Social Development	199
Table 6.3	Taiwan's Economic Performance During the 1990s	202
Table 6.4	Electoral Support of Major Parties in Taiwan	212

Figures

Figure 2.1 Gross Value of Industrial Output by Ownership, 1975–1994 62

Figure 2.2 China's Foreign Sector, 1983–1994 75

Preface

China Briefing: The Contradictions of Change is the first volume in the 17-year-old series to be copublished by the Asia Society and M. E. Sharpe. A biennial review of current political, economic, and social issues in China, Taiwan, and Hong Kong, the series ranks among the best in analysis of regional contemporary affairs. Since its inception in 1980, *China Briefing* has followed the regime of Deng Xiaoping; 1990s editions have focused on the succession question and the need for major institutional reform to accompany Deng's radical change in economic course. The defining moment in the period covered by the last *Briefing* occurred when Deng called for accelerated economic reform in early 1992. In the late 1990s, Deng Xiaoping still looms large, but mostly by virtue of his impending departure from the scene.

Broad and often subtle changes occurring below the level of national leadership occupy the foreground of the 1997 edition. From the limited reform of the early 1990s, governmental institutions have gained the momentum required to further transform themselves. For example, in 1996 the National People's Congress, once a pro-forma parliamentary showpiece, passed a revision of the 1980 criminal code that laid significant emphasis on the rule of law. But serious discrepancies between the party's economic and political goals may still threaten China's economic development. The existence of inefficient state-owned enterprises, for example, continues to drain the national budget. Economic changes are having an impact on two areas of Chinese society covered in this *Briefing*. The role of women is evolving, for better and worse, as more women enter the workforce and more girls suffer the negative effects of the one-child policy. And a mass popular culture has been born of powerful market forces. The final chapters turn to compelling issues outside the domestic sphere: Hong Kong's transition to Chinese sovereignty, Taiwan's unresolved relationship with the mainland, and the United States and China's inability to find a solid common ground.

Special thanks are due to William A. Joseph for his excellent choice of authors and superb job of editing the chapters. The Asia Society is grateful to the contributors for their fresh ideas and polished writing. Karen S. Fein, editor in the Society's division of Contemporary Affairs and Corporate Programs, oversaw the various phases of the project, and was assisted by editorial interns Lili Cole, Alison Ostrer, and Les Baquiran. We thank Philomena Mariani for her thorough copyediting and Nancy Hearst for her meticulous proofreading and checking of facts. Finally, the time and efforts of Douglas Merwin, Angela Piliouras, and Mai Shaikhanuar-Cota at M. E. Sharpe have contributed to the success of the volume.

Nicholas Platt
President, Asia Society
January 1997

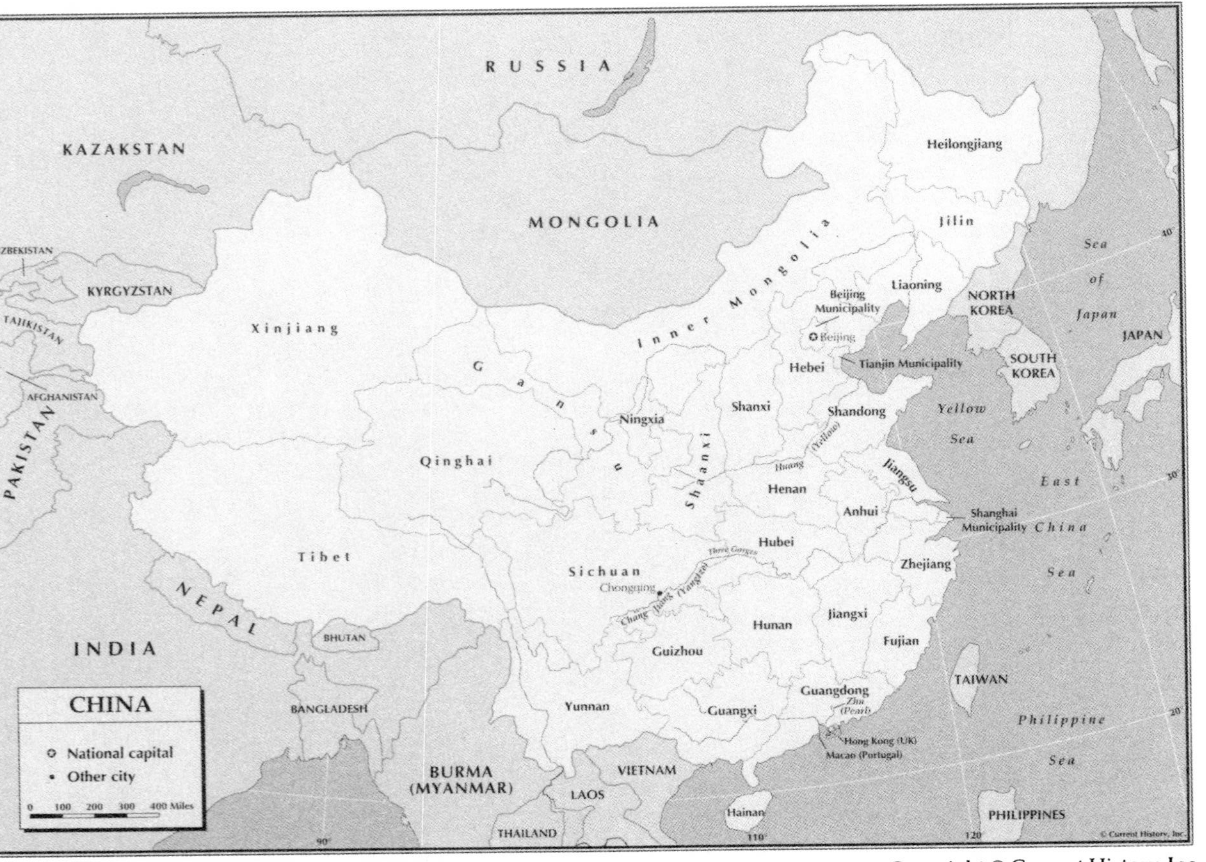
CHINA
National capital
Other city
0 100 200 300 400 Miles
RUSSIA
KAZAKSTAN
MONGOLIA
UZBEKISTAN
KYRGYZSTAN
TAJIKISTAN
AFGHANISTAN
PAKISTAN
INDIA
NEPAL
BHUTAN
BANGLADESH
BURMA (MYANMAR)
THAILAND
LAOS
VIETNAM
PHILIPPINES
TAIWAN
NORTH KOREA
SOUTH KOREA
JAPAN
Sea of Japan
Yellow Sea
East China Sea
Philippine Sea
Xinjiang
Tibet
Qinghai
Gansu
Inner Mongolia
Ningxia
Shaanxi
Shanxi
Hebei
Beijing Municipality
Beijing
Tianjin Municipality
Liaoning
Jilin
Heilongjiang
Shandong
Henan
Jiangsu
Anhui
Shanghai Municipality
Zhejiang
Hubei
Sichuan
Chongqing
Hunan
Jiangxi
Fujian
Guizhou
Yunnan
Guangxi
Guangdong
Hainan
Hong Kong (UK)
Macao (Portugal)
Huang (Yellow)
Chang Jiang (Yangtze)
Three Gorges
Zhu (Pearl)
90°
110°
120
© Current History, Inc.

Introduction: The Contradictions of Change

William A. Joseph

Near the southern end of Beijing's Tiananmen Square, not far from the Martyrs' Monument where pro-democracy demonstrators made their last stand in June 1989, sits the Chairman Mao Memorial Hall. This huge edifice, which opened in September 1977, is principally a mausoleum where Mao Zedong's preserved remains are on display for public viewing.[1] It has often been remarked that if the embalmed Chairman could see the changes that have taken place in China since Deng Xiaoping became the country's paramount leader in the late 1970s, his corpse would spin furiously in its crystal coffin: rural communes replaced by family-based, profit-driven farms; billboards touting not class struggle and unity with oppressed peoples around the world, but Coca-Cola and Sony TVs; young people flocking not to mass political rallies, but to discos; stock markets, private businesses, multimillionaires, beggars, and bankruptcies—everywhere trappings of the capitalism he fought so long and hard to stamp out!

Yet one consequence of Deng's reverse-course revolution might meet with Mao's approval: the many contradictions that have emerged from the rapid and far-reaching transformation

1. For more on the mausoleum, see Shang Rongguang, "Mao's Memorial Hall: The Attraction to Millions," *Beijing Review*, October 25, 1993, pp. 29–31. In Li Zhisui, *The Private Life of Chairman Mao: The Memoirs of Mao's Personal Physician* (New York: Random House, 1994), Dr. Li recounts both the process of and the political struggle over the embalming of Mao's remains after his death in September 1976. See also, Lincoln Kaye, "Mummy Dearest: The Expensive Art of Preserving a Great Leader," *Far Eastern Economic Review* (Hong Kong), September 1, 1994, p. 17.

of nearly every aspect of life in China in the last two decades. Chairman Mao was a passionate advocate of the power of contradictions—diametrically (or, as he would say, dialectically) opposed aspects of a situation—that he believed to be ever present in both the physical world and human society. "There is nothing that does not contain contradiction," he wrote in 1937 at the height of the civil war that pitted the Chinese Communist Party (CCP) against the Kuomintang (KMT); "without contradiction nothing would exist."[2]

Mao saw contradictions as the source of creative tensions that propelled history forward, and it was the task and the test of a revolutionary political party to grasp correctly the essence of those contradictions—such as that between the "people" and their oppressors—in order to steer the nation toward liberation and progress. Even after the communist victory in 1949, many of Mao's radical policy initiatives, including the Great Leap Forward (1958–60) and the Cultural Revolution (1966–76), can be seen at least in part as a reflection of the Chairman's determination to stir up and resolve the contradictions he perceived as lying at the heart of China's development under socialism.[3]

Mao would most certainly not agree that the CCP of the 1990s has correctly grasped the principal contradiction facing China by promoting economic pragmatism, cultural openness, and nearly unlimited ideological flexibility in pursuit of national modernization and prosperity. But he might get some wry satisfaction that the dramatic changes in post-Mao China and in its relations with the outside world have produced, along with remarkable economic progress, some truly epic contradictions.

The chapters in this edition of *China Briefing* describe and analyze the causes and consequences of the momentous changes taking place in the People's Republic of China (PRC), Hong Kong, and Taiwan in the mid-1990s. But it is the *contradictions* of

2. "On Contradiction," in *Selected Readings from the Works of Mao Tse-tung [Mao Zedong]* (Beijing: Foreign Languages Press, 1971), p. 93. For more on Mao's theory of contradictions, see Stuart Schram, *The Thought of Mao Tse-tung* (Cambridge: Cambridge University Press, 1989); Schram calls the theory of contradictions "the philosophical core" of Mao's thinking (p. 84).

3. See Lowell Dittmer, *China's Continuous Revolution: The Post-Liberation Epoch* (Berkeley: University of California Press, 1987).

change that particularly stand out as a conceptual thread running through the range of issues and places covered in this volume. Each chapter draws attention to the competing tendencies, divergent directions, and delicate balances that change has produced. The tensions and uncertainties that emerge from these contradictions not only define this particular moment in China, Hong Kong, and Taiwan, but will also profoundly shape the future of these areas as they each move toward decisive turning points in their distinct yet intertwined histories.

The title of Minxin Pei's chapter, "Racing Against Time: Institutional Decay and Renewal in China," highlights a major contradiction in contemporary Chinese politics: China's party and state organizations are becoming in some ways less, and in other ways more, capable of effectively governing the nation.

Pei dissects the who's who and what's what in the power struggle among China's potential post-Deng leaders, with an emphasis on the maneuvers of CCP general secretary and PRC president Jiang Zemin to consolidate his position as Deng Xiaoping's chosen successor. After all, which individuals and factions triumph in that struggle will greatly affect the country's future course. But Pei also wisely warns that given the uncertainties of power politics at the top, it is equally important to "focus on China's underlying political institutions" in order to understand the deeper trends in China's recent political development.

Thus, the "race" between institutional renewal and decay merits special attention. As of the mid-1990s it seems as if decay is outpacing renewal. Pei notes that Deng Xiaoping's "most important failure" has been his "inability to construct durable political institutions that can safeguard [his] economic legacies." This failure has already enmeshed China in a "governability crisis" manifest in ways that Pei details in his essay, including the growth of a "predatory state" that feeds on corruption and other abuses of public authority for private gain, declining social services, soaring crime rates, labor unrest, rural riots, and the continuing suppression of dissent.

However, alongside this decay, Pei detects "signs and seeds of institutional renewal" in China's political development. As evidence, he describes the evolution of China's legislature, the National People's Congress, from a party "rubber stamp" to an important (if still constrained) forum for debate and consultation in the policy-making process; the growth of the country's legal system and "public legal activism"; and the emergence of "experimental self-government" in the rural areas in the form of directly elected village committees and representative assemblies that give people in the countryside a political voice in local affairs. All these initiatives have been sanctioned by the CCP in the belief that they serve the interests of economic development, but to a large extent they have taken on a momentum of their own that the party may find increasingly hard to contain.

Minxin Pei's framework juxtaposing decay and renewal is a useful one for understanding China's political development in the 1990s. Furthermore, which of these contradictory tendencies prevails will greatly influence whether the country's political future will be some combination of autocracy and chaos or stability and transition to a less repressive form of government.

Perhaps nothing captures better the essence of the contradictions present in Deng's China than the notion of a "socialist market economy," the official designation given the PRC's economic system in a 1993 amendment to the country's constitution.[4] Penelope B. Prime's chapter assesses the record, current status, and future prospects of this hybrid economy, which is increasingly responsive to capitalist market mechanisms such as the profit motive, yet retains important elements of socialist-style central planning. Indeed, Prime notes that "many of the pillars of China's prereform economic and political system are still in place" and that, along with a number of other "bottlenecks and imbalances" in the economy, they pose a serious threat to the future sustainability of the country's phenomenal record of development over the last 15 years or so.

Prime's survey of China's contemporary economic terrain begins with the rural sector (70 percent of the Chinese people still live and work in the countryside) and features a discussion of the debate over whether China can produce enough food to feed its

---

4. The opening sentence of Article 15 of China's constitution was amended in March 1993 to read as follows: "The state practices a socialist market economy." This replaced the sentence, "The state practices economic planning on the basis of socialist public ownership."

people. She then turns her attention to the less-than-successful efforts to reform those resource-devouring dinosaurs of central planning, the state-owned enterprises; despite the growing importance of nonstate industries, Prime argues that continued economic progress in China will depend on making the state sector "more productive and profitable." China's leaders will also face critical challenges in providing the infrastructure (transportation, telecommunications, and energy) needed to support modernization and growth, devising effective macroeconomic policies (taxation, banking, and foreign exchange regulations), and keeping the international sector (investment, loans, and trade) a vibrant part of the country's development strategy.

Deng's reforms have certainly deeply affected the lives of all Chinese, but Nancy E. Riley's chapter on gender equality and inequality in contemporary China shows how the reforms have clearly had different effects on women than they have had on men. Riley's essay calls our attention to the critical importance of analyzing, in China and elsewhere, both the gendered impact of change and the impact of change on gender relations.

Riley finds that "economic reform has had mixed effects" on China's women. Changes since the late 1970s have brought Chinese women in general "unprecedented opportunities in many areas of their lives." As a result, more women are in the labor force and in schools than ever before, they have more sources of independent income and therefore increased influence in family decision making, and they have wider and more autonomous lifestyle choices, including in matters of courtship and clothing.

Yet gender contradictions still abound in the China of the 1990s. Inequalities between men and women as measured by indicators such as the gender gap in wages or educational attainment remain evident—and in some ways are increasing. Certain reforms have had ambiguous, negative, or even outright tragic consequences for Chinese women and girls. Mixed messages about female adornment and pressure on young girls to drop out of school so they can contribute to the family income before marriage pale in comparison to the gendered effects of the

PRC's efforts to sharply reduce population growth. China's population control policies have forced women into a difficult position between "competing pressures" from a state that wants to limit fertility and a patriarchal family system that values sons above daughters. This has led to the spread of sex-specific abortions, the death by neglect of baby girls, and the nonregistration or even the abandonment of female infants, marring China's demographic profile with the appalling phenomenon of many thousands of "missing girls." Nothing could remind us more starkly of the need to keep gender in mind when assessing the contradictions of change in China.

The 1990s has witnessed, in Jianying Zha's view, "a dramatic shift in China's cultural landscape," particularly in the area of popular culture, which is the focus of her chapter in this volume. She examines the appearance and stunning popularity of completely apolitical television soap operas, sensationalist tabloid journalism, rock musicians who sing of disillusionment and alienation, best-selling and sometimes even pornographic novels that "make fun of everything sacred and serious," and a cinema that has produced some of the world's most acclaimed young filmmakers.

Zha explores several dimensions along which contradictions have emerged in this vibrant cultural scene. First, there is the contradiction between the climate of political repression and official censorship that still exists in China and the wide-open popular culture that constantly seems to be testing the limits of the possible and "has helped to breed a new generation more interested in lifestyle than revolution." There is also the tension between the *mass* appeal of this multimedia popular culture and the likes and dislikes of China's *elite* intellectuals who consider much of it to be trash. Finally, there are the sharply opposing views about how to assess the overall impact of these cultural trends: the optimists see hope in the fact that popular culture has greatly expanded cultural pluralism in China and created "a range of new spaces and forms for both personal and social expression," while the pessimists see popular culture in China today as characterized by unabashed commercialization, irresponsible political apathy, and crude foreign influences. Cultural rebirth or cultural morass? In either case, it is just these kinds of contradictions that make Chinese popular culture such an interesting and important aspect of a changing China.

The final three chapters in this volume shift our focus beyond China's borders to developments in Hong Kong, Taiwan, and Sino-American relations. In each of these areas, recent changes have also created contradictions that both shape the present moment and will influence the future.

Much of the world's interest about what lies ahead for Hong Kong after it becomes a Special Administrative Region (SAR) of China on July 1, 1997, has focused on the question of whether Chinese rule will suffocate the colony's vibrant, freewheeling, and tremendously successful form of capitalism. Suzanne Pepper's chapter emphasizes the equally crucial political dimension of this historic transition. The contradiction between British efforts to promote democratic reforms in Hong Kong since 1992 and Chinese insistence that it will not tolerate such unilateral political changes is the source of some of the greatest uncertainty about what lies ahead for the territory.

Pepper analyzes the political roller coaster that Hong Kong has been on since the 1984 signing of the Sino-British Joint Declaration on the transfer of sovereignty. She emphasizes the importance of the Tiananmen crisis of 1989 and its aftermath (especially the collapse of East European and later Soviet communism) in setting the stage for the confrontation between the territory's past and future rulers by "politicizing Hong Kong, energizing the British, and provoking China." In the years since then, Hong Kong has witnessed many momentous political developments, including the tug-of-war over the contents of the Basic Law that will be the SAR's post-1997 constitution, British governor Christopher Patten's bold program for electoral and institutional reform, the establishment of parties on both sides and in the middle of the pro-democracy, pro-China divide, and the increasingly important role of the media and interest groups in the territory's public life.

These developments raise important questions: What role will Hong Kong people play in determining their own political destiny? How firmly rooted have democratic values become in Hong Kong after Patten's "five-year crash course in Western-style democratic development"? What will China's leaders decide "about the degree to which they should try to force Hong Kong into the Chinese political mold"? Suzanne Pepper's chapter highlights historical influences, political forces, and simmering tensions that will greatly influence Hong Kong's fortunes well after the Union Jack has ceased to fly over the territory.

The transformation of Taiwan over the last few decades from a rather poor island to one of the world's economic dynamos and from a harsh police state to a nearly full-fledged democracy is surely one of the great development tales of the second half of the 20th century. Cal Clark's chapter provides an overview of the origins and evolution of this transformation, but his focus is on the latest installments of Taiwan's economic and political miracles. He analyzes the "fundamental structural change" now occurring on the island as it moves from the manufacturing-based, export-led stage of its initial economic takeoff in the 1970s and 1980s to a high-tech, service-oriented economy in the mid-1990s. Taiwan reached a new level of political maturity with its first free, multiparty, direct presidential election in March 1996, a powerful symbol of the legitimacy of the island's "claim to be the first democracy in a Chinese society." Clark also looks at the considerable successes of Taiwan's use of "pragmatic diplomacy" to overcome its international isolation and reclaim a recognized role in world affairs.

However, another important theme of Clark's chapter is the downside to Taiwan's many achievements, such as the widening gap between rich and poor after decades of highly equitable economic growth, serious environmental dilemmas, and a contagion of Japan-like "money politics" and other forms of unscrupulous government-business collusion. But the primary threat to Taiwan's prospects for continued progress comes from the persisting influence of what Clark refers to as "ghosts of the past," issues that hark back to the Chinese civil war and the cold war. These "ghosts" include tensions with the People's Republic over questions of sovereignty and the still fragile, if much-improved relations between native Taiwanese ("islanders") and the mainlanders whose personal or family histories can be traced to the Kuomintang's last-gasp flight from China in the late 1940s. All in all, Clark remains "cautiously optimistic" about Taiwan's future. Nevertheless, his depiction of the contradictions in the island's economic and political development and in its international and cross-strait relations is a sobering reminder not to overlook the serious challenges that still confront Taiwan in its quest for prosperity, peace, and democracy.

According to Steven I. Levine, relations between the United States and the People's Republic of China are "drifting toward disaster." At the core of an escalating series of strains in Sino-American ties over the last few years are the contradictions that ensue when, "Like other rising powers before it, China inevitably challenges the superior position of the dominant great power." And compounding the problems of conflicting interests are the perceptions the two nations have of one another: Beijing sees the United States as "a meddlesome and arrogant superpower," while Washington believes that the PRC is a "troublesome upstart in global politics."

Levine reviews the "series of contentious issues" on which U.S.-China relations have lately stumbled, including vastly differing perspectives on the subject of human rights, charges of unfair trade practices and copyright piracy, arms sales and other security matters, and political and diplomatic developments in Taiwan—a situation that actually led to a show of military bravado by both sides in the summer of 1995 and early 1996. He argues that in the area of security (including the security aspects of the Taiwan issue) the United States and China must work particularly hard and urgently to build a mutually acceptable modus vivendi that adjusts their bilateral relations to the sometimes contradictory impulses of the PRC's growing economic and military power, the "trend toward global interdependence," and the balance of power in the Asia-Pacific region. To achieve this goal and get Sino-American ties back on a more positive track will require an infusion of "political will and diplomatic craftsmanship" that Steven Levine finds has been lacking in both Beijing and Washington in recent years.

Each of the Chinese areas covered in this volume is at an historic crossroads: for China, the passage to the post-Deng era; for Taiwan, the transition to a developed economy and mature democracy; for Hong Kong, the changeover from British to Chinese sovereignty. It is not possible to know with any certainty what lies beyond these crossroads, and attempts to forecast the future of these areas usually offer a spectrum of possible outcomes. For example, one scholarly effort to lay out what the PRC after Deng might look like weighed the likelihood of a wide range of different scenarios, including neoauthoritarianism, neo-Maoism, military intervention, democratization, and political fission (one variant of which is chaos).[5] This edition of *China Briefing* does not offer readers a crystal ball for peering into the future. But by probing some of the many changes under way in China, Hong Kong, and Taiwan—and the contradictions of those changes—it hopefully can contribute to a more informed understanding of that future as it unfolds into the next century.

5. Richard Baum, "China After Deng: Ten Scenarios in Search of Reality," *China Quarterly* (London), no. 145 (March 1996), pp. 152–175. Baum's own handicapping of possible scenarios for post-Deng China favors a "neoconservative" regime that maintains tight (but nonideological) political and economic control and bases its legitimacy largely on nationalist appeals; a close second in his estimation is "neoauthoritarianism," which would combine further marketization with "rudimentary 'rule by law' but only minimal political pluralism—as in Singapore" (p. 156). For a very pessimistic forecast of what may happen in Hong Kong after 1997, see Bruce Bueno de Mesquita, David Newman, and Alvin Rabushka, *Red Flag over Hong Kong* (Chatham, N.J.: Chatham House Publishers, 1996).

Racing Against Time: Institutional Decay and Renewal in China

Minxin Pei

One of the most serious flaws of any dictatorship is its lack of an institutionalized procedure for transferring power. This conventional wisdom was again proved in China in the mid-1990s when the paramount leader, Deng Xiaoping, became incapacitated, and the collective leadership around president and Chinese Communist Party (CCP) general secretary Jiang Zemin was nearly paralyzed by competition for power and delayed taking critical steps to deal with serious economic and political problems. The mid-1990s is a crucial juncture in China's tortuous and difficult transition from a hard-line communist regime to a somewhat softer one, as the country goes through a complex process of both institutional decay and renewal that will profoundly shape its political destiny.

The anxiety over whether Deng's monumental legacy of reform can be safeguarded by his successors is widely shared among many observers of China and reflected in the recent spate of works on various scenarios for China's prospects.[1] While the Deng era saw the most dynamic economic growth and rapid social change in modern Chinese history, the same period witnessed rapid decay of the political institutions of the old regime. Deng may be credited with a bold program of economic liberalization that has unleashed the entrepreneurship of the Chinese people, but he may also take the blame for an in-

1. See, e.g., Jack Goldstone, "The Coming Chinese Collapse," *Foreign Policy*, no. 99 (Summer 1995), pp. 35–53; Yasheng Huang, "Why China Will Not Collapse," *Foreign Policy*, no. 99 (Summer 1995), pp. 54–68.

ability to establish a solid institutional foundation to sustain his reforms.

The succession struggle is still unfolding in Beijing in the mid-1990s, with no clear indication of a decisive outcome. In the midst of such uncertainty, prudent analysts can only focus on China's underlying political institutions to search for clues to the most important and intriguing puzzles of contemporary Chinese politics: What are the causes and signs of the decline of the old political institutions? Is there a simultaneous process of reinvigorating China's governing institutions, such as political parties, the legal system, and representative organs? If so, can this renewal eventually produce the deep institutional changes that Deng himself was unable or unwilling to bring about during his reign?

The central concern of this essay is the declining capacity of the CCP and other existing institutions to govern China. The basic cause of the governability crisis in China (manifested in the loss of government authority and rising incidence of violent anti-regime activities) lies in the fact that the erosion of the institutional capacity of the country's political institutions has not been adequately offset by new institutions designed to replace the dysfunctional organizations and procedures of the old regime. The extensive signs of institutional decay (i.e., declining organizational effectiveness, rules, and norms of a political system) provide ample cause for alarm over a breakdown of China's economic and political transition. Nevertheless, there is at least enough tentative evidence of institutional renewal to provide hopes for a continuing evolutionary process of change.

The Politics of Succession

For all practical purposes, poor health forced Deng Xiaoping to cede his decision-making power to other leaders in 1994, although two years later his presence continued to cast a long shadow over politics in Beijing. A strong indication of the effective passage of Deng as China's supreme leader was the emergence of Jiang Zemin's political agenda and a series of moves by Jiang to consolidate his power. One sign of this came in early 1995 with the launching of a new anti-corruption campaign that bore the Jiang imprimatur.[2]

The collective leadership under Jiang first demonstrated its new resolve against corruption in February 1995 by arresting a high-profile entrepreneur, Zhou Beifang. The corruption charges against Zhou were initially vague (unspecified "economic crimes"), although it was reported that the police found a large stash of cash (several million yuan) in his residence. In a low-profile trial held in November 1996, Zhou was convicted of embezzlement of state funds and taking bribes, and received a suspended death sentence. Zhou's case was particularly noteworthy because of his status as a "princeling," the son of an influential official, in this case, Zhou Guanwu, the head of one of the country's largest steel makers, Shougang (the Capital Iron and Steel Corporation). The Zhou family also had strong ties with Deng Xiaoping's family. The younger Zhou was the chairman of Shougang Concord International Enterprises and Shougang Concord Grand, two of Shougang's five publicly listed subsidiaries in Hong Kong. Deng Xiaoping's youngest son, Deng Zhifang, was a senior executive of one of the companies associated with the Shougang Concord group. Within 24 hours of the arrest of the younger Zhou, his father was abruptly "retired."

Jiang used the anti-graft drive to target political rivals who were tainted by illegal activities. In April 1995 Beijing was shocked by the alleged suicide of its executive vice-mayor, Wang Baosen, who was closely associated with the city's party chief, Chen Xitong, one of Jiang's major political competitors. As the government's investigation of Wang's case unfolded, details of one of the largest corruption scandals since the founding of the People's Republic of China (PRC) began to emerge. Wang reportedly embezzled public funds and accepted bribes totaling $37 million. He was accused of living a decadent life and illegally lending the city's funds to his cronies and mistresses. Evidence obtained from the investigation

2. Jiang was also responsible for the adoption by the PRC of a more conciliatory line toward Taiwan (the so-called Eight Points) in early 1995. Jiang's soft line on Taiwan abruptly ended when Taiwan president Lee Teng-hui made a highly publicized visit to the United States in June 1995. Cross-strait relations deteriorated rapidly afterward. For more on this, see the chapters in this volume by Steven I. Levine and Cal Clark.

implicated Chen, a party hard-liner who had ruled Beijing for 12 years and played a leading role in the Tiananmen crackdown in 1989. Unofficial reports alleged that Chen had pocketed $24 million in public funds and led a life of debauchery. The CCP Central Committee launched an official investigation of Chen. At the Fifth Plenum of the CCP Central Committee in September he was formally expelled from the Politburo on charges of corruption, although he was spared criminal indictment. By early 1996, the government's investigators were able to establish the magnitude of the corruption in the Beijing municipal government under Chen's rule. More than 18 billion yuan ($2.2 billion) was missing from the treasury of the Beijing city govern- ment, making this case the country's largest corruption scandal ever. Most of the funds were transferred by Wang through various illegal schemes and accounts. More than 18 senior government officials connected with the scandal had been arrested by April 1996.

The campaign also ensnared officials of lesser standing. The government prosecuted 2,262 senior officials for corruption in 1995, a 27.9 percent rise over 1994 and a record in CCP history.[3] An important factor in the higher arrest and conviction rates of government officials was the active participation by a public that had been repelled by rising corruption in society. One official report claimed that about 70 to 80 percent of all the corruption-related cases prosecuted by law enforcement agencies in China were built on tips provided by the public.[4] Public anger at rampant official corruption forced the government to make several symbolic gestures. One of them was the imposition of a strict rule on the possession and use of official cars; imported luxury automobiles carrying officials have become one of the most irksome symbols of unchecked abuse of government privileges. In October 1994 the central government ordered that only officials at or above the rank of provincial governor or central government minister could be assigned their own cars, and these must be domestically made and have an engine no larger than three liters.

The crackdown on official corruption was accompanied by a

3. Reuters dispatch, March 17, 1996.

4. *Liaowang* (Outlook Weekly/Beijing), November 21, 1994, p. 8. See also Michael Johnston and Yufan Hao, "China's Surge of Corruption," *Journal of Democracy*, Vol. 6, no. 4 (October 1995), pp. 80–94.

hardening of government policy on internal dissent. Fourteen dissidents were put on trial in July 1994—the largest public prosecution of regime opponents since 1989. Coming shortly after U.S. president Bill Clinton delinked human rights from China's most favored nation (MFN) trade status, this move by Jiang and his supporters to accommodate party hard-liners seriously undermined Clinton's case for "comprehensive engagement" with China and was indirectly responsible for the downward spiral of Sino-U.S. relations in 1995. The most costly action by the Chinese government was the trial of the country's leading dissident, Wei Jingsheng, in December 1995, which ended with a 14-year jail term for Wei (who had already served 14 years in prison for a previous conviction of "counterrevolutionary" activities in 1979). Most analysts were puzzled by the poor timing of this move by Beijing and the enormous damage it did to China's image abroad. There appeared to be no practical urgency or necessity to put Wei in the headlines again, since Wei had in fact been detained by the Chinese police since April 1994 following his meeting in a Beijing hotel with the U.S. assistant secretary of state for human rights John Shattuck.

In part, the new crackdown was the government's response to resurgent dissident activities following a long post-Tiananmen hiatus. In mid-1995 more than 200 individuals, including many intellectuals and veteran dissidents, signed six different petitions calling on the government to adopt a more tolerant policy and reverse the official verdict that the Tiananmen protests had been a counterrevolutionary rebellion that was justifiably suppressed by the authorities. This represented the most audacious demonstration of opposition since 1989. The government acted immediately by arresting 22 and detaining 45 for questioning.[5]

When Deng's health deteriorated in 1994, Jiang Zemin began to consolidate his power at the top of the ruling hierarchy. He relied primarily on promoting his former colleagues in Shanghai, where Jiang had served as mayor and party secretary in the late 1980s. At the Fourth Plenum of the CCP Central Committee

5. *Far Eastern Economic Review* (Hong Kong), June 15, 1995, p. 15.

in September 1994, Jiang elevated two top Shanghai officials—Wu Bangguo (Shanghai's party chief) and Huang Ju (the city's mayor)—to central leadership positions. Wu was appointed to the party Secretariat and Huang to the Politburo. Another Jiang ally, Jiang Chunyun, who was the party secretary of Shandong Province, was promoted to the Secretariat. In March 1995, both Wu and Jiang Chunyun were given additional power as vice-premiers at the annual session of the National People's Congress.

In the meantime, Jiang Zemin, who is also the chairman of the CCP's Central Military Commission (CMC) and China's commander-in-chief, courted support among the military and elevated his allies to key positions in the military high command. At the Fifth Plenum of the CCP Central Committee in September 1995, Jiang managed to push through important leadership changes in China's top military command. He appointed two loyal supporters, Defense Minister Chi Haotian and People's Liberation Army (PLA) chief of staff Zhang Wannian, as vice-chairmen of the CMC. This move was widely viewed as the first step in easing out two incumbent aging CMC vice-chairmen, Zhang Zhen and Liu Huaqing.

While Jiang was arranging the personnel lineup inside the party, government, and military establishments to his political advantage, potential challengers to his position took a different approach. The most notable example was Qiao Shi, chairman of the National People's Congress (NPC), whose strategy was to strengthen China's parliament as a credible political institution to counterbalance the dominance of the CCP and the state bureaucracy. As one of the members of the Standing Committee of the CCP Politburo and a former chief of China's security apparatus, Qiao is a formidable leader and a force to reckon with in the succession struggle. Ever since he took over as chairman of the NPC in 1993, Qiao, who is regarded as a moderate reformer, has methodically strengthened the autonomy and power of the NPC as a lawmaking body, an important trend which is discussed in detail below. One of the most contentious issues in making the post-Deng ruling arrangement has been determining the choice of the next premier and the political future of the incumbent, Li Peng. Li's term expires in March 1998, when the NPC convenes its full session and approves the CCP's nomination of the new premier. Although Li, a political hard-liner tainted by the Tiananmen

Square incident, seems to have no other choice than to abide by the two-term limit set by the Chinese constitution, he is said to be unwilling to retire. Reportedly, he aspires to be either the PRC president or the general secretary of the CCP, both positions currently occupied by Jiang Zemin. Li's plans, if they are true, will surely raise troubling questions about whether Jiang will relinquish one of his posts in order to accommodate Li.

Equally problematic is the selection of Li's successor. Executive vice-premier and economic czar Zhu Rongji is perhaps the most qualified leader to take over the premiership. However, Zhu has antagonized many provincial leaders with his policy of recentralization and does not have a strong power base. Other leaders being mentioned as possible successors are generally considered lightweights, such as Wu Bangguo and Li Lanqing, both vice-premiers who have yet to establish a track record demonstrating their administrative and political skills. Therefore, the conflict over Li's new position and the choice of his successor will be the first, and probably the most crucial, test for the post-Deng leadership.

The high drama of the succession struggle in Beijing did not seem to have a significant impact on the mood of ordinary Chinese, as suggested by the results of several public opinion polls.[6] Most polls in the early 1990s showed no widespread anxiety about the possibility of political turmoil arising from a major power struggle at the top. Instead, several polls revealed a general willingness on the part of the Chinese public to allow the government to continue its gradualist reform and avoid a Soviet-type collapse.

For example, a poll of 2,500 residents in ten Chinese cities conducted in October 1994 by a private firm, the Beijing-based Market Research Consultancy, strongly suggests that the level of public satisfaction with the government had recovered slightly by the mid-1990s. The respondents considered the first decade of reform (1978–88) the "golden years," with 49.1 percent expressing satisfaction with the government during this period. Public support for the government plunged after the crackdown

---

6. As an indication of the political and social loosening produced by economic reforms, public opinion surveys have become frequent and reliable since the late 1970s. Aside from government-approved polling organizations, foreign market research firms and Chinese private polling organizations and researchers now conduct such polls.

in Tiananmen, with only 32.8 percent indicating satisfaction with the government during 1989–91. The level of satisfaction with the government rose a little after economic reform accelerated in 1992: 36.8 percent expressed satisfaction with the government's performance during 1992–94. Two-thirds of the respondents said that the country's economic conditions were improving; only 11.7 percent thought the economy was deteriorating. Nearly half of the respondents (47 percent) expected their standard of living to rise in the following three years, with only 6 percent fearing that it would fall.

The poll also revealed that a majority of the respondents (54 percent) placed a higher priority on economic development than on democracy. This seemed to be caused by a widespread fear of a Soviet-type collapse: 63.4 percent of the respondents agreed that "it would be a disaster for China to experience a similar change as that in the former Soviet Union." Such fear may also explain the considerable public support enjoyed by the CCP. About 40 percent of the respondents (excluding members of the CCP) said that they voluntarily maintained the same political position as the CCP. A different poll of 2,000 urban residents conducted by an official opinion survey organization in November 1995 showed similar results, with 70 percent holding a positive view of the government's policy of promoting economic growth and social stability.

Polls clearly show that official corruption remains the most important source of public discontent with the regime. The poll revealed that 71 percent of the respondents were dissatisfied with the integrity of government officials; only 4 percent said they were satisfied with official integrity. This was a sharp decline from the results of a similar poll in 1987, which showed that 28 percent were satisfied with the integrity of government officials. The November 1995 poll showed that half of the respondents called on the government to take more forceful measures against corruption.[7] Such polling data suggest that Jiang's anti-corruption drive was a carefully conceived political move

7. The above polls were reported in Min Qi and Li Wei, "Dalu shimin zhengzhi taidu diaocha" (Survey of Political Attitudes in Mainland China), *Zhongguo Shibao* (China Times Weekly/New York), October 15–21, 1995, pp. 48–49; UPI dispatch, April 13, 1996; *Far Eastern Economic Review*, December 7, 1995, p. 36.

aimed at not only damaging the reputations of his potential political rivals, but also appealing to ordinary Chinese in his consolidation of power.

Finally, the polls indicate that there were more channels for the public to express and address their grievances. This confirmed what many informed analysts of Chinese politics had long suspected: the slow evolution of China's political system during economic reform had created multiple avenues for redressing public grievances, thus helping reduce the pressure on the government. This was evident in the trend that fewer people went to the party or the state bureaucracy to press their grievances. In 1988, for example, about 43 percent of the respondents said that they would go to the "relevant authorities" (i.e., party and state officials) to make complaints. In 1994, 38 percent chose this option. On the other hand, the media and the People's Congress gained influence as forums to air private grievances. In 1994, nearly a quarter of the respondents said that they would choose the media to voice their complaints (compared with only 9 percent in 1988); about 22 percent said that they would present their complaints to the deputies of the People's Congress (compared with 13 percent in 1988). In both surveys only a negligible minority (less than 4 percent) chose public protest as an option.[8]

China's Predatory State

Compared with most of the former communist regimes, China appears, on the surface at least, to have made enormous strides in its transition to a market economy. The real size of its economy has quadrupled since reform was launched in 1979. In purchasing power parity (PPP) terms, the Chinese economy is estimated to be the third largest in the world (after the United States and Japan). It has also become a major player in international trade (the 11th largest trading nation in the world in 1995) and attracted the largest flow of foreign direct investment to

8. *Far Eastern Economic Review*, December 7, 1995, p. 35. However, the respondents had low expectations of the efficacy of their complaints. Only 29.7 percent thought that their complaints would produce results. See Min and Li, "Survey of Political Attitudes," p. 49.

emerging markets, and it had accumulated the world's fourth largest foreign currency reserves (about $80 billion) by the beginning of 1996. This list of impressive economic achievements, however, conceals the most important failure of Deng's reformist regime—its inability to construct durable political institutions that can safeguard its economic legacies. The fragile institutional foundations of the political system are the basic source of declining governability in contemporary China.

In the early 1990s, evidence of China's governability crisis was pervasive. Centrifugal forces have severely eroded the authority relations between Beijing and provincial governments. The central government's budgetary revenue had fallen to the dangerously low level of 12.2 percent of gross domestic product (GDP) in 1994.[9] Incidence of labor unrest was rising rapidly. Official sources reported that the number of labor disputes rose to 12,358 in 1993, a 50 percent increase over 1992.[10] In the countryside, peasant income remained stagnant in most areas, while the urban-rural income gap was larger in the early 1990s than it had been *before the reforms*.[11] Relative deterioration in the peasants' economic well-being was behind the rising level of rural discontent. Large-scale rural riots were reported in 11 major provinces in China in the first half of 1993.[12] The government's social control was evidently slipping, with surging crime waves in cities and the breakdown of law and order in villages. A poll in 1994 showed that half of the respondents were dissatisfied with the state of public security.[13]

Generally speaking, a governability crisis stems from the decay of key political institutions and the subsequent erosion of

9. State Statistical Bureau, *Zhongguo tongji nianjian/China Statistical Yearbook, 1995* (Beijing: China Statistical Publishing House, 1995), p. 26; hereafter *China Statistical Yearbook.*

10. *Far Eastern Economic Review*, June 16, 1994, p. 32.

11. Between 1989 and 1991 real rural income rose only 0.7 percent a year; although the rate of increase reached 5 percent in 1992, it fell to 3.2 percent in 1993, much slower than the rise in urban income. See *Jingji Cankao Bao* (Economic Information Newspaper/Beijing), March 5, 1994, p. 2. At the end of the 1970s the ratio of urban-rural income was 2.3 : 1; in the early 1990s it rose to 2.4 : 1. See *Shijie Ribao* (World Journal/New York), July 7, 1994, p. A16.

12. *Far Eastern Economic Review*, July 15, 1993, p. 68.

13. *Far Eastern Economic Review*, December 7, 1995, p. 36.

the state's capacity to meet the demands and needs of its citizens. Such institutional decay is reflected in a deterioration of the norms controlling the behavior of the ruling elite, which results in unrestrained abuses of power by the state's coercive and administrative agencies. This creates what political scientists refer to as a "predatory state" in which the government preys upon society to extract economic resources which are used more to support the privileged lifestyle of the elite than to benefit the nation as a whole.[14] There is substantial evidence that China is becoming a predatory state and that corruption and other forms of abuse of power for private gain—or "state predation"—has reached alarming proportions.

The most important measurements of state predation are the share of the economy the state demands from society as tax payments and the size of the administrative personnel in the state's employ. Using government revenues as a percentage of GDP and the size of the state's bureaucracy to measure the level of predation in China leads to a paradoxical conclusion: although the state's total revenues have steadily declined as a share of GDP since reform began, the size of its bureaucracy has grown enormously. Counting both budgetary revenues (mainly taxes) and extrabudgetary revenues (mostly ad hoc fees such as those levied in the name of improving public sanitation, environmental protection, and education), the total revenues of the government (both central and local) have declined significantly as a share of GDP between the late 1970s and early 1990s. (See Table 1.1.) Although the causes of the declining central government revenues are complex, three factors seem to have been most responsible for this trend: reforms of state-owned enterprises that have resulted in increased retained earnings by state-owned enterprises and lower revenues to the central government; poor performance of state-owned enterprises after economic reform increased market competition; and administrative decentralization that has permitted local governments to reduce their contributions to the central treasury.[15]

14. For more on the predatory state, see Margaret Levi, "A Theory of Predatory Rule," *Politics and Society*, Vol. 10, no. 4 (1981), pp. 431–65.

15. World Bank, *China: Macroeconomic Stability in a Decentralized Economy* (Washington, D.C.: World Bank, 1995), pp. 27–30.

Table 1.1

Total Government Revenue in China, 1978–1993

	1978	1980	1984	1986	1990	1992	1993
Revenues as a share of GDP (%)[a]	40.2	35.2	36.6	38.2	31.4	29.2	17.8

Source: Based on the data in *China Statistical Yearbook, 1995* (Beijing: China Statistical Publishing House, 1995), pp. 32, 223.

[a]Including both budgetary and extrabudgetary revenues.

On the surface, the fact that the state's revenues have declined drastically seems to contradict the claim that the Chinese state has become excessively predatory. However, several pieces of evidence suggest that the magnitude of the state's revenues as a share of total economic output represent an incomplete measure of state predation in the Chinese case.

First, the absolute size of the Chinese state, measured in terms of its personnel, has grown greatly in recent years despite the fact that 15 years of market-oriented reforms have significantly reduced the state's role in the economy and made redundant many administrative functions. The number of government administrative personnel in 1990 reached 31 million, compared with 13 million in 1980.[16] Cautious government figures indicate that in the early 1990s there were 600,000 excess personnel in party and government agencies at and above the county level and 2.1 million in township governments.[17]

Second, the predatory state exhibits a highly parasitic characteristic in that the huge state apparatus has been claiming a much higher relative share of *dwindling* state resources for its own consumption. This is most evident in the surge of the state's administrative expenditures in the 1980s. Such expenditures include salaries, benefits, certain capital costs (office buildings and official vehicles), operating expenses, and meetings and entertainment. Measured in absolute terms, government expenditures in 1990 were nearly eight times those in 1978. In

16. *Minzhu yu Fazhi* (Democracy and Law/Shanghai) (May 1992), p. 9.
17. *Jingji Cankao Bao*, December 21, 1993, p. 2.

Table 1.2

Share of the Budget: Selected Central Government Expenditures in China, 1978–1994 (Percent)

Year	Administrative expenditures	Investment in agricultural infrastructure	Pensions and social welfare	R&D expenditures
1978	4.76	4.59	1.62	4.76
1980	6.22	3.96	1.65	5.33
1982	7.87	2.42	1.82	5.66
1984	9.04	2.13	1.61	6.13
1986	9.43	1.84	1.50	4.83
1988	10.03	1.44	1.51	4.48
1990	12.00	1.91	1.59	4.03
1992	10.54	1.93	1.50	—
1994	14.62	1.84	1.64	—

Sources: China Statistical Yearbook, 1993 (Beijing: China Statistical Publishing House, 1993), pp. 215, 221, 224, 225; *China Statistical Yearbook, 1995* (Beijing: China Statistical Publishing House, 1995), pp. 215, 219, 221; *China Finance Statistics, 1950–1991* (Beijing: Science Press, 1992), p. 330.

relative terms, they more than tripled between 1978 and 1994 as a share of the central government's total budgetary expenditures. (See Table 1.2.) The central government expenditures in the early 1990s show that its administrative expenditures were from 150 to 170 percent of those for rural development and from 52 to 58 percent of the combined expenditures on education, science, and health care.[18] The data in Table 1.2 demonstrate that fiscal resources were shifted from more legitimate economic and social goals to the maintenance of the state. The share of agricultural infrastructure investment in the state budget fell from 4.59 percent in 1978 to 1.84 percent in 1994, budget allocation for research and development decreased from 6.13 percent in 1984 to 4.03 percent in 1990, and social welfare expenditures (poverty and disaster relief) in the budget remained stagnant through the 1980s—in sharp contrast to the rapid rise in government administrative expenditures.

Third, even though the state's formal extractive capacity (e.g., taxation) has declined, state predation in China may be assum-

18. *China Statistical Yearbook, 1993*, pp. 222–23.

ing a different, but no less rapacious, form. The deterioration in the formal revenue-producing capacity of the Chinese state has been accompanied by a proliferation of arbitrary fees and other informal levies.

Anecdotal press reports reveal that the levying of arbitrary fees by government agencies has reached epidemic proportions. Many Chinese government agencies (such as courts of law, police departments, government regulatory agencies, customs, and auditing and tax collection departments) have started charging fees for services that used to be provided free to the public. Prior to reform, extrabudgetary revenues equaled about 30 to 35 percent of the tax-based budgetary revenues. In 1992, mostly fee-based extrabudgetary revenues equaled 97 percent of the government's tax-based budgetary revenues.[19] And this does not take into account the extrabudgetary revenues collected by the agents of the state but not recorded in official statistics. This trend seems to point to the growth of a predatory state in China, since tax-based revenues are more tightly controlled and monitored than nontax revenues, which are less transparent, less subject to central control and supervision, and therefore more likely to lead to abuse.

This change in China's fiscal system has produced severe detrimental effects on public finance, created one of the most important sources of official corruption, and fueled public discontent. The Chinese peasantry has been the most vulnerable victim of this mutated fiscal system and borne a disproportionate share of the nontax levies.[20] Furthermore, a large body of evidence strongly indicates that a significant portion of extrabudgetary revenues is used to the direct or indirect advantage of officials. In 1986, 16 percent of the extrabudgetary revenue was allocated for government employee benefits, bonuses, and administrative expenditures. In 1990, 20 percent of the extrabudgetary income (53.6 billion yuan out of 166.9 billion

19. Ibid., p. 223.

20. One official study showed that, in one municipality surveyed by the government, levies and fees on peasants amounted to 16.4 percent of their net annual income in 1989 and 22 percent in 1992; the rate of increase in the amount of levies and fees they paid was 234 percent that of the rate of increase in their income. See *Minzhu yu Fazhi* (October 1993), p. 24.

yuan) was used for these purposes, exceeding the amount allocated to capital investment (52 billion yuan) and dwarfing the amount of extrabudgetary income spent on education (9 billion yuan).[21]

A large number of government agencies, motivated to generate off-budget revenues to increase their incomes and offset the dwindling appropriations from the formal state budget, have spun off their regulatory departments into separate for-profit "service companies," which typically earn money by charging high processing fees to business firms and private citizens. In 1994, 137,088 commercial firms were operated by government agencies and party organizations to generate income for these components of the party-state, a direct violation of the rules set by the central government.[22] Many of these government-affiliated firms provide for-fee regulatory, legal, consulting, and intermediary services that private entrepreneurs and other economic entities are required by local government agencies to use in conducting routine business. Other government-run monopolies (such as post offices, telephone companies, utilities, and railroads) imitated this practice by charging unexplained additional fees. In many localities, government agencies linked the bonuses and benefits of government officials to the amount of fines and fees collected, thereby reinforcing the incentives for levying arbitrary fees. A central government document disclosed that "most [off-budget] revenues have gone into cash slush funds *[xiaojinku]* and are used to finance automobile purchases, bonuses, wasteful consumption, and expansion of employee benefits."[23]

Finally, the most revealing measure of the degree of parasitism of the Chinese state is the officially reported sum of resources spent by the Communist Party organizations, government agencies, and state-owned enterprises on what may be called "privatized public consumption," which is govern-

21. *China Finance Statistics, 1950–1991* (Beijing: Science Press, 1992), pp. 212–13, 334–35.

22. Even after the central government issued a ban on such firms, only 25 percent of them ostensibly "delinked" their ties. See *Chingpao* (Mirror/Hong Kong) (September 1994), p. 37.

23. *Jingji Cankao Bao*, October 25, 1993, p. 2; see also the central government's document on the anti-corruption movement issued on October 5, 1993, *Jingji Cankao Bao*, October 23, 1993, p. 1.

ment consumption that benefits mostly the elite. Until 1995, the Chinese government regularly published the amount of *shehui jituan xiaofei* (social group consumption, or purchases of consumer goods by government agencies and state-owned enterprises). Such consumption included big-ticket consumer goods (automobiles, air conditioners, cellular telephones, color televisions, and stereo systems). Since the 1950s, the government's purchase of consumer goods has accounted for about 10 to 11 percent of the total retail value of consumer goods in China.[24] Throughout the 1980s and early 1990s annual increases in social group purchase of consumer goods rose dramatically, reflecting increasing levels of privatized public consumption amid China's economic boom. (See Table 1.3.) In the 1990s, a huge portion of government expenditures on consumer goods was used to purchase imported automobiles. One news report in an official publication estimated that, in 1992, automobile purchases and related expenses accounted for 60 to 70 billion yuan, about 70 percent of social group consumption and equivalent to the total amount of foreign and domestic debt borrowed by the government that year.[25] In addition, privatized public consumption in China also includes government expenditures on official junkets and entertainment. One figure disclosed by a government disciplinary agency, the Ministry of Supervision (Jianchabu), showed that such expenses amounted to 120 billion yuan, or 4.5 percent of GDP, in 1992 (excluding gifts purchased with government funds).[26]

Institutional Decay and Declining Governability

The degree and scope of state predation discussed above are symptoms of a more serious malady in China's political system: the decay of its ruling institutions. This process of decay produces both increasing state predation and declining governability.

24. *China Statistical Yearbook, 1993*, p. 611.

25. *Liaowang*, June 30, 1994, p. 15. The government borrowed about 67 billion yuan in 1992; see *China Statistical Yearbook, 1993*, p. 219.

26. *Cheng Ming* (Hong Kong) (July 1993), pp. 33–34.

Table 1.3

Increases in Social Group Purchase of Consumer Goods, 1983–1992

	Expenditures (billion yuan)	Change over previous year (%)
1983	25.6	13.7
1984	32.4	26.5
1985	41.0	26.5
1986	46.2	12.6
1987	55.3	19.6
1988	66.5	20.2
1989	69.7	4.8
1990	74.1	6.3
1991	88.7	19.7
1992	108.3	22.0

Source: China Statistical Yearbook, 1993 (Beijing: China Statistical Publishing House, 1992), p. 611.

Political institutions deteriorate for many reasons. For example, they may decay because of the weakening ideological appeal of a political doctrine that defines the missions and upholds the norms of such institutions. Such decay can also be the consequence of the emergence of rival social and political forces that compete for public support and talented individuals. A sudden change in the overall operating environment (for example, the introduction of economic and political liberalization) tends to generate shocks to established political institutions. Organizational decay of political institutions in authoritarian states often accelerates with the decreasing use of coercion.

Institutional decay may take several forms, ranging from massive abuse of power by members of the ruling elite to the progressive deterioration of organizational cohesion and effectiveness of the ruling party and the state bureaucracies. As the most striking manifestation of institutional decay in China, systematic and unrestrained abuse of power for private gains has become a pervasive feature of the party-state and has greatly alarmed the country's top leadership. One leaked internal party document revealed that the ruling elite had identified the following causes and effects of the decay of the CCP: erosion of the official ideology; loss of faith in communism; a growing gap between the slow institutional development of the party and government and the fast-paced socioeconomic changes; cadres' weakening identification with the party; low sense of party discipline; rising localism; declining authority of the party's central institutions; and decreasing frequency of organizational activities among a large number of party cells.[27]

Such institutional decay is reflected in the declining organizational effectiveness of the CCP and the government. Another internal CCP Central Committee document, which rated the effectiveness of provincial, prefect, and county governments, disclosed that nearly 40 percent were considered "poor" and only about a quarter "very good."[28] At the grassroots level, organizational decay of the CCP was similarly advanced. Two internal studies conducted by the CCP in the mid-1980s revealed that of the thousands of CCP branches in the countryside surveyed about one-third could be termed "effective," while 20 to 25 percent were rated as "poor" or "defunct." About half of them were considered mediocre.[29] In state-owned enterprises, long considered the bastion of social support for the CCP, it was reported that about 35 percent of factory workshops did not have a single party member in the mid-1990s.[30]

Institutional decay has severely affected the vital organizations of the state, such as the military, law enforcement agencies, and customs. The most visible symptom of the deterioration of China's military has been its unprecedented commercialization and extensive involvement in many forms of illicit activities. By the late 1980s, the Chinese military had set up more than 10,000 companies encompassing businesses ranging from manufacturing of consumer goods, real estate,

27. *Cheng Ming* (September 1993), p. 9.

28. *Cheng Ming* (March 1993), p. 17.

29. Dai Zhou and Kang Nongcheng, *Nongcun zhengdang wenti wenda* (Questions and Answers on the Rectification of the Party in the Countryside) (Beijing: Hongqi Publishing House, 1986), pp. 6, 56.

30. *Liaowang*, October 24, 1994, p. 5.

tourism, and weapons exports. In the early 1990s, one estimate put the number of military-owned firms at about 20,000.[31] The U.S. Central Intelligence Agency estimated that these companies generated revenues of more than $5 billion each year.[32] The military has also been implicated in several major smuggling cases. One of the most notorious cases allegedly involved the North Sea Fleet, which was caught using its warships to smuggle 2,200 cars from Russia and South Korea (valued at $23 million) in 1993.[33]

Law enforcement agencies in China have succumbed to the same process of institutional decay. The Ministry of Public Security's disciplinary committee acknowledged that between 1988 and 1992 more than 400 senior police officers (at or above the level of county public security bureau) were punished for corruption. A senior state councillor called the public security apparatus a "disaster area" of official corruption.[34] Increasingly, these state institutions charged with providing public services have turned their power into a means of extracting resources from the public. In Hunan, Guangdong, Yunnan, and Guangxi, there have been reports of police departments and local courts demanding fees from business firms that filed lawsuits and complaints.[35] Numerous official reports indicate that the corrosive effect of institutional decay has also reached the court system in China. Like police departments, Chinese courts must secure some funding on their own, since government appropriations meet only part of their expenses. One Beijing district court was forced to raise one-third of its total budget. In some areas, courts were given numerical targets for attracting investment and capital from overseas. According to a survey of the chiefs of local courts, they were forced to devote one-third of their time to raising money.[36]

The degree of institutional decay is most alarmingly regis-

31. *Far Eastern Economic Review*, October 14, 1993, p. 64.
32. *New York Times*, May 24, 1994, p. A6.
33. *Cheng Ming* (September 1993), pp. 20–21.
34. *Cheng Ming* (July 1993), p. 16.
35. *Cheng Ming* (September 1993), p. 30.
36. *Liaowang*, January 31, 1994, p. 23.

tered in the large numbers of reported cases of official corruption. The Central Committee's Discipline Commission reported that between 1983 and 1992 it had investigated 2.24 million cases of corruption and wrongdoing involving CCP officials and prosecuted and punished 1.8 million CCP members and officials. More than 63,600 government agencies and about 150,000 state-owned enterprises were implicated.[37] Official figures reveal a rising level of criminal penetration of China's state and political institutions. For instance, of the 41,866 criminals prosecuted for "economic crimes" in 1991, 5,390 (12.9 percent) worked in CCP organizations and government agencies; 16,879 (40.3 percent) worked in state-owned enterprises; 12,106 (28.9 percent) were agents of local government organizations; 7,491 (17.9 percent) were employees of collective firms.[38]

The institutional decay of a political system inevitably produces declining governability for two reasons. First, such decay negatively affects the level of government performance, especially in maintaining an acceptable level of provision of basic public goods (law and order, education, and protection of property rights). Whether a state can provide an adequate level of public goods is one of the most rudimentary measurements of a country's governability. Deterioration in the supply of public goods is a main source of popular discontent and rising ungovernability. Second, decay of key political institutions reduces the government's capacity to build and maintain social support and to solve social conflicts through noncoercive means. As such decay advances, the regime is forced to undertake more costly measures in order to maintain power, such as excessively high social spending or intensified political repression. Evidence from China indicates that declining governability has manifested itself in the deterioration in the state's provision of basic public goods, as reflected in recent trends in the areas of education and public health, law and order, and investment in rural infrastructure.

37. *Cheng Ming* (April 1993), p. 33.

38. *Xinhua Yuebao* (Xinhua Monthly/Beijing) (April 1992), p. 570.

Education and Public Health

Compared to other developing countries, China has been relatively successful in the last few decades in raising its overall level of human development, as measured by such indicators as the education and health of the Chinese people.[39] However, there are worrisome trends in both these areas of public welfare. The state's investment in education has stagnated or even declined slightly since the late 1970s. Its outlays on education decreased, from 3.3 percent of GDP in 1980 to 2.4 percent in 1994, despite repeated pledges by the government to increase spending on education.[40] In some provinces, the government could meet only 70 percent of the amount of the payroll for schoolteachers. By the end of May 1993 the total amount of unpaid salaries for rural teachers alone was 1.43 billion yuan. In the first five months of 1994 unpaid salaries for all teachers increased by another 500 million yuan, in addition to the hundreds of millions of yuan in back pay.[41] A direct consequence of the underfunding of public education was a rising dropout rate for both students and teachers. Between 1984 and 1993 more than 41 million students dropped out of primary and middle schools; in each year of the early 1990s low pay and poor working conditions forced 200,000 primary and middle school teachers to seek other jobs.[42]

The rural areas in China have so far borne the brunt of the declining provision of government-funded health care. Between 1980 and 1990, the number of rural hospitals and clinics fell from 55,413 to 47,749. The number of hospital beds fell from 0.95 to 0.81 per 1,000 rural residents. The number of health-care workers fell from 1.27 to 0.99 per 1,000 rural residents. In 1983, 12.9 percent of China's villages had no medical facilities. In 1990, the figure rose to 13.8 percent.[43] An official study showed

39. United Nations Development Program, *Human Development Report 1993* (New York: Oxford University Press, 1993), pp. 135–37.

40. *China Statistical Yearbook, 1993*, p. 927; The World Bank, *The Chinese Economy: Fighting Inflation, Deepening Reform* (Washington, D.C.: 1996), p. 53.

41. *Liaowang*, October 18, 1993, p. 8; July 11, 1994, p. 20.

42. *Shijie Ribao*, April 6, 1994, p. A19.

43. Population Research Institute of the Chinese Academy of Social Sciences, *Zhongguo renkou nianjian* (Almanac of China's Population) (Beijing: Jingji Guanli Publishing Co., 1992), pp. 520–21.

that in one region the state's budgetary allocation for health expenditures fell from 5.8 to 4.6 percent between 1980 and 1990; expenditures for preventive care fell from 25.7 to 14.3 percent. In another region, rural health-care professionals suffered an attrition rate of 86.9 percent in less than five years as many gave up health-related careers for more lucrative work. Such dramatic underinvestment in public health has created a deep anxiety among the rural population. In a survey of more than 1,000 peasants in the early 1990s, 99 percent reported "getting sick" as their number one concern.[44] The effects of reduced government spending on public health were registered in a slight but detectable deterioration of China's health statistics. The death rate, which declined in the late 1970s after reform began, rose in the late 1980s.[45] Some infectious diseases eradicated in the 1970s returned in the late 1980s. For instance, schistosomiasis, which had been nearly wiped out by the end of the 1970s, reemerged as a major health threat in the late 1980s, with more than 100 million people in China living in areas affected by the parasites responsible for the debilitating disease.[46]

Law and Order

In China, one of the most serious symptoms of growing ungovernability has been the rapid rise of crime rates and the government's declining capacity to cope with the breakdown of law and order. Table 1.4 shows that the number of criminal cases filed increased nearly fourfold from 1985 to 1990 while the case resolution rate declined from nearly 80 percent in the mid-1980s to 57 percent in 1990. An official survey of 12 provinces for 1992 showed that law and order was considered "mediocre" and "poor" in 28 percent of the jurisdictions.[47] The surge of lawlessness hit China's countryside particularly hard. Official statistics showed a doubling of the homicide rate between 1980 and 1988 in rural areas; it rose about 30 percent in the urban

44. *Minzhu yu Fazhi* (February 1993), p. 10.

45. In 1977 the death rate was 6.87 per 1,000; in 1979 it fell to 6.21, but it began to rise in 1980; in 1992 it reached 6.64. See *China Statistical Yearbook, 1993*, p. 82.

46. *Minzhu yu Fazhi* (February 1993), p. 16.

47. *Zhongguo falu nianjian, 1993* (Law Yearbook of China, 1993) (Beijing: Press of the Law Yearbook of China, 1993), p. 118.

Table 1.4

Rising Crime Rate and Declining Case Resolution Rate in China, 1985–1990

	Criminal cases filed[a] (1,000)	Criminal cases solved (%)
1985	542	78.8
1986	547	79.2
1987	570	81.3
1988	828	75.7
1989	1,972	56.4
1990	2,117	57.1

Source: Zhongguo shehui fazhan ziliao, 1992 (Data on Chinese Social Development, 1992) (Beijing: China Statistical Publishing Co., 1992), p. 263.

[a]Including murder, assault, robbery, rape, fraud, and theft.

areas in the same period.[48] The problem of banditry, long eliminated under communist rule, has returned on an alarming scale. In the first half of 1993 more than 10,000 cases of armed robberies of public transportation in six provinces (Yunnan, Guangdong, Fujian, Jiangxi, Guangxi, and Hainan) were reported.[49] Drug trafficking and addiction also reemerged as major problems. The official press reported that between 1991 and 1995 Chinese law enforcement officials caught 46,000 drug traffickers and sentenced more than 7,300 to death or life imprisonment. By the end of 1995, 520,000 addicts were registered; government officials estimated that there were at least one million drug addicts in China.[50]

Rural Infrastructure

Underinvestment in rural infrastructure is another dramatic example of the state's declining provision of public goods. The government's allocation for agricultural infrastructure fell

48. *Zhongguo shehui tongji ziliao, 1990* (China Social Statistics, 1990) (Beijing: China Statistical Publishing Co., 1990), p. 298.

49. *Cheng Ming* (October 1993), p. 23.

50. Reuters dispatch, April 12, 1996.

significantly in the 1980s. Government investment in irrigation projects in 1977 was 7.5 percent of the country's total capital investment; it fell to 2.9 percent in 1990.[51] Such underinvestment led directly to the atrophy of China's irrigation system and loss of irrigated farmland. The amount of reservoir-irrigated farmland declined from 252 million *mu* (approximately one-sixth of an acre) in 1979 to 237 million *mu* in 1990; in per capita terms, in 1979 each rural resident had 0.89 *mu* of irrigated land; this figure fell to 0.81 *mu* in 1990 (nearly a 10 percent decline in a decade). Soil erosion also worsened, resulting in massive loss of China's scarce arable land. In 1978 serious soil erosion affected 1.18 million square kilometers of land; in 1990 it affected 1.36 million square kilometers (an increase of 15 percent).[52]

Whereas declining governability attributable to the decreasing provision of public goods may be quantitatively documented, it is more problematic to gauge its political effects. In democratic systems, declining governability often exhibits itself in the form of weak and unstable coalition governments, political gridlock, and rising frequency of public protest. In authoritarian systems, its chief manifestation is an increase in mass anti-government political and social movements. In this sense, the massive nationwide waves of protest sparked by the Tiananmen Square movement in 1989 were probably the most evident symptom of declining governability in China. Similar evidence includes the large-scale peasant riots that swept major grain-producing provinces in 1992 and increasingly frequent labor strikes. Such incidents show that the government's deteriorating capacity to maintain social support and solve conflicts peacefully led to, on the one hand, more open and destabilizing forms of public protest, and, on the other, more frequent resort to repression.

Facing the problem of rising ungovernability due to the organizational decline of its ruling institutions, the regime is forced to adopt two costly measures, one economic and the other political. Economically, the government keeps providing

---

51. *Zhongguo shuili nianjian, 1991* (Almanac of China's Water Resources, 1991) (Beijing: Shuili Dianli Publishing Co., 1992), p. 701.

52. Ibid., pp. 656–57, 659.

large subsidies to money-losing state-owned enterprises to prevent massive unemployment and social unrest. In 1993 alone such subsidies amounted to nearly 5 to 7 percent of GDP.[53] Since most such subsidies were channeled through state-owned banks as loans, they have put enormous pressures on the banking system. It was estimated that by the end of 1993 nonperforming and unrecoverable loans to state-owned enterprises had reached 300 to 400 billion yuan (about 30 percent of all bank loans to state-owned enterprises made that year).[54] It is inconceivable that such subsidies can continue without causing a banking crisis.

Politically, the government has displayed an unusually high feeling of insecurity when challenged by the small but active dissident community. The government's sense of insecurity probably stems from its awareness of the declining effectiveness of its political institutions in countering such challenges with noncoercive means. As the regime is increasingly unable to mobilize support from its traditional social bases (such as the peasantry and industrial workers), it has begun to rely almost exclusively on the repressive organs of the state to confront internal challenges to its power. Such a hard-line policy has exacted a high toll on China's international image in the post–cold war world and made it a central target of international human rights groups. China's relations with the United States, which in ideological terms has shifted its global strategy from the defeat of communism to the promotion of human rights and democracy, deteriorated rapidly as Beijing's hard-line positions made it increasingly difficult for President Clinton to defend his policy of comprehensive engagement with China.

Signs and Seeds of Institutional Renewal

The alarming degree of institutional decay and its troubling political implications are causes for pessimism about China's pros-

53. Harry G. Broadman, *Meeting the Challenge of Chinese Enterprise Reform,* World Bank Discussion Paper, no. 283 (Washington, D.C.: World Bank, 1995), p. 15.

54. Chen Yuguang, "Yinqi zhaiwu weiji yu tonghuo pengzhang" (The Crisis of Bank Loans to State-Owned Enterprises and Inflation), *Caimao Jingji* (Financial and Trade Economics/Beijing), no. 6 (1995), p. 24.

pects in the post-Deng era. However, political reality in China is complex, and the same process of economic reform and social change that has produced such decay has also created forces of institutional renewal.[55] Both the rising demands of emerging social forces and the limited government-initiated reforms aimed at meeting such demands have driven this tentative renewal.

The transformation of deeply embedded economic and political institutions, such as the command economy and the Leninist political system, first entails the dismantling of many of their key components. Of course, the form and speed of such dismantling may differ from one country to another. In the former Soviet Union and Eastern European countries, the dismantling of communism assumed a more revolutionary form and was accomplished within a short span of time. In China and Vietnam, it has taken a more evolutionary form and proceeded at a slower speed. Moreover, the phasing of reform can also explain why pervasive institutional decay precedes institutional renewal. In the Chinese case, the first phase of reform (1979–92) was liberalization, which succeeded in breaking down the barriers to economic growth and individual initiatives. The unleashing of various social forces, such as private entrepreneurs, through liberalization was a prerequisite for generating the initial momentum for reform. However, the liberalization process at the same time severely weakened the old institutions of the party-state and reduced their effectiveness and integrity. In the early 1990s, as China entered the second phase of reform, commonly referred to as "institutional deepening," its leaders became more aware of the pressing need to construct new economic, social, and political institutions to safeguard the initial achievements of liberalization.

In the early 1980s, shortly after launching its economic reforms, the Chinese government undertook some limited political institutional reforms of the state bureaucracy, the legal system, and the representative organs. An important incentive for adopting such limited reforms was to avoid repeating the

55. For a brief survey of this process of institutional renewal, see Minxin Pei, "Creeping Democratization in China?" *Journal of Democracy*, Vol. 6, no. 4 (October 1995), pp. 64–79.

catastrophe of the Cultural Revolution (1966–76). An unforgettable lesson learned by the top elite who survived the Cultural Revolution was that political power must be constrained by certain rules. Mutual security would be enhanced and the costs of defeat in interelite power struggles would be reduced if firm rules of the political game were established and enforced. Since well-established institutions can stabilize expectations, reduce uncertainty, and lead to more efficient utilization of resources, limited political reform was also in the self-interest of a regime that experienced a serious decline of legitimacy following the Cultural Revolution. Its dwindling social support would not allow it to maintain the costly form of comprehensive and direct repression of society characteristic of Mao's regime. Such considerations provide an important explanation for the tentative signs of institutional renewal reflected in the limited political reforms adopted by the Deng regime since 1979–80, including the strengthening of the National People's Congress, the enhancement of the legal system, and the introduction of free elections of village governments in rural China.

The National People's Congress

A centerpiece of political institutionalization in the Deng era has been the strengthening of the autonomy of the NPC. In the prereform era, although the NPC was nominally China's supreme lawmaking institution according to the constitution, it was effectively a rubber stamp of the CCP and played the merely symbolic role of formalizing decisions made by the CCP. In fact, during the Cultural Revolution, the NPC ceased to function completely. In the Deng era, the regime allowed the NPC an increasing degree of autonomy. This process enabled the NPC gradually to become an important player in the decision-making process.[56]

A key factor for the growing role of the NPC in China's law-

56. See Murray Scot Tanner, "The Erosion of Communist Party Control over Lawmaking in China," *China Quarterly* (London), no. 138 (June 1994), pp. 381–403; Tanner, "How a Bill Becomes a Law in China: Stages and Processes in Lawmaking," *China Quarterly*, no. 141 (March 1995), pp. 39–64.

making process was the decentralization of power that was part of the general trend of reform since 1980. As the CCP relaxed its control of society and the economy, it delegated many routine governmental functions to specialized agencies (including the NPC) that are, in nominal institutional terms, separate from the CCP. In one researcher's view, the relocation of the day-to-day control of lawmaking from the CCP to the NPC accelerated the evolution of the latter as an increasingly autonomous political institution.[57] The CCP leadership aided this process by assigning a succession of party heavyweights—Peng Zhen, Wan Li, and Qiao Shi—to head the NPC and by clarifying, in a 1991 directive, the division of labor in the legislative process among the NPC, the State Council (the executive branch), and the CCP.[58]

This explicit arrangement of institutional power sharing enormously enhanced the legitimacy of the NPC in protecting its "turf." Its delegates now propose new legislation, subject proposed laws to lengthy debate, and offer amendments. Although the NPC has rarely voted down a law (except for one case in 1989 involving a law on urban neighborhood committees), China's lawmakers can now force substantive revision in the contents of legislation and openly voice their disapproval by voting against or refusing to vote for certain legislation as a form of political protest. Such assertiveness was clearly demonstrated in the passage of several important laws, such as the Enterprise Bankruptcy Law (1986), the Central Bank Law (draft, 1995), and the Education Law (draft, 1995).[59] In 1993, after the NPC rejected five drafts of a law on the formation and governance of corporations written by the ministries under the State Council, it wrote its own version and approved it in December 1993, marking a legislative milestone in NPC history; this was the first law exclusively written by the NPC, and not by the CCP or the State Council.

---

57. Tanner, "The Erosion of Communist Party Control," p. 387.

58. Ibid., p. 381.

59. Although all three laws were passed by the NPC, heated public debate accompanied all of them. The Central Bank Law and the Education Law encountered substantial opposition in the NPC's 1995 session, with a third of the deputies voting against the former and a quarter against the latter.

The NPC and local people's congresses have emerged as potential counterweights to the power of the Communist Party as these legislative bodies begin to have an influence in the selection and confirmation of key government officials. In several provinces, local people's congresses voted down the nominations of senior provincial officials and selected candidates not endorsed by the local party organizations. As a testimony to the changing political norms in China, the CCP accepted such outcomes. In the March 1995 session of the NPC, a third of the deputies effectively voted against the nomination of CCP Politburo member and Jiang Zemin protégé, Jiang Chunyun, to be one of the deputy premiers.

The NPC's 1996 session provided new evidence of the institution's increasing assertiveness. As a display of their dissatisfaction with the government's performance in law enforcement, 30 percent of the NPC deputies voted against or abstained from supporting the report given by China's top prosecutor on law enforcement and corruption. Nearly 20 percent of the deputies refused to approve the report given by the chief judge of the Supreme People's Court. More important, the NPC pushed through a landmark legal reform with a sweeping revision of the 1980 criminal code. Among other major changes, the new law, which would take effect on January 1, 1997, establishes the assumption of innocence of defendants. It bans the police from holding a suspect for more than 30 days without an arrest warrant (under the old law, administrative detention can last three years). The new criminal code has expanded suspects' rights to legal counsel by allowing them to consult a lawyer after being interrogated by the police (the old law allowed access to legal counsel only shortly before trial). The enacted reform measures, if fully implemented, would also give judges more power and permit them to be impartial referees in the court proceedings.

The NPC has also gained a role as a privileged forum for voicing public sentiment and redressing individual grievances. As mentioned above, an increasing number of citizens now choose to contact NPC and local people's congress delegates to make complaints. Each year the NPC's central office receives more than 100,000 letters from private citizens requesting help. Chinese media often report personal interventions by influential

NPC members in cases of miscarriage of justice by the government. In a much-publicized case in 1992, the NPC intervened successfully on behalf of a wrongfully imprisoned deputy in a city in Hunan who had initiated impeachment proceedings in the local congress against the city's corrupt mayor.[60] On another occasion, a group of political activists managed to secure the support of 32 NPC deputies in proposing a resolution demanding that Japan make war reparations to private Chinese citizens because the Chinese government has renounced its official right to seek reparations. This incident occurred in March 1992 during the annual NPC session and embarrassed the Chinese government as it was about to host the first visit by a Japanese emperor to China.

At the subnational level, provincial and municipal people's congresses have begun to guard their emerging autonomy by nominating their own candidates as deputies to the NPC, rather than simply accepting those designated by the government. In 1988 such locally initiated nominees made up about 15 percent of the candidates for deputies of the NPC.[61] There were also reports of local deputies abstaining in large numbers from voting for government-designated deputies to the NPC. In the elections of deputies of the Eighth NPC in 1993, local deputies filed more than 1,200 protests and complaints about "undemocratic practices" by local authorities.[62]

The Changing Legal System

China's efforts to establish a system of law through legal reform since the late 1970s have been extensively studied by Western scholars.[63] Although the leadership's original intention was not

60. For a fascinating account of the incident, see *Falu yu Shenghuo* (Law and Life/Beijing) (June 1993), pp. 4–8, although in that case the mayor was not punished but promoted instead.

61. Deputies of the NPC are indirectly elected. Typically, they are handpicked by the CCP and formally nominated by the presidiums of municipal and provincial people's congresses. See *Liaowang*, February 15, 1993, p. 5.

62. *Tung Hsiang* (Trend Magazine/Hong Kong) (March 1993), p. 10.

63. See Pitman B. Potter, ed., *Domestic Law Reforms in Post-Mao China* (Armonk, N.Y.: M.E. Sharpe, 1994); Stanley Lubman, "The Future of Chinese Law," *China Quarterly*, no. 141 (March 1995), pp. 1–21.

to build a rule of law, which would be inherently in conflict with the CCP's monopoly of power, its program of limited legal reforms has generated considerable momentum toward establishing legal rules and norms that play an increasing role in China's political, economic, and social activities. As measured by sheer numbers of laws passed by the NPC in a given period of time, China's record of legal reform looks impressive. Between 1979 and 1992, the NPC enacted more than 600 laws; provincial and local people's congresses passed 2,300 laws during the same period.[64] In this fast-paced process of legislation, China's law writers heavily borrowed from Western legal doctrines, concepts, frameworks, and technical terms. On the surface, therefore, many Chinese laws appear quite similar to Western laws.

The real difficulty of establishing a rule of law is, of course, not in the content of the law, but in the enforcement of it. China's progress in this area has been frustratingly slow, owing to its poor record of enforcement of existing laws. According to the office of research of the Supreme People's Court, of the 302,497 commercial cases adjudicated by the courts in 1993, 146,801 (about 50 percent) had not been enforced at the end of the year.[65] This finding was consistent with other estimates that suggested that the enforcement ratio of court decisions was about 50 percent.[66]

Despite such a poor enforcement record, China's embryonic legal system has had a subtle impact on social and political norms and the public's awareness of its legal rights. This has resulted in a form of public legal activism that bodes well for the eventual development of the rule of law in China. A telling case in point is a law that permits Chinese citizens to take the government to court for wrongful exercise of administrative power. Known as the Administrative Litigation Law, it became effective in October 1990 and marked a milestone in China's legal reform. Before its passage, victims of abuse of power by Chinese offi-

64. *Liaowang*, March 8, 1993, p. 13.

65. *Liaowang*, February 2, 1994, p. 20.

66. Institute of Sociology of the Chinese Academy of Social Sciences, *Zhongguo zhuanxing qi shehui fazhan de zonghe fenxi* (A Comprehensive Analysis of Social Development During China's Transition), *Shehuixue Yanjiu* (Sociological Studies/Beijing) (April 1991), p. 84.

cials had no recourse to justice, although a handful of bold citizens had tried to take the government to court for violations of their constitutional rights. Government figures show that about 44,000 such lawsuits had been filed by private citizens between 1983 and 1990 (averaging about 10,000 a year at the end of the 1980s). After the passage of the law, the number of lawsuits filed against the government rose dramatically, reaching 25,600 in 1991.[67] The number of such suits filed in 1992 and 1993 averaged 27,000, with citizens winning about 20 percent of the suits.[68] A large proportion of these suits brought against the government fell in the category of the definition and protection of private property rights and economic freedom. Typical cases reported in the Chinese media featured suits by peasants whose properties were seized or damaged by government agents and by private entrepreneurs whose businesses were closed down or who were harassed by local officials. These instances suggest that such laws have provided a valuable resource for ordinary Chinese in asserting their civil and economic rights.

The most pervasive impact of China's legal reform is on the country's economic activities. In an unreformed planned economy, laws played almost no role in enforcing contracts. But as China hurtled toward a market economy, the demand for legal enforcement of contracts arose. In the mid-1990s, China's courts assumed a central role in adjudicating economic disputes. In 1984, the legal system handled only 90,000 cases related to commercial disputes. By 1993, the number had risen to 900,000.[69] Although the poor enforcement record of court decisions in China creates serious doubts about the exact extent to which property rights are effectively protected, the removal of the day-to-day power of adjudicating economic disputes from the CCP and the state bureaucracy to courts of law is very likely to create a strong institutional incentive for these organizations to build and defend their autonomy and reputation, initiating a process of transforming a system of law into the rule of law.

---

67. *Falu yu Shenghuo* (October 1990), p. 19; *Minzhu yu Fazhi* (October 1990), p. 15; *Liaowang*, March 30, 1992, p. 3.

68. *Minzhu yu Fazhi* (January 1995), p. 6. The numbers here do not add up to 100 percent.

69. *Liaowang*, November 15, 1994, p. 11.

Another important factor for the gradual development of the rule of law in China has been the rapid growth of a professional legal community. The number of lawyers rose to 90,000 in 1995 and was expected to exceed 150,000 by the end of this century. In 1995 this community formed a national association, the All-China Lawyers Association. It is officially independent from government control. As a sign of its autonomy, the association's members voted out the officials of the association who had been appointed by the Ministry of Justice and elected a new slate of candidates.[70] Some members of China's legal community have become active in social causes. For example, the law school of Wuhan University has set up a Center for the Protection of the Rights of the Weak. It has more than 40 members, who come from the school's faculty and graduate and undergraduate student body. They perform pro bono legal work for ordinary citizens unjustly treated by the legal system or the government. They have gained a national reputation for defending citizens' rights. In one case, they successfully sued the police in Hangzhou for illegally detaining and searching a suspect and won a 700 yuan judgment against the police. They also defended a private entrepreneur wrongly accused of sexual harassment and sentenced to hard labor.[71]

Ironically, China's handful of dissidents have also tapped available legal resources in their struggle against the government. Zhang Weiguo, a well-known lawyer-turned-journalist jailed shortly after Tiananmen for his political views, used his legal knowledge skillfully to exploit loopholes in the Chinese legal system and freelanced for the overseas Chinese press from 1991 until he was forced into exile in 1992. He claimed that it was possible for individual dissidents to defend their rights and push for democratization using the methods deemed legal by China's existing laws.[72] Guo Luoji, another prominent dissident who taught philosophy at Nanjing University, sued the CCP branch of the university and the State Education Commission for violating his constitutional rights by banning him from the

70. *Far Eastern Economic Review*, March 7, 1996, p. 28.

71. *Liaowang*, July 21, 1994, p. 37.

72. Zhang Weiguo, *Hefa duoli he gongkai de liliang* (The Power of Legality, Autonomy, and Openness), *Cheng Ming* (October 1993), pp. 51–53.

classroom. Although the court refused to take up his case, the suit created a sensation, and the dissident was cheered on by his students and colleagues. Wang Meng, the reform-minded former minister of culture, filed a lawsuit against a conservative newspaper in 1991 for libel and "political persecution" after the paper printed an article attacking one of his short stories (although the court refused to handle the case).

The above signs indicate that China's evolving legal system will most likely become a focal point upon which the emerging political and economic forces in China—politically conscious citizens trying to defend their rights, private entrepreneurs seeking to protect their property and enforce contracts, and opposition groups attempting to challenge the regime in new institutional settings—will converge. The increasing autonomy of lawyers and judges comes at the expense of the CCP's power and, for that reason, might be opposed by party hard-liners. However, a politically neutral legal system might also benefit the CCP in the long run by taking some of the pressure from aggrieved and angry citizens off the party and enhancing its legitimacy.

Experimental Self-Government in Rural China

As described above, the institutional decay of the communist party-state has been most severe in China's rural areas. There is strong evidence that many of the 1.3 million CCP grassroots organizations in the countryside have ceased to function effectively. The erosion of the CCP's organizational presence, coupled with rapid social and economic changes, has generated both the demand and the opportunity for rural self-government. First, the collapse of the grassroots cells of the CCP has opened up opportunities for new political entrepreneurs to control local resources. Second, the decline of state authority and enforcement capacity in villages has led to rising insecurity of peasants' lives and property, which they now seek to protect through other political means. Third, random and arbitrary imposition of taxes and fees by local governments, as well as poor management of village finances, has aroused strong resentment from peasants who want the power to curb such abuses. Finally, self-governing bodies meet a vital need to organize collective efforts to solve local social problems and provide public services abandoned by the state.

To be sure, top CCP leaders have become keenly aware of the vital need to fill the political vacuum created by the deterioration of the CCP grassroots organizations. Although the first local rural self-governing body, the village committee, was organized spontaneously by peasants in the early 1980s without any support from the government and the CCP, the Chinese leadership immediately recognized the usefulness of such self-governing institutions in rural China. Rejecting the options of reimposing tight CCP control and of appointing village officials, the government endorsed the idea of allowing rural residents to elect their own leaders. Some senior CCP leaders, most notably Peng Zhen, who was then head of the NPC, enthusiastically promoted self-government in rural China. In 1982, the amended Chinese constitution granted legal recognition to village committees as a form of local civic organization. Peng was the driving force behind the passage by the NPC, in November 1987, of the Organic Law of the Village Committees of the PRC, which further sanctified the legal status and administrative functions of village committees.

This form of rural self-government spread quickly. By the beginning of 1985, the government reported that nearly one million village committees had been formed. By 1995, 24 provinces (out of 30) had passed local legislation on village committees. Despite the temporary setback following the Tiananmen crackdown in 1989, rural self-government continued after the revival of economic reforms in 1992. According to a report by a U.S. mission sent to observe rural self-government in China, more than 90 percent of the village committees were formed through local elections in the mid-1990s, and 20 provinces had held two rounds of elections by 1992.[73] In 1996, 18 provinces were scheduled to hold the third round of village elections. In addition to encouraging all villages to hold elections, the central government selected 63 counties (comprising 3,917 towns and 82,266

73. International Republican Institute, *People's Republic of China: Election Observation Report* (Washington, D.C.: International Republican Institute, 1995), p. 1.

villages) from 1990 to 1995 as "demonstration sites," which received more technical help and supervision from the Ministry of Civil Affairs in conducting elections.[74]

In terms of administrative function, the village committees perform the role of executive councils that manage day-to-day affairs. However, the newly formed village committees frequently are faced with difficult decisions that they lack the necessary authority to make. Therefore, between the late 1980s and early 1990s, another institutional form, the villagers' representative assembly, was adopted to expand political participation in rural China. Such assemblies complement the village committees and provide their decision making with a higher degree of popular legitimacy. Elected assembly representatives participate in the most important decisions made by the village committee (such as the budget and major public expenditures) and monitor and evaluate the work and performance of the members of the village committee. Surveys of Liaoning, Jiangsu, and Shandong show that an average assembly consists of 35 representatives (one for 10–15 households), all of whom are elected together with the members of the village committees (i.e., there are two concurrent elections, one for the village committee and the other for the representative assembly). By 1994, a government study estimated that at least half of the Chinese villages had elected such assemblies.[75]

Because of the relatively short history of this experiment in self-government and the enormous regional variations, it is difficult to assess its impact on the governance of rural China. While some newly elected village committees performed the role of local government effectively, others barely functioned. According to one news report, about 20 percent of village committees in Fujian were "paralyzed or semiparalyzed" in the late 1980s.[76] In villages where experimental self-government has

---

74. China Rural Villagers' Self-Government Research Group, *Zhongguo nongcun chunmin daibiao huiyi zhidu* (Report on Villagers' Representative Assemblies in China) (Beijing: Zhongguo Shehui Publishing Co., 1994), pp. 9–13. See also Susan V. Lawrence, "Democracy, Chinese-Style: Village Representative Assemblies," *Australian Journal of Chinese Affairs* (Canberra), no. 32 (July 1994), pp. 61–68.

75. *Beijing Review*, March 11–17, 1996, p. 14.

76. *Minzhu yu Fazhi* (November 1992), p. 40.

been successful, voter turnout was high. One official document reported a turnout rate of 90 percent in seven provinces sampled by a study team.77 The level of competition in these elections differed from one area to another. While some elections featured multiple candidates for slots on the village committees, others were hardly competitive. One report showed that non-CCP candidates won about 30 percent of the elections for director of village committees in demonstration jurisdictions in three provinces.[78] Many CCP incumbents have failed to be reelected. In the 1991 elections in Fujian, 51 percent of the 11,930 directors of village committees were members of the CCP.[79]

Although no comprehensive study has been carried out to measure the improvement of local governance as a result of the introduction of self-government in rural China, there is some indication that this institutional innovation may offer a viable solution to the decay of the communist party-state in the countryside. The Chinese official press has carried numerous reports on the improvement in law and order in those villages where free elections have been held. The management of village finances, provision of social services, and implementation of government policies reportedly have also improved in these villages.[80]

This bold experiment in rural self-government represents an historic step toward democracy in a part of China where nearly 70 percent of the population resides. Despite its slow progress and flaws, the enormous potential of this institutional innovation should not be underestimated. The electoral procedure will gradually gain legitimacy, and the electoral cycle can constrain the exercise of power by rural officials. A higher standard of local governance and greater transparency may also come out of the competitive dynamics of elections. This process may have

---

77. China Rural Villagers' Self-Government Research Group and the Chinese Research Society of Basic Level Government, *Zhongguo nongcun jumin weiyuanhui xuanju de diaocha baogao* (Study of the Election of Villagers' Committees in Rural China: Main Report) (Beijing: Zhongguo Shehui Publishing Co., 1993), pp. 88–90; hereafter *Main Report.*

78. *Minzhu yu Fazhi* (November 1992), p. 40; *Main Report*, p. 76.

79. International Republican Institute, *People's Republic of China*, p. 9.

80. See, e.g., Chinese press stories in *Minzhu yu Fazhi* (April 1992), pp. 32–35; (May 1992), pp. 39–40.

already started in villages where the experiment has taken root. Several elected village officials professed that they remembered the number of votes they received in the last election and knew when they were up for reelection. The trend toward genuine self-government in rural China seems hardly reversible. According to Chinese officials and social scientists closely involved in the experiment, "The dispute about whether village committees should be elected has been settled; the issue now is how to hold the elections and what type of rules to set in order to solve the political and social problems of the rural community."[81]

Conclusion

The evidence and analysis of institutional decay and renewal in China in the mid-1990s show a country in a revolutionary transition but with uncertain prospects. The parallel process of decay and renewal makes any firm prediction about China's political future hazardous and unreliable. On the one hand, the degree and scope of political decay are profound causes for concern. The erosion of state capacity and governmental authority is the primary cause of transitional ungovernability in China. The political weakness of the transitional collective leadership further hampers the government's ability to take firm action to reverse the alarming trends of declining governability portrayed in this chapter. Left uncorrected, there is little doubt that these trends would culminate in a systemic crisis threatening the regime's survival.

On the other hand, the tentative signs of institutional renewal provide some grounds for cautious optimism for a managed gradual transition to a relatively consolidated soft-authoritarian system based on a market economy. The institutional innovations embodied in the autonomy of the NPC, the establishment of the rule of law, and the consolidation of rural self-government will counter the trends of decay and provide some of the fundamental solutions to declining governability in China. The greatest challenge to Deng's successors is to slow the process of institutional decay while accelerating that of renewal. Experi-

81. *Main Report,* p. 111.

ence from the last 16 years in China suggests that, in this race against time, it will be in the CCP's interest to speed up these institutional reforms. Although such reforms may force the CCP to share some of its power with other political institutions and social groups, they will also allow the CCP to divest many of its old political liabilities. In effect, these new institutions may become political buffers that shield the regime from the powerful and uncontrolled social and political pressures that have been unleashed by the momentous changes in China since the end of the Maoist era.

China's Economic Progress: Is It Sustainable?

Penelope B. Prime

China's economy in the mid-1990s looks very different than it did over a decade ago when the country began its ambitious market-oriented reform program. While not all the changes have been positive, people's economic lives have, overall, seen great improvement. (See Table 2.1.) Since 1978 real income per capita has more than trebled. Wages have risen substantially. Even buying an automobile is now possible for some households. Since 1984 agricultural output has increased an average of 8 percent per year while industry has increased 13 percent. International exports and imports have increased an average of 13 percent per year. With these growth rates, China's prospects have looked comparatively very promising internationally, leading to record levels of foreign investment.[1]

These impressive achievements are the result of both domestic economic reform and growing interactions with the global economy. Many changes were initiated by government policy, while others were spontaneous, coming from local communities. But the process has not been smooth. The reform period has been characterized in part by a series of growth cycles reflecting a macroeconomic imbalance that has caused serious problems, including high inflation rates; this, in turn, has caused policymakers to retrench and slow down the process of change. Politically Deng Xiaoping's leadership throughout this period of immense change has presented an image of organization and

1. These figures are from State Statistical Bureau, *Zhongguo tongji nianjian/China Statistical Yearbook, 1995* (Beijing: China Statistical Publishing House, 1995); hereafter *China Statistical Yearbook.*

Table 2.1

Indicators of China's National Economy

	1978	1980	1985	1990	1993	1994
Gross national product (GNP) (billion yuan)	362.4	451.8	899.5	1,854.5	3,447.7	4,491.8
GNP per capita (yuan)	379	460	856	1,634	2,926	3,679
Gross value of agricultural output (billion yuan)	139.7	192.3	361.9	766.2	1,099.6	1,575.0
Gross value of industrial output (billion yuan)	423.7	515.4	971.6	2,392.4	5,269.2	7,690.9
Exports (billion $US)	9.75	18.12	27.35	62.09	91.74	121.04

Source: China Statistical Yearbook, 1995 (Beijing: China Statistical Publishing House, 1995), pp. 20–25, 32.

unity. But the party has been under tremendous pressure to justify the market-oriented reforms as "socialist" and to redefine its role within the new, emerging system.

The economic changes that have taken place in China have been far-reaching and challenging to make. Nevertheless it could be argued that they have been achieved through relatively easy and straightforward reforms. For example, major increases in farm production were largely due to altering individual incentives by dismantling the commune system. Likewise, easing restrictions on the development of nonstate enterprises contributed greatly to increased industrial output. But many of the pillars of China's prereform economic and political system are still in place: natural resources, including farmland, are still owned by the state; the core of the industrial structure continues to be state-owned enterprises; the legal system is set up primarily to support the government; and political expression remains severely curtailed. It may be, then, that to sustain economic progress in the next 10 to 20 years China will have to deal with some intractable and politically sensitive problems.

This chapter analyzes key economic bottlenecks and imbalances that represent potential constraints on China's future development, with particular attention to challenges in the areas of agriculture, state-owned industry, infrastructure, macroeconomic management, and foreign exchange. How China deals with these challenges will shape the country's future economic system and its prospects for development. A related theme of this chapter is the extent and nature of China's increasing interaction with the global economy, which will greatly influence both the economic opportunities and difficulties China will face as it approaches the 21st century.[2]

Agriculture

One of the earliest reforms of the Deng era was to dissolve the rural communes and replace them with the "household responsibility system" as the basis of China's agricultural economy. In a sharp break with the previous system of collectivized control of production, families could now contract with the village government for the use of land and, in return, sell a predetermined amount of output to the state at set prices. The rest they could keep to consume themselves or sell at market prices. Government procurement prices for grain and produce were raised to give families an additional incentive to bear the inherent risks of such a system and to produce as much as possible.

The introduction of the household responsibility system led to major increases in agricultural output largely because of the new tie between hard work and increased income. Between 1978 and 1988 growth in the gross value of agricultural output increased an average of 15 percent per year compared with only 4 percent between 1952 and the late 1970s.[3] But relying on the incentive effects of the household responsibility system to increase agricultural output is likely to work only in the short run.

---

2. Much of this chapter is based on fieldwork in China in 1994 and 1995. I would like to thank Ms. Cheryl Xiaoning Long for her research assistance while I was in Beijing in 1995.

3. Shwu-Eng H. Webb and Francis C. Tuan, "China's Agricultural Reforms: Evaluation and Outlook," in *China's Economic Dilemmas in the 1990s: The Problems of Reforms, Modernization, and Interdependence: Study Papers Submitted to the Joint Economic Committee, Congress of the United States*, Vol. 1 (Washington, D.C.: U.S. Government Printing Office, 1991), pp. 366–67. Reprinted by M.E. Sharpe, Armonk, N.Y., 1992.

Indeed, since the mid-1980s increases have slowed substantially.[4] To achieve continued growth in agriculture after the incentive system has been well established other steps have to be taken, such as increasing the use of fertilizer, developing new strains of seeds, and raising the state purchasing price of grain, all of which have been part of recent official policy.

A major concern in assessing the future of Chinese agriculture has been the decline in arable land in a country where already only 7 percent of the area is cultivatable.[5] Land is in greater and greater demand for uses other than farming such as housing and rural industries. In 1957, 111 million hectares were cultivated; by 1990 this had fallen to 95 million hectares.[6] Between 1983 and 1993 the average annual decline in cultivated land was 325,000 hectares.[7] A 1984 conference on land management in China was followed by a series of land-use surveys, which led in turn to the passage of a land management law in 1986 that set guidelines and application procedures for using land for nonagricultural purposes; nevertheless, declining arable land remains a serious problem for Chinese agriculture.

Another major concern about food production is the size and growth of the country's population. China's population of over 1.2 billion people has been growing at approximately 1.1 percent per year, adding approximately 12 million people per year. Projections generally are optimistic that the population growth rate will fall to .9 percent between 1995 and 2000 and to .8 percent between 2000 and 2005. However, this still means that China's population will not stabilize until approximately 2030 when there will be about 1.5 billion people to support.[8]

The population, land use, and environmental challenges that China faces have created a concern in some quarters about

4. Terry Sicular, "China's Agricultural Policy During the Reform Period," in *China's Economic Dilemmas in the 1990s*, pp. 340–64.

5. Leo Orleans, "Loss and Misuse of China's Cultivated Land," in *China's Economic Dilemmas in the 1990s*, pp. 403–17.

6. Susumu Yabuki, *China's New Political Economy: The Giant Awakes*, trans. Stephen M. Harner (Boulder, Colo.: Westview Press, 1995), p. 93.

7. D. Gale Johnson, "Chinese Farmers Can Feed the Future," *China Daily* (New York), July 12 and 13, 1995, p. 4.

8. Based on figures from the U.S. Bureau of the Census, International Programs Center.

whether China—or even the world—will be able to supply the country with enough food to feed its people adequately. In the early 1990s several forces came together to cause alarm among some experts in China and abroad about the future of Chinese agricultural production. Between 1992 and 1995 China went from having net exports of grain of about 7.5 billion tons to net imports of about twice that amount. This was a huge turnaround and profoundly affected world grain markets. This swing called attention to several related trends. Consumption of meat in China was growing quickly, which led to a substantial increase in the demand for grain to feed the livestock. Arable land was declining due to rural industrialization and suburban sprawl, and land for planting grain was decreasing as other crops became more profitable. Because of growing demand and poor conservation, water supplies were dwindling quickly. And due to more profitable alternatives, investment in agriculture was low and falling.

In 1994 Lester Brown published an article in *World Watch*, the journal of the Worldwatch Institute, and a book the next year entitled *Who Will Feed China? Wake-Up Call for a Small Planet*.[9] Brown predicted that, based on a conservative estimate, China's grain production would fall by one-fifth by the year 2030 due primarily to the loss of cropland and growing scarcity of water. Based on China's 1990 harvest, he argued that this implied that annual output would be approximately 272 million tons. On the demand side Brown analyzed two scenarios. In the first scenario, average consumption of grain would remain at its current level of 300 kilograms per person per year. In the second scenario, average consumption would rise to 400 kilograms, which is equal to Taiwan's grain consumption and about half that of the United States. In the "status quo" scenario, demand would equal 479 million tons of grain per year, while in the "growth" scenario, it would rise to 641 million tons. These scenarios imply that China will have a grain shortfall of between 207 and 369 million tons by 2030, which might be met with imports. With the 369 million tons being more than double current *total* world

9. Lester R. Brown, *Who Will Feed China? Wake-Up Call for a Small Planet* (New York: W.W. Norton, 1995).

grain exports, Brown suggested that such huge imports by China would have serious negative impacts on the supplies and prices of food worldwide.

The gloomy projections put forth by Brown caused reevaluations and reactions by other analysts and by Chinese policymakers. Analysts who tend to disagree with Brown's calculations offer several counterarguments that suggest a more optimistic scenario.[10] The main critique is that Brown's estimates simply extend current trends into the future without considering how the world and China will respond to the growing value of food production. First, if grain prices rise, both Chinese and foreign farmers will be willing to grow more grain. Higher grain prices would also help reduce the speed at which farmland in China is being converted to other uses and reduce the amount of grain and meat that people are willing to buy. Second, it is argued that instead of experiencing an absolute decrease in grain production over the next few decades, China actually has room for continued growth in output. This argument is based on the fact that the amount of cultivated land is substantially underestimated in China. Third, improvements in the transport and storage of grain alone would increase available grain by 10 to 20 percent. Fourth, there is the prospect that improvements in seed strains and other technological changes will have a positive effect on grain production. Finally, some analysts point to a number of policy reforms that could have a positive impact on the availability of food.[11] For example, they recommend that China develop a national grain market rather than rely on state distribution and regional markets; use the international market to make up short-run deficits and absorb short-run surpluses; allow buying and selling instead of just contracting of land so that farm size can adjust to improve efficiency; and allow more market incentives to guide the development of agriculture. Even those who see a less dire situation, however, acknowledge that

10. Frederick Crook and Bill Coyle, "China's Rising Imports Will Not Cause Global Grain Shortage," *APEC Agricultural and Trade Report*, Economic Research Service, USDA, AER734 (May 1996), pp. 1–4; D. Gale Johnson, "Does China Have a Grain Problem?" *China Economic Review*, Vol. 5, no. 1 (1994), pp. 1–14.

11. Sicular, "China's Agricultural Policy," argues that the decline in agricultural growth in the mid-1980s was due primarily to policy changes.

China has a number of major challenges ahead in terms of improving its agricultural sector, including solving the already serious water shortage and slowing the decline in the amount of arable land.

Within China, policymakers take the issue of grain production very seriously and are wary of too much dependence on international markets. Brown's predictions spurred more discussion of these issues, and he was invited to visit China in the summer of 1995. China's official estimate of grain needs by 2030 is 600 million tons per year, which is close to Brown's estimate of 641 million. More at issue is how much output can be increased. By Chinese estimates, grain output needs to increase by over 62 million tons per year on average for the next five years compared with an average annual increase of only 55 million tons since 1985.[12] In the mid-1990s policy responses to this challenge included standard government directives combined with some market incentives. For example, in 1995 the central government directed provincial leaders to increase grain production in each of their provinces, presumably primarily by contracting with households for more grain production and regulating more closely what land is converted to industrial uses. The Ninth Five-Year Plan (1996–2000) gives a fairly high profile to agriculture, and to grain in particular. The goal is to increase grain output to 500 million tons by the year 2000 by increasing investment, protecting land, reducing pollution, and adjusting prices.

While Lester Brown's estimates of China's potential grain production may be too low, Brown and others are probably correct in their predictions that China will become a net importer of grain and other food as its industrialization continues, despite policies designed by Chinese leaders to stimulate continued agricultural growth. But the question remains: how large will net imports be? The more optimistic estimates are around 100 million tons by 2030—rather than more than 350 million tons as Brown suggests. In either case, since China's low percentage of arable land area means its global comparative advan-

12. "More Land Sown to Grain" and Wang Xin, "Green Revolution," *Beijing Review*, April 8–14, 1996, pp. 7 and 12 respectively.

tage is most likely not in agricultural products, a trend toward increased food imports is not necessarily a bad development. In addition, farmers in other countries will benefit greatly from the fact that increases in China's demand for food imports will raise the prices for their products and the value of their land.

Industry

While sustained agricultural growth is required to meet China's increasing need for food and industrial inputs, industry itself is also a key component of China's future economic progress. In 1996 there were an estimated 80 to 100 million underemployed people in China, mostly in rural areas, to be employed by industry or services, in addition to the growing numbers of young people entering the labor market. Furthermore, major increases in productivity need to come from industry if wages are to rise and improve the average standard of living. And through industry China can best meet growing domestic demand and produce exports to earn the foreign exchange it needs to pay for imported technology, food, and consumer goods.

China's industrial sector is divided into two general categories: state-owned and nonstate-owned enterprises. State-owned enterprises are in principle owned by all the people and supervised by one or more levels of government administration, including the central, provincial, municipal, county, township, or village levels. Workers earn a wage and often a bonus, housing and other services are provided, and jobs are generally secure. China has approximately 108,000 state-owned enterprises, employing over 100 million workers. About 13,700 of them are classified as large- or medium-sized. State-owned enterprises dominate certain sectors, especially materials used in production, producing over 70 percent of the output value of coal, petroleum and natural gas, smelting of ferrous metals, logging, electric power, and water supply.

State enterprise reform has been an important part of the overall reform program. State enterprises were the backbone of the centrally planned economy. They were given output targets and matched inputs, all with fixed planned prices, in monthly, annual, and five-year planning periods. Investment was also decided by planners, as was the allocation and transport of the final products. Planning took place at central, provincial, and local levels. In the mid-1990s, relatively few items are still produced in this way. Central allocation of materials used in production ("producer goods") declined from 837 kinds of commodities in 1980 to 19 by 1992 (including commodities such as steel products, coal, and nitric acid); only 14 consumer goods (including grain and vegetable oils) were subject to central allocation by 1992, down from 274 in 1980.[13] In addition, none of these goods were 100 percent controlled by the central government. In the early 1990s prices were still centrally planned for about a thousand products, even if output targets were not.[14] Although government agencies had less to say than they did in prereform China about what was produced and at what prices, they continued to play an important, if declining, role in the distribution system.

With the decline of central planning, state enterprises have increasingly made their own decisions about what products to produce and where to sell them. For the first time managers had to be concerned with what potential customers would buy, as well as increasing the demand for their products through advertising and competing on the basis of quality and price. Correspondingly, under the reforms enterprises pay a profit tax of approximately 33 percent, retaining the rest for their own use (e.g., to buy new technology or build new worker housing) rather than turning most of their profit over to the state. They also have the discretion to offer their employees bonuses based on job performance and more leeway to determine wages than ever before.

Some state enterprises have responded positively to the market and enterprise reforms as evidenced by changes in their output mix, improvement in the quality of their products for domestic and foreign customers, and improvement in produc-

---

13. Anjali Kumar, *China: Internal Market Development and Regulation* (Washington, D.C.: World Bank, 1994), pp. 58–60.

14. Yabuki, *China's New Political Economy*, p. 128.

tivity measures. However, making the changes necessary to survive in this new economic environment is a major challenge. Many state enterprises are experiencing serious problems, with up to half losing money annually. In the first quarter of 1996 losses by the state sector outweighed profits for the first time.[15] This situation has not helped government tax revenues, and even more important, has been a drain on central and provincial resources to keep them operating. These enterprises also owe a great deal of money to other enterprises and to banks. Dynamic growth in the nonstate industrial sector has helped give China some time to figure out how to improve the performance of these firms, but the resource drain is becoming increasingly severe.

Throughout 1995 there was much discussion in China about what should be done to save the floundering state sector, especially as policymakers were formulating the Ninth Five-Year Plan. Large-scale privatization has been ruled out, at least for the time being. Some state enterprises will go out of business—reportedly almost 2,000 went bankrupt in 1995;[16] however, bankruptcy is not seen as a general solution either, because of the major labor dislocation it would cause. Laying off unneeded or unproductive workers is difficult for the same reasons. The focus, instead, is on revitalizing and technologically upgrading the state-owned enterprises by encouraging foreign investment and establishing a "modern enterprise system." In such a system enterprises would be run by boards of directors as corporate entities, which would allow a separation of ownership and management, with the owners still being largely the Chinese government rather than private investors. The goal is described as maintaining a socialist form of ownership while reaping the benefits of modern management techniques and a semicompetitive environment.

While this approach is getting started, other techniques are also being used to revamp state-owned enterprises. One popular way is to find a foreign partner and create a joint venture

---

15. Cheung Lai-kuen, "Record Loss Suffered by State Sector," *South China Morning Post International Weekly* (Hong Kong), June 29, 1996, Business, p. 1.

16. Craig S. Smith, "China Is Revitalizing State Sector, Starting at the Factory Level," *Wall Street Journal*, March 26, 1996, pp. A1, A8.

with part of the enterprise's facilities. In an extreme example an investor from Singapore bought 41 state factories from one city in Fujian Province. Another trend is to merge ailing enterprises with healthy ones. For example, when a major textile factory with over 3,000 employees in Wuhan declared bankruptcy in 1994, another state firm was already set to buy it.[17] In a few cases, smaller enterprises have been sold or leased to individuals to run as private or collective businesses. Some have issued shares to employees to raise money; others have been listed on one of China's two stock exchanges; and a few have been listed on one of the international stock exchanges.

While state-owned enterprises are still prominent in terms of the value of assets and as producers of key machines and inputs, their share of China's industrial output has fallen from over 81 percent in 1975 to under 35 percent in 1994. (See Figure 2.1.) The growing importance of China's nonstate sector has been widely publicized. This sector includes enterprises with foreign investment, urban collectives, rural township and village enterprises, joint ventures between domestic firms, private firms, and individual and small family businesses. These enterprises now account for over 65 percent of China's gross domestic product (GDP) and have contributed greatly to China's export growth.

A key question with respect to the nonstate sector is how much longer it can continue to be the main source of industrial growth and exports. The bulk of China's investment still goes to the state sector; the rules, credit access, and market environment do not encourage—or sometimes even allow—small nonstate companies to grow large; and the nonsocialist nature of these enterprises continues to be a concern for some Chinese leaders. Foreign investment in Chinese enterprises will continue to grow but will probably not be maintained at the relatively high levels of the early 1990s. Some key concessions to foreign companies are being phased out and the problems of intellectual property rights and technology transfer are ever more apparent. Taking all of these factors into consideration, it is not likely that the nonstate sector alone can absorb the unemployed or even even-

17. "Wuhan Textile Firm Goes Bankrupt," *China Daily*, August 25, 1994.

Figure 2.1
Gross Value of Industrial Output by Ownership, 1975–1994 (Percent)

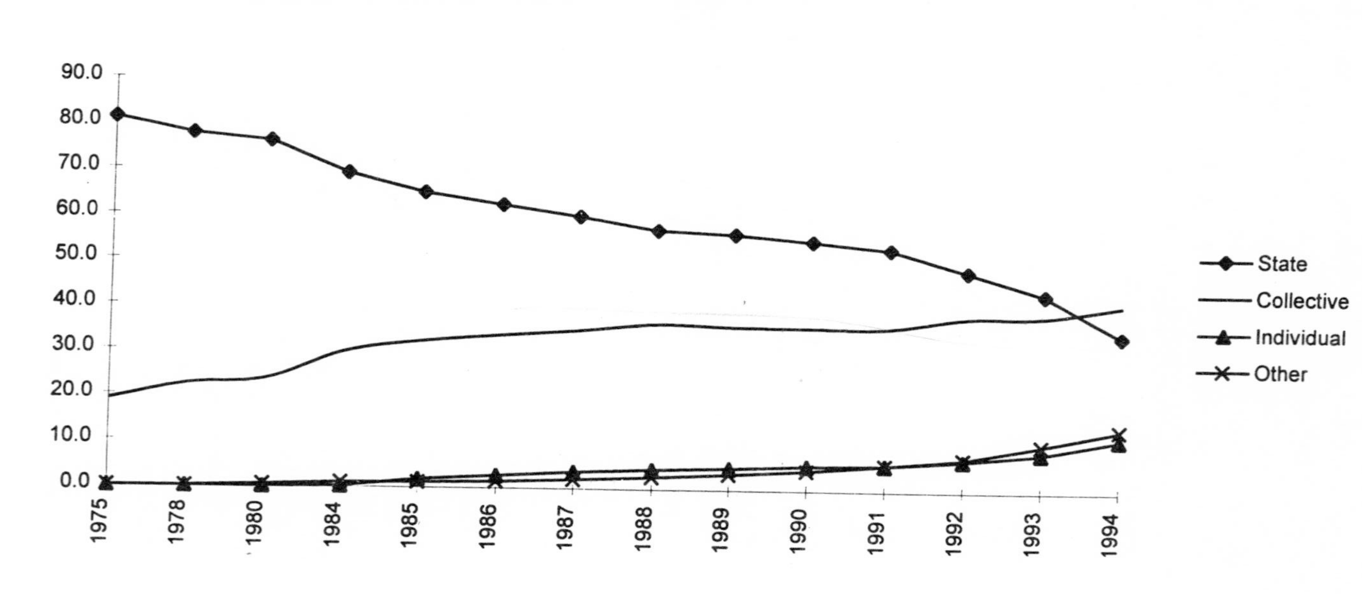

Source: China Statistical Yearbook, 1995 (Beijing: China Statistical Publishing House, 1995), p. 377.

tually produce all that China requires. It certainly cannot make up for all the losses and debts of the state sector. For the Chinese economy to continue to make progress, the state sector will have to become more productive and profitable.

Infrastructure

Another key constraint that affects both production and distribution in all sectors of the economy is infrastructure. Transportation, telecommunications, and energy all represent serious bottlenecks in China's economy.

Transportation

As a result of rapid increases in demand for transport in the 1980s, China's leadership directed resources to update its transport systems. In the 1990s transport was given even higher priority. Existing transportation capacity was already far less than demand, and the situation is likely to worsen as economic output is expected to grow 8 to 10 percent per year, but road and rail capacity at only 2 to 4 percent.[18] Although China relies mostly on rail, it can take nearly a month to ship goods from Beijing to Guangdong by train. Roads are an alternative, but they are often of poor quality and represent a minimal system. China has approximately 541 miles of roads per one million people compared with 1,070 in India, 5,457 in Japan, and 15,195 in the United States.[19] (See Table 2.2.)

The central government's transport plans for 1996–2000 are ambitious. In 1995, the State Planning Commission announced projects that would increase the length of China's railways from 54,000 km in 1994 to 70,000 km, and highways from 1.11 million km in 1994 to 1.25 million km (including 5,000 km of expressway). The number of deep water coastal ports would be raised as well. Three major airports are also scheduled to be built or

18. Emily Thornton, "Distribution: Detour in China," *Far Eastern Economic Review* (Hong Kong), November 23, 1995, pp. 74–78.

19. Patrick E. Tyler, "China's Transport Gridlock: Cars Versus Mass Transit," *New York Times*, May 4, 1996, p. 3.

Table 2.2

Comparative Infrastructure Indicators, 1992

	Rail traffic units (per $1,000 of GDP)	Telephone mainlines (per 1,000 persons)	Electric power (kwh per person)
China	847	10	647
India	488	8	373
Brazil	61	71	1,570
Japan	147	464	7,211
United States	344	565	12,900

Source: World Bank, *World Development Report, 1995: Workers in an Integrating World* (New York: Oxford University Press, 1995), pp. 224–25.

improved in Beijing, Shanghai, and Guangzhou. Adequate funding for all of these projects is a problem, however, especially in the face of the growing central budget deficit. This has led the central leadership to encourage provincial and local investment in transport infrastructure, to seek loans from the World Bank and Japan, and to open this sector to foreign investment in the mid-1990s. Even so, by early 1996 some of these projects were already being postponed or canceled altogether.

Central to China's transport issue is the question of how to manage the increased use of cars and trucks by businesses and households. On the one hand China would like to build its own capability in auto production. Chinese car companies will need to sell domestically for this to happen. In the early 1990s the State Council moved forward with plans to invest in auto plants and announced that it was now acceptable for private individuals to own vehicles. The ramifications for gridlock on streets and highways and for the environment are potentially staggering, since China's huge population can only magnify similar problems already being experienced by cities such as Bangkok and Jakarta.[20] Since then scientists and city officials who are becoming worried about such a strategy have increasingly expressed their concerns.

20. Ibid. For an overview of China's plans in this area, see "China's Strategy for Development of Private Cars," *Beijing Review*, December 12–18, 1994, pp. 11–16.

Telecommunications

China possesses a diversified telecommunications system that links all major cities by telephone, telegraph, radio, and television. Growth in China's economy has put enormous pressure on these systems, but has also led to many efforts to respond to the rising demand. Urban areas are far better served than rural areas.

The primary form of telecommunication in the 1990s is local and long-distance telephone service administered by six regional bureaus that serve as switching centers for provincial and regional subsystems. The number of telephones and telephone lines in use has grown rapidly in the 1990s but is still well below international standards. (See Table 2.2.) In 1993 China had 420,323 long-distance telephone lines; 26 million telephones, of which only 4.6 million were in rural areas; and a switchboard capacity of over 30 million telephones. By 1994 the number of telephones jumped to over 40 million and by 1995 an estimated 50 million.[21] Direct international and domestic dialing services are available in hotels in many major cities. Wireless and mobile phone services are also available in some areas and growing fast. In the mid-1990s an estimated 26 million people subscribed to pager services.[22] In 1995 alone over 2 million new subscribers signed on to cellular phone services, making China the world's fourth largest cellular market with over 4 million subscribers. The Ninth Five-Year Plan includes major investments in switching capacity, lines, and cellular and telephone usage.

Use of the Internet in China is limited but expanding. In 1995 the Ministry of Posts and Telecommunications began an official, commercial link to the Internet called ChinaNet.[23] Controversy about access to the Internet has surrounded this and a few other fledgling on-line services from the beginning.

---

21. "China's Telecoms Industry: Hung Up," *Economist*, July 22, 1995, pp. 64–65.

22. Alexandra Rehak and John Wang, "On the Fast Track," and John Wang, "Walking and Talking," *China Business Review* (March-April 1996), pp. 10 and 14–15 respectively.

23. "China Logs on to the Internet," *Economist*, January 7, 1995, p. 27. ChinaNet's World Wide Web address is http://www.bta.net.cn.

Using two dedicated lines to Beijing and Shanghai and help from a Hong Kong company, China Internet Corporation, central government officials have announced that they will select what is accessible to Chinese citizens on the Net.[24]

Energy

Few would deny that China is experiencing a dramatic shortfall in energy, but it is difficult to estimate with any accuracy how much demand exceeds—and will exceed—supply. One estimate by China's Academy of Social Sciences suggests that energy supplies would have to grow 7 percent per year to the year 2000 as compared with an actual rate of 4 percent between 1979 and 1988.[25] Since such a large increase is unlikely, even with stepped up conservation efforts, the same report predicted a 15 to 20 percent shortfall. While China has relatively extensive reserves of oil and coal and great hydroelectric potential compared with most other countries, the limits of these reserves are apparent if examined on a per capita basis. In rural areas millions of people still rely on grasses, stalks, and other biomass for cooking fuel.[26] Seventy-five percent of China's energy is supplied by coal, a figure that is not expected to change much in the near future. Coal burning is a major pollutant; furthermore, China's coal deposits are concentrated in certain parts of the country, so much of the country's limited transport capacity is required to move the coal to areas that need it.[27]

As with other areas of infrastructure, China's Ninth Five-Year Plan addresses the energy problem. For example, the plan calls for the Ministry of Electric Power to become a national power company and for electric power-generating capacity to equal 1,400 billion kilowatt hours per year by 2000 compared

---

24. "Chinese Firewall: Beijing Seeks to Build Version of the Internet That Can Be Censored," *Wall Street Journal*, January 31, 1996, pp. A1, A4; Louise Lucas, "Net for China: No Smut, No Politics, No Decadent Culture," *Financial Times*, July 10, 1995, p. 9.

25. Vaclav Smil, *China's Environmental Crisis: An Inquiry into the Limits of National Development* (Armonk, N.Y.: M.E. Sharpe, 1993), p. 122.

26. Ibid., pp. 100–101.

27. Yabuki, *China's New Political Economy*, p. 141.

with 1,000 in 1995.[28] But as with the other parts of the national infrastructure, there is the problem of financing. Here too China hopes that foreign investment will contribute some of the needed investment; however, restrictions on allowed rates of return, the uncertainties involved with such major projects, and questions about the controversial environmental impact of some projects such as the gigantic Three Gorges Dam on the Yangzi River have so far kept foreign involvement relatively small.[29] Furthermore, the amount of the funds needed to solve China's energy and other infrastructure bottlenecks means that foreign funds could help only marginally, even in the best of investment climates.

Macroeconomic Management

For ideological and political reasons China's leaders have been willing to go forward with economic reform only when major dislocations of people and imbalances of demand and supply could be controlled. Each time inflation has risen above an acceptable level, price controls have been reimposed and credit curtailed, forcing construction projects to a halt and slowing economic activity generally. In 1989–90 inflation reached its highest levels since reforms began, nearly 30 percent on an annualized basis. Strictly enforced price and credit controls succeeded in bringing inflation down but also caused the growth rate of output to slow. During such austerity programs, the reform process was often put on hold as well. China's leaders recognize this constraint on the nation's progress, so in 1993 when rapid growth again led to high inflation, which in turn prompted a renewed austerity program, their stated goal was to bring inflation under control without causing an economic downturn.[30] After

28. Dusty Clayton, "End to Tax Perks in Changing Economy," *South China Morning Post International Weekly*, February 24, 1996, Business, p. 3; Wu Naitao, "Energy Sector Seeks More Foreign Cooperation," *Beijing Review*, April 24–30, 1995, pp. 7–9.

29. For more on the Three Gorges project, see Richard Louis Edmonds, "China's Environment," in *China Briefing, 1994*, ed. William A. Joseph (Boulder, Colo.: Westview Press, 1994), pp. 143–70.

30. Penelope B. Prime, "The Economy in Overdrive: Will It Crash?" *Current History* (special issue on China), Vol. 92, no. 575 (September 1993), pp. 260–64; U.S. Central Intelligence Agency, *China's Economy in 1993 and 1994: The Search for a Soft Landing* (EA 94–10016, August 1994).

reaching over 20 percent in 1994, inflation fell to an official level of 14.8 percent by the retail index and 17 percent by the cost of living index by the end of 1995. Significantly, growth in GDP averaged 12 percent between 1992 and 1995.[31] The goal of reducing inflation without causing a major slowing in growth had been achieved, but the experience exposed the difficulty of trying to introduce market incentives into a planned system. As a result, the latest round of major reform measures has been aimed at those institutions directly affecting monetary and fiscal health: the tax, banking, and exchange-rate systems. These systems, if designed properly, will allow Chinese policymakers to indirectly influence, or manage, inflation by incremental changes in tax rates, the money supply, or exchange rates rather than by administrative decree.

Public Finance

With the decreasing importance of planning and the growth of nonstate-directed economic activity, major changes in the financing of central and local governments were necessary. Various experiments and institutional reorganizations had already occurred in the 1980s. For example, the former system whereby enterprises turned over most of their profits to the state budget was replaced by a profit tax combined with a number of other taxes. Local and central government finances were also increasingly separated, using a variety of revenue-sharing systems.

Several distinct fiscal trends occurred as a result of these changes combined with other developments in the economy. Of particular interest to central leaders was that the center's share of total revenue collected fell while localities' share rose, and the share of all government resources fell relative to the size of the economy. From the perspective of outside analysts these trends were not extreme when compared with other countries nor were they surprising in light of the decentralizing nature of the reform program; however, within China they created much concern.[32]

To stop, and perhaps reverse, the fall in the center's share of

31. *China Statistical Yearbook, 1995*, pp. 233, 32.

32. Bert Hofman, "An Analysis of Chinese Fiscal Data over the Reform Period," *China Economic Review*, Vol. 4, no. 2 (1993), pp. 213–30.

revenue, another round of major tax reforms was initiated in 1994.[33] The system whereby enterprises contracted (and therefore bargained) for the amount of tax they would pay, the so-called enterprise contract responsibility system, was formally ended. Instead a standard 33 percent tax rate on profits was instituted for all types of domestic enterprises. The personal income tax, the value-added tax, excise taxes, and business taxes were all streamlined and rationalized. Negotiations over revenue sharing between the central and provincial or municipal governments were also replaced with standardized tax assignments and fixed sharing arrangements.

Despite the progress made on the taxation side, severe central budgetary problems still exist. The national budget deficit continued to rise in 1994 and 1995, causing financial problems ranging from late payments to farmers for their produce to cancellation of some major construction projects.

Banking

Along with public finance, the banking system is one of the pillars of a country's macroeconomic infrastructure because of its key role in determining money and credit supply and interest rates. Despite reform in many areas of the economy, China's banking system is still largely patterned on the former planned system where the primary goal of the government-run banks is to support the state sector. In the past, the government's fiscal budget funded investment and covered losses for state-owned enterprises. As planning has been gradually phased out, these funds have begun to be provided by banks as loans. But as before, there continue to be few penalties for not repaying loans. As a result, the banking system is burdened with carrying increasing debt. Forcing bankruptcy is not politically desirable because thousands of enterprises and millions of jobs would be in jeopardy.

To begin to deal with this problem, and to make the banking

33. This section is based on Wanda Tseng et al., *Economic Reform in China: A New Phase*, IMF Occasional Paper, no. 114 (Washington, D.C.: International Monetary Fund, 1994).

system a usable tool for macroeconomic management, plans to reorganize the system were begun in 1994.[34] The People's Bank of China was designated as the central bank, which would regulate the rest of the system. China's four specialized banks, the Industrial and Commercial Bank, the People's Construction Bank (known as the Construction Bank of China as of 1996), the Agricultural Bank, and the Bank of China, were designated to become commercial banks that would be expected to earn profits, although they would remain state-owned. To aid in the economic viability of these existing banks, three new policy banks were created to handle the state funds designated to subsidize policy-oriented investment and long-term projects: the State Development Bank aimed at financing infrastructure projects; the Export and Import Bank would provide trade-related credits; and the Agricultural Development Bank would cover key agricultural projects and the purchase and distribution of grain and cotton. These three policy banks would be expected to loan judiciously but not to be profitable organizations. Within the banking system there are also corporate state commercial banks, such as the Industrial Bank associated with the China International Trust & Investment Corporation (CITIC), a proposed system of urban cooperative banks, and one private commercial bank, the People's Livelihood Bank. Outside the banking system, but increasing in importance, are nonbank financial intermediaries, which include trust and investment companies, securities companies, financial leasing companies, and the People's Insurance Company.

Although reform of the banking system has occurred in name, as of the end of 1996 there had been little fundamental change. One of the main problems is that the financial losses of state-owned enterprises are now covered by lending from banks rather than by direct subsidies from the state budget—hence the unrecoverable loans that plague China's banking sector. In addition, to fund the policy banks and their various undertakings, the People's Bank has been issuing bonds that the specialized banks are required to buy at unfavorable rates; thus, the goals of reform to

34. This section is based on an interview with the deputy general manager of the State Development Bank, Beijing, May 9, 1995; Tseng et al., *Economic Reform in China*, pp. 12–20; and Agatha Ngai, "Reforms Sinking in a Sea of Debt," *South China Morning Post International Weekly*, April 22, 1995, Business, p. 5.

relieve the specialized banks of the burden of subsidizing development projects and to transform them into profitable, market-sensitive commercial institutions are far from being achieved.

In other ways the financial system has made progress. March 1994 saw the passage of a national Budget Law, which was designed to convert the budgetary process from one of planning to one of macroeconomic management. For example, two of its provisions were that central budget deficits would be funded by selling bonds rather than printing money and that the central government would no longer cover local government deficits. In addition, the backbone of the system has been a credit plan with quotas or ceilings allocated to each of the major banks. In recent years this plan has been supplemented with lending guidelines, interest rates, and reserve requirements to develop indicative guidance—rather than direct administrative control—over the macroeconomy.

Exchange Rates

Partly as a result of its attempts to join the World Trade Organization, China has announced its intention to move toward a system in which its currency (the renminbi) could be freely converted into the currencies of other countries. In the 1980s and first half of the 1990s, companies used local "swap markets" to exchange renminbi (also called yuan) and foreign currencies. In these markets, companies could trade the foreign exchange they had earned from the products they had sold abroad for renminbi supplied by the earnings of foreign-invested companies in China. The yuan per dollar rate in these swap markets was lower than the official exchange rate, implying that the renminbi was overvalued at the official rate in comparison with major foreign currencies.

In January 1994 several changes were implemented. Foreign exchange management was reorganized so that the State Administration of Foreign Exchange, the China Foreign Exchange Trade Network (located in Shanghai), and 14 banks were designated to deal in foreign exchange.[35] This was a key step toward

35. Lucille A. Barale and Thomas E. Jones, "Getting Strict with Foreign Exchange," *China Business Review* (September-October 1994), pp. 52–56.

the establishment of a full national foreign exchange market where businesses could purchase foreign exchange directly from the banks. Swap markets would then be phased out as they would no longer be needed.[36] As of early 1996, the banks and swap markets still operated parallel foreign exchange markets, although they both went through the Exchange System in Shanghai. Beginning on July 1, 1996, foreign companies began switching from swap markets to banks to exchange currencies, although the full transition to banks was expected to take some time.[37] The State Administration of Exchange Control announced in mid-1995 that in its view current account convertibility had already been achieved, meaning that anyone needing foreign exchange or renminbi for trading purposes could obtain it through a simple market transaction at one of the designated banks.[38] These changes amount to a managed float system where the People's Bank of China would buy or sell currencies to affect the value of the renminbi only if its value moves outside a predetermined range.[39] Capital account convertibility, which would mean market transactions for currency needed for foreign investment in or outside of China, is not expected to occur anytime soon. Throughout 1995 and 1996 the value of China's currency was quite stable, fluctuating around 8.5 yuan per dollar.

Earning Foreign Exchange

Not having foreign exchange to pay for needed imports of technology, intermediate goods, food, and consumer goods limits China's options in terms of its modernization program. Hence increasing access to foreign exchange through foreign investment, foreign loans, and exports has been a priority.

Foreign commitments to China grew slowly in the early 1980s and then began to increase substantially in the second half of the

36. Wang Yong, "Drop in Investment Dismissed," *China Daily*, June 22, 1995, p. 5.
37. Seth Faison, "China Further Eases Trading of Currency," *New York Times*, June 21, 1996, p. 3.
38. "RMB Reform Runs Ahead of Schedule," *China Daily*, April 27, 1995, p. 7.
39. Tseng et al., *Economic Reform in China*, p. 10.

decade. The inflow of foreign capital temporarily slowed as a result of the June 1989 Tiananmen incident but picked up dramatically in 1992. Then in 1993 businesses, governments, and international organizations committed an unprecedented $123.27 billion of investment and loans to over 83,000 projects in China. This represented a substantial annual increase in foreign capital; for the previous 14 years from 1979 to 1992 total cumulative commitments were $191 billion. Investment and loan contracts fell some in 1994 compared with 1993 but still were high at $93.76 billion. In terms of foreign capital actually used, by the end of 1994 the cumulative amount reached $181 billion, of which $95 billion represented direct foreign investment.[40]

China's success in attracting foreign investment led central leaders in the mid-1990s to begin to phase out the preferential incentives in the coastal areas and to encourage capital flows to less developed, interior areas. Also targeted for foreign investment were bottleneck sectors, including infrastructure, energy, agriculture, raw materials, and advanced technology. Simultaneously, restrictions were eased on foreign investment in services, including retail sales, advertising, insurance, engineering, and financial services. New forms of investment were also allowed, including issuing equity shares for joint ventures and "build, operate, transfer" arrangements, in which a project is built and operated by a foreign company for a specific period after which ownership is transferred to the Chinese partner. A consistent focus in the 1990s has been a desire to upgrade technology, and some people have even suggested a type of competition wherein the foreign company willing to transfer the most technology wins the deal. The German auto-maker Daimler-Benz may have beat out Chrysler to build minivans in China for just such a reason.

Throughout the reform period, the Chinese government has borrowed abroad conservatively, maintaining a good credit rating internationally. Between 1979 and 1985 China signed loans totaling $20.3 billion.[41] Most loans supported infrastructure projects, such as energy and transportation, or funded imports of

40. *China Statistical Yearbook*, various years.
41. *China Statistical Yearbook, 1994*, p. 527.

key raw materials. By the mid-1980s China's demand for foreign loans had increased appreciatively. Outstanding foreign debt increased from $30 billion in 1987 to over $100 billion by the end of 1995.[42]

Since the beginning of reforms in the late 1970s, China has increasingly become a world player in international markets. This situation is in stark contrast to the previous three decades when trade played a minor role in the planned economy and Chinese leaders were opposed to global interdependence. In the 1970s, China's trade volume represented less than one percent of total world trade, ranking it as the 30th largest trading nation.[43] But by 1985 Chinese foreign trade had risen to $69 billion, putting China in 16th place in world trade rankings. In the second half of the 1980s growth in trade accelerated. By 1995 total trade had increased to an impressive $281 billion, with exports totaling $149 billion and imports totaling $132 billion. This represents an annual average increase in exports of 14 percent and an increase in imports of 13 percent.[44]

China has been successful in earning foreign exchange through trade and investment, and to a lesser extent, loans. For the last decade reserves grew steadily and then increased substantially in the mid-1990s. (See Figure 2.2.) Foreign exchange reserves were almost $3 billion in 1987; by the end of 1995 they had risen to over $70 billion. The increases were due to China's running a merchandise trade surplus every year since 1990 except for 1993 and to foreign capital inflows. With many outstanding foreign loans and a desire to maintain a stable exchange rate, these reserves provide a comfortable cushion.

China's goal to gain membership in the World Trade Organization (WTO) has created pressure to make its trading rules transparent and less restrictive, especially with respect to imports. For example, in 1994 China's first foreign trade law came into effect, which unified and made more transparent the framework for conducting foreign trade in China. In another example

42. *China Statistical Yearbook, 1995*, p. 225; *Beijing Review*, May 6–12, 1996, p. 4.

43. Nicholas R. Lardy, *China in the World Economy* (Washington, D.C.: Institute for International Economics, 1994), p. 1.

44. *Haiguan Tongji* (Customs Statistics/Beijing), Vol. 36, no. 12 (1995), p. 1.

Figure 2.2
China's Foreign Sector, 1983–1994

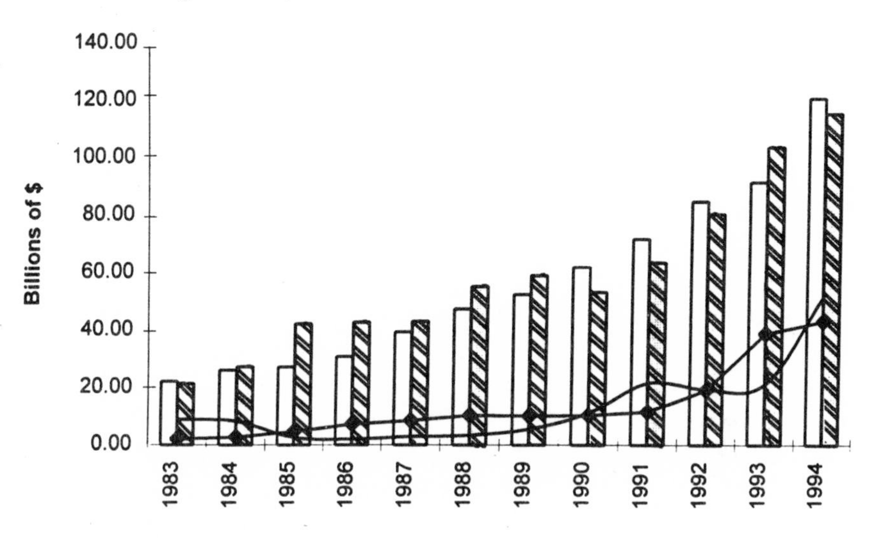

Exports
Imports
Total Foreign Investment
Foreign Exchange Reserves

Source: China Statistical Yearbook, various issues.

of China responding to WTO guidelines, at the end of 1995 President Jiang Zemin announced a trade liberalization plan to decrease tariffs on 4,000 imports and end import controls on 170 tariff categories. This announcement came one day after meetings with the United States concerning China's membership.[45] As of mid-1996, China has held observer status in the WTO which allows the Chinese delegation to participate in discussions but not to vote in the organization. A number of current members, especially

45. Vivien Pik-kwan Chan, "Beijing Unveils Trade Reforms," *South China Morning Post International Weekly*, November 25, 1995, p. 1.

the United States, are lobbying for China to reform its economy and legal system further before being allowed to join.

Prospects for Sustained Progress

Three broad trends can be identified from recent changes and emerging constraints in China's economy. First, although impressive agricultural performance has been one of the hallmarks of China's reforms, environmental and population pressures are taking their toll and increasingly raising questions about the long-term viability of this sector. Second, the Chinese government's role in the economy is under increasing strain with the interconnected problems of unproductive state-owned enterprises, inadequate public infrastructure, rising budget deficits, and nonviable financial institutions. This strain is growing at the same time that the government's ability to maintain economic growth with stability and equality is increasingly the test of its legitimacy. And third, the international sector of the Chinese economy stands out as a major success in terms of trade, investment, and foreign exchange. Not surprisingly, then, there is a tendency to look outside the country for ways to solve the myriad problems facing China's economy today, including using foreign investment to ease energy, transport, and telecommunications bottlenecks and importing technology to revitalize state enterprises. The sheer size of China's economic problems and the investment necessary to solve them, however, mean that progress must depend ultimately on domestic resources and institutional change. In addition, continued growth will increasingly have to come from domestic consumption, since further export growth will be dampened over time as foreign markets become saturated with Chinese goods.

One potential constraint on expanding the role of the international sector in China's economic development is the recent deterioration of relations between China and the United States. As Steven I. Levine discusses in his chapter in this volume, there are rising tensions over the growing U.S. trade deficit with China, China's noncompliance with intellectual property rights agreements, and restricted access to China's markets, in addition to the political issues of Taiwan, human rights, and arms sales. Depending on the statistics used, the U.S. market absorbs between 18 and 25 percent of China's exports and the United States is one of the four largest investors in China.[46] These two large economies have grown increasingly interdependent, but have difficult political relations as well as weak communication and negotiation structures for dealing with their problems. Continuing conflicts with the United States could seriously undermine a major source of access for China to much-needed trade, investment, and credit.

Although China faces many serious problems in its quest for sustained development, it is also working with some solid preconditions for economic growth. These include an educated labor force, high savings and investment rates, and an increasingly open economy. These strengths have helped China go forward with its relatively gradual reform program and will help it to overcome its development bottlenecks. China's very success, however, is making it harder and harder for its leaders to balance their socialist, self-reliant political goals with the increasing marketization and globalization of their economy. Thus political change may be the biggest challenge of all to China's sustained economic progress.

46. Penelope B. Prime and Loraine A. West, "U.S.-China Trade: Avoiding Conflict Ahead," paper prepared for the International Trade and Finance Association, San Diego, May 1996.

Gender Equality in China: Two Steps Forward, One Step Back

Nancy E. Riley

In September 1995 Beijing hosted the United Nations International Women's Conference. The conference attracted attention to the situation of women and girls across the world, but in many ways it was particularly appropriate that such a conference took place in China. After centuries during which women occupied a clearly subordinate status to men, China has ostensibly placed gender equality on its national agenda. Since the communist revolution of 1949 government rhetoric about improvement in women's status has been constant and strong, with leaders asserting that raising women's status was a high priority of the state. The official rhetoric and the direct and deliberate role of the state in the many social and economic changes that have taken place in recent decades partly account for the interest shown by outsiders in the lives of Chinese women and in the 1995 conference. Whether state efforts have matched rhetoric in the area of gender equality is a significant question for those around the world who support this goal.

In some areas of women's lives the efforts of the Chinese state have indeed had a visible positive effect. Because of direct state intervention, women in China have one of the highest labor force participation rates in the world. Birth rates have plummeted, at least partly because of strictly enforced fertility restrictions. But in other key areas rhetoric has not been matched by action. Although overall women in China are not as subordinate today as they were when the practice of footbinding was prevalent, they remain unequal to men in the political arena, in family life, and in many other areas, where their lower status resembles that of women in societies vastly different from China.

Of course, there is great variety in the lives of women across China, especially in recent years as China has undergone rapid and extensive changes in both its economy and social organization and as differences among people generally—in income, opportunities, and living standards—have increased. Differences between rural and urban areas are especially important to keep in mind. Urban-rural differences are present in nearly all aspects of life, in access to new opportunities and exposure to the world outside China, but also in the ways of daily life, including the way that gender is organized. At the same time, increases in migration within China have meant that rural residents are having more and more contact with urban areas.

Another point to keep in mind is related to the differences between China and Western societies. Using the same standard for evaluating gender equality and organization for all societies is problematic, because it ignores the importance of culture in the construction of gender in any society. On the other hand, it is useful to make comparisons with other societies in order to put in perspective China's achievements and shortcomings in this area. Balancing China's comparative record on gender equality with its unique history and culture is a difficult but important endeavor.

This chapter will examine women's lives in China and the ways that gender shapes Chinese society. It begins by briefly setting the historical context, which is key in understanding Chinese women's lives today. It then describes women's roles and position in contemporary social, political, and economic life and compares China's progress with that of other countries. The last half of the chapter is devoted to examining three aspects of Chinese society that reflect the shape of gender inequality in China in the mid-1990s and suggest what might be expected in the future. Family planning restrictions have been crucial in shaping key aspects of most women's lives; many women are now facing competing pressures from their families and from the state, which have different reproductive goals. A second recent influence has been economic changes which have not only provided women with new opportunities but have also been the source of new forms of gender inequality. Finally, images of women in the mass media reflect some of the contradictory messages that women face in the China of the mid-1990s and some of the challenges they will face in the future.

The Legacy of Gender Subordination

For centuries, the lives of Chinese women were circumscribed by ideas, ideology, and practices that resulted in gender inequality and female subordination. All individuals in Chinese society were bound by Confucian notions of hierarchy and practices of patriarchy, patrilocality, and patrilineage. The family patriarch (usually the eldest male) wielded enormous power over the lives of those in his sphere of influence, determining who they married, whether and what kind of training they received, and what work they undertook. Marriage patterns, which mark a pivotal family and social event in all societies, reveal how Chinese females were particularly disadvantaged in this system. At marriage, women moved from their homes to those of their husbands. This practice (called patrilocality) affected the lives of females from birth, long before marriage. Because females would marry out of the family, they were not considered part of their natal, or birth, families. Girls grew up knowing they were valued less than their brothers, since they would be gone before they could make any significant contribution to their families. They were seen mostly as potential drains on the resources of their natal families.

The loneliness and hardships of new brides in this system is legendary. At marriage, they not only moved to a new household but usually to a new and unfamiliar village as well. Thus as a total stranger a bride entered her new home, where she took her place at the bottom of the age and gender hierarchies.

In this system, most women's lives were confined to the sphere of the family, where childbearing was a woman's raison d'être: a woman's central contribution to her husband's family was to provide the family with (male) heirs. A woman herself was usually eager to bear a son, for it made her place in her new household more secure. In addition, her children—her "uterine family"—were a woman's source of emotional and economic security, people she could forever count on amidst a group of strangers.[1] Through childbearing, then, a woman found a way to make her own family; and as these children, especially sons, grew up, a woman could count on them to guarantee her some status and comfort in her old age.

Since the beginning of the 20th century the lives of women in China have undergone enormous change. Efforts toward reform began early in the century and have continued through the present. Although earlier reform movements worked for important changes such as the abolition of footbinding and the promotion of girls' education, some of the most radical efforts were part of the May 4th Movement of 1919. This movement, promoted mostly by urban educated elites, focused in part on the ways that Confucian ideas harmed Chinese society, its progress, and its place in the world. At the center of its attack was the traditional Chinese family and particularly the role of women in it. Judith Stacey has noted that during the May 4th era, "the logic of Confucian patriarchy made family transformation the primary idiom of political discourse and induced Chinese radicalism to assume a feminist cast."[2]

Many of the radical ideas of the May 4th Movement were adopted by the growing Chinese communist movement in the 1930s and 1940s. However, the focus on the family as a means of transforming society soon lost its primacy for the communists; in the process the priority of women's equality also became less central. Nevertheless, gender equality remained an important part of early Chinese Communist Party (CCP) policy and rhetoric for several decades. Focusing on class inequality and the role of production on social and economic organization in Chinese society, communist leaders argued that it was through entering the productive sphere that women would gain an equal place in society.

What happened to those goals of gender equality which seemed to be so important to early communist revolutionaries? Why have they not been realized, even now, more than 50 years later? Some have argued that if gender equality had been made a priority in the years after 1949, other goals of the CCP might

1. See Margery Wolf's *Women and the Family in Rural Taiwan* (Stanford: Stanford University Press, 1972), for a discussion of the role of the uterine family in women's lives.

2. Judith Stacey, *Patriarchy and Socialist Revolution in China* (Berkeley: University of California Press, 1983), p. 75.

have gone unrealized. The successes and shortcomings in improving women's lives in China, in fact, illustrate how deeply entrenched notions of gender shape the direction of even the most intense revolutionary movements.

One of the most important factors in early communist successes in China was enlisting peasant support. Chinese peasants had suffered greatly during the decades before the communists came to power and communist leaders were dedicated to improving peasant lives and livelihoods. In the early 1950s the government enacted a series of reforms that were meant to aid peasants while allowing the government to gain peasant support and strengthen its control over Chinese citizens. These included land reform, which resulted in redistribution of land and gave poor peasants greater access to this important resource. The government also began to restructure village life, gradually taking ownership of the means of production (such as farmland) out of the hands of individuals and putting them under state control. Marriage reform was also enacted; by outlawing arranged marriage and early marriage (before the age of 18 for women and 20 for men) and making divorce legal, the state hoped to weaken the control of the family over its individual members and give less powerful members (especially women) increased independence.

These early reforms reflected the state's continuing interest in improving women's lives. But their uneven enforcement also meant the continuing subordination of gender equality to other revolutionary goals. Although land reform and the socialization of the economy all proceeded apace, officials were more reluctant to push reforms, such as the Marriage Law, that might have given women further voice or freedom. Scholars disagree about how deliberate the lack of sustained attention to so-called women's issues was during this period. Some argue that China's leaders did not recognize their own biases about women and therefore were not likely to see how early reforms were insufficient to change women's lives.[3] Others argue that these leaders recognized that to push for gender equality might have meant

3. See Kay Ann Johnson, *Women, the Family, and Peasant Revolution in China* (Chicago: University of Chicago Press, 1983).

the loss of male peasant support, without which the revolution would fail.[4] Whatever the reason, gender equality received less effort than did other goals of the new regime.

In fact, many of the reforms in the first years of communist rule in China actually increased or reestablished women's inequality. One clue as to why this happened can be found by looking at the "family crisis" that existed in rural China in the years before the CCP came to power. Because of the severe economic problems and social instability of the 1920s–1940s, peasants were unable to maintain the Confucian tradition of a strong patriarchal family, considered the cornerstone of a successful Chinese life:

> [T]he agrarian crisis posed a serious threat to the physical survival, reproduction, household size and complexity, and the legitimacy of traditional peasant family life. . . . The domain of a peasant patriarch's authority contracted: he had fewer workers to oversee, less income to manage or invest, fewer marriages to arrange, and fewer ceremonies and rituals over which to officiate. In consequence, there was less deference for him to enjoy or old age security and ancestor worship to anticipate.[5]

Communist revolutionaries recognized the importance of efforts to resolve this peasant family crisis and restore family stability if they wanted to garner peasant support. In their focus on satisfying the desire of male peasants for the kind of family Confucian principles dictated, officials ignored, or even discouraged, efforts toward correcting gender inequality. The same fear of alienating male peasants helps explain why the CCP did not promote radical changes in gender relations after it came to power.

But women's family lives also did not receive concerted or sustained attention because communist leaders believed that gender equality could be achieved through promoting female participation in the labor force. Following the writings of Engels and Marx, they believed that if women became equal contributors to the productive sector of Chinese society, the basis of their

4. Stacey, *Patriarchy and Socialist Revolution in China.*
5. Ibid., p. 97.

inequality would be destroyed, and they would achieve equality in all aspects of their lives. Consequently, in the 1950s the party began to work toward the goal of bringing women into the labor force in record numbers rather than focusing on women's issues specifically.

During the 1960s and 70s—especially during the Cultural Revolution—gender neutrality was promoted and in some ways women gained enormous ground.[6] The official slogan of the times was that women "hold up half the sky," and in fact women were brought into production in record numbers and their political representation reached an all-time peak in these years. Still, in key ways women's position was hurt during this period. When examples of correct revolutionary behavior were promoted, the model used was male, revealed in a slogan popular at the time—"women can do anything men can do"—which suggests that the evaluation of women was based on how well they fulfilled male roles. A reciprocal change was not suggested for men. Women thus ended up doubly burdened, expected to take on new male roles and to be responsible for traditional female roles as well, particularly in the spheres of childrearing and household chores. In addition, the party's efforts at this time were focused on issues of class, not gender; "concessions" to women were seen as potentially harmful to the ultimate goals of proletarian unity. Leaders argued that women did not need "special" treatment, and that it was individual women's responsibility—not the state's—to handle the family and work conflicts that women's increased responsibilities were creating. The abolition of the All-China Women's Federation (a party-controlled organization that played a watchdog and organizing role in many areas of women's lives) reflected many of the gender ideas of the late Maoist era:

> Not only was it claimed that the federation had been infiltrated by bourgeois ideas, leading it to dwell on "narrow" family and

6. For an insightful look at women during the Cultural Revolution, see Marilyn B. Young, "Chicken Little in China: Women after the Cultural Revolution," in *Promissory Notes: Women in the Transition to Socialism*, ed. Sonia Kruks, Rayna Rapp, and Marilyn B. Young (New York: Monthly Review Press, 1989), pp. 233–47.

> welfare issues and to ignore the "class education" of women, but this ultra-left line also claimed that under the dictatorship of the proletariat, women had no special interests, only common class interests with men. Therefore, women did not need a separate organization, which in any case only served to divide the proletariat.[7]

In sum, although gender equality has nearly always been on the official agenda and part of government rhetoric in China since 1949, it has often taken a backseat to what the leaders have felt are more immediate or more important goals, whether that be engaging support of the male peasantry or class struggle. Although the CCP recognized the inequalities women faced in Chinese society, it attributed much of it to old ideas or "feudal remnants," rather than attending to the structural bases of that inequality, including the family. As discussed below, family organization, especially the traditions of women marrying out of their own village and moving to their husbands' village have continued to reinforce women's subordinate status in China.

Chinese Women's Lives in the 1990s

What are the lives of Chinese women like in the mid-1990s? Again, it is important to keep in mind the huge variations among different geographical areas and groups of women. The concerns of college graduates are not likely to be the same as those faced by women in remote rural areas. Where a woman lives, her access to particular jobs, her educational background, and other factors will all influence her life in significant ways.

A distinction must also be made between women's experience in the public and private spheres of their lives. It is not that these areas of women's (or men's) lives are always separable; indeed, they are interrelated in many complex ways. But particularly in China, this distinction remains important for several reasons. First, state efforts toward changing women's lives have focused—heavily and, at times, exclusively—on women's *public* roles, such as in the workplace or in politics. This emphasis on

7. Johnson, *Women, the Family, and Peasant Revolution in China*, p. 181.

one rather than the other or both aspects of life comes from Marxist ideology about the central role of work and production in the organization of society. But, as the May 4th radicals recognized, family organization and ideology (i.e., the private sphere) are key factors in Chinese society; they understood that if the society was to undergo revolution, the family would have to be part of the change. Although CCP leaders since then have sometimes recognized the key role that family life, organization, and ideology plays in women's subordination, it has rarely been given priority. And yet, for women especially, the family has been absolutely central to the shape and direction of life, and, in turn, a source of gender inequality in China. Prohibited from the public arena for centuries, women have come to define their position in Chinese society primarily through their role in the family, as daughters, wives, and mothers. Therefore, although it is important to examine the public lives of Chinese women today, their lives in families and households must also be kept in mind.

Although Chinese women have a better record of political involvement than women in some other societies, women's political representation still lags far behind men's, especially at higher levels of the party and state. In the mid-1990s only 6 percent of ministerial positions are held by women, and they make up only 21 percent of the National People's Congress.[8] Women do occupy many positions at the lowest levels of government; for example, in the cities neighborhood-level officials are often women. Although these officials do important jobs, their duties are often very unpopular with the people among whom they work. For example, they are responsible for negotiations surrounding divorce and for monitoring the state's stringent family planning program.

Within the Communist Party, women also fare poorly, comprising only 13 percent of party members.[9] This figure is important, for party membership confers key advantages. Local leaders are more likely to be party members, and membership involves

8. United Nations, *The World's Women, 1995: Trends and Statistics* (New York: United Nations, 1995), p. 174.

9. Elisabeth Croll, *Changing Identities of Chinese Women* (London: Zed Books, 1995).

social and political connections that can help an individual in all aspects of daily life and work.

One of the most visible, public aspects of Chinese women's lives is their extensive participation in the labor force. As the government and party promised in the early years of the People's Republic, women's representation in the labor force is nearly equal to men's. About 90 percent of working-age women in urban areas work at full-time jobs. The rate for rural women is estimated to be lower, because rural women are more likely than urban women to work only for their family, at home or in the fields.[10] Nevertheless, even given the lower estimates of their participation in paid labor in rural areas, women in China have one of the highest female labor force participation rates in the world. That participation is a key factor in women's efforts to gain a place equal to men in Chinese society. It means that most women are involved in public life on a daily basis and are visible in public arenas. As discussed below, this public work has also affected women's family lives.

But in many ways, the numbers of women working in China tell only part of the story. Examining more closely what is happening to women at work shows that they are not equal to men in anything except that they are working. Although a comparatively high percentage of Chinese women work, the reality of women's participation in the labor force is not much different from that in many other societies, be they socialist, capitalist, or more or less industrialized. For example, in China and elsewhere, women tend to be clustered in jobs that are considered appropriate for women, such as in textiles or light industry. The unique structure of the Chinese economy gives this special meaning. In terms of ownership, industries and enterprises are categorized as state, collective (mostly local government), private, or joint ventures by foreign and Chinese owners. Although private industries are starting to increase in China, only about 10 percent of the labor force is employed in them. State firms are given priority by the state and command a higher share of re-

10. John Bauer, Wang Feng, Nancy E. Riley, and Zhao Xiaohua, "Gender Inequality in Urban China: Education and Employment," *Modern China*, Vol. 18, no. 3 (1992), pp. 333–70.

sources; for workers, this translates into higher salaries, better benefits such as health care, housing, and day care, and better access to such perquisites as travel. Women make up only between 35 and 40 percent of workers in these state industries.[11] The salaries of women in nonagricultural work averages 59.4 percent of men's;[12] but in addition to these lower salaries, they have access to fewer benefits as well.

Within the industries that they work in, women are also less likely to be in leadership positions. Although sex discrimination is technically illegal, by all reports women face discrimination in hiring and promotion throughout the labor force. Whereas there are only 13 women per 100 men in administrative and managerial positions (see Table 3.1), they are relatively more numerous in sales positions, where there are 88 women per 100 men. And, as in many other societies, women dominate the service sector (which includes sales clerks and restaurant workers), which has 107 women per 100 men.

Part of women's poor showing in high-level jobs can be traced to their lower levels of education. Since 1949 Chinese women have made significant gains in schooling; the percentage of girls enrolled in school has risen at all levels in the last 15 years. But changing the lens of comparison from one that compares contemporary women with past women to one that compares current experiences of women and men reveals disparities, especially as one moves up the education ladder. There are 95 girls per 100 boys enrolled in primary school, but this ratio declines to 78 girls per 100 boys in secondary school and to 75 per 100 at the university level.[13] In addition, dropout rates at all levels, especially in rural areas, are higher for girls than boys. Even literacy is skewed by gender. Compared to the 88 percent of women over age 45 who are illiterate, only 6 percent of women aged 15 to 19 cannot read or write.[14] Nevertheless, 70 percent of all illiterates aged 15–19 are female. One

11. Yanjie Bian, *Work and Inequality in Urban China* (Albany: State University of New York Press, 1994).

12. United Nations Development Program, *Human Development Report 1995* (New York: Oxford University Press, 1995), p. 36.

13. Ibid., p. 52.

14. Bauer et al., "Gender Inequality in Urban China," p. 336.

Table 3.1

Indicators of Gender Equality in Selected Countries

	China	South Korea	India	Sri Lanka	Philippines	Thailand	Italy	Sweden	U.S.
GNP per capita	530	8,220	310	640	960	2,210	19,270	23,630	25,860
% Women in labor force	70	41	28	29	36	65	30	55	50
Number of women per 100 men in									
Administration/management	13	4	2	33	38	29	60	64	67
Production/transportation	56	43	15	46	25	46	24	18	22
Service sector	107	156	22	NA	138	128	NA	332	150
% Illiterate, ages 15–24									
Female	13	NA	59.7	9.8	3.1	2.1	0.4	NA	0.6
Male	4	NA	33.7	8.1	3.7	1.5	0.3	NA	0.7
% Illiterate, age 25+									
Female	54	NA	80.6	22	8.7	25.2	5.5	NA	3.1
Male	23	NA	50.2	9	7.2	11.8	3.4	NA	3.4
Females per 100 males in									
High school	73	92	52	106	99	93	96	100	103
University	50	46	42	68	143	111	91	116	120
% Females in									
Parliament	21	1	7	5	11	4	15	34	11
Ministry	6	3.8	2.9	3.2	7.7	0	12	30	13.6
Administration/management	12	4	2	25	28	22	NA	39	40
Total fertility rate	2	1.6	3.4	2.3	4.1	2.2	1.2	2	1.7
% Married women using contraception	70	79	41	66	40	66	NA	78	71
Maternal mortality ratio (per 100,000 live births)	95	26	460	80	100	50	4	5	8
Sex ratio at birth	113.8	113.1	NA	104.3	109.3	105.5	106.4	105.3	105

Sources: United Nations, *The World's Women, 1995: Trends and Statistics* (New York: United Nations, 1995); Population Reference Bureau, *1996 World Population Data Sheet* (Washington, D.C.: PRB, 1996).

reason for this pattern of gender inequality in schooling is that the continuing marriage practice in which girls move away from their families at marriage makes parents less willing to invest time or money in education for their daughters than they are for their sons. In school girls are also given different messages from boys and are channeled into less challenging (and less well-paid) fields. Some have argued that girls will move closer to boys in the amount of education they receive as the economy changes, but in fact trends toward equal numbers of girls and boys in school slowed during the 1980s as the Chinese economy grew.

Women's lives in China have been greatly affected by the extensive changes that have taken place in many aspects of family life over the last several decades. For example, there has been a transformation in how and when families form. No longer are women likely to marry someone their parents have chosen. Although parents continue to have important influence on their children's marriages, young people—including women—are now able to have a say in that decision as well.[15] Marriage is also occurring later than it did in the past. Because of marriage regulations and the influence of schooling in delaying marriage, the average age of marriage for women is now above age 22, compared to about 20 in 1971. Young couples are also less likely to spend their married lives under the roof of the husband's family. Greater mobility and changing ideals have meant that couples increasingly live by themselves. This trend is especially apparent in urban areas; in rural areas, although there is greater mobility, most couples continue to live with the husband's parents after marriage, although they might move out of the house after several years.

The kinds of changes that have been occurring within Chinese households after marriage have been less fully studied, but some clues are beginning to emerge from recent research. Women continue to have primary and overwhelming responsibility for household concerns. Their double burden means that they work full-time in a paid job and then put in many more hours of domestic work at home. Although the government reg-

15. Nancy E. Riley, "Interwoven Lives: Parents, Marriage, and *Guanxi* in China," *Journal of Marriage and the Family*, Vol. 56, no. 4 (November 1994), pp. 791–803.

ularly pronounces the importance of men helping their wives at home, husbands rarely put in as much time in household work or child care as their wives do. Men, especially younger men in urban areas, do seem to be spending more time on domestic chores, but they rarely take as much responsibility as their wives have in this realm. In a survey of urban Shandong Province, nearly three-quarters of women report that they are primarily responsible for daily tasks such as laundry, housekeeping, and cooking, while men are likely to do chores that can be done less frequently, such as buying grain or fuel. Women also retain primary responsibility for child care; in Shandong, for example, nearly 90 percent of women report being primarily responsible for child care.[16] Although some younger fathers are spending more time with their children than fathers did in the past, mothers are still considered to be better parents, and thus do most of both early infant care and later childrearing. Even when husbands claim to be sharing these tasks equally with their wives, data show that the reality is that women spend significantly more time than their husbands in providing child care.[17]

Have women gained more power at home? Has their greater access to work and income given them a larger voice in the household? Although data is scarce, there is some indication that women have indeed gained some power in their families. Research done in Hohhot, the capital of Inner Mongolia, found that men and even women insisted that the power of wives in the home has increased in recent years.[18] Wives are now able to assert some decision-making power in key areas, from domestic consumer purchases to decisions about contact with and financial support of parents and parents-in-law. Despite this increase in domestic power, women remain subordinate in their households and families. In both urban and rural areas, husbands are

16. Nancy E. Riley and Xiong Yu, "Women's Power in Chinese Households," paper presented at the American Sociological Association Annual Meeting, Los Angeles, August 1995.

17. Ester Ngan-ling Chow and Kevin Chen, "The Impact of the One-Child Policy on Women and the Patriarchal Family in the People's Republic of China," in *Women, the Family, and Policy: A Global Perspective*, ed. Ester Ngan-ling Chow and Catherine White Berheide (Albany: State University of New York Press, 1993), pp. 71–98.

18. William R. Jankowiak, *Sex, Death, and Hierarchy in a Chinese City: An Anthropological Account* (New York: Columbia University Press, 1993).

usually twice as likely as their wives to have primary say in consumer purchases and in most cases command far more leisure time.[19] Women's income has not always or easily translated into family power, and wives continue to be saddled with most household and child-care tasks.

Women now have unprecedented opportunities in many areas of their lives. But at the same time, gender inequality, which has been a part of Chinese society for centuries, remains and has been re-created in many of these new structures, institutions, and even opportunities. The government recognizes many of these continuing inequalities. In mid-1995 it issued a "Program for the Development of Chinese Women," which addressed issues such as the need to reduce dropout rates for female students and the problem of discrimination against girl children, although this resolution has not yet resulted in specific actions.[20] The next sections of this chapter, which examine three important areas of women's lives which have undergone recent change, suggest just how difficult achieving gender equality will be.

Women and China's Family Planning Program

In an essay on Chinese women, Marilyn Young wrote, "always, of course, the effect of policy [is] gender-specific, whether or not it was framed with gender in mind."[21] China's family planning policies since the 1970s are perhaps the clearest examples of the truth of this statement. The main purpose of these policies was to reduce population growth so it would not be a drag on economic development. But officials also argued that the population programs would benefit women, by freeing them from the health dangers of repeated childbirth and allowing them to spend less time in child care and more in other pursuits. Furthermore, they argued, women would benefit because reducing fertility and population growth would prevent the recurrence of severe economic crises and famines, in which women and girls,

19. Riley and Xiong, "Women's Power in Chinese Households."

20. "Five-Year Program for Women Advanced," *Beijing Review*, August 28–September 2, 1995, p. 4.

21. Young, "Chicken Little in China," p. 234.

being sold or dying in higher numbers, suffered more than males. But the program has had specific and sometimes negative consequences for females that reveal the continuing persistence of women's subordination in Chinese society.

State-directed family planning efforts began in the 1960s with campaigns to encourage couples to use birth control and have fewer children. But it was in 1979 and 1980 that the current restrictions were put into place.[22] Although the policies have varied somewhat during different time periods and in different localities, they basically restrict all urban couples to one child. Rural couples have been allowed to have two and sometimes three children, although today most areas restrict allowable births to two if the first child is a girl. These policies have met strong resistance in most parts of China but especially among the peasantry.

The strength of rural resistance to state-imposed limits on childbearing reflects the role of children, and particularly sons, in rural life. In the cities most workers have state pensions after retirement, which make elderly citizens less dependent, especially financially, on other family members in their old age. But in the countryside pensions are rare, and rural residents (nearly 70 percent of the population) must rely on family members for financial and other support in time of need. In addition, decollectivization has turned farm production back over to the family, so families need labor to succeed economically. Therefore, they are often eager to have more children than the government allows.

In this situation sons are especially important. For Chinese families that trace the family line through males (a practice called patrilineage), sons represent family continuation. In addition, marriage in rural China continues to be patrilocal, which means that daughters are effectively lost to their parents at marriage. Therefore, if parents need support in old age, they must look to their sons. Sons have always been preferred over daughters in most parts of China. Since peasants have been restricted

22. For recent history of the family planning program, see Tyrene White, "The Population Factor: China's Family Planning Policy in the 1990s," in *China Briefing, 1991*, ed. William A. Joseph (Boulder, Colo.: Westview Press, 1991), pp. 97–117.

in the number of children they can have, the desire for sons is often intensified.

Under these pressures, women are affected in important and often dire ways. The wives and daughters-in-law of those who desperately want sons can be under enormous pressure to bear boys and are blamed if they bear a girl. Women themselves want sons, since their lives too will be adversely affected if the family has no male children. But it is women who bear much of the brunt of the consequences of the competing pressures of family and state. The government's family planning program directs most of its efforts to women: women must undergo abortion if they are pregnant when they already have the maximum number of children allowed; women are the targets of local and national campaigns to get people to use birth control; female sterilization is much more common than male sterilization; and IUDs, requiring surgical implantation, are one of the most common forms of contraception.[23]

But it is not only adult females who have suffered under these pressures. Since the program has gone into effect, infant and girl children have also been affected. It is widely believed that the strong desire for sons has produced the "missing girls" phenomenon: since the early 1980s, thousands of girls are "missing" in China. Demographic data reveals that the sex ratio at birth—a measure of the number of girls born for every hundred boys—is highly skewed. (See Table 3.1.) Whereas this ratio is normally about 105 (i.e., 105 boys born for every 100 girls), most recent data show the sex ratio to be 113.8 in China, and even as high as 117 in some provinces.[24] Although the difference be-

23. For interesting and provocative discussions on the role of gender in China's population control program, see Susan Greenhalgh, "Controlling Births and Bodies in Village China," *American Ethnologist*, Vol. 21, no. 1 (1994), pp. 3–30; and Ann Anagnost, "A Surfeit of Bodies: Population and the Rationality of the State in Post-Mao China," in *Conceiving the New World Order: The Global Politics of Reproduction*, ed. Faye D. Ginsburg and Rayna Rapp (Berkeley: University of California Press, 1995), pp. 22–41.

24. For further details, see Zeng Yi et al., "Causes and Implications of the Recent Increase in the Reported Sex Ratio in China," *Population and Development Review*, Vol. 19, no. 2 (1993), pp. 283–302; Sten Johansson and Ola Nygren, "The Missing Girls of China: A New Demographic Account," *Population and Development Review*, Vol. 17, no. 1 (1991), pp. 35–52; and Terence Hull, "Recent Trends in Sex Ratios at Birth in China," *Population and Development Review*, Vol. 16, no. 1 (1990), pp. 63–84.

tween 114 and 105 might not seem great, that difference suggests that tens of thousands of girls are missing, some 12 percent of all girls born in recent years. What has happened to these girls is not fully known. But it is clear that four practices contribute to these skewed ratios. Infanticide, nonreporting of girl births (either because the parents don't consider such a birth worthy to report or because they hope to hide the birth so they can try to have a boy), abandonment, and sex-selective abortion all play a role in this phenomenon. Underreporting accounts for some missing girls, but abandonment and infanticide—although strongly condemned by the government—is inevitably the fate of some Chinese baby girls. Reports indicate that girls are being abandoned by their parents in increasing numbers. Many of them end up in state-run orphanages, where nearly all of the children are girls. A large proportion of these abandoned girls die in infancy, because of the precarious state of their health upon arrival and because these institutions often do not have the means to care for them adequately.[25] Sex-selective abortions apparently account for a large proportion of the missing girls. Such abortions appear to be on the rise, as technology (particularly ultrasound) becomes increasingly available; when parents find out that they are carrying a girl, they abort the fetus. The government has attempted to outlaw this practice, but because of the widespread availability of abortion, and because the technology to detect the sex of the fetus is often privately owned, government control has not been very effective.

Why is it that females bear the burden of China's family planning program, subjecting them to enormous pressure and sometimes even costing them their lives? The answer to this question is twofold. First, the Chinese government has not addressed the gender-specific effects of its policies in this area. Not only are women the targets of the program, reinforcing centuries-old beliefs that reproduction is women's—and not men's—responsibility. But in addition, although the outcomes of the program have become clear,

25. See Kay Ann Johnson, "The Politics of the Revival of Infant Abandonment in China, with Special Reference to Hunan," *Population and Development Review*, Vol. 22, no. 1 (1996), pp. 77–98; and Nancy E. Riley, "American Adoptions of Chinese Girls: The Sociopolitical Matrices of Individual Decisions," *Women's Studies International Forum*, Vol. 20, no. 1 (1997).

the government has not taken concrete steps to ameliorate the negative impact on females. Even faced with increasing evidence of larger and larger numbers of missing girls, the government chooses to prioritize population control rather than the health and well-being of females. Many observers have argued that there are alternatives to this program (such as more emphasis on female education or the provision of pensions to rural residents) that would have the same effects on reducing population control without the negative consequences for women, but the state has not changed its direction in this matter.[26]

Second, women are particularly affected by the population policy because of the way the program highlights and even reinforces longstanding devaluation of females in Chinese society. Girls and women are less valued than males especially because the foundations of the Chinese family system—including marriage practices, the way that family lineage is traced, and an ideology that gives more power to males than females—dictate that boys are necessary for the family's survival and future. The population control program, by restricting the family's childbearing goals, has reinforced China's longstanding son preference. As Elisabeth Croll has noted, "if there was any doubt before reform that sons were preferred to daughters, the resistance to the single-child family policy has offered continuing proof that daughters not just cannot substitute for sons but indeed they may even be sacrificed for sons."[27]

The Gender Consequences of Economic Reform

In rural areas, the major impact of China's economic reforms of the early 1980s and 1990s has come through the dismantling of the commune system of farming and distribution. This decollectivization has given households and individuals more

---

26. See, e.g., D. Gale Johnson, "Effects of Institutions and Policies on Rural Population Growth with Application to China," *Population and Development Review,* Vol. 20, no. 3 (1994), pp. 503–31; and Amartya Sen, "Population: Delusion and Reality," *New York Review of Books,* September 22, 1994, pp. 62–71.

27. Elisabeth Croll, *From Heaven to Earth: Images and Experiences of Development in China* (London: Routledge, 1994), p. 197.

control over production, distribution, and consumption.[28] In urban areas especially, reform has resulted in the privatization of many means of production and a decreasing presence of the state in many areas of economic life. Whereas once goods and services were rationed and controlled by the state, they are now more often sold and bought on the open market. Individuals have opportunities for jobs in new fields, as foreign investment and technology become increasingly common. What have these economic changes meant for women?

There are many indications that reform has brought women increased economic opportunities. Private employment has increased significantly in both urban and rural areas, and jobs created by the development of new factories, businesses and industries, the influx of foreign investment, and the increased flexibility of the marketplace have given women access to previously unavailable jobs. To illustrate: In Northeast China, foreign companies have been setting up factories in the Dalian Economic and Technical Development Zone, which was created to attract foreign as well as Chinese businesses. These companies are hiring hundreds of young women to work in all aspects of their businesses, from assembly-line workers to floor managers to administrative personnel. In addition, the businesses created to support this industrial development—such as hotels, restaurants, and transportation—have also been hiring new workers. Who are these new workers? While many are from neighboring Dalian City and commute daily to their jobs, most come from the rural areas surrounding the zone, some from hundreds of miles away. The young women often see these new jobs as positive changes, arguing that they provide them opportunities unavailable in their rural villages.[29] They get a chance to go to the city, see new ways of life, receive training and skills in a new area of work, earn higher salaries, and have more freedom than they would at home with their families. Flexibility and increased mobility mean that employed

28. See Huang Shu-min, "Rural China in Transition," in *China Briefing, 1994*, ed. William A. Joseph (Boulder, Colo.: Westview Press, 1994), pp. 87–112, for a discussion of rural economic reform. Ellen R. Judd, *Gender and Power in Rural North China* (Stanford: Stanford University Press, 1994), discusses the effects of rural reform on women's lives.

29. Personal interview files, Dalian, March–April 1996.

women have been able to find more satisfying or better paying jobs.

In rural areas decollectivization has meant that households are freer than before to choose what crops to grow, how to dispose of what they produce, and what other sources of income to pursue. In recent years many households have increased their incomes many times over as they develop new lines of production, from growing vegetables to raising animals or developing small-scale businesses. The standard of living in rural China has subsequently been rising steadily. In some areas women have opportunities to earn cash that belongs to them rather than to the household. Whereas work done in the context of the family (such as farm work) often means that women's earnings are pooled with those of other family members, income generated through sideline activities such as raising chickens or handicraft production is often seen as belonging to the woman who earned it, to be used at her discretion. In this way, women might literally earn more power in their families and family decision making and can increase their power as consumers as well. This is especially likely to be the case in situations where women are involved in sideline activities that contribute a large share to the total household income. In urban areas too, new jobs are giving women an independent source of income, even in those cases (as in the case of rural women working in the Dalian factories) where they remit much of what they earn to their families.

Thus, in both rural and urban areas, the era of economic reform has ushered in major changes for women that have resulted in increased power and independence. At the same time, however, Chinese women's lives are still bounded by a gender ideology that continues to favor men and to limit the opportunities women have. These ideas have been a part of Chinese society for centuries; in addition, along with new technology, foreign enterprises have introduced their own, often Western, versions of gender inequality, which are demonstrated in practices such as unequal hiring and promotion policies. As discussed above in the context of the family planning program, many new institutions are built on or actually reproduce traditional ideas about women's roles.

As in the case of labor force participation and educational attainment, it is important to compare Chinese women's lives today not only with those of women in the past but also with their male peers. In other words, are the opportunities that economic reform has opened up for women similar to or as extensive as those for men? This perspective reveals continuing gender inequality.

Because financial success increasingly depends on individual initiative, contacts and mobility have become more important than they were when the state controlled production and distribution. Rural peasants and urban entrepreneurs alike now need to find markets for their products, business partners, and sources of supply; to do so, individuals travel to other villages or cities to develop business relationships and draw up agreements with others. Theoretically, women have as much access to these new channels as men do. But in reality, women are disadvantaged for a number of reasons. Given the discrepancies between female and male levels of education, women's training is likely to be less than men's, putting them at a disadvantage at an early stage in the process. The discrimination they face in hiring and promotion means they often have had less experience in jobs with responsibility and have developed fewer of the necessary contacts through work, putting them at further disadvantage in the resources they bring to negotiations with others.

The number of migrants, especially from countryside to city, has risen steeply in recent years. But men are more likely than women to travel away from their villages and take short- or long-term jobs elsewhere. This pattern of migration is partly a function of men's greater freedom of movement and partly because the jobs they travel for, such as construction jobs, are considered "male" work. And women are seen much less often than men in restaurants or other gathering places, drinking and associating with current or potential business partners; in addition to general disapproval of women socializing in that manner at night, their responsibilities at home usually preclude such activities.

Many reports indicate that women are actually facing increased discrimination in hiring and promotion. As the state relinquishes some of its surveillance and control over workplaces, employers are freer to hire and promote as they want. And many of these employers are not eager to hire women, since to do so means contending with the family responsibilities that continue to be women's domain. Unwilling to provide child care or maternity leave, employers—both Chinese and foreign—hire men, or hire only single women, letting them go when they marry. For women especially, working in private firms or factories carries with it certain risks; their equal right to hiring and promotion is less well protected there than in state-run firms, where they are guaranteed such benefits as a fully paid maternity leave.

Rural areas are experiencing a rapid spread of so-called township and village enterprises (TVEs), local industries that are providing new work opportunities for women as well as men. But although the work itself may be new for women, it has not led to a higher status for them. Women often have lower pay and more marginal positions in the TVEs than their male counterparts and they are also excluded from most leadership positions.[30]

In other ways as well, these economic changes have served to undermine some of the gains women and girls have made in recent decades. For example, with the return to family farming, rural households must carefully manage their labor resources. Households have to balance the financial needs and responsibilities of all family members and the amount and kind of labor power they can elicit from their members. As discussed above, this sometimes results in women taking control of important sideline production. But it can also result in girls and women being shortchanged when the labor of females is subsumed by the family; in such instances, the females work side by side with other family members but do not earn a separate income. All profits accrue to the head of the household (almost always a male), who can decide how to distribute them. In these cases, compared with their lives in the commune system, where at least they earned their own workpoints, women have actually lost economic independence to male family members.

The growth in male labor migration to urban areas has meant that farm work in some areas is becoming increasingly feminized. It is true that the movement of men off the farms has given women who are assuming responsibility for farming more decision-making power and independence, but it also means that

30. Judd, *Gender and Power in Rural North China*, pp. 86–93.

women often struggle alone to manage the family agricultural pursuits as well as keep the household running.

As discussed above, women continue to be responsible for most housework and child care, and rural women's lives are especially difficult in this regard. As government support of social services declines and family responsibility increases, it is often women who are burdened with the increased responsibility of caring for ill or elderly family members. Furthermore, the household needs as many hands as possible to increase family prosperity, and older women are often called upon to take care of sideline activities or to take over household or child-care responsibilities as younger members go off to work outside the home.

Perhaps even more serious have been recent reports indicating that, especially in rural areas, girls are losing out in schooling as families decide they need their labor power on farms or in family businesses. Child labor is generally increasing in parts of China, and children in poor rural areas are not likely to attend school for long. The cost of educating children is often difficult for poor rural families to sustain; these costs include not only school fees which can use a substantial proportion of a family's annual income, but also the lost opportunity costs of the money or the labor power that children do not contribute to the family while they attend school. Chinese children are leaving school early in spite of the fact that, as recent research indicates, education is an important means for them to get an off-farm—and ultimately better paying—job. In the process that parents go through to estimate the benefits and costs of sending a child to school, girls are particularly vulnerable. If they can invest in only one child's education, it is better, they reason, to invest in a son's, since the family is more likely to benefit from his education than from a daughter's; better to put a daughter to work at an early age, for then her family will receive some benefits before she leaves the family at marriage. In some ways, females are doubly disadvantaged here because education is now likely to aid females more than males in getting an off-farm job; educated peasant women have a higher chance than others to move into nonfarm jobs, such as work in small factories or in the service sector.[31] This fact may not have much effect on parents' decisions about whether to educate their daughters or put them to work, since girls are unlikely to contribute financially to their families after marriage. However, a pattern may develop in China similar to that which currently exists in other parts of East Asia. In Taiwan and Hong Kong, parents allow their daughters to remain in school; these girls then take well-paying jobs until they marry. During the time between leaving school and getting married, they turn most of their income over to their families. Both daughters and parents see advantages to this arrangement; daughters are glad to have academic opportunities, and parents feel they get some return on their educational investment, especially if marriage is delayed, which it often is because of employment.[32]

The timing of China's economic reform has been crucial for its effects on women's lives. The reforms began at about the same time as the more stringent population control policies, and in the conflict between these two changes women have sometimes been made quite vulnerable, especially in rural areas. In order to take full advantage of the economic opportunities that the reforms have made available, families have had to find ways to increase their labor power and to use it efficiently. One of the solutions to the need for labor in the past was to bear more children, but this avenue has been blocked by fertility restrictions. Consequently, they rely on other means, sometimes hiring outside labor or exchanging it among households. But marriage is another source of new labor, and with the practice of patrilocal marriage, it is the husband's family that benefits from having a new working daughter-in-law enter the household. Because of increasing need for labor power and restrictions on where they can seek it, such families often pressure young women into

31. William L. Parish et al., "Nonfarm Work and Marketization of the Chinese Countryside," *China Quarterly* (London), no. 143 (September 1995), pp. 697–730.

32. On the experience of women in Taiwan and Hong Kong, see Lydia Kung, *Factory Women in Taiwan* (New York: Columbia University Press, 1994); Janet W. Salaff, *Working Daughters of Hong Kong: Filial Piety or Power in the Family?* (Cambridge: Cambridge University Press, 1981); and Susan Greenhalgh, "Sexual Stratification: The Other Side of 'Growth and Equity' in East Asia," *Population and Development Review*, Vol. 11, no. 2 (1985), pp. 265–314.

early marriage with their sons; the sooner a marriage takes place, the sooner they have access to two more hands to work in the family business or on family lands. Although marriage age in general has risen in recent years, in rural areas it is estimated that 20 percent of weddings take place before the legal age of 20 years, and that in some, usually very poor, areas 90 percent of women marry before the legal age.[33]

In sum, economic reform has had mixed effects on the lives of Chinese women. Far from being a panacea, or a completely positive change that might push women toward equality with men, it holds both positive and negative possibilities for women. Opportunities have increased, but they often exist within structures such as the family that have themselves developed on the basis of gender inequality. China's new economy is still unfolding and how women fare within it remains to be seen.

Changing Images of Women in China

In less than two decades, the images and appearance of women in public spaces in China have undergone drastic change. The contrast between the images of Chinese women now and those of the Maoist years is especially sharp and heightens the significance of this change.

In the early years of the communist regime, women dressed in austere, plain, and simple clothes, shunning makeup or other adornments, arguing that these things were not needed, since women were to be judged not by their ability to attract men but by their skills and capabilities. This style of dress was also encouraged and sometimes required by state and party officials, who supported such attire as in keeping with the spirit of the revolution.[34] Sexuality was also downplayed and rarely mentioned.

During the Cultural Revolution (1966–76), simple, functional, and unadorned dress for women truly became compulsory. Not only were other styles unavailable, but they were also openly

33. Croll, *From Heaven to Earth*, p. 169.

34. Emily Honig and Gail Hershatter, *Personal Voices: Chinese Women in the 1980s* (Stanford: Stanford University Press, 1988), pp. 42ff; see also Croll, *Changing Identities of Chinese Women*.

and publicly discouraged. Pictures of model "iron maidens" inevitably depicted women dressed in a style of clothing identical to that of men. The message was clear: the energy of these women was dedicated to the lofty pursuits of work, not to something as frivolous as looks or dress. During this decade, sexual interest or sexuality in general was considered to be a sign of lack of loyalty to the party, the state, and the society. Individuals were expected to choose mates not based on some individual desire or interest such as love or attraction, but on shared revolutionary goals.

It was partly as a reaction to these attitudes that the interest in dress, clothing, and appearance began to take hold in the 1980s. People were eager to put the instability and suffering of the Cultural Revolution behind them and had a strong interest in changing lifestyles to mark a break with the past. Brightly colored clothes, new styles, and articles of adornment became increasingly available, and women especially began to develop a real interest in these new fashions. Some claimed that dressing stylishly was a way of self-expression; individual preference or having a unique style, banned during the previous decade, was now becoming more acceptable. Although discussions of sex were still limited during the 1980s, sex and sexuality were nevertheless more visible.

Now, in the mid-1990s, what was considered daring and unusual even in the 1980s is common. Varieties of style, color, and fashion have proliferated, even outside urban areas. Shopping for clothing and other articles of adornment, along with consumer goods, has become a favorite pastime. Fashion magazines, with new Chinese, Hong Kong, and Western styles, are available on many street corners. Signs of a burgeoning fashion and clothing industry are everywhere.

Although men's clothing has also undergone change, much of the interest in clothing and fashion comes from women and, as in many societies, the fashion industry directs its sales pitches to them. Images of women in the public sphere reinforce the interest women have in their own appearance. In a variety of ways, they are being encouraged to pay attention to their appearance, to wear clothing that enhances it, and to find ways to address physical "flaws." Women's magazines contain advertisements for breast enhancers and for cosmetic surgery to "fix" eyes, i.e., make them look more Western. Even the official Women's Federation, reorganized in 1979, which once promoted images of strong revolutionary women on its publications and in its rhetoric, has changed its approach. For example, the head of the Shanghai Women's Federation encouraged the use of makeup, arguing that it allows women to do their jobs better.[35] The Women's Federation Community Center in Dalian, opened in 1995, has dedicated a room to classes that teach women how to apply makeup.[36] In books and magazines, on TV and in advertising, women are being told that they need to look good to succeed. Success here is defined in two ways: on the one hand, attractive women will do better in their jobs and, on the other hand, beauty and care of physical appearance is necessary to be successful in marriage.

Sexuality and sexual expression is no longer as taboo as it was in the past. Holding hands in public is now common practice among young couples. Discussions about sex are much more widespread and manuals on sex are now available. There are even telephone hot lines in many cities where callers can ask about sexual problems. And sex is now being used in China, as it is used elsewhere, to sell goods. Not only are images of beautiful women increasingly widespread in all public arenas in China, these images are more and more likely to exploit sex as well as beauty to sell products. Sultry women posing in scanty clothing adorn magazine covers or are plastered on billboards, inducing consumers to buy products from washing machines to tires to foods. New statues of bare-breasted women are scattered around, and one often sees women as well as men posing for pictures in front of them.

What is the significance of these new images of women, for society, for gender equality, and for women themselves? As in other countries, women are getting mixed messages from such images about what is important: Should they aspire to be strong, independent women who are capable of working hard and well? Or should their goal be to look as attractive as possible to men? Or are these different aspirations at all compatible?

35. Honig and Hershatter, *Personal Voices*, p. 46.

36. Personal observations, March 1996.

Chinese women have to negotiate these mixed messages, finding a pathway to their own goals. But Chinese women today also have to contend with the way in which China's unique history has defined women, men, and the differences between them.

Comparing the images of Chinese women from the Cultural Revolution with those today gives some idea of the weight of this history. Some scholars believe that during the Cultural Revolution women had a status closer to men than at any other time in China's history. It seemed to be a time when gender differences were minimized. However, the Cultural Revolution is now seen as a terrible period in China's recent past, and nearly all aspects of life during that time have been criticized. Therefore, it has been hard for anyone in China to see the situation of women during that time as something positive. Many also argue that it was only because women were forced to act and even look like men that gender differences were not obvious during the Cultural Revolution. In other words, the archetypal Maoist citizen was a male model. Women were not allowed to express their feminine traits. The following statement made by a Chinese man in the 1980s reflects the views of the many people in China who are now reacting against the Cultural Revolution's image of women: "A woman who becomes masculine is a mutant. Capable women should be different from men. They have their own special charm, for example exquisiteness and depth of emotions, and well-developed imaginistic thinking. Women's own latent abilities should be called forth."[37]

Personal adornment, a search for beauty, and highlighting female/male differences are now seen as ways for women to present themselves as women. The twist here, of course, is that in doing so women have also begun to be looked at and even to think of themselves as commodities, much as they have in other societies. Chinese women have to learn to negotiate the legacy of past images and current practices to find a place in society that builds on female models of success without compromising their independence and abilities in public spheres.

37. Honig and Hershatter, *Personal Voices*, quoted in Young, "Chicken Little in China," p. 242.

Conclusion

In sum, the position of Chinese women and the opportunities open to them have improved in many ways in the last two decades. For example, women are going to school in increasing numbers and achieving higher educational levels, and they continue to make up a large percentage of the work force. Yet there are many areas of life in China in which gender inequality is evident and strong. The passage of the 1995 Resolution to improve women's lives reflects the government's open recognition of the continuing difficulties that women face and suggests that even in those areas where state effort has been concentrated, such as work or politics, gender inequality remains. The double burden of paid work outside the home and responsibility for most household chores, the demeaning images of women in the media, the lower status and pay of women in the work force, and the many privileges available only to men are just some of the things that Chinese women share with women throughout much of the world. But this chapter has also stressed the unique and often contradictory influences of China's turbulent history, its enduring cultural traditions, the interventions of the modern Chinese state, and recent, dramatic economic reforms and family planning policies on the lives of women. Thus, women in China today, like women elsewhere, are struggling to define their role in society, but they are carrying on this struggle in a context that must be recognized as uniquely Chinese.

China's Popular Culture in the 1990s

Jianying Zha

When the 50-part television soap opera *Yearning* (*Kewang*) became a national craze in China at the beginning of 1991, almost everyone was taken by surprise. A year and a half had passed since the Tiananmen massacre, and the fact that the Chinese population was rallying around an officially endorsed melodrama about ordinary family life and traditional values rather than displaying continued enthusiasm for political dissent and intellectual culture caused considerable dismay among many educated Chinese.

Few realized, however, that the *Yearning* phenomenon was merely the opening curtain of a dramatic shift in China's cultural landscape. With the wild success of *Yearning,* and a renewed surge of economic reforms, China in the 1990s has witnessed a striking rise of multimedia popular culture, including domestic and imported products. Soap operas, sitcoms, radio talk shows, tabloid newspapers, mass-market books, pop music, and action movies have all mushroomed and grown with explosive speed in recent years, capturing public attention nationwide. Some of these genres have appeared in China for the first time. Thriving in the cracks between political repression and economic opening, between old-style elite culture and official censorship and recent international influences, this new popular culture has played a complex and intriguing role in changing Chinese attitudes, tastes, and thinking. It reflects widespread public fatigue and indifference toward politics in post-Tiananmen China and has helped to breed a new generation more interested in lifestyle than revolution. It has also fostered new spaces for personal expression, debate over social issues, and development of mass entertainment.

While its long-term implications remain ambiguous, popular culture has clearly turned into one of the most volatile and important arenas for battling ideologies and social forces in China, especially as the country becomes increasingly involved in the global economy and international media. Examining the development of China's transformed popular culture illuminates many paradoxes and ironies in contemporary Chinese society and politics.[1]

Historical Background

Traditionally, popular culture in China existed in various forms, including folk religion, regional opera and drama, and storytelling by traveling artists, as well as vernacular literature. It was spread throughout the country, yet highly localized in its many variants. Popular culture in the modern sense, which is overlaid with and to some extent displaced by a national, officially mediated and controlled mass culture, is largely a phenomenon of the 20th century.

Until the 1950s, electronic media were rare in China, and there were few newsreels to inform people about politics and national affairs. Modern newspapers and magazines appeared first in the major Chinese treaty ports in the early 1890s. Radio came to China in 1922, and by 1937 there were 93 broadcasting stations, of which almost half were in Shanghai. China had about 300 movie theaters at that time, with foreign films dominating the Chinese film market. The movie theaters and audiences were also concentrated in Shanghai and a handful of other large cities. But the wars of the coming decade (the Sino-Japanese War and then the civil war between the Nationalists and the Communists) set back this growing mass culture industry: with rare exceptions, further developments of movie, radio, and print media were put on hold.

It was not until after the communist victory in 1949 that a

---

1. Much of the information in this chapter is based on research and interviews conducted in China. For more on some of these sources, see Jianying Zha, *China Pop: How Soap Operas, Tabloids, and Bestsellers Are Transforming a Culture* (New York: New Press, 1995).

truly mass culture with a mass audience was created. Using ceaseless grassroots campaigns and mass movements as tools of mobilization, the new government thoroughly reorganized China's economic, political, social, and cultural life into an extensive vertical structure of control and administration. As part of this process, all public communication channels were nationalized, that is to say, newspapers, publishing houses, radio stations, theaters, and cinemas all came under the control of the Communist Party.

Furthermore, because of its emphasis on the moral and ideological education of all citizens, the Chinese Communist Party (CCP) had long viewed culture in general as an important tool for the party's cause and a sensitive area of power and influence. Mao's view that culture must always serve the revolution and the masses was expressed in 1943 in his famous talk on literature and art at Yan'an, the Red Army base, several years before the CCP actually had the power to impose this mandate on artists nationwide.[2] According to Mao, culture, elite and popular, could never be considered independent of politics and left outside the party's leadership and regulation. Therefore, in addition to nationalizing the major media, the regime also systematically disbanded, destroyed, or took over all the independent vehicles and institutions of public culture that had existed before 1949, such as artists' guilds, folk art troupes, literary associations, and publications. All artists and writers were regrouped into state-sponsored units and went through "thought reform," or indoctrination in Maoist ideology, to become workers for socialist culture. After all the institutional bases of old culture were thus swept away or taken over, the party emerged as the country's only cultural authority in full control of a new national culture that could now begin to penetrate every corner of Chinese society on an unprecedented scale.

Of course, the content of this mass culture had to reflect the spirit of the changed times. The break with tradition was astonishing. From the outset, the communist regime declared hostil-

---

2. Bonnie S. McDougall, *Mao Zedong's "Talks at the Yan'an Conference on Literature and Art": A Translation of the 1943 Text with Commentary*, Michigan Papers in Chinese Studies, no. 39 (Ann Arbor: Center for Chinese Studies, University of Michigan, 1980).

ity toward the past, intending to eradicate ruthlessly all traces of what it considered feudal or bourgeois elements in Chinese culture in order to affirm the dominance of the newly established socialist culture. For this purpose, the regime's cultural workers produced new songs and dances, new poetry and fiction, new paintings and journalism, all following the party's guidance on what was suitable for the education and consumption of the proletarian masses. Many writers and artists willingly collaborated in the creation of this mass culture, as they believed that the party was leading the nation toward a strong, rich, and just society. But the real outcome was the end of intellectual and cultural freedom in China, a didactic, impoverishing cultural tyranny that would only grow with time.

In the three Maoist decades (1949–76), an all-encompassing, monolithic official culture, consciously engineered, propagated, and controlled from the top and systematically disseminated through institutional networks and media channels, gradually washed over the minds of the entire Chinese population. Not only did intellectuals and artists conform, but various forms of traditional popular culture (such as folk religions or regional operas) were displaced or transformed. In a sense, a cultural revolution started the moment the CCP came to power in 1949, and each decade marked its further advance with fresh campaigns, until it culminated in the hysterical heights of the Great Cultural Revolution from 1966 to 1976.

By the time Deng Xiaoping began his reign as China's top leader in 1978, this highly politicized mass culture had effectively saturated the lives of nearly all China's people. In print media alone, China in 1979 had more than 1,800 official magazines, newspapers, and other periodicals with a combined circulation of more than 150 million copies. And there were reports of plans to increase the circulation of the central party newspaper, the *People's Daily*, from 5.3 million to 50 million by the year 2000.

The late 1970s through the eve of the Tiananmen massacre in 1989, with Deng Xiaoping's market-oriented economic reforms and policies of opening to the outside world, proved in retrospect to be a golden decade for the revival of Chinese intellectual life. After decades of persecution and living in ideological straitjackets, intellectuals rejoiced at the more liberal and tolerant political atmosphere. Debates over past errors and tragedies, albeit still carefully circumscribed by official lines, raged in newspapers and journals. Poetry and fiction captured the attention of the general public with their taboo-breaking subjects and emotional honesty. Writers, artists, and scholars became famous overnight and served as a kind of moral voice of the people, venting their grievances and providing the spiritual nourishment they hungered for. By the 1980s, the publication of foreign translations was booming, making much of important 20th-century Western literature and social sciences available to Chinese for the first time. A lively scene of literary and artistic experimentation emerged, with writers and artists now more interested in form and style than political propaganda. Talks about reexamining and reinventing China's cultural tradition and catching up with the West became an increasing obsession among educated Chinese.

Elite intellectual discourse with its lofty idealism, critical energy, and highbrow aspirations dominated China's cultural landscape in the 1980s. Popular culture existed only in the margins during that period. It lacked legitimate production and distribution venues, since the state still held firm financial and political control of the mass media and cultural production. Deng's economic reforms provided some fresh opportunities for daring entrepreneurs, especially in the more freewheeling southern coastal towns. This resulted in the emergence of an underground industry that smuggled and pirated popular videos and literature from Hong Kong and Taiwan, as well as an alternative, semiprivate network that sold and distributed more commercially viable books. But, on the whole, opportunities for independent action in the field of culture remained quite limited. The potential of popular culture remained latent, and to most Chinese intellectuals, it was simply a blind spot.

The turning point was Tiananmen. It is ironic that an event that ended in the brutal suppression of a popular political movement should give rise to a rebirth of Chinese popular culture. The remainder of this chapter will describe this rebirth by looking at recent trends in television, newspapers and tabloids, music, literature, and film.

Television

Drama

Up to the end of the Cultural Revolution in 1976, the sight of a small black-and-white television in a Chinese living room had been a sure sign of luxury and privilege. To most Chinese families, not having a television set was no loss: fresh local productions were pathetically few, and for decades the government had banned foreign movies and television shows, except for about a dozen from "socialist brother countries"—movies like *Lenin in October* and *Lenin in 1918* from the Soviet Union, or *The Flower Girl* from North Korea.

Only in the past 15 years or so has television begun to enter the living rooms of ordinary Chinese families. Given China's generally low standard of living, the increase of television sales has been sudden and remarkable. In 1978, only roughly half a million sets were sold—a tiny figure in a large country like China. But a surge began in 1979 when nearly two million sets were sold.[3] In the 1980s nearly every family managed to buy a television, a rapid spread comparable to what happened in the United States in the 1950s. By the end of 1990, about 166 million TV sets were installed in people's homes, that is to say, one of every six or seven Chinese owns a television set. More than any other modern device, television has become a symbol of material prosperity.

Naturally, the popularization of television led to higher demand for good programming. Now more than 400 television stations broadcast throughout China, of which about 100 produce original programming. The dominant force is the national network, Central China Television (CCTV), whose presentation of official news and information, politically correct entertainment, and educational programs can be seen throughout the country on hundreds of stations that receive signals from Beijing via satellite links and retransmission facilities. While all stations fall under the administrative and

3. James Lull, *China Turned On: Television, Reform, and Resistance* (London: Routledge, 1991), p. 20.

censorship umbrella of the Ministry of Radio, Film, and Television in Beijing, regional stations that originate some of their own programming enjoy a certain autonomy in their day-to-day operations. They can, for example, import foreign shows without observing the regulations that CCTV would have to abide by. But on the whole, regional officials have a clear understanding of the national guidelines regarding the purpose and rules of television, and since ultimately their jobs are at stake, they are more than willing to play it safe on programming. As a result, the main staples from CCTV, usually banal and didactic, dominate Chinese television, along with a dose of innocuous "local color" programming. The more popular offerings such as foreign movies, drama series, news, and sports remain quite limited. By official stipulation, imported shows and films belong to a category of programs that cannot exceed 8 percent of total airtime.[4]

Throughout the 1980s people brought their new sets home and complained about television programs with equal amounts of zeal. This was in part caused by the lack of other forms of entertainment. Even for the residents of Beijing, there was not much night life. Until the boom of recent years, restaurants and shops tended to close early in the evening, leaving even the major avenues deserted by ten o'clock. Movies, concerts, and theater of any kind were infrequent and were also plagued regularly by censorship or lack of quality offerings. Museums were in notoriously bad condition, with great classical paintings often tucked away in storage rooms for protection. With government backing, the old traditions of public teahouses, local opera performances, and folk art festivals were revived to some degree, but their appeal was limited mostly to a small sector of the older generation. On the whole, Chinese cities remained largely provincial and boring in spite of a splash of fancy new hotels and commercial buildings that catered to foreign business people and a tiny number of local nouveaux riches.

So, naturally, for the millions who could count only on television for daily entertainment, its poor programming was disappointing. Any mention of "what's on TV" would elicit a litany

4. Ibid., p. 27.

of complaints: the international news was too short, the domestic news too dull; the drama shows had laughable plots, laughable characters and laughable acting, and the stand-up comedians were not funny at all—the complaints ran on and on.

Against this backdrop of widespread viewer unhappiness the soap opera *Yearning* exploded onto Chinese TV screens. Since the show is now widely acknowledged to be a watershed event in Chinese television and the rise of popular culture in mass media, it is worth discussing its origins and impact in some detail.

The timing of the show's appearance was both crucial and intriguing. According to the producers' account and newspaper reports, plans for the show started before the tragic events of June 1989. The impetus for creating a new type of TV drama derived from a blend of professional exasperation and ambition. By the late 1980s the multiple woes of Chinese television had created a sense of urgency among some people in the field. For example, experts calculated that the country needed some 2,000 episodes of television drama each year to fill up the available time slots, but available programming fell far short of this.

For one thing, funding was in severe shortage. While censorship remained intact, government financial support had dropped steadily in the name of economic reform. By one reporter's account, the state gave roughly two billion yuan (about $364 million) to TV networks each year, which in 1990 averaged out to less than $2.20 for each TV set in the country. From this meager sum had to come the salaries of every network employee, funds for basic infrastructure maintenance and development, and so on. Advertising was only beginning to appear in China at the time and had a long way to go before becoming a major means of funding television production.

Much of this limited budget was also being allocated to expensively made TV shows; many television producers and directors had been trained at film school and believed that a television drama would gain respectability if it resembled a movie. They not only squandered money this way, but also revealed their lack of professionalism in modern television production.

The situation distressed some young television employees at the Beijing Television Art Center (BTAC). For years they had watched with envy the success of a host of soap operas imported from countries like Japan, Mexico, Brazil, and, later, from Taiwan and Hong Kong. They were fascinated by the way these long, sentimental series captured the average Chinese audience. Later on, in interviews, several of them recollected a collective sense of shame and agitation over the phenomenon, which motivated them to create their own series. Lu Xiaowei, future director of *Yearning,* said that he was driven by a sense of honor and a desire to prove that a Chinese director could produce equally good TV series. Li Xiaoming, the show's future chief scriptwriter, said his fingers itched to write as he watched those imported series and thought how easy it would be to make a mainland Chinese version: "All the main scenes were shot indoors; you could tell at one glance that they didn't cost much." This genre of television series, shot mostly with studio-made indoor scenes, later received the Chinese name *shineiju,* or indoor drama. Its attractions were obvious: low production cost, high emotional appeal. For a true television professional, herein lay the best use of the strength and limits of the media.

Luckily, BTAC's leaders were thinking along the same lines. In 1988 they built a new studio on Beijing's outskirts where the Center could develop its own indoor dramas. Studio construction used up nearly all of BTAC's program money that year, and Chen Changben, the head of the Beijing Broadcasting Enterprise Bureau, of which the Center is a subsidiary, had put his career on the line by approving the budget. As a result, the Center was under intense pressure to succeed quickly. Its first show had to get high ratings.

The story of how BTAC formed a team of authors who wrote the script for *Yearning* has become legend among Chinese TV professionals. The team of five men included two well-known novelists, Wang Shuo and Zheng Wanlong; two BTAC staff members, Li Xiaoming, the Center's chief literary editor, and Zheng Xiaolong, the Center's young deputy director; and Chen Changben, the party boss at BTAC who had also been a writer in the past. From the outset, these men understood that their job was to create a popular show with mass appeal that would attract audiences like the foreign hits. When they first gathered in a hotel suite late in the winter of 1988, they had very little raw material. Zheng Xiaolong brought in a newspaper report about a divorced working mother raising her deaf son, and Zheng Wanlong had an idea about an abandoned baby. From this skimpy beginning, through a series of intense "script talk sessions," a story gradually took shape and characters were added and fleshed out. The team then appointed Li Xiaoming to write up a full script from the notes. A devoted TV professional, Li rolled up his sleeves and focused on writing the soap opera for five months, oblivious to the student demonstrations in Tiananmen Square, and produced a draft that was the equivalent of a 1,500-page book. BTAC then hired two unknown writers to polish the draft.

In the finished script, the project had evolved into a 50-episode saga about two Beijing families and their daily lives and struggles during the Cultural Revolution and the years of reform in the 1980s. The Lius are a working-class family living in an old working-class neighborhood, while the Wangs are an intellectual family living in a modern apartment. The two families first come into contact during the Cultural Revolution. The Wangs suffer persecution and become social outcasts, which offers a chance for the two central characters to meet. Assigned to a factory job, Husheng, the son of the Wang family, comes under the supervision of Huifang, the daughter of the Liu family. They soon become lovers and eventually get married, thus starting off a long, convoluted melodrama of interactions between the two families over their class and moral differences and through the ups and downs of their political fortunes. However, contrary to usual Chinese treatment, politics is largely pushed to the background, reflected in the way the obligatory portrait of Chairman Mao hangs as an unobtrusive decoration on the walls of various homes depicted in the show. The series focuses instead on everyday life in the Liu and Wang families, especially on various romantic relationships. While the important political events of the time remain vague, there are endless scenes depicting mundane details such as family meals, household chores, gossip between friends, quarrels and misunderstandings between lovers and family members. And like other TV soaps, the show provides a heavy dose of tear-jerking scenes and many improbable but convenient twists and turns to keep the audience hooked on the story.

The program formulates a sharp contrast between the two central characters. Liu Huifang, a simple worker with a sweet temper and a heart of gold, is forever kind, patient, modest, and giving. The well-educated Wang Husheng, on the other hand, is an egotistical, whining, spineless man of weak morality. With a few exceptions and variations, similar differences are shown to exist between the two families. Consequently, the working-class Lius come off in a generally favorable light, while the sophisticated Wangs are often portrayed in unsympathetic ways. Caught between the two families is an abandoned baby girl raised by Huifang through all manner of hardship. The child later turns out to be the daughter of Wang Husheng's sister. Fate being cruel to the saintly Huifang, she is eventually divorced from her ungrateful husband (pressured by his family to pursue a woman of his privileged background), hit by a car, paralyzed, bedridden, and forced to give back her beloved adopted daughter.

This script, designed to appeal to a large audience with its working-class values and melodrama, was quickly approved and produced by BTAC. The creative method of talk sessions and teamwork would later be emulated by almost all writers of Chinese TV series. The shooting of *Yearning* was as speedy as the writing: 50 episodes done within ten months, an average of six days per episode.

The Center had practically no money left when the shooting ended and had done little advertising for *Yearning* when it first aired in Nanjing in November 1990. But by the end of the month the news had spread by word of mouth. By January 1991, all the major television stations in China had picked up the show, and the viewer ratio was unusually high. In the greater Beijing area, for instance, the rating was 27 percent, surpassing all previous foreign hits. In Yanshan, an oil and chemical industrial town with a population of over 100,000, the audience share was a stunning 98 percent.

A *Yearning* craze set in.[5] Letters and phone calls flooded the

5. For a discussion of the *Yearning* craze (and some production photos), see "TV Series Touches Longed-For Nerve," in the semi-official Chinese publication *China Today* (Beijing) (August 1991), pp. 46–48.

stations daily, the time slot allotted for the show was increased, and reruns began even before the first run had ended. The show emptied the streets in cities like Nanjing and Wuhan. People everywhere talked about *Yearning* and hummed its theme songs. Eighteen cassette versions of the series' music were hurriedly produced and sold like hot cakes. The press churned out all sorts of stories, interviews, and analytical essays about the show. By the time the cast and crew went on promotional tour, the stars of the show were already household names and they were mobbed by huge crowds wherever they went.

If the spectacular popularity of *Yearning* took many by surprise, the official reaction was even more unexpected. On January 8, 1991, Li Ruihuan, the CCP Politburo member in charge of ideology, received the program's crew at Zhongnanhai, the party headquarters, and warmly praised the show. Li said the success of *Yearning,* a show about ordinary life, taught party leaders an important lesson: an artistic work must entertain first, or it is pointless to talk about using it to educate people. According to Li, leaders had come to realize that the influence exerted by the party must be subtle and imperceptible, and the people should be influenced without being conscious of it. In order to make socialist principles and moral virtues acceptable to the broad masses, the party must learn to use cultural forms that appeal to them. According to Li, these principles and virtues—honesty, tolerance, harmony, mutual help among the people—were well portrayed in *Yearning*. He called the show "a worthy model for our literary and artistic workers." On the following day, all the major Chinese papers reported Li's remarks as front-page news.

Despite the standard propaganda and the sinister talk about subtly influencing people, to many of those seasoned in Chinese-style politics, Li's true message lay between the lines. A shrewd, moderate politician assigned to the sensitive post of ideological chief right after Tiananmen, Li's tone was clearly conciliatory, considering the still tense, gloomy political atmosphere of the time. While the hard-liners had been drumming about deepening class struggle, Li was obviously using *Yearning* to highlight a set of temperate values, sprinkling his remarks with revealing words like "harmony," "unity," "tolerance," and "prosperity."

Yearning became wildly controversial in China's cultural community. Those who liked it more often than not tended to be writers of old-school socialist realism or cultural apparatchiks who were simply following the lead of Li Ruihuan. The younger and more experimental writers and critics, if they bothered to watch the show at all, found *Yearning* generally repulsive. To them, the show was offensive in many ways: its (in their view) vulgar style and cheap sentimentality, its endorsement and use by officials, its derogatory portrayal of intellectuals, and its promulgation of traditional Chinese values such as self-sacrifice and submission (as opposed to modern, Western values such as individualism and initiative). To these critics, the scriptwriters sold out to curry favor with both the regime and the working people. Some detractors even suspected that the whole thing was a conspiracy by the Ministry of Culture to placate the post-Tiananmen population with harmless conservative entertainment. And as if to give this suspicion some credence, Chen Changben, the BTAC leader who had supervised the production of *Yearning,* was promoted to vice-minister of culture.

Given *Yearning*'s ambiguous content and timing and its bizarre mixture of cynicism and sentimentalism, the fiercely different reactions to it were perhaps inevitable. The seeming paradox and irony were difficult to swallow: the same Chinese people who had followed the students and elite intellectuals to Tiananmen Square shouting "freedom" and "democracy" now embraced the conservative values the government eagerly lauded: they gushed sympathy for the passive conventional Huifang and denounced the villianized, pretentious intellectual characters. Furthermore, the popularity of *Yearning* stood in jarring contrast to the sudden post-Tiananmen decline of the intellectual avant-garde scene. After the massacre, writers continued to produce and magazines continued to be published, but the literary atmosphere changed, the spirit and energy sagged. All of a sudden, it seemed, readers of serious literature dwindled, magazine subscriptions dropped, and nobody seemed to care.

Thus, the *Yearning* craze raised the curtain for China's transition from the 1980s idealistic, oppositional cultural scene to the 1990s market- and mass-audience-oriented, politically ambiguous popular culture. The former had been led by the intellectual elite, who were gradually marginalized by a new breed of commercial talent. Inevitably, ambivalence toward post-Tiananmen pop culture has continued to plague many Chinese intellectuals.

Amid the stormy debate over *Yearning,* two key elements largely escaped analysis. The first was the working method of the scriptwriters: teamwork, rather than individual writing, is nothing new in the West, but in China the *Yearning* team did it for the first time. Second, there was the significance of ordinary life as a main subject for the media. After *Yearning,* works depicting major political events and big historical moments declined, while daily life with all its mundane aspirations, emotions, charms, and troubles has become an increasingly dominant theme on Chinese television.

In 1992, BTAC produced its second hit, China's first situation comedy, *The Story of an Editorial Office* (*Bianjibu de gushi*). Again, the script team included Wang Shuo, who was on his way to becoming the most famous post-Tiananmen Chinese writer, and Feng Xiaogang, who was soon to be another high-profile television writer/director. Unlike *Yearning,* which had a continuous plot line, *The Story of an Editorial Office* was episodic and loosely arranged around six magazine editors and a series of characters who constantly drop in and out of the office. Structurally, it resembles American shows like *Murphy Brown* or *Mary Tyler Moore,* even though the themes and styles are very different. After the creative team worked out an outline, the 30 or so episodes were divided among six authors to write up separately. Set in current times, *The Story of an Editorial Office* took up a slew of topics the scriptwriters considered hot: rumors about natural disasters, money, fame, romance, power struggle within a work unit, baby-sitter troubles, and so on. Although the quality of writing was uneven, the show on the whole had a more urbane, whimsical, humorous flavor, the pace was faster, and the acting was better than *Yearning.* The program was a huge success in numerous large northern cities, perhaps owing to its combination of certain truly hilarious scenes, some very funny dialogue, and a measure of social and political satire. Of course, the show toed the official political line with consummate caution and shrewdness: the writers made sure that no matter how pungent certain satirical lines were, the characters always uttered them in a lighthearted, buffoonish fashion, and each episode would invariably end on a politically correct tone. This time, it won universal praise: not only the average audience and the officials liked the show, university students and intellectuals enjoyed it too. Although it did not set off another nationwide craze—viewers in the south did not respond with the same enthusiasm, probably because they found it difficult to appreciate the show's dense, garrulous Beijing humor—the general consensus among critics seemed to be that *The Story of an Editorial Office* was in some ways a better made TV show than *Yearning*.

After *Yearning* and *The Story of an Editorial Office,* indoor drama became the rage among the general public. Many stations were on the lookout for promising new programs, and more novelists began to try their hands at television team writing. With two popular shows, BTAC assumed the role of the flagship for making TV series, enjoying an easy relationship with the Beijing municipal officials and attracting public attention with each of its new projects.

Another turning point came in early 1992, when Deng Xiaoping made important speeches calling for deeper and wider market reform. The paramount leader's call stimulated further economic deregulation and set off a frantic race for material wealth among the Chinese population. Culture shifted gears, too. To encourage more individual initiative and relieve some of the government's financial burdens, television stations and professional writers were allowed more flexibility. Although the final product was still subject to official approval, some programming was now contracted out. Producers could now solicit advertising on their own for TV shows and receive a fat percentage. Writers in demand got much higher pay per TV episode. Excited by these new measures, more and more people began putting their energies into television work.

BTAC's next drama series, *No Choice in Loving You* (*Ai ni mei shangliang),* a chatty, contrived, and long-winded love story written by a team (again including Wang Shuo) turned out to be a flop: the audiences were lukewarm, the critics openly sarcastic. And it made no impression on the southern cities. But it made the news anyway because of two things that were considered breakthroughs in Chinese television. First, the show enjoyed a well-prepared, noisy publicity campaign that long preceded its release: professional media hype was born. Second, it was the first time that a TV show actually pulled in good money for its producers. Despite the high ratings of its previous shows, BTAC had remained poor, gaining nothing but professional prestige. Quick to take advantage of the laissez-faire, entrepreneurial environment, BTAC was able to sell the new show for a handsome sum. The duped buyer of the flop turned out to be none other than CCTV, the headquarters of official television!

Once the floodgates had opened, the tide of commercialism washed over Chinese television quickly. The number of TV commercials shot up, as did that of programs selling merchandise and providing shopping directories. Indoor dramas came and went; as the audience's taste in the genre grew more selective, there were flops and hits. But two more popular shows proved BTAC's professional savvy and helped keep its leading position in the field. *Beijinger in New York* (*Beijing ren zai Niu Yue*), a well-shot, well-acted series based on a best-selling book about struggling new Chinese immigrants in New York, became the hottest show in 1993. The show's petty, xenophobic tones and unflattering portrayal of capitalist American society didn't seem to bother its Chinese audience; its patriotic sentiment, on the other hand, obviously rang a bell among the general public.[6] Officials showered praises on it; curiously, many intellectuals liked it too. In 1994 the short series *Have a High, Then Die (Guo ba yin jiu si)*, based on a novella by Wang Shuo, enjoyed a quiet yet substantial success for its sympathetic treatment of mundane daily life and ordinary love.

News

Government control of televised news reports has remained very tight, especially of news that is considered politically sensitive. CCTV continues to oversee what is permissible in this area,

---

6. For more on *Beijinger in New York* and on the issue of hypernationalism and xenophobia as a theme in contemporary Chinese popular culture, see Geremie Barme, "Soft Porn, Packaged Dissent, and Nationalism: Notes on Chinese Culture in the 1990s," *Current History*, Vol. 93, no. 584 (September 1994), pp. 270–75.

issuing daily its carefully filtered edition of prime-time domestic and international news for the entire nation. In May 1993, however, a new CCTV morning news program called *Eastern Time and Space* (*Dongfang shikong*) was aired, and after a few months many people in the media began to murmur about the show as "a quiet revolution in Chinese television." To those familiar with standard Chinese television news, the program indeed has some refreshing traits: more direct interviews (people actually answer questions and speak in their own voices) and on occasion more neutrality of reporting. The format is also new to Chinese viewers: designed somewhat like TV news magazines such as CBS's *60 Minutes*, *Eastern Time and Space* is divided into four slots, each featuring a main story, thus enabling more in-depth reporting. The chief source of these changes was a mostly young crew, who in the climate of reform have been given a freer hand to design their programs. But the finished product still has to go through CCTV's official censors, so it is easy to recognize the stamp of censorship and self-censorship in the program's halfhearted, cautious efforts toward freer reporting. Switch to other channels, though, and you are back to more orthodox news with the usual stiff anchors reading out dull official lines. Compared with that fare, *Eastern Time and Space* is quite an improvement.

All the same, the producers of the program know that certain lines are not to be crossed when it comes to real hard news. In this respect, Chinese in the southern parts of the country enjoy a privilege. In cities like Guangzhou or Shenzhen, for example, anybody can set up an antenna to watch Hong Kong television, even though this is officially illegal. Up north, word of mouth is still the best way to learn the real news.

Newspapers and Tabloids

In 1949, the new communist government inherited fewer than 400 functioning newspapers. Since then, the number of newspapers and the size of their circulations have fluctuated greatly, depending on China's political and economic situation. A great surge in the number of newspaper titles and readers and in the size of circulations took place in the reform years of the early 1980s, a period of relatively open political climate in which public enthusiasm about the affairs of the nation seemed to rise to a new height. According to an official statement, there were about 180 newspapers before 1978, but by 1993 the number had jumped to nearly 2,000. In 1993 alone, more than a hundred new papers appeared.[7] By 1986, circulation of the national and provincial press reached more than 200 million, meaning that there is a copy of a newspaper for about every five Chinese citizens, more than a threefold increase from 1978.[8]

Newspapers have always been subject to the party's close control, since they are considered to be on the front line of ideological battles. Structurally, Chinese newspapers are set up like many regular work units, receiving both subsidies and orders from various levels of party and government; but control has loosened to varying degrees at different papers and at different times. With the exception of certain unusual political times (i.e., during the chaotic, early period of the Cultural Revolution when various Red Guards and other rebellious factions ran wild with their own publications), no genuine private newspapers were allowed to exist. As always, whatever is printed in the papers is not supposed to go beyond limits and guidelines from above. And the party, of course, ultimately sets all the limits and the guidelines.

Although newspapers, like other public media in China, were never free even before 1989, the Tiananmen crackdown cast an even darker shadow over the press. It would not be easy for Beijingers to forget the brief few days in the spring of 1989 when reporters from the *People's Daily*, the central party newspaper, demonstrated on the streets shouting, "We don't want to lie anymore!" Journalists and staff from many other major papers joined the students and openly petitioned for a free press and free speech. Such actions were unprecedented in communist China. But even before the massacre in Beijing, the government abruptly shut down the *World Economic Herald*, a reformist Shanghai newspaper popular among educated Chinese, and

7. *Shijie Ribao* (World Journal/New York), December 24, 1993.
8. Lull, *China Turned On*, p. 19.

dismissed its highly respected chief editor, Qin Benli. The incident was symbolic of how a newspaper and its staff were completely at the mercy of the party. After Tiananmen, hard-liners reclaimed the leadership of many national papers, pushing a campaign of investigation and reprisal that led to the purging of many liberal-minded newspaper staff and setting an ultraconservative tone in the press. Subsequently, Chinese newspapers became little more than sheets of governmental propaganda and boldfaced lies.

In addition to political repression, periodicals' financial concerns had grown graver by the end of 1989. With the reforms, and with new papers and journals springing up to compete with the old ones, complacency over absolute financial security had steadily eroded. Even though inflation continued and the price of paper climbed, the government still doled out the same old subsidies. And for the first time a lot of papers realized that the party would not bail them out of debt.

Opportunity for change came in 1992. As in other areas, Deng Xiaoping's speech calling for wider and deeper market reform and his open rejection of the rigid division between socialism and capitalism proved to be a powerful stimulus for China's newspapers. Following Deng's orders, the PRC Press and Publishing Administration announced new guidelines. Publishers were given more power to decide on matters such as printing adult erotic materials and kung fu novels; the previous ban on printing pictures of girls in bikinis, foreign movie stars, and pop singers on Chinese calendars was lifted, and publishers in specialized fields could now cross over to general subjects in order to boost sales. Many newspapers began to allow willing, capable individuals to take charge of sections of a newspaper as long as they signed a contract of responsibilities. In effect, this means the contractor has the power to hire or fire staff and to design his or her own section of the newspaper, as long as he or she turns in the pledged percentage of profit from sales and advertisements.

In this auspicious atmosphere, many newspapers began to toy with a more relaxed image. The most obvious change took place first among the official but not so major newspapers such as the *Beijing Youth Daily*, the *China Youth Daily*, and the *China*

Business Times. In interviews conducted in 1993 with some of the younger editors of these papers, a sense of excitement and pent-up energy came across very strongly. The editors talked with pride about the various incremental improvements they were able to achieve at their papers: more power given to the younger editors and reporters, fresh, lively social news and human interest stories (versus the usual dull political propaganda), and in terms of format, more colors and better typesetting (imitating the eye-catching style of Hong Kong and Taiwan newspapers). In some ways, it was the first time that the generation of editors and reporters in their thirties was allowed to take charge at these papers. Many were becoming section chiefs or program directors around this time, and they quickly took up Deng's call for marketization to make their papers profitable by lightening them up.

In this wave of competition for readership, some papers attempted rather curious shifts and strategies. For example, Yang Lang, a young section chief at the *China Youth Daily*, planned with his colleagues to put out a special edition of fake news on April 1. The idea was to get readers' attention by playing a joke on April Fool's Day. But Yang and his colleagues were severely criticized by their superiors who saw this sort of flippancy as going too far for a newspaper that was, after all, the organ of the Chinese Communist Youth League.

But the colorful transformation of *Cultural Weekend*, the weekend edition of the official *China Culture Gazette* (CCG), provides a rather revealing case of how commercial pop culture stole into the heart of a party organ. Like many other newspapers in Beijing, CCG had long been a bastion of the hard-line apparatchiks, always echoed the party line, and printed nothing but standard party propaganda. As the economic reforms spread, however, the paper's financial situation worsened. Its debt piled up and the paper was on the brink of folding toward the end of 1992.

Under these pressures Zhang Zuomin, a former Red Guard in his late 30s, became one of the first bold contractors to take charge of *Cultural Weekend*. Zhang's method of saving the paper was radical. On January 1, 1993, the New Year edition of *Cultural Weekend* beckoned readers with four sheets filled with photographs of nude and barely clothed women (most of whom were busty Westerners). It also ran a front-page interview on the subject of nudity with the famous movie star Liu Xiaoqing, who was well known for her frank public confessions even before the birth of China's tabloid industry. The issue was an instant hit: it not only sold out quickly from the newsstands but also earned Zhang's paper a reputation as "the most breezy paper in Beijing."

The ensuing controversy over whether such practice crossed the line over to pornography did not shake Zhang's power at the paper. *CCG*'s hard-line chief editor backed him up even under pressure from his own bosses at the CCP's Propaganda Department and the Ministry of Culture. The wily old apparatchik cleverly defended his paper's new moves by invoking Deng's call for market reforms and used his own clout to fend off Zhang's critics. Economic survival and profit, of course, were now the real motive behind such farcical political struggle.

The pragmatic approach triumphed. *Cultural Weekend* soon became known for its often racy front-page coverage of women, sex, and the pop culture scene. Its circulation soared to 260,000, far surpassing *CCG*'s old record. In Beijing journalist circles, Zhang Zuomin's taste for sensationalism earned him a rather dubious reputation, but he took personal pride in the fact that *Cultural Weekend* under his leadership became one of "the four little dragons of the Beijing press."

Indeed, in many ways the Chinese tabloid press was born in 1992 and blossomed rapidly in 1993, with hundreds of small papers mushrooming everywhere. The format of a small-size weekend edition carrying only "soft news" about culture, society, and amusements, sold separately from the weekday paper, became such a vogue that Chinese journalists referred to the phenomenon as "the weekend edition craze." The influence came partly from the Western newspaper tradition of the weekend supplement, but more directly from Taiwan and Hong Kong newspapers to which many mainland journalists had access. Personal contacts and exchanges with the outside world were also increasing. Among the thousands of Taiwan and Hong Kong investors who flocked to the mainland each year were some newspaper and magazine editors looking for joint-venture opportunities. As they met and socialized with their mainland counterparts, information and ideas were transmitted and discussed.

Naturally, not all of the weekend editions went as far as *Cultural Weekend,* and some, such as the popular *Southern Weekend,* were clearly a notch too genteel and serious to be called tabloid papers. Instead of "selling cheap stuff" as many considered Zhang Zuomin to be doing at *Cultural Weekend, Southern Weekend* took pains to solicit and print columns by famous writers such as Wang Meng and Liu Xinwu. Of course, these well-respected authors of serious literature, while lending prestige to the paper, would naturally adjust their style, tone, and topics for the readers of a weekend paper. More often than not, their contributions fit with the generally light and breezy tone of the paper.

On the whole, there is no denying that these papers share a set of common characteristics: gossipy, often prone to sensationalistic topics and reporting, and obsessed with the pop culture scene. With this formula, many papers have begun to support themselves, attract advertisements, and relieve the government of its financial burden. But the lively competition among the weekend editions has broken more than new economic ground. For average Chinese readers who have long been fed up with the official propaganda papers, the weekend editions and the evening dailies, with their lively, interesting coverage of popular events, have provided a refreshing alternative. Once dominant organs, such as the *People's Daily* and the *Guangming Daily,* are still delivered to the offices of all state enterprises and other organizations nationwide, but they have lost their monopoly over readers. They simply cannot compete with the colorful, sexy weekend editions now available at newsstands.

The trend is controversial within the journalist community. Many frown at the vulgarity of the tabloid papers. In an interview, a young editor at the *People's Daily* described them as "various intestines boiled into a thick, greasy soup." He was certain that readers would get tired of them soon. Some journalists feel that, since China has no real news freedom to speak of, peddling soft news is just an easy way of evading the country's harsh political reality. Some older intellectuals privately worry that the new trend may play right into the regime's hand by helping to provide a kind of new opiate for the masses. Others are dismayed by the spread of bribe-taking by journalists and other compromises of professional ethics. "I'm deeply disappointed by our reporters," said the prominent dissident journalist Dai Qing in 1993. "They are totally corrupted by commercialization."

On the other hand, there are many defenders of the new trend, such as Chen Xilin, the young director of the weekend edition of the *China Business Times*. By shunning political propaganda and focusing on the economy and lifestyle issues, Chen's paper embodies a brand of journalism that is smart, slick, and politically moderate. Chen's opinion of papers like *Cultural Weekend* is not high, but his views about Chinese media reflect the optimism of many Chinese journalists. In a long interview, Chen speculated:

> After a while, some of these small, gossipy papers will fold, some will remain. The society always needs this sort of reading, but not so much of it. They play an important role in the eventual freeing of the press: they've broken up the official news language, shifted the concerns from the government and state affairs to ordinary people and social lives. They are already affecting the big papers, forcing them to loosen up a bit, to compete, to be more attractive to readers. Isn't this a victory in itself?

So far, Chen Xilin's prediction has largely turned out to be correct. The initial craze over the weekend editions and other tabloid papers has subsided; some of them have disappeared from the streets. But a great number of them have survived and are doing well. Forced to adapt and compete, many big papers, including the *People's Daily*, have moved to enliven their pages or add lifestyle supplements.

In some ways, these upstarts have become a new establishment within China's print media, and the line between them and the official papers can be blurry sometimes. To a certain degree, the smaller, lighter papers belong to the new pop culture they promote and report on. Even with their soft positions or silence on certain political issues, they have managed to widen the range of coverage by bringing new subjects and styles into Chinese print. Because of their energy and flair, the Chinese newspaper scene in the mid-1990s has grown more diverse and lively, if not free.

Music

To discuss contemporary Chinese pop music is to discuss the various outside influences that have inspired music trends in China since the late 1970s. A singer from Taiwan named Deng Lijun was the first to capture the mainland Chinese fresh out of the Maoist decades during which all music had to be "revolutionary" and suit the tastes of workers, peasants, and soldiers. In sharp contrast to the rigidity and grand zeal of revolutionary songs, Deng's sweet face and soft, sentimental songs about unrequited love and a cozy home melted millions of Chinese hearts. Affectionately nicknamed "The Little Deng," the Taiwan singer became a household name in China and for years the object of imitation by many young mainland singers.

Traditional Chinese music—operas, folk songs, instrumentals—enjoyed a revival around the same time, finding its followers largely among older people and the rural population. Western classical music came back to China in the late seventies, attracting an audience mainly of educated urban professionals. This audience is likely to expand as the Chinese standard of living improves and more people can afford to buy stereo systems and compact discs. One indicator of interest is the circulation of *Philharmonic* (*Ai Yue*), the first Western classical music and stereo review in Chinese; launched around 1993, it sold about 2,000 copies in Beijing alone.

Contemporary Western pop music like rock 'n' roll, jazz, and country western was still hard to come by in China in the mid-1980s because of its reputation as a source of bourgeois decadence. But through foreign visitors, some Chinese musicians gained access to this "alien music." China's own rock scene did not begin until 1986, the year a 25-year-old trumpeter named Cui Jian listened to the Beatles, Elvis Presley, Bob Dylan, and Sting for the first time.[9] Cui had already been playing the guitar and writing his first pop songs, but only through this powerful foreign music was he to find a unique voice. That year he wrote

9. Zhao Jianwei, *Cui Jian zai yiwusuoyouzhong nahan: Zhongguo yaogun beiwanglu* (Cui Jian Cries Out from Nothingness: A Memorandum of Chinese Rock 'n' Roll) (Beijing: Beijing Normal University Press, 1992), p. 121.

and by a fluke was able to perform "Nothing to My Name" at a concert in Beijing Workers' Stadium. The song has become a classic in the short history of Chinese rock 'n' roll, and Cui Jian has emerged since then as China's first and most celebrated rock star.

From the beginning, Cui Jian elicited an impassioned response from his audience. His husky voice, rugged image, and intense music that sounds like explosives to Chinese ears sent shock waves through the sleepy Chinese music scene. But above all, it was his lyrics that conquered millions of fans. Angry, passionate, intensely personal and political, Cui's beautifully written lyrics expressed the disillusionment, the alienation, the confusion, and the yearning of an entire generation. His music quickly became a release valve for the emotions of the young. Sensing its subversive power, the government banned rock from television and frequently sent plainclothes police to maintain order at Cui's concerts. Although Cui Jian performed mostly in small concerts and did not release his first album until late 1989, by then he had become a symbol for rebellious youth in big cities. Beijing University students even formed a Cui Jian *houyuan dui* (support team), bringing their red streamers and loud cheers to every Cui Jian concert in town. In the spring of 1989, students on Tiananmen Square expressed their defiant spirit by singing and dancing to various rock songs by Cui and other Chinese groups. Hou Dejian, a popular balladeer from Taiwan most famous for his romantic, nationalist song "The Dragon's Descendants," galvanized students on the Square with his performance and personal participation in a last-minute hunger strike. In those emotional moments, the classic union between rock and pop music, idealistic passion, and political protest came together openly for the first time in China.[10]

By the time Cui Jian's first album, *Rock 'n' Roll on the Road of the New Long March,* was released, the massacre on Tiananmen had once again silenced political protest in China. The album, however, confirmed Cui's stature as a sort of Chinese Bob Dylan and started a new frenzy over his music. In 1990 he received

10. For an analysis of rock music as a form of cultural protest in the Soviet Union and postcommunist Russia, see Thomas Cushman, *Notes from Underground: Rock Music Counterculture in Russia* (Albany: State University of New York Press, 1995).

permission for a fund-raising concert tour for the Asian Games, and the concerts in Beijing, Wuhan, Zhengzhou, and Xi'an turned out to be huge successes.

In the wake of Cui Jian's popularity, a lively rock scene unfolded in China, heavily concentrated in Beijing. Although rock was still not allowed on television, a dozen or so bands performed regularly in private restaurants in Beijing; from time to time, they broke through censorship and played sold-out concerts in big stadiums. These new bands featured a variety of styles from heavy metal (Tang Dynasty, Breathing) to soft rock (Black Panther) to ballads (Ai Jing). Younger singer-songwriters such as He Yong, Zhang Chu, and Dou Wei released albums around 1994, each striving to get out of Cui Jian's shadow and fashion an individual style. Cui has produced two more albums. His music has grown more complex, his lyrics more mature and a shade darker, but it seems clear that after Tiananmen even he must struggle to keep the flames of true emotion alive in his fans.[11]

The Chinese music scene has changed a good deal since 1992. After the engine of economic reform shifted into overdrive, the mood of the country shifted too. With more opportunities to pursue money and a merrier lifestyle, society is becoming fragmented and culture commercialized. Political lectures are out, elite sentiments are generally ignored, and ordinary people, particularly younger ones, are demanding new cultural forms, including soft pop songs, kung fu videos, late-night radio talk shows, sitcoms, variety shows, and karaoke bars. One after another, slickly packaged Hong Kong and Taiwan teen idols with perfect makeup and glittering stage clothes fly in to give sold-out shows in mainland cities, offering themselves to thousands of screaming, worshipping fans. With songs in the universal style of light pop about young love, adolescent alienation, and so on, their albums and cassettes have come to dominate the music market nationwide. As is the case with many other electronic products, piracy of music CDs and tapes runs rampant. More and more mainland pop singers have sought or

11. For more on Cui Jian, including audio files of some of his music and a variety of information on Chinese rock music, see the following Internet Web site: http://www.ecf.toronto.edu/jiangy/rock.html.

been picked up by Hong Kong and Taiwan music companies for recording, packaging, and marketing. In the face of this commercial wave, the more rugged, angry voice of indigenous Chinese rock has faded into cult circles. No longer capable of claiming a wide, highly political audience, rock in China has taken on an increasingly commercial flavor. As Taiwan recording and distribution companies have begun to tap into the mainland rock talent pool and successfully joined with mainland music entities in various endeavors, Chinese rock has increasingly come to look like any other safe category on music store shelves.

As Deng's subjects chase after wealth and entertainment in the 1990s, they are not only casting off the stoic resignation Mao's people once displayed, but also some of the piety and seriousness about their past. One of the best-selling cassettes in China in 1992 was *Red Sun,* a tape that adapted famous hymns praising Mao to soft rock rhythms with electronic synthesizers. This vogue spread quickly: all sorts of revolutionary songs were dug up and adapted to the beat. Is this a sly act of deconstructing revolutionary history or an ingenious marketing strategy? Perhaps both. In today's China, turning socialist nostalgia into marketable kitsch has become an industry. Not only music but also other arts are susceptible to this phenomenon. Most remarkable, nobody in China seems to find it offensive or absurd. Listening to an old Cultural Revolution song with a soft, cheerful pop beat in a glitzy karaoke bar, sung warmly by a middle-aged entrepreneur who may well have been a Red Guard in his youth, how can one escape a sense of irony?[12] Yet such cultural contradictions are abundant in 1990s China.

In 1995 a Hard Rock Café opened in the heart of a new commercial district on the east side of Beijing, complete with the international chain's signature wall ornaments of rock icons' personal belongings. Despite its steep prices and outlandish decor, the café seems to fit right into the new landscape of the old socialist capital. Night after night, with beer flowing, a

12. See Philip Shenon, "Chinese Sup on the Sweet and Sour Days of Mao," *New York Times,* July 25, 1994, for a description of a restaurant in Beijing that serves food and has a decor reminiscent of the Cultural Revolution.

crowd of foreigners and hip young locals merrily dances away to new tunes and old favorites belted out by Western singers. Business is also bustling in karaoke and other small local bars with live or recorded pop music. For the time being, it looks as though commercialism has infused China's music scene with jaded normalcy.

Literature

The 1980s were triumphant years for contemporary Chinese literature. Coming out of the party's tight grip and a literary vacuum of three decades, poetry and fiction were the first powerful vehicles to voice people's anger and grief. At first underground poetry printed by mimeograph machines and posted on public walls gained a large following in the cities. Deftly mixing modernist images with passionate political protest, young poets like Bei Dao, Mang Ke, and Shu Ting became counterculture heroes in the late 1970s and early 1980s even as the police shut down their influential literary samizdat *Today*. Around the same time, the reading public devoured so-called scar literature, which consisted largely of sentimental stories about personal or family travails and atrocities of the Cultural Revolution. These stories and novellas helped the public to vent its grievances and brought about catharsis. Then came so-called reform literature, depicting social and economic reforms of the day using the conventions of socialist realism, but with more plausible characters than before and with plots that sometimes broke into taboo topics like sex. But these works aged quickly and they soon declined in popularity.[13]

By the mid-1980s China had grown more open, the government had become more tolerant, and translations of many 20th-century foreign works had become available to the Chinese for the first time. Propelled by desires to reexamine China's own cultural heritage in order to understand the present and to catch

13. For samples of these early post-Mao literary trends, see Perry Link, ed., *Stubborn Weeds: Popular and Controversial Chinese Literature after the Cultural Revolution* (Bloomington: Indiana University Press, 1983); and Helen F. Siu and Zelda Stern, eds., *Mao's Harvest: Voices from China's New Generation* (New York: Oxford University Press, 1983).

up with the contemporary world, anxious and ambitious young writers began to produce more complex and experimental fiction in this period. As if in a frantic race to make up for the past, writers and critics hastily embraced and abandoned one style, theory, trend, movement, "-ism" after another, all in a matter of a few years. Consequently, the eighties literary scene changed with numbing frequency.

This period, which Chinese intellectuals generally refer to as the "Culture Craze," turned out to be a short-lived peak for contemporary Chinese literature. As the elite literary scene was going strong, with critics busy both picking and dropping writers, other wider publishing and reading trends were quietly developing. Along with new translations of highbrow Western authors such as William Faulkner, Saul Bellow, and Jorge Luis Borges, popular novelists like Sidney Sheldon also came to China. Kung fu novels from Hong Kong and romance paperbacks from Taiwan were being reprinted cheaply in the mainland and conquering the hearts of millions. Average readers found many more options in bookstores and bookstalls and it did not take long for them to drop serious literature for more entertaining material. But elite writers and critics, absorbed in their own lively literary scene, did not wake up to the new reality until sometime after Tiananmen.

Reflecting this trend, subscriptions for and sales of literary journals have dropped. Gone is the feeling that a writer is the voice of the people and the conscience of society. The public no longer seems to rely on literature for "venting grievances" or "purifying the soul." Rather, amusement and relaxation have become the main functions of reading. Experimental literature is still in print, but it has turned into an intellectual activity with a very limited reach.

The publishing system has changed too. As soon as the government relaxed its economic control, Chinese entrepreneurs sprang into action, establishing a tremendous network of private and semiprivate book distribution channels that linked both state and private publishers with booksellers across the country. Today, this "second channel," as it is commonly known in the publishing trade, is a parallel structure alongside the old state-run distribution system.

Unlike its outmoded, inefficient official sibling, however, the second channel operates primarily by profit motive and market laws. Given the transitional, poorly regulated nature of the Chinese publishing market, second-channel entrepreneurs have a collective reputation for running their businesses in a crass, free-for-all style. Many stories circulate in state publishing circles about how untrustworthy the second channel is, how as often as not a private distributor will take books and disappear without paying a cent in return. However, despite this common image of a semi-underground mafia dominated by a bunch of immoral, cash-hungry swindlers, the second channel is also often credited with bringing into Chinese publishing an unprecedented degree of professional savvy and business acumen. Forced to use and to compete with the second channel, the state-run publishing houses have gradually learned not only to keep close tabs on party and elite preferences, but also on those of the average reader. And these groups' opinions don't always converge: a book disapproved of by the party or snubbed by the elite might be a hit with the average reader. As state subsidies and readership for serious literature dwindle, more and more publishing houses are trying to make ends meet by publishing popular books for the market.

The one Chinese writer who rode beautifully—and perhaps anticipated—the tide of the commercialization of literature was the young Beijing novelist Wang Shuo, discussed above as one of the scriptwriters for *Yearning* and other TV soap operas. Labeled a "hooligan writer" by critics, Wang uses rich, colorful, contemporary Beijing speech to portray the lives of young streetwise hustlers who make fun of everything sacred and serious. Under his merciless pen, both the official party culture and the intellectual scene look ridiculous and are constantly disparaged through sly jokes and comic situations. Wang did not go to college but moved from job to job after serving several years in the military. He began to publish fiction in the mid-1980s, gradually building up a loyal following among urban youth. Then, beginning with *Yearning,* he moved on to writing scripts for movies and television. While many literary careers languished, Wang's fame soared in the early 1990s. Owing in part to the sweeping success of nearly every TV series he helped write,

Wang's readership also grew. By the time his hefty four-volume selected works appeared in bookstalls across the country, Wang had become a superstar on the Chinese pop culture scene.

With his constant mockery of the pretensions of high culture, his quick humor, and his slippery tongue, Wang easily endeared himself to the popular media. A darling of the tabloid press, Wang often talked about fame and money. He admits that his commercial instincts were honed from his early days as a hustling small businessman: "I learned to watch what my customers need."

People remain passionately divided over what the "Wang Shuo phenomenon" means. For some, the typical Wang character—a young urban hooligan with no sense of belief or purpose, but possessing self-confidence and a quick tongue—embodies the nihilistic sensibilities of the young generation. Some people find this worrisome because, while it subverts and ridicules an outmoded official ideology, it also dissolves the impulse to construct or believe in something. Intellectuals especially have a deep ambivalence toward the Wang Shuo phenomenon because of its flagrant anti-intellectualism. Some perceive a set of conventional values behind Wang's sarcastic veneer and ambiguous politics: ultimately, Wang's hooligan characters are decent and lovelorn; they are just against people putting on airs.

Wang's supporters consider his works the voice of a generation. Sharing Wang's contempt for China's educated elite, they believe that the Wang Shuo brand of cynicism is long overdue. They are quick to point out the difference between Wang, a freelance writer and independent spirit, and most Chinese intellectuals, who remain economically dependent on the state.

Politics aside, Wang's literary gift has been widely recognized. He is often praised for infusing fresh energy and vitality into Chinese fiction with his original portraits of contemporary urban life and creating something original in the pungent dialogue and narrative that blend the Mao-speak of the Cultural Revolution, Beijing street-talk, black humor, and certain classical literary expressions.[14]

---

14. For a further discussion of Wang Shuo's style and influence, see Geremie Barmé, "Wang Shuo and *Liumang* (Hooligan) Culture," *Australian Journal of Chinese Affairs* (Can-

Despite the publicity and the controversy, Wang Shuo's works enjoy a large following only in China's northern cities; in the south, probably in part because of their dense Beijing dialogue and humor, his works have not won the same kind of popularity. The nationwide best-sellers are books such as kung fu novels by the Hong Kong author Jin Yong, formulaic love stories by the Taiwan author Qiong Yao, and certain topical books that few critics consider well written enough to be reviewed as serious literature. Two crudely written autobiographical novels, *A China Lady in Manhattan (Manhadun de Zhongguo nuren)* and *Beijinger in New York*,[15] belong to this genre of popular best-sellers, which resemble supermarket paperbacks in the United States. Both of these are melodramatic accounts of the struggles and successes of recent Chinese immigrants to the United States, and they play right into the common Chinese fantasy about an America that is both gold mine and hell.

In 1993, however, a new national best-seller stirred up a huge literary controversy: *The Abandoned Capital* (*Feidu*), a thick, juicy novel about the corruption of contemporary life in China by the well-known and respected author Jia Pingwa. Centering around the unraveling career and numerous sexual exploits of the famous middle-aged writer Zhuang Zhidie, the novel is broadly taken to be autobiographical. It features a wide variety of characters and offers a realist picture of a decadent daily life that revolves around eating, talking, cheating, scheming, exchanging favors, making shady deals, and generally gypping other people. Life may seem hollow and lacking in meaning, but sex, especially adultery, is a force to be reckoned with. The author provides abundant bedroom scenes that qualify as hard-core pornography; however—to satisfy potential censors or titillate readers—Jia cuts out the last juicy detail of many passages by replacing the missing words with blank squares.

Within the first few months of its publication, *The Abandoned*

---

berra), no. 28 (July 1992), pp. 23–66. A small sample of Wang's writing can be found in Geremie Barme and Linda Jaivin, eds., *New Ghosts, Old Dreams: Chinese Rebel Voices* (New York: Times Books, 1992).

15. This novel is available in English translation: Glen Cao, *Beijinger in New York*, trans. Ted Wang (San Francisco: China Books and Periodicals, 1994). It was also the basis of the popular 1993 TV soap opera.

Capital sold half-a-million copies and, with more than ten pirated versions, countless more later on. From both critical and popular sources, the novel received rave reviews. It has been hailed, for instance, as "an epic work of the Chinese intellectual soul" and "an extraordinary monument of contemporary Chinese literature." Booksellers trumpeted the book's explicit sexual scenes; newspapers speculated about the large advances the author was supposed to have received. Many intellectuals and Chinese literati, on the other hand, have condemned the novel, outraged by its "unbearably vulgar sex scenes" and "despicable male sexual psychology." Some called the novel a cheap imitation of the late Ming erotic classic *The Golden Lotus;* others deplored yet another case of a serious writer "selling out" under commercial pressures and "degenerating" into the low ranks of pornography and "literature for the sidewalk stalls" (*ditan wenxue*).

Government anti-pornography officials had a tough case on their hands. Accustomed to battling the "yellow" trade (yellow being the color that signifies sex and pornography in China) with arrests, bans, and confiscation, they did not know how to deal with this odd situation: can a famous novelist with a previously stainless political and moral record and a reputation for having produced in the past only "pure literature" have written a yellow book?

Meanwhile, the novel kept on selling and generating debate. Some even took the phenomenon as a sign of the public's renewed interest in literature. Zhang Yiwu, a young literary critic teaching at Beijing University, sees the novel's success in a different light. He considers it to be a sign that the trend of "quality writing for leisurely reading" is making a comeback in China. Back in the 1920s and 1930s, many talented Chinese novelists wrote good, amusing, readable fiction about daily life for mass consumption. But after 1949 this kind of literature was displaced by politically correct literature for the proletariat. Only in the late 1980s and early 1990s did young mainland Chinese writers begin to produce such works again. In fact well before the publication of *The Abandoned Capital,* a group of southern writers were publishing stories and novellas that can easily be described as "quality writing for leisurely reading." Two prominent examples are Nanjing novelists Ye Zhaoyan and Su Tong, both well known for their popular, readable novellas with mildly erotic overtones depicting ordinary life in small southern towns.

Eventually, in late January 1994, Chinese authorities did announce a ban on *The Abandoned Capital* on anti-pornography grounds. But by then both the sales and the controversy over the book had begun to cool. Curiously, when *White Night (Bai ye)*, a new, similarly erotic novel by the same author written in a similar style, came out in 1995, it received almost no attention at all.

The debate over *The Abandoned Capital* highlights a set of tensions prevalent in Chinese literature and publishing in the 1990s. The transformation of culture into a commodity is still so recent that many people—writers, critics, readers, and publishers—find it hard to distinguish the boundaries between high and low, serious and pop, soul-probing literary works and manipulative entertainment. Opinions vary about whether a novel like *The Abandoned Capital* is a clever but trashy potboiler or a literary masterpiece. The media hype surrounding the novel focused so heavily on issues of sex and money that it drowned out any serious discussion of the novel's interestingly dark, apocalyptic vision of China as an abandoned, sick, and spiritless civilization.

Since *The Abandoned Capital* no other novel has generated nationwide debate. On the whole, the public seems restless and increasingly jaded toward literature. In 1995, when the first complete Chinese translation of James Joyce's *Ulysses* came out, sales quickly climbed to about 80,000. This surprised many in the publishing industry, but illusions of a surging public taste for highbrow literature were soon dispelled. Experts list the following reasons for the appeal of *Ulysses:* its Chinese translators are famous, it is reputedly one of the greatest literary breakthroughs of the 20th century, and it has sections that contain explicit depictions of sex. But most important, all of these facts were well reported in the popular media before the book's publication. In other words, it is a story of successful marketing in which the literature itself is largely incidental.

Nevertheless, a large amount of fiction and other forms of literary work continue to be published each year in China, even though the steady sellers in the bookstalls tend to be formulaic fiction. As more novelists turn to television scriptwriting for better money and more visibility, there is a general sense of crisis among writers that serious literature in the 1990s is facing tough challenges from the thriving, fast-food popular culture. In this atmosphere, few literary works can win the kind of sustained public attention they had even in the recent past.

Movies

Chinese films have won much international attention in recent years, largely because of the works of a handful of young directors. In 1991 and 1992 movies by Zhang Yimou, *Ju Dou* and *Raise the Red Lantern (Dahong denglong gaogao gua)*, respectively, were nominated for Academy Awards in the foreign-language film category. In 1993 Chen Kaige's *Farewell My Concubine (Ba wang bie ji)* was awarded the Palme d'Or at the Cannes Film Festival. In general, Chinese movies have demonstrated a strong competitiveness in many prestigious international film festivals. Such critical recognition helps to boost popular interest in Chinese movies in the West, even as Chinese filmmakers struggle to cope with rapid changes in the troubled film industry at home.

Much has been written about the relatively recent rise of the Chinese cinema and its most innovative force, the "fifth generation," a label often used for the first post–Cultural Revolution graduates from the Beijing Film Academy, China's only film school.[16] This group of brilliant young directors burst onto the screen in the early 1980s with fresh and powerful new works and created a Chinese "New Wave" cinema. Some of the earliest fifth generation works, such as Chen Kaige's *The Yellow Earth* (*Huang tudi,* 1984) and Zhang Junzhao's *One and Eight* (*Yige yu bage,* 1984), dazzled film critics with their inventive cinematography, striking images, and ingenious reworking of the contents of orthodox revolutionary Chinese cinema. Although they became the darlings of foreign film festivals and avant-garde Chinese critics, these films often sold few copies at film conventions in China and did not have wide domestic distribution. Many

16. See Paul Clark, "Chinese Cinema Enters the 1990s," in *China Briefing, 1992,* ed. William A. Joseph (Boulder, Colo.: Westview Press, 1993), pp. 125–47.

mainstream Chinese filmmakers held disparaging views of the fifth generation's work, arguing that it was elitist and had limited audience appeal in China. Confronted with questions of accessibility, one of the leading fifth generation directors, Tian Zhuangzhuang (*Horse Thief* [*Dao ma zei*], 1987), said half jokingly that his films were made for 21st-century audiences. Fortunately, until the late 1980s, even as tension between cinematic camps grew, the new generation continued to receive financial support from state studios, often subsidized by the earnings of other, more popular B movies.

The one exception among the fifth generation is Zhang Yimou. His debut film, *Red Sorghum* (*Hong gaoliang,* 1987), not only won the Golden Bear at the 1988 Berlin Film Festival but also filled local movie houses in China. From the beginning, Zhang appeared different from his other prominent classmates: he emphasized not only original camera work and visual brilliance but also strong story lines, faster pace, and the importance of stars (*Red Sorghum*'s leading actor, Jiang Wen, was China's most famous movie star, and Gong Li, who rose to stardom after her debut in *Red Sorghum,* has been the leading lady in all of Zhang's later films). *Red Sorghum* was the first fifth generation film that found a mass audience; but to the critics who still viewed it as an art film, its popular appeal seemed largely incidental.

By mid-1988 the state film industry began to experience serious problems. Because of the pressures of economic reform, the state grew increasingly reluctant to subsidize the 16 or so feature film studios, some of which were on the verge of bankruptcy. To improve the situation, a new policy was announced that allowed studios some flexibility in negotiating the sales terms of some of their films. The studios could now share a percentage of the box-office returns with provincial distribution corporations. This in turn encouraged the studios to pay more attention to the market and their audiences. Such minor changes, however, proved to be a drop of water on a forest fire. Since film was too important a communication and educational medium to be allowed completely free play, the state still imposed censorship, assigned quotas to studios to make a certain number of films with approved political content, and continued to dominate film finances. Trapped in a vicious cycle of bad films, bad politics, and bad management at the end of the 1980s, China's cumbersome, Soviet-style film industry needed a major overhaul.

To make a bad situation worse, the audience for domestic movies had steadily dropped off. One report had it that the urban film audience had declined from roughly seven billion moviegoers per year in the late 1970s and early 1980s to about half that level in 1993.[17] Television and imported foreign movies were luring audiences away. Since new Western blockbusters were too costly to import, Hong Kong martial art and horror movies and old European and American B movies dominated mainland theaters. To attract larger audiences, many local theaters offered cafés with cable TV, special all-night shows with box seats for lovers, and videocassette projection rooms. And again, these new facilities featured the latest movies or videos from Hong Kong rather than domestic fare. Renovated small theaters provided a cozy atmosphere but also caused ticket prices to skyrocket, another reason to make the average moviegoer balk.

In response to this crisis several things happened. Many top mainland filmmakers turned to coproductions with foreign investors who would cover most of the budget and assume control of production and distribution outside China. The pressure to win international prizes intensified: with the domestic film market in a slump and foreign distribution growing more important, such prizes provided not only sorely needed critical recognition but also a seal of commercial viability. And many filmmakers who had not distinguished themselves artistically resorted to making officially assigned projects, such as the numerous 1991 "commemorative films" celebrating the 70th anniversary of the founding of the CCP. These films actually filled theaters for various reasons, not the least of which was the fact that party organizations and unions purchased blocks of seats for their members. Young filmmakers who came after the fifth generation faced an especially tough situation. Struggling in the shadow of the fifth generation's success, they also had little state

17. Ibid., p. 137.

support or foreign funds. Most of them shot commercials or MTV-type videos, and only a small number of them could scrounge enough private funding to make small films on a shoestring budget.

Against this complex background of transition, adjustment, and struggle, fierce debates broke out over the meaning of Zhang Yimou's continued success abroad. Within Chinese intellectual circles in and outside the mainland, many wondered if Zhang owed his popularity to the shrewd marketing of oriental exotica to the West. His films seemed so outlandish and looked so different from ordinary Chinese life yet captured so many foreign prizes and praises that some suspected they were made precisely with that aim in mind. After listing the many "grating inauthenticities" in a film like *Raise the Red Lantern,* some critics concluded, "this kind of film is really shot for the casual pleasures of foreigners."

This kind of criticism did not seem to affect Zhang Yimou's popularity abroad or at home. Official bans on *Ju Dou* and *Raise the Red Lantern* only added to their attraction, and when they were eventually released in China, Chinese audiences showed considerable enthusiasm too. With so many young filmmakers striving to emulate his success and the media's tireless coverage of him and his star Gong Li, Zhang emerged as one of the country's superstars on the pop culture scene.[18]

But the shift in Chinese filmmaking appeared to be complete when the other leading fifth generation director, Chen Kaige, came out in 1993 with *Farewell My Concubine,* a movie based on a Hong Kong novel and financed mainly by Hong Kong. This lush three-hour melodrama about the passions and sufferings of two Peking Opera performers spans the precommunist era to the Cultural Revolution and resembles a Hollywood epic more than Chen's earlier experimental films. Reaping both prestigious prizes and commercial success, *Farewell My Concubine* provided a much-needed boost for Chen's troubled career and put him back on the top of China's directorial chart.[19] Inevitably, the film and Chen's move toward the commercial mainstream aroused

18. For more on Zhang Yimou and Gong Li, see *China Today* (January 1993), pp. 55–61.

19. For more on Chen Kaige, see *China Today* (November 1993), pp. 44–47.

some criticism and controversy within the Chinese intellectual community. By then, however, such criticism sounded increasingly like isolated, academic grumbling as almost all filmmakers took stock of the reality of the bottom line and made various efforts to adjust and adapt. Many young and middle-aged directors were making thrillers or urban comedies. Tian Zhuangzhuang, one of the most intractable enfants terribles of the fifth generation, had made *Rock 'n' Roll Kids* (*Yaogun qingnian*) as early as 1988 to prove that he was capable of shooting flashy commercial entertainment. In 1990 he directed two of China's most popular stars in an historical drama, *Li Lianying, the Imperial Eunuch* (*Da taijian Li Lianying*). Like Chen Kaige, Tian no longer insisted on upholding relentless avant-garde standards but instead attempted now to infuse his artistic vision and style into more entertaining historical films. Of course, in the more restricted atmosphere after Tiananmen, shooting films set in the precommunist era also provided political safety. *Blue Kite* (*Lan fengzheng,* 1994), Tian's personal and subtle portrait of growing up during the Cultural Revolution, was immediately banned by Chinese censors. By then, there was a mounting sense that China's avant-garde filmmakers had splintered into different directions.

Among numerous younger filmmakers, independent productions gradually became common practice in the 1990s. Although often obliged to carry a state studio's insignia, these films were independent projects shot with privately raised funds and by privately organized crews. Whenever a finished product failed to pass the official censors and was blocked from domestic release, copies of it often cropped up in foreign film festivals where it frequently won an award. Many younger directors whom some critics have loosely labeled as the "sixth generation," such as Zhang Yuan, Wu Wenguang, and Wang Xiaoshuai, started off this way. After getting some overseas attention, each was able to raise more private funds or receive film grants from abroad to do his next project. Shot on a small budget and often with extremely limited distribution, these works have been uneven. Perhaps reflecting certain fixations of the filmmakers' common age and background, these films almost all deal with themes of contemporary urban alienation. So far none of the directors have been able to capture the kind of critical or popular attention the fifth generation filmmakers did in their early days. But by manipulating the loopholes of the official studio system and obtaining the support of various foreign festivals, they have tenaciously carved out a lively subcultural existence on the margins of China's film scene.

Although the industry is still in the throes of reform and revamping, the crop of Chinese films that came out in 1994 and 1995 seems to offer hope: there was a greater variety of subjects and a collective improvement in technical quality. While in general this is not a period of major breakthroughs like the 1980s, Chinese filmmaking appears to have gained a higher level of professionalism. Zhang Yimou once again demonstrated his technical mastery in *Shanghai Triad* (*Yao a yao, yao dao waipo qiao*), his film about the 1930s Shanghai crime world, although aspects of the movie seemed repetitious of his earlier works, and it received mixed reviews in China. Ye Daying's *Red Cherry (Hong yingtao),* about Chinese communist children in the Soviet Union during World War II, and Li Shaohong's *Rouge* (*Hongfen*), about the reforming of prostitutes in the 1950s, were well-shot, well-acted films on offbeat subjects. *In the Heat of the Sun* (*Yangguang canlan de rizi*), film star Jiang Wen's directorial debut, turned out to be the sleeper of 1995. This story about a Beijing boy and his teenage pals growing up in the mid-1970s takes an unusual angle on the Cultural Revolution: political history becomes largely a backdrop for the intense personal drama of adolescent violence and romance. Through Jiang's lens the Cultural Revolution is not only about suffering, betrayal, and fanaticism, as it was in the hands of the fifth generation; it is about having fun, falling in love, and asserting one's masculinity, an approach that is disturbing to some and refreshing to others. In a sense, *In the Heat of the Sun* is really the first accomplished work from someone whose age would qualify him as a sixth generation director. When the film opened in Beijing in the fall of 1995, it played to theaters packed with young audiences and caused such a buzz that some local reporters claimed it was beating imported Hollywood blockbusters in box office returns.

Indeed, China had made ground-breaking deals in 1995 to import foreign films. Previously the government paid only a low, flat rate for second-run Hollywood pictures; in 1995 authorities allowed ten recent blockbusters to be released, agreeing to share the box office receipts with the studios that made them. These movies, which included *True Lies, Speed, The Fugitive,* and *The Lion King,* helped revive theater attendance and gave hope to Hollywood studios for further collaboration—and profit! Lured by China's potentially huge film market, executives from almost every major Hollywood studio flew in to attend the Shanghai Film Festival in October 1995, eager to position themselves for future efforts. Although the generally archaic ways of China's film bureaucracy shocked and confused many of the visitors, they also received encouraging words from the Chinese. "China's film industry is in a time of transition," said Wu Mengchen, president of the China Film Import and Export Corporation. "One of the main characteristics is that it is changing from a welfare-state mode to a moneymaking mode." Another official announced at the festival that a state-run monopoly on film distribution would be broken in 1996, allowing individual studios and producers to distribute American movies for the first time.[20]

Hollywood's dreams of huge Chinese audiences, American-style theater complexes, and movie-related theme parks may come true. But its entrepreneurs will have to contend with China's shifting culture policy and wrestle with Chinese film bureaucrats who are likely to fight to preserve control over their fiefdoms. It should not take long for Hollywood executives to figure out what many foreign investors learned in the 1980s: China may be a gold mine, but it is also a minefield.

Conclusion

Popular culture has been the spearhead of the explosive cultural changes that have taken place in post-Tiananmen China. Opinions about the current state of Chinese culture and what the future might hold for it remain divided. Some see hope in a fast growing, depoliticizing commercial culture, some emphasize pop culture's positive function in building a more open, relaxed,

20. Seth Faison, "A Chinese Wall Shows Cracks," *New York Times*, November 21, 1995.

and pluralist atmosphere. To these optimists, commercialized pop culture—whether in print media or in the sight and sound industries—has broken the Communist Party's cultural monopoly by creating a range of new spaces and forms for both social and personal expression. They see these spaces and forms as giving new energy and richness to Chinese cultural life and, in time, they hope they might develop into even more independent mediums and structures. Others, who consider such hopes naive, are alarmed by the growth and spread of commercial pop culture, perceiving it as a new form of mass cultural tyranny and political apathy. To them, neither the old party culture nor the new pop culture is palatable. In their view, the future of Chinese culture does not look bright, with, on the one side, communist authorities learning to control and manipulate commercial culture and, on the other side, the invasion of China by global capitalist mass culture from the United States, Hong Kong, and Taiwan.

These debates reflect the complexity of the many cultural changes going on in today's China. But whatever its long-term influences, popular culture has already established itself as an important fact of life in contemporary China.

Hong Kong on the Eve of Reunification with China

Suzanne Pepper

Probably at no time since its founding has the attention of Hong Kong's inhabitants been so uniformly and precisely concentrated. Their focal point is, of course, July 1, 1997, when the colony will be reunited with China after 150 years of British rule. Preparations for this event have continued unabated since 1982. During that year, Chinese leaders in Beijing confirmed their intention to regain sovereignty over the entire colony as of 1997, when the 99-year lease on most of its territory expires. The remaining land area was granted to Britain in perpetuity under 19th-century treaties, the legitimacy of which had been disavowed by many generations of Chinese who regarded them as impositions by an unwelcome colonial power. Sino-British negotiations thus began on a sour note in 1982, when British prime minister Margaret Thatcher tried to bargain for a continued British presence after 1997 by proclaiming the validity of the old treaties. Chinese leaders angrily dismissed such claims and soon demonstrated their resolve to regain full sovereignty. A sequence of agreements then ensued spelling out the terms of Hong Kong's return to China, marking its penultimate struggle to create a single, sovereign Chinese state.

In the Sino-British Joint Declaration of 1984, China promised Hong Kong a "high degree of autonomy" and a 50-year guarantee against changes in its way of life. Capitalism would be retained and the socialist system would not be introduced during that time. Popularized under the slogans "one country–two systems" and "Hong Kong people ruling Hong Kong," the aim reiterated in every official statement was to preserve Hong

Kong's economic prosperity and social stability. The promises spelled out in the Joint Declaration were formalized in the Basic Law of 1990, intended to serve as Hong Kong's post-1997 constitution.

Yet despite the preparations and the already well-advanced economic integration of Hong Kong and China, by 1996 its impending "date with destiny" had become the colony's number-one attraction and the main preoccupation of its six million citizens. Their mixed mood of guarded optimism and apprehensive uncertainty is not any less genuine for the glare of international publicity which has suddenly surrounded them. In fact, the significance of the occasion is belied by its concentrated nature in time and space; rarely can a day in the life of a city be seen to symbolize so much of 20th-century history as July 1, 1997. Given the peculiar circumstances of its existence as an acknowledged part of China, Hong Kong could not embark along the more conventional route from colonial rule to self-government and independence. Hong Kong also did not come under Communist Party rule when the People's Republic of China (PRC) was established in 1949 and so did not proceed along with the rest of mainland China through the subsequent phases of its communist-led revolution. Furthermore, the Chinese Communist Party (CCP) did not follow the course of its major counterparts in the early 1990s by collapsing or evolving toward a more democratic political system.

July 1, 1997, will thus signify multiple transitions. For Hong Kong, it will mean moving directly from British to Chinese sovereignty and from colonial status to an as yet ill-defined system of administrative autonomy under Beijing's communist-led government. But for Beijing—heir to the national memory of 19th-century Western intrusion and early 20th-century political decay—1997 is an equally momentous date. Hong Kong's return symbolizes both an end to the colonial era of national humiliation and the next-to-last step in China's long climb back from chaos to national reunification. After Hong Kong, Taiwan is the only part of China that remains beyond Beijing's grasp and has become its next preoccupation, if the daily volume of Chinese media output can be taken as an accurate indicator.

Remembrance of Things Past

For the people of Hong Kong, however, these historic events are less significant than their potential for changing individual lives and fortunes. The key concern in this regard derives from Hong Kong's fear of communism. This fear has not been newly created by the imminent arrival of 1997, but is rooted in memories of firsthand experiences from the past that have been replenished and passed on from one generation to the next since 1949. Hence, despite its unique colonial status, Hong Kong's people have not remained isolated from all the century's political trends. And to say that the territory has escaped the direct consequences of those trends is not to say that its people have themselves always been politically inert. On the contrary, the colonial government until recently exerted considerable effort to discourage political activity in order to prevent the spillover into Hong Kong of China's endemic 20th-century political conflict between the CCP and its opponents.

New arrivals were thus obliged to put their political pasts behind them, and the territory became a safe haven for every generation of émigré produced by the Chinese communist revolution. Hong Kong's population in the mid-1990s is 95+ percent ethnic Chinese, the great majority being post-1949 migrants from the mainland together with their children and grandchildren. The hopes and fears of Hong Kong people about their future under CCP rule therefore derive from the same set of experiences, namely, those associated with Chinese communism. The recollections are, moreover, largely negative and all the stronger from being rooted in so many personal lives and family histories.

Three phases loom largest in the public's memory, with variable impact on its current mood: the late 1940s civil war period, ending in communist military and political victory; the major social and economic changes after 1949, culminating in the 1966–76 Cultural Revolution; and the "postrevolutionary" years after Mao Zedong's death, including the student-led protests of the late 1980s, the subsequent clampdown on dissent, and the repressive backlash which continues at present.

The pre-1949 phase provides lessons in the fickleness of political fortune and the shifting tides of world history. During the 1920s and 1930s, the Kuomintang (KMT, Nationalist Party) had been the rising power in China. But by the end of World War II, the KMT-CCP power balance shifted dramatically and by 1949 was reversed. The CCP had exploited its rural isolation to full advantage by building its army and its party into a peasant-based fighting force and revolutionary movement with which the KMT could not compete. The latter, meanwhile, had dissipated its mandate many times over. Corruption, incompetence, and oppression were the attributes commonly evoked with reference to the KMT's decline, along with rampant inflation, rural poverty, bureaucratic capitalism, and moral decay.

In *China on the Eve of Communist Takeover*, Doak Barnett chronicled the country's civic disintegration. From Shanghai in October 1948, he described the "prevailing feeling of cynicism and despair," the "bankruptcy" of KMT rule, and the "near-complete" collapse of public confidence. Last-ditch economic reforms had failed. The army was demoralized and defeated. Intellectuals, almost universally disaffected and estranged from the KMT government, had drifted steadily leftward. From Hong Kong in December 1948, Barnett summarized his impressions: people everywhere in southern China were preparing for the prospect of a communist-led order "with emotions that mix resignation, relief, and apprehension in varying degrees."[1]

The contrast between China in 1949 and 1996 is, of course, striking. Far from disappearing after its remnant forces fled to Taiwan, the KMT has risen from the ashes of defeat. It presided over a development strategy that placed Taiwan at the forefront of Asia's fast-growing economies, and consequently Taiwan's per capita gross domestic product has doubled during the past decade to $12,200 in 1995. Political liberalization followed economic success, with KMT leader Lee Teng-hui becoming the first popularly elected president in Chinese history. The end of the cold war has allowed capitalism and democracy to emerge as the dominant world trends and Taiwan under KMT rule to ride the crest of the wave.[2]

---

1. A. Doak Barnett, *China on the Eve of Communist Takeover* (New York: Praeger, 1963).
2. For more on Taiwan's political and economic development, see the chapter in this volume by Cal Clark.

In contrast, China's communist government is seen as an historical anachronism. Its per capita gross domestic product of about $550 is regarded as the legacy of a discredited socialist economy, and its neo-Marxist polemics as the last gasps of a dying regime. By century's end, the victor in 1949 had even taken on the erstwhile characteristics of its opponent. Images that marked the KMT's past, like corruption, rural poverty, and repression, are regularly invoked with reference to its CCP successor.

Contemplating these reversals of fortune, Hong Kong people have been made keenly aware of the continuities that lie within the shifting currents of history. Thus, the single unbroken thread that runs from the 1940s to the 1990s, binding China then and Hong Kong now, is the CCP's determination to achieve national reunification under its rule. And however great the ironies, or perhaps because of them, popular sentiments in Hong Kong today seem to differ only in degree from those noted by Doak Barnett in China 50 years ago on the eve of communist victory.

Yet had the prospect of reunification not been reinforced by other intervening memories, 1997 might have passed as little more than another date on modern China's political calendar. Instead, the prospect of reunification is underlined in people's thoughts and emotions by all the stages of China's revolution. Each phase targeted different groups to produce a new wave of Hong Kong arrivals. Because of their sensitivity, the events that marked these periods have not been subjects for systematic study in the territory's schools. Yet their cumulative impact is constantly reinforced by a multitude of eyewitness accounts transmitted privately from one generation to the next and by an avid news-reading public. It sustains dozens of locally published dailies, weeklies, and monthlies, in which reporting on China is a basic stock in trade. Current events, old stories, personal memoirs, anecdotes, gossip, and rumor all recount again and again the episodes that make up the Chinese revolution as seen through local eyes.

Urban entrepreneurs and rural landlords represented the first wave of émigrés. Following the expropriation of their property in the 1950s, many fled south and their stories are still among Hong Kong's most often repeated, since they concern so many of its now wealthiest families. Similarly, Hong Kong's prominent Christian minority harbors memories and grievances dating back to the earliest years of communist rule. After the CCP consolidated its economic base, the party turned its attention to the political and cultural aspects of China's revolutionary transformation. This phase began to accelerate with the 1957 antirightist campaign against intellectuals and others critical of the new communist order. In popular Hong Kong historiography, 1957 has thus become a key date heralding the onset of the CCP's cultural or anti-intellectual crusade in a final assault against the modern successors of China's traditional ruling elite. The economic depression that followed in the Great Leap Forward in 1958, an adventure in high-speed socialist development, produced another upsurge of migrants in the early 1960s and stories of famine which are still attracting Sunday-feature-page readers 30 years later.

The radicalism that began in 1957 developed into increasingly divisive class-based concerns during the 1960s. These culminated in Mao's strategy to stave off capitalist restoration with his last great mass campaign, the Cultural Revolution. Hong Kong still remembers that upheaval primarily in terms of the violence that characterized its inaugural 1966–67 stage, during which the colony's own small leftist community activated a riotous equivalent to the Red Guard sagas unfolding across the border. Hong Kong also did not extend more than the coolest of welcomes to immigrant Red Guards from China, who had failed to grasp the shifting laws of Maoist mass movement politics and found themselves among its losers. They nevertheless migrated southward in variable numbers (along with their former targets and victims) throughout the 1970s, as Chinese political currents ebbed and flowed. Once China's official view turned definitively against the Cultural Revolution, however, the memories of perpetrators and victims alike fused into a critical mass with seemingly limitless media appeal in Hong Kong.

Marking as it did the end of Mao's radical career, and given its repudiation by his successors, even the Cultural Revolution might have been discounted as past history but for the military suppression of unarmed protesters in Tiananmen Square. With public opinion primed by the 1997 reunification issue, Hong

Kong in effect became like any other Chinese city in May 1989, when Beijing students protested and demonstrators everywhere identified with their causes. But for Hong Kong especially it became a rare defining moment with an estimated one million people marching in support of the Tiananmen protesters.

Never in all the territory's past had so many people cared enough to join together in any form of political exercise, much less take to the streets in several consecutive weeks of public demonstrations. The accumulated grievances against China's communist-led government seemed to coalesce and the worst fears about Hong Kong's future seemed to be confirmed. Memories and emotions mixed to produce an unprecedented display of common purpose as the territory's disparate communities marched out together, including local leftists and migrants from every Chinese political generation.

It would be an exaggeration to claim that those events transformed Hong Kong people—who do not easily cross the various invisible boundaries that divide them—into a commonality of six million public-spirited citizens. But in so forcefully galvanizing popular concerns, the impact of 1989 on Hong Kong's political development during the final years of transition to Chinese sovereignty and beyond would be difficult to exaggerate. The net result has been finally to give the territory not only a political life of its own but one wherein the principal players are trying to make up for lost time. It seems like the past is being replayed in fast-forward mode for Hong Kong's benefit, with all the political lessons of the 20th century compressed into a few years.

The Response to Tiananmen and Its Aftermath

The territory's response to Tiananmen came first from the streets and then from the halls of power in Hong Kong and London. According to some, Tiananmen provided the inspiration and example for Eastern Europe's popular uprisings against communist rule which began later in 1989. The dominoes did not stop falling until the Soviet Union collapsed in 1991; their momentum evidently emboldened London to strengthen its management of Hong Kong's transition to Chinese rule. This effort was launched in 1992. Shaken by the collapse of communism elsewhere but defiant, Beijing leaders responded in kind to Britain's initiative, producing the heightened tensions that have characterized Hong Kong's final years of transition to Chinese rule.

In *China Briefing, 1990,* Hong Kong journalist Frank Ching described the initial repercussions of Tiananmen on the preparations for Hong Kong's future. "Virtually overnight," he wrote, "a consensus emerged that the colony needed to hasten the development of democracy."[3] In 1987 Governor David Wilson had easily won agreement within the Executive Council (Exco, his cabinet of top local advisers) to delay introducing direct elections for the Legislative Council (Legco, then still a colonial-style consultative body of indirectly elected and appointed members). This delay conformed to the tradition of "benevolent autocracy" by which Hong Kong had always been governed.[4] In 1987 that tradition was reinforced by Chinese pressure and the gradual arrangements for Hong Kong's future political development then being drafted under Beijing's direction for inclusion in the Basic Law.[5] After Tiananmen, Hong Kong political leaders agreed unanimously that the pace of building democracy should be hastened. Hong Kong's executive and legislative councillors reached a rare consensus in July 1989, agreeing that at least half the legislature should be directly elected by 1995, and the entire body and the chief executive by the year 2003.[6]

In early June, Governor Wilson had flown to London to urge among other things the restoration of full British nationality to Hong Kong citizens, including the right of abode in Britain, which had been taken from them in earlier years. The aim was

---

3. Frank Ching, "One Country, Two Systems: The Future of Hong Kong," in *China Briefing, 1990,* ed. Anthony J. Kane (Boulder, Colo.: Westview Press, 1990), p. 117.

4. On the scuttling of earlier attempts at political reform, see Steve Yui-sang Tsang, *Democracy Shelved: Great Britain, China, and Attempts at Constitutional Reform in Hong Kong, 1945–1952* (Hong Kong: Oxford University Press, 1988).

5. For more on the 1987 episode, see Mark Roberti, *The Fall of Hong Kong: China's Triumph and Britain's Betrayal* (New York: Wiley, 1994), pp. 197–210. See also Norman Miners, *The Government and Politics of Hong Kong,* 5th ed. (Hong Kong: Oxford University Press, 1991), pp. 26–27; and William McGurn, ed., *Basic Law, Basic Questions* (Hong Kong: Review Publishing Company, 1988), Appendix C.

6. Stephen Davies and Elfed Roberts, *Political Dictionary for Hong Kong* (Hong Kong: Macmillan, 1990), pp. 332–33.

to allow an escape route in the event of a post-1997 calamity. In early July a parliamentary foreign affairs report recommended full democracy for Hong Kong *before* 1997 as the best means of improving its chances for maintaining a "high degree of autonomy" afterward. Foreign Secretary Geoffrey Howe told Parliament that Britain would indeed strive to hasten the development of Hong Kong's democracy prior to 1997 and try to convince China to continue such development afterward.[7] Also in early July and after equivocating for years, the Hong Kong government announced its intention to draft a Bill of Rights. The ordinance was completed in March 1990 and promulgated a year later.[8]

As post-Tiananmen passions cooled, however, the brave deeds and grand gestures of 1989 yielded something less impressive. But the goals of 1989 would come to be seen as having laid the foundation (by politicizing Hong Kong, energizing the British, and provoking China) for subsequent developments that would change the course of the transition. Thus, in December 1989 Britain's response to the nationality problem was only a modest package offering full British citizenship to 50,000 Hong Kong individuals and their families (or 225,000 people total) to be selected from different categories including civil servants, professionals, and entrepreneurs.

British efforts to influence the Basic Law drafting process, by then in its final stages, bore equally modest fruit. If Hong Kong was outraged by events in 1989, so were the Chinese, and a tense stand-off ensued as transition work resumed. For every safeguard demanded in Hong Kong's name, Beijing inserted a provision to enhance its own interests. Accordingly, the final draft of the Basic Law completed in February 1990 stipulated (as earlier drafts had not) that no more than 20 percent of all future Hong Kong legislators could have the right of abode in foreign

---

7. "Statement by the British Foreign Secretary in the House of Commons," July 5, 1989, reprinted in *The Hong Kong Basic Law: Blueprint for "Stability and Prosperity" Under Chinese Sovereignty?*, ed. Ming K. Chan and David J. Clark (Armonk, N.Y.: M.E. Sharpe, 1991), pp. 246–47.

8. *Hong Kong's Bill of Rights: Problems and Prospects* (Hong Kong: Faculty of Law, University of Hong Kong, 1990); Raymond Wacks, ed., *Human Rights in Hong Kong* (Hong Kong: Oxford University Press, 1992).

countries (Article 67)—a payback for the British citizenship plan. Furthermore, Article 14 stipulated that Chinese armed forces would indeed be garrisoned in the Hong Kong Special Administrative Region (SAR), which is the future formal designation for Hong Kong. Article 18 gave the central government in Beijing the right to declare a state of emergency in Hong Kong should "turmoil" develop. Most unnerving of all, given the moral and material support that Hong Kong people had extended to participants in the Tiananmen uprising of 1989 (officially designated subversive or "counterrevolutionary" by the Chinese), was the Basic Law's Article 23, greatly strengthened by comparison with earlier drafts. The article now prohibited Hong Kong–based "subversion" against the central Chinese government as well as political activities by foreign organizations in Hong Kong.[9]

From China's perspective, the most sensitive issue was that of electoral arrangements for Hong Kong, since these were now clearly rooted in its demand for popular sovereignty as a safeguard of autonomy. According to Percy Cradock, a key player in the Sino-British negotiations over Hong Kong, Britain fought hard for expanding the scope of elections. But it succeeded in gaining only five additional directly elected seats for the Legislative Council in comparison with the pre-1989 Basic Law draft. The net result was an increase from 15 such seats in a 55-seat chamber to 20 in a 60-seat body to be achieved by 1997, and no more than half the council was to be directly elected by 2003.[10] The demand for a directly elected chief executive was dropped altogether.

Despite the gap between their 1989 aspirations and Basic Law realities, Hong Kong councillors reverted to their old cooperative mode and gave a stamp of approval to the new arrangements. The Hong Kong government also remained committed to the principle of "convergence" established in 1986. This controversial goal, known as the "through train" from Hong Kong to China, aimed to achieve continuity of institutions and personnel in order to promote a smooth transition. This, in turn, served

9. For a useful analysis of the Basic Law and its various drafts, see Chan and Clark, eds., *The Hong Kong Basic Law*.

10. Percy Cradock, *Experiences of China* (London: John Murray, 1994), pp. 226–36.

to check and balance British and Chinese influence within each other's respective time zones, that is, before and after 1997.[11] Thus in February 1990 the Hong Kong government announced arrangements for the scheduled 1991 Legislative Council election that dovetailed with those stipulated in the Basic Law and related decisions. Eighteen seats would be directly elected in 1991 and 20 in 1995, allowing the 1995 council to meet the stipulated post-1997 requirements for the first SAR legislature (1997–99) and ride the through train, that is, complete its four-year term of office (1995–99). In other words, the aim of both the British and Chinese arrangements was to allow the last legislature elected under British rule in 1995 to continue sitting without change as the first legislature under Chinese sovereignty.

Given the initial course of events from high emotion in 1989 to low-keyed accommodation in 1990, what precisely motivated Britain to shift gears in 1992 with an aggressive new political program for Hong Kong has yet to be revealed. Percy Cradock has suggested that the ideas originated during Margaret Thatcher's term as British prime minister (May 1979–November 1990) and were implemented by her successor, John Major.[12] The ideas in any case produced a new British governor and a new policy for Hong Kong. Christopher Patten, a leading Conservative Party politician, succeeded scholar-diplomat David Wilson in 1992, and the new policy was as different from its predecessor as Patten was from his.

Patten's 1992 Reform Program: Throwing Down the Gauntlet

Two intervening considerations—one global, one local—possibly influenced the timing of Britain's 1992 initiative on Hong Kong. Presumably Britain would not have initiated its Hong Kong reform program without the massive shift in opinion against China after Tiananmen and, more importantly, in the global balance of power that followed the Soviet Union's demise.

11. Roberti, *The Fall of Hong Kong,* pp. 161–64; Robert Cottrell, *The End of Hong Kong: The Secret Diplomacy of Imperial Retreat* (London: John Murray, 1993), p. 183.

12. Cradock, *Experiences of China,* p. 244.

In Hong Kong the 1991 Legislative Council election proved that the emotions of 1989 had not been forgotten and could easily make the transition from street politics to ballot box. Throughout the 1980s, Hong Kong's politicization had taken organizational form, if at all, only in small discussion and pressure groups. With direct elections now enshrined in the Basic Law, however, old restrictions on political party activity were lifted and several groups moved from discussion to participation in advance of the 1991 elections. Hong Kong's formal political development was now underway. The strongest of the political groups, with only a few hundred members, was the United Democrats of Hong Kong (UDHK) led by lawyer Martin Lee (Li Zhuming), teacher Szeto Wah (Situ Hua), and other activists. Many were also concurrently members of the Hong Kong Alliance in Support of the Patriotic Democratic Movement in China. This latter group, born during the 1989 protests and labeled subversive by the Chinese government, has organized the June 4 memorial activities in Hong Kong each year since and continues to assist dissidents leaving China.[13]

The experts and authorities had anticipated that the novice electorate would vote for personalities in 1991, rather than parties or ideologies. The territory was divided into nine districts with each district electing two councillors and each voter able to vote for two candidates. This system was designed ostensibly to produce a cross section of community representation among the 18 new directly elected legislative councillors. Instead, the poll produced a "liberal" landslide, liberal being the local designation for candidates advocating a faster pace of democratization and as much autonomy from China as possible.

In the pro-democracy/pro-China dichotomy that swiftly emerged, the pro-China side produced only one successful candidate who was subsequently disqualified. After the by-election to replace him the pro-China side lost even this seat. Initially

13. On Hong Kong's emerging political spectrum, see, e.g., Louie Kin-sheun, "Political Parties," in *The Other Hong Kong Report, 1991*, ed. Sung Yun-wing and Lee Ming-kwan (Hong Kong: Chinese University Press, 1991), pp. 55–75; Jane C. Y. Lee, "The 1997 Transition and Hong Kong's Evolving Political Leadership," in *One Culture, Many Systems: Politics in the Reunification of China*, ed. Donald H. McMillen and Michael E. DeGolyer (Hong Kong: Chinese University Press, 1993), pp. 63–93.

worried that they lacked sufficient candidates, UDHK leaders were able to capitalize on their popularity by pairing stronger and weaker candidates in the same district, winning both seats through a coattail effect. The net result (after the by-election) was 17 liberals and one independent. The new liberal lineup comprised 12 UDHK members, 4 from other like-minded groups, and journalist Emily Lau (Liu Huiqing), who ran as an independent but was actually the most outspoken liberal of all.[14]

Christopher Patten as politician-turned-governor arrived in Hong Kong at this juncture. To the democrats, he was a breath of fresh air. Others saw him as being out of his element. Gone were Wilson and Cradock, heirs to the British Foreign Office tradition of mandarin scholar-diplomats who took pride in their understanding of the so-called Chinese mind. They had labored for over a decade, shuttling from Hong Kong to London to Beijing and back again, as they negotiated their way through the endless contradictions of Hong Kong's transition. Now they were sent into retirement with shouts of "shame" and "betrayal" echoing from the subtitles of one book after another reflecting the doubts provoked by their labors.

Patten, by contrast, spoke not a word of Chinese and gleefully set about breaking conventions right and left. His new political reform program seemed designed to lead the territory through a five-year crash course in Western-style democratic development with the hope of laying constitutional foundations that might survive into the post-1997 era. Some established negotiating positions came crashing down , including the principles of convergence, consensus, and cooperation, together with certain rules of political deference cherished on both sides of the mainland–Hong Kong divide.

Governor Patten introduced his reforms at the start of Hong Kong's legislative year in October 1992, breaking an established

---

14. Ian Scott, "An Overview of the Hong Kong Legislative Council Elections of 1991," in *Votes Without Power: The Hong Kong Legislative Council Elections, 1991*, ed. Rowena Y. F. Kwok, Joan Y. H. Leung, and Ian Scott (Hong Kong: Hong Kong University Press, 1992), pp. 1–28; Lau Siu-kai and Louie Kin-sheun, eds., *Hong Kong Tried Democracy: The 1991 Elections in Hong Kong* (Hong Kong: Institute of Asia-Pacific Studies, Chinese University, 1993).

rule at the start by not first consulting the Chinese about proposed changes with post-1997 implications.[15] Electoral reforms were the most important part of the package to be submitted to legislators for appraisal and possible amendment. This legislative procedure was delayed for a year while 17 rounds of talks were conducted between Britain and China during 1993 in a vain effort to win the latter's approval.[16] When that was not forthcoming, Britain proceeded unilaterally. The electoral reform proposals were approved by Legco and implemented in essentially the same form as they were introduced by Patten in 1992.

Overall, the reform program was a concerted attempt to promote the cause of autonomous self-government by introducing a comprehensive set of adjustments throughout Hong Kong's political system. The adjustments had been designed to converge with the post-1997 structures laid down in the Basic Law. But the 1992 reforms also improvised creatively, exploiting certain loopholes and points of silence within that law. Those points concerned especially the sequence of council elections in 1994 and 1995, the results of which would straddle 1997.

Following standard British colonial practice, Hong Kong's government is led by an appointed governor sent from London, his cabinet or Executive Council, and the Legislative Council. By tradition, the latter was a consultative body, and both councils were made up solely of members appointed by the governor. Lower levels of government administration have gradually evolved into the present territory-wide system of districts, led by 18 District Boards responsible for various public works and amenities at the neighborhood level. Additionally, two intermediate bodies, the Urban Council and Regional Council (often referred to simply as the municipal councils), serving urban and suburban areas respectively, have similar responsibilities which include sanitation, entertainment, public libraries, and parks.

The first concerted effort to democratize this political struc-

15. Christopher Patten, "Our Next Five Years: The Agenda for Hong Kong," speech to the Legislative Council, October 7, 1992; text in *South China Morning Post* (Hong Kong, hereafter *SCMP*), October 8, 1992.

16. Britain and China each published separate versions of these talks (full texts in *SCMP*, February 25, 1994, and March 1, 1994, respectively).

ture occurred in the 1980s, after China's intentions for 1997 were made known, with China's sometimes qualified approval. The 1992 reforms accelerated the effort without such approval. By 1994 all boards and councils (except Exco, the cabinet) contained a mix of appointed and elected members; after 1994 all but Exco became fully elected bodies. The District Boards and municipal councils also became not just fully elected but directly elected, their seats filled on a one-person one-vote basis with constituencies determined by the voter's place of residence.

Legco arrangements were more complicated, since they combined Western-style direct election with Chinese-style indirect representation similar to China's people's congress system. Such complexity was necessary in order to keep within the letter of the Basic Law on Legco's composition. Under the new plan, the 60–seat chamber would be composed of 20 seats directly elected by geographic constituencies, 30 seats elected by a restricted franchise arrangement based on occupation and known as functional constituencies, and ten seats indirectly elected by an election committee. This division had been negotiated with China and written into the Basic Law and related decisions, as the foundation for the 1995–99 legislative term which would straddle the 1997 divide.

Patten's reforms, however, changed quite drastically the arrangements for filling the two indirectly elected categories. The election committee responsible for filling ten seats was, under Patten's plan, to be composed of the new directly elected District Board members. This arrangement contrasted sharply with that stipulated in the Basic Law decisions, which called for a complicated mix of appointees, most of whom would never have been directly elected.

As for the 30 functional constituency seats, the old occupational categories remained much as before, electing 21 representatives. The nine remaining seats were filled by nine new constituencies designed to enfranchise employees as well as employers, who dominated selection in the old categories. These latter were designated for representatives of business, industry, finance, real estate, tourism, medicine, law, and other professions, with only two seats reserved for organized labor. By contrast, the nine new constituencies were clearly artificial creations and they were meant to be all-inclusive. For example, the ninth category known as "community, social, and personal services" provoked the most comment, since it combined journalists, bar hostesses, civil servants, and domestic workers (but not housewives). As a result, virtually all *employed* persons could claim two votes, that is, one each in the geographic and new functional constituencies. Without actually admitting as much, this change meant in effect nine additional directly elected seats under cover of the "functional constituency" label.

Equally significant, according to the Chinese record of their abortive 1993 talks with Britain, the British also proposed using the election committee (composed of directly elected District Board members) not only to fill ten Legco seats in 1995, but to choose the post-1997 chief executive as well. This would have partly salvaged the 1989 consensus in favor of a directly elected chief executive, since it would have produced the nearest possible equivalent given the Basic Law constraint for post-1997 arrangements. The Basic Law stipulates the same dual use of the election committee (to select a small number of legislators and the chief executive), but with a very different kind of appointed committee.

Meanwhile, Patten's arrival marked the onset of Legco's metamorphosis into the center of Hong Kong's political life with enhanced status, oversight authority, and above all publicity. The old Exco power elite almost disappeared from public view, anticipating an eventual shift from executive-led government to one with legislative checks and balances. All elective offices ceased to be called administrative or advisory. Instead, the councils—Legco, the municipal councils, and the District Boards—were referred to as the "three tiers of government." The aim was to root autonomy if not actual sovereignty in the people of Hong Kong with a comprehensive set of popularly elected self-governing institutions from the neighborhood level upward. The British have persevered in implementing this agenda, including its most sensitive electoral items, even in the face of China's unrelenting opposition.

China's Response: The Battle Joined

CCP hard-liners emerged victorious from the Tiananmen crisis of 1989, just in time to find the tides of global change rising in the opposite direction. Rather than let themselves be swept away by the anti-communist current, China's leaders decided to swim against it, and their opposition to Britain's new Hong Kong agenda was consistent with that resolve. Their defiance was based on the timing of Britain's initiative and its assumption of inevitable communist decline in China as elsewhere. Beijing also sees multiple dangers within the two-way relationship between China and Hong Kong, including the threat to Chinese sovereignty inherent in Patten's reform package; practical concerns about post-1997 governance and control; and the potentially subversive impact of a democratic Hong Kong on China.

By 1992, Chinese negotiators were well versed in the intricacies of Western electoral politics and the significance of direct democracy as the basis of popular sovereignty, autonomy, and independence. These questions had been debated throughout the Basic Law drafting process (1985–90). One of the most frequently cited summations of China's position dates from that time and came directly from Deng Xiaoping. "Hong Kong's system cannot be completely westernized; it cannot just indiscriminately imitate *[zhaoban]* the West," he told members of the Basic Law Drafting Committee in 1987. To copy everything and set up an Anglo-American system of representative government with a bicameral legislature, multiparty elections, and a division of executive, legislative, and judicial powers would not be suitable.

Furthermore, Deng noted, "the people managing Hong Kong affairs should be Hong Kong people who are patriotic, with love for China and Hong Kong *[ai zuguo ai Xianggang]*. Can such people really be elected by universal suffrage?" Conditions were not yet ripe for Western-style democracy in China either, he said. But he anticipated that perhaps after 50 years, China would have evolved into a system with universal suffrage. Nevertheless, he warned that trying to hasten the process by turning

Hong Kong into a base for subverting the mainland "under cover of democracy" would not be tolerated.[17]

Hence, just as the British have persisted in implementing their reform agenda, so China has opposed it every step of the way. And just as Patten set about giving the territory a crash course in democratic development, so the Chinese arguments against it are reaching back to evoke lessons from every age of modern China's political history.

There is no little irony in this result, since a major Chinese argument against Patten's agenda has been that it risks turning Hong Kong into a "political city." The most direct warning on this point came initially from Lu Ping, the senior Beijing official responsible for Hong Kong affairs. After boycotting Hong Kong for two years while the Sino-British dispute over Patten's reforms continued, Lu Ping arrived for a visit in the spring of 1994. His message was that "the value of Hong Kong to China" had always been economic and people should preserve that value or beware the consequences. He acknowledged that some believed Hong Kong's increasingly democratic system could only be guaranteed if China changed likewise. China's leaders were dead set against such a course, he said, for fear of "chaos and disruption." He therefore warned those "so naive" as to think they could turn Hong Kong into a "political city" with the aim of influencing mainland politics as well.[18] But rather than follow Lu Ping's logic and set a nonpolitical example by saying little and doing nothing, Beijing picked up the gauntlet and joined the political battle on all fronts.

Negating Patten's Reforms

In concrete terms, Patten's agenda is rejected by China as a "triple violator," that is, it violates the 1984 Joint Declaration, the 1990 Basic Law, and other relevant Sino-British agreements.

17. Deng Xiaoping, "Huijian Xianggang tebie xingzhengqu jibenfa qicao weiyuanhui weiyuan shi de jianghua" (Talk to Members of the Hong Kong SAR Basic Law Drafting Committee), April 16, 1987, in *Deng Xiaoping lun Xianggang wenti* (Deng Xiaoping on Hong Kong Questions) (Hong Kong: Sanlian, 1993), pp. 35–36.

18. Text of Lu Ping's speech in *SCMP*, May 7, 1994. Lu heads the Chinese State Council's Hong Kong and Macao Affairs Office.

The Joint Declaration had promised consultation and cooperation between London and Beijing on all major issues relating to Hong Kong. The Basic Law assumed convergence between political institutions before and after 1997. And the reforms were said to violate agreements reached in principle over the composition of the election committee responsible for choosing a small number of legislators and also the chief executive for the first SAR government.

The Chinese therefore began making their own unilateral preparations for the transfer of sovereignty. While talks with Britain were still underway over the new program, a Preliminary Working Committee (PWC) was created by Beijing in mid-1993, ahead of the formal SAR Preparatory Committee that was scheduled to begin work in early 1996. The PWC was an ad hoc appointed body composed of 30 mainland and 39 sympathetic Hong Kong members, empowered to deliberate and advise only. From its founding until it was disbanded at the end of 1995, the PWC's four subgroups met frequently to consider all aspects of the transition. In fact, these meetings served as regular occasions for publicizing China's counterproposals to virtually every item on Britain's political agenda for Hong Kong with the electoral reform and human rights provisions singled out for special attention.

At the same time, Chinese officials have continually reiterated that Patten's reforms will become null and void as of July 1, 1997. Instead of remaining in office until their terms end, following the through-train principle, all bodies elected under the new reformed rules will be reconstituted. As of mid-1996, procedures for reorganizing the District Boards and municipal councils (which the Chinese insist on referring to as lower levels of administration, not government or self-governing bodies) had yet to be finalized. Legco is to be replaced by a caretaker provisional council which will sit for about a year until fresh elections conforming to China's interpretation of the Basic Law can be held in 1998.

The Polemics of Confrontation

Public issues tend to be aired most intensely during election campaigns, and Hong Kong's experience has been no exception. Pro-China partisans entered the fray with an enthusiasm that belied China's formal fear of Hong Kong politics. The elections held under Patten's new rules proceeded in a three-part sequence: District Boards were elected in September 1994, the municipal councils in March 1995, and Legco in September 1995. During each sequence, China's case was put to the Hong Kong public most fully not by pro-China candidates, who had to focus on other issues as well in order to win votes, but by the pro-China press.

Hong Kong's most popular news publications are highly critical of China; most others are somewhat less so. By contrast, the pro-China press includes a handful of newspapers serving primarily those Deng Xiaoping referred to as "patriotic" *(aiguo)* Hong Kong people. This pro-China patriotic minority has long been part of Hong Kong life but its members (until recently) were effectively excluded from local leading political and intellectual circles. The pro-China minority attended its own schools, read its own newspapers, and worked for China-owned or China-oriented organizations and businesses. The largest of these is the Federation of Trade Unions with a current membership of about 210,000.

The most authoritative of the pro-China news publications is the Hong Kong edition of the daily *Wen Wei Po.*[19] Its main editorials are vetted by the Hong Kong branch of the Xinhua News Agency which has, since the People's Republic was established, doubled as a news agency and China's official representative body or de facto embassy in Hong Kong. In addition to its main editorials, the *Wen Wei Po* carries daily commentaries by its own writers and sometimes by those of other patriotic organizations and sympathetic freelancers. It is to these columns that Hong Kong readers can turn for a unique range of pro-China views on any given issue, and these writers have excelled in defending China's stand against Patten's program. The most concentrated collection of such views appeared during the 1995 Legco election campaign offering up a rich and often vitriolic assortment of political arguments.

Two themes in particular stood out amid this campaign cover-

19. *Wen Wei Po* is the standard transliteration from Cantonese; the mainland or pinyin equivalent is *Wenhui bao.* The Chinese is difficult to translate and this paper does not have an English name. It is cited hereafter as *WHB;* all references are to the Hong Kong edition.

age which spelled out China's case on its own terms with little regard for the impact on mainstream Hong Kong sensitivities or the votes that might be lost as a consequence. The first theme warned about "mechanical copying" by China of dominant world trends, a concern surviving from the early decades of the century. The second theme was more self-evident and highly partisan, being tied not just to 20th-century Chinese history but to China's revolutionary communist history. This can be termed the political struggle theme—using images from the past, it reminded everyone that the next-to-last struggle for Chinese reunification under Communist Party rule is underway in Hong Kong.

Why did Hong Kong's governor introduce such a political reform plan?, queried an official pre-election *Wen Wei Po* commentary.

> A major reason is that after 1989, the British government began to change its policy toward Hong Kong, feeling that its past policy toward China had not been strong enough. After 1989, Britain felt that with the disintegration of the Soviet Union and the changes in Eastern Europe, China would follow these countries and change similarly. Hence, Britain should adopt an even stronger policy toward China than before.

The political reform plan was therefore introduced "absolutely not by chance but because the British policy toward Hong Kong changed."[20] Nothing could have been better calculated than the British reform plan to stiffen Chinese resolve and trigger an antagonistic reaction. China's leaders did not need to be reminded in so direct a manner of the power balance shifting against them. The 20th century has made Chinese leaders of every generation and every political persuasion especially sensitive to the effect of such shifting world trends on China.

Mechanical Copying and Dominant World Trends

China's apprehension about its relationship to global trends originated in the country's sudden rush to learn from the out-

20. *WHB*, September 11, 1995 (from the "Special Column on Hong Kong's Basic Law," published jointly by *WHB* and the Central People's Broadcasting Station).

side world that took hold at the beginning of the 20th century when the last imperial dynasty was overthrown. Once traditional precedents were broken, China's leaders looked to the outside world for the ideal model of national reconstruction. Although those leaders came to diverge over what model to follow, the designs were always sought in the dominant world trends of the day. The main problem with this approach was that there were many dominant trends during the century. The consequent experience of rushing too quickly from one to the next before any could yield true national reconstruction has provided many painful lessons, most commonly derided as "mechanical copying."

The sequence has become an ongoing fact of Chinese political life. Someone is always promoting a dominant or rising foreign model as the key to national salvation. Yet the consequences of actually attempting such crash-course emulation of foreign ways have regularly been so destructive that they produce a countervailing critique of mechanical copying. This dialectical sequence could be seen at work in the 1980s, when some began advocating "complete westernization" again for China, and for Hong Kong, only to be contradicted by opponents across the political spectrum. By 1995 the collapse of international communism strengthened further the pressures for westernization. China's response to Britain's 1992 agenda for Hong Kong reflected China's historic predicament with arguments and actions that tried to deflect the world trends arrayed against it. Beijing proclaimed its defiance by categorically rejecting Patten's political reform program and everything it contained.

With this background, *Wen Wei Po* commentators invoked the classic mechanical copying argument before, during, and after Hong Kong's Legco election to justify China's opposition. "Radical" demands for full democracy were repudiated as an example of "wholesale copying" without concern for Hong Kong's actual conditions.[21] The low turnout rates proved that Patten's exercise in expanded representation was "divorced from Hong Kong's social realities."[22] As pressures mounted after the Legco

21. *WHB*, September 14, 1995.
22. *WHB*, September 19, 1995.

election to reverse China's decision so that legislators might remain in office after 1997, people were reminded that "mechanically copying the form of Western democratic political systems does not correspond with Hong Kong's concrete realities."[23] In fact, the pro-China side argued that the democrats were "going against the tide" of history by associating their political interests with the departing British colonials and others intent on perpetuating Western influence in Hong Kong. Meanwhile, pro-China forces were on the rise, and they represented the wave of Hong Kong's future when cooperation with China would become the dominant trend.[24]

Political Struggle and the Rhetoric of Liberation

Erudite points of history may have graced the strategic heights of China's defensive posture, but its tactical barbs were pitched at a much lower partisan level. An interesting contradiction developed within the pro-China camp as the elections progressed. Its candidates fought good defensive campaigns and were on the receiving end of much provocative democratic oratory. But while pro-China candidates concentrated on winning votes with their fixed-smile rebuttals and grassroots concerns, the pro-China Hong Kong press seemed bent on trying to even the score against their opposition. Hence, just as had always been feared in Hong Kong, electioneering did inspire an upsurge of anti-communist rhetoric confirming for the Chinese side the dangers of democracy. But instead of holding their peace, pro-China writers responded in equally inflammatory terms confirming democratic fears of communist logic if not communist rule. In this manner, the political struggle between the forces of dictatorship and democracy was fully joined in the microcosmic world of Hong Kong's election campaigns.

The arguments were in all respects consistent with the mechanical copying theme. But at this partisan level, the dominant trends of world history were rephrased as an international con-

23. From Foreign Minister Qian Qichen's address to the second plenary session of the Hong Kong SAR Preparatory Committee; text in *WHB*, March 25, 1996.

24. See, e.g., *WHB*, September 13 and 20, 1995; *Renmin Ribao* (People's Daily/Beijing, overseas edition), September 19, 1995.

spiracy of Western forces deliberately closing ranks to bring down the last major communist power. Toward this end, the United States had purportedly revived George Kennan's old policy of containment to complete the West's cold war mission against communism. Many weapons were being used against China in this effort: human rights, most favored nation trade status, arms sales, Tibet, Taiwan, and Hong Kong. The latter's role was to serve as a spearhead for this last great anti-communist crusade, and Britain's plan to expand democratic self-governance in Hong Kong was part of the West's attempt "to seek a final solution in the disintegration or gradual evolution of China's state power."[25] Patten's electoral reforms were "actually an attempt to change Hong Kong into an independent or semi-independent political entity" by giving political power to the people rather than returning the colony to China. Hence the interest of the international community in providing aid, encouragement, and advice to the anti-China side of the electoral contest.[26]

In language not heard since the height of the cold war, those in Hong Kong who supported Patten's plan were denounced not just as mechanical copiers but as "running dogs," "pawns," and "servants," doing the bidding of their "colonial masters." They had also become "proxies" and "a special detachment of secret agents" working tirelessly to help the United States contain China.[27]

As China's chief Hong Kong adversary, the Democratic Party (DP), successor to the UDHK, was singled out for special polemical attention. DP leader Martin Lee may have said (as charged) that they were all "riding the through train to hell" and that giving Hong Kong back to China was like returning Jews to Nazi Germany. And he may have lobbied against proportional representation in order to keep pro-China candidates from winning any Legco seats. But China's main charge against Lee was his effort to "internationalize" Hong Kong by actively soliciting support among foreigners for his cause.

In this way, the mechanical copying argument was transformed into a patriotic appeal, following another time-honored

25. *WHB*, September 13, 1995.
26. *WHB*, August 29, 1995; also *WHB*, August 23, 1995.
27. *WHB*, September 13, 1995; also *WHB*, September 14, 16, and 20, 1995.

political tactic. Historically, the reaction against mechanical copying of foreign models was not necessarily synonymous with Chinese nationalism; but the two had often been paired for maximum effect in times of perceived national urgency and political struggle. This being such a time, Martin Lee and like-minded colleagues were accused not just of preferring Anglo-American forms of governance but of "betraying their own nation."[28]

Finally, even the old Maoist concept of class struggle was recycled in the attack against pro-democracy forces, albeit carefully adapted and for limited use. Instead of simply promoting class struggle as of old, the Chinese side accused its opposition of trying to make mischief by fomenting such antagonisms. The electoral reform program contributed toward that end. The nine new functional constituencies sharpened contradictions between labor and capital, a result the old groupings had been designed to avoid. In most of the nine, candidates representing workers and employers were in direct competition for the same seat which served to highlight the conflicts of interest between the two sides.[29]

Meanwhile, Martin Lee and the democrats were accused of aggravating the same contradictions, having "not learned the good things of socialism but only the bad." The reference was to their alleged free-lunch Fabian socialist demands such as higher taxes for the rich and more social security for the poor. In fact, the democrats were blamed for advocating such "extreme left" aims not just for the economy but for the political system as well. Their motives were deliberate: to return an unstable and weakened Hong Kong to China in 1997.[30]

Implementing Patten's Reforms: Western Democracy Hong Kong–Style

Having introduced the reform package and guided its passage to conclusion in the 1994–95 elections, Governor Patten could look upon his labors with some satisfaction. He proclaimed that the foundations of democratic government had been laid in

28. *WHB*, September 13 and 14, 1995.
29. *WHB*, September 5, 1995.
30. *WHB*, September 9, 1995.

Hong Kong and that there would be no turning back. He could hardly have said otherwise, amid all the talk about lame ducks, imperial sunsets, and "too little too late." Still, the foundations *have* been laid. And even assuming a worst-case scenario wherein the Chinese actually succeed in dismantling every last item on Patten's 1992 agenda, the territory's gradual evolution toward democratic rule has been written into the Basic Law. Thus, by the year 2003 half the legislature is to be directly elected and (according to Articles 45 and 68) "the ultimate aim" is the election of the chief executive and all Legislative Council members by universal suffrage. Since the achievement of those aims must be realized by the people of Hong Kong, their response should be seen as the first test of Patten's labors. By this standard, the results to date have been mixed at best.

Election Results in 1994 and 1995

The election campaigns were sedate and low key, although whether this was despite or because of the political tumult surrounding them remains unclear. Public opinion polls and survey research projects have proliferated as a by-product of Hong Kong's new democracy, but many basic answers remain frustratingly elusive.[31] Among them is the impact on voters of China's declaration to halt the through train and reconstitute all the councils after July 1, 1997. This and other unanswered questions surround the low voter turnout which, as noted, quickly became a major point in the Chinese arsenal of arguments against Patten's reforms. Also not available are definitive profiles of Hong Kong's developing political spectrum. But in general, business is known to ally with pro-China forces, or capitalists with communists; middle-class professionals are said to favor the democrats; and organized labor is split between the two sides.

Several small political groups have taken their places along this spectrum. The Democratic Party remains the strongest in

31. The main university-based survey work is being done by Robert Chung at the University of Hong Kong's Social Sciences Research Centre; the interuniversity Hong Kong Transition Project led by Michael DeGolyer, Baptist University; and Lau Siu-kai and Kuan Hsin-chi, directors of ongoing research at the Chinese University of Hong Kong.

terms of voter appeal and the most unequivocal in its stance. The party's platform calls for repudiation of the 1989 anti-democracy crackdown in Beijing as well as amendment of the Basic Law before 1997, to allow the full direct election of Hong Kong's governor and legislature. Also on the pro-democracy side of the ledger is the Association for Democracy and People's Livelihood (ADPL) which differs from the DP over the latter's confrontational stance toward China. The ADPL also regards itself as purer in its grassroots orientation.

After their rout in the 1991 elections, pro-China forces organized the Democratic Alliance for the Betterment of Hong Kong (DAB) to further their electoral prospects. The patriotic community did not unanimously embrace this idea. But despite China's opposition to Patten's new rules, it allowed supporters to contest the elections and DAB politicians emerged as strong campaigners. Their position has been bolstered by a handful of other small united front groups with which the DAB has coordinated campaign strategies and tactics. Business is represented by the Liberal Party (LP) which lacks grassroots support and tries to occupy a centrist position on the democracy/China spectrum.

The voters were not particularly inspired, however, despite an energetic registration drive, massive publicity, and their characteristics as part of a literate, well-informed, almost entirely urban electorate. Turnout rates were only 33 percent of all voters registered for the 1994 District Board elections; 26 percent for the 1995 municipal council elections; and 36 percent for the 1995 Legco election.[32] However, the number of voters in *absolute* terms continued to grow over time. The turnout rate was highest in 1991, before the advent of Patten's reforms. Some 1.92 million people registered that year, of whom 750,000 or 39 percent voted in the first direct Legco election to fill 18 seats. Comparable figures for the 20 directly elected Legco seats in 1995 were 2.57 million registered voters, of whom 920,567 went to the

32. Studies on the nonvoter are useful but inconclusive, e.g., Alfred Ko-wei Hu, "Who Voted in the 1995 Hong Kong Legco Election and Why: A Comparative Study of Election Turnout in Hong Kong and Taiwan," Transition Project conference paper, November 1995; Lau Siu-kai and Kuan Hsin-chi, "The Attentive Spectators: Political Participation of the Hong Kong Chinese," *Journal of Northeast Asian Studies*, Vol. 14, no. 1 (Spring 1995), pp. 3–25; Kuan Hsin-chi and Lau Siu-kai, "The Partial Vision of Democracy in Hong Kong," *China Journal* (Canberra), no. 34 (July 1995), pp. 239–64.

polls or one-sixth the total population. About 500,000 voted in both old and new functional constituencies producing a combined turnout rate of 40 percent. But these electors were all assumed to have cast a second ballot and were not counted as additional voters in calculating the official 36 percent turnout rate for the 1995 Legco election.[33]

The democrats could not reproduce their 1991 landslide victory, although they did remain the strongest bloc in terms of voter appeal. But the DP itself won only 22 percent of the total 346 District Board seats, 32 percent of the 77 municipal council seats, and 32 percent of the 60 total Legco seats. By contrast, the pro-China DAB won 11 percent of the District Board seats, 13 percent of those on the municipal councils, and 10 percent of all Legco seats.[34]

In Hong Kong's fragmented system, the real winners were the small groups and parties plus independents who together make up the majorities on most councils. Nevertheless, most of these groups and independents are also inclined toward one of the two dominant power blocs. At the District Board level, for instance, independents won 167 seats or 48 percent of the total. But constituencies are small, averaging about 17,000 voters each, and leftists have strong ties in many urban neighborhoods as well as in the rural suburbs. Therefore analysts calculated that up to 120 of the independents could be counted on to support pro-China forces, and they predicted the latter would be able to secure three or four of the ten Legco seats to be filled by the District Board election committee in 1995. The prediction proved too conservative: pro-China candidates actually won six of those ten seats.

Thus, success in the Legco election was correlated with the voting method. By and large, democratic candidates were strongest in the direct (geographic constituency) contests whereas pro-China politicians did best under the "least" demo-

33. Percentages on voter turnout are as given with the official figures: *SCMP*, September 19, 1994, March 6, 1995, and September 18, 1995, for the three elections respectively. Hong Kong government statistics on the 1991 Legco direct elections and 1995 final voter roll, from the "Press Kit," September 17, 1995, pp. 54 and 31, respectively; and Government Information Services, press release, "Voter Turnout," September 18, 1995. Statistics do not record those who may have voted only in a functional constituency.

34. Success rates for the two parties are from the official vote count for the three elections in *SCMP*, September 20, 1994, March 7, 1995, and September 19, 1995, respectively.

cratic or indirect election committee method. But given the new standards of Hong Kong's developing democracy, popular esteem was also correlated with the number of direct votes won. The greatest strength of pro-business candidates remained where it had always been, in the old functional constituencies which had been designed just for them and where broader popular support did not matter. So clear were the political implications of their status, however, that LP chairman Allen Lee (Li Pengfei) insisted on running for a geographic rather than a functional seat in order to earn the added legitimacy that only direct election could bring under the new rules. Similarly, his colleagues who won "new" functional constituency seats reminded everyone that their vote-counts were as high as those of the directly elected councillors. DAB leaders contested in geographic constituencies for the same reason, even going so far as to vow that they would not join the provisional legislature in 1997, if it was constituted by appointment rather than by election.

Consequently, the democrats, including the DP and like-minded independents, predominated in the geographic constituencies winning 14 of the 20 directly elected seats. The remaining six seats were allocated as follows: DAB, two; ADPL, two; LP, one; independent, one. Heightening the sense of partisan victory, all leading democratic politicians won easily, while pro-China forces lost their three strongest leaders to defeat in the geographic constituencies, including DAB chairman Tsang Yok-sing (Zeng Yucheng).

Defeated as well was Elsie Elliott Tu, Hong Kong's most venerable British personality, renowned as an anti-establishment champion of just causes. She had held her municipal council seat (initially won under an old restricted franchise formula) for almost 30 years and moved on to Legco where opinion polls consistently ranked her its most popular member—until she began siding with China and criticizing Patten's reforms. Her political career ended in symbolic and bitter defeat after a deliberate democratic "raid" into her district. The challenger was Szeto Wah who had begun his political life in patriotic circles and moved on to lead Hong Kong's "subversive" efforts for democracy in China. Elsie Tu's last campaign also marked the clear passage of Hong Kong's colonial era with the evolution of Legco from a body that had once been wholly British to one with only Chinese members.

China's reasons for opposing more directly elected seats—and Deng Xiaoping's above-mentioned doubts about copying Western democracy—become much clearer on contemplating the cross section of Hong Kong political interests reflected in Legco's diverse 1995 constituencies. The overall popularity of anti-communist concerns makes it impossible for patriotic candidates to win substantial victories within an Anglo-American winner-take-all electoral system. In 1995, election districts were redesigned to eliminate the 1991 coattail effect but proportional representation was ruled out and the polls were organized on a one-person one-vote basis to elect one representative from each of 20 districts with a simple plurality of votes cast.

Yet a relatively large minority of voters was still willing to stand on the Chinese side, its strength concentrated in various organizations and in neighborhoods scattered throughout the territory. The direct elections showed the extent of public support for pro-China forces more precisely than had ever been possible before. Such candidates ran in almost all the geographic constituencies where, despite winning only two contests, they received about 280,000 votes (or 30 percent of the total cast).[35] This suggests that active pro-China strength has not grown much beyond its traditional leftist base, but is much greater than indicated by the few seats won.

Moreover, the total Legco lineup including both directly and indirectly elected members is about evenly divided along the democracy/China spectrum. Twenty-five legislators are solidly in the democratic camp (19 DP plus six others), with an almost equal number in the pro-China (16)/pro-business (10) alignment. The balance is held by a handful of "true" independents and the four ADPL members.

---

35. Calculations are mine, based on the official election result (*SCMP*, September 19, 1995). One pro-China source calculated 34 percent of the popular vote in the geographic constituencies for its candidates and 61 percent for the democrats (*WHB*, September 22, 1995). Governor Patten claimed that democrats received about 60 percent of the popular vote both in 1991 and 1995 (*SCMP*, October 2, 1995).

Empowering Legco: "Class Struggle" at Last

Once pro-China candidates decided to follow the electoral route after 1991, they discovered wider public interests beyond the confines of their community, which had tended to look after its own. These candidates found themselves at a double disadvantage, since many democrats had originally built their careers as social activists upon the more mundane concerns of big city life. Racing to reclaim turf that should have been theirs, DAB leaders quickly targeted these issues. In this manner, only the big political question seemed to separate platforms. Election analysts therefore presented two balance sheets: one for political issues, the other for grassroots concerns. On the latter, populists emerged with a clear majority in the 1995 Legislative Council. One such tally counted 37 seats for "labor" including all DP, DAB, and ADPL councillors, with only 18 for "business and industry."[36]

As a result, Hong Kong's business community was challenged as never before. The colony had been built by and for this sector and its members had dominated the political establishment ever since, even as its ethnic composition changed from British to Chinese. This configuration of power was responsible for several aspects of Hong Kong life that had remained, along with its political development, well insulated from 20th-century trends. For example, rights long assumed elsewhere—such as labor protection, unemployment insurance, retirement benefits, social welfare, equal opportunity—had been held at bay by the Hong Kong government in concert with business leaders. During the 1980s, business rebuffed growing demands for reform in these areas by evoking the specter of free lunches to explain Britain's decline. The term is still routinely used in Hong Kong as a shorthand reference for British-style welfare-state economics and for business fears about the consequences of too much mass participation in politics. And sure enough, once electioneering began in earnest parties and candidates all reflected grassroots demands for social welfare reform.

36. *Mingbao* (Ming Pao Daily News/Hong Kong), September 19, 1995.

This unprecedented fall from grace and power of business interests helps explain the ironic spectacle of Hong Kong's capitalists falling out with Patten, a conservative British governor, to seek patronage from their future communist sovereign (and despite the populist inclinations of China's newly activated Hong Kong mass base). These were the contradictions, developing throughout Patten's tenure, that erupted into international headlines after *Newsweek* magazine's May 13, 1996, interview with the governor on "Betraying Hong Kong." In that interview, Patten emphasized the business community's opposition to democratic reforms in Hong Kong. But another unanticipated factor had already been at work heightening tensions all-around in the colony for over a year.

By a coincidence of bad timing, election year 1995 was the worst for Hong Kong economically in two decades. According to the official year-end figures, Hong Kong's gross domestic product, adjusted for the terms-of-trade or real income measure, grew only 1.5 percent, the lowest growth rate since 1974. Throughout 1995, economists insisted that Hong Kong's fundamentals were sound and the upturn "just around the corner." By mid-1996, they were beginning to predict no end in sight. Causes were both external and internal but included declining consumer confidence that no one would admit to being 1997-related.[37]

Yet causes for such reluctance were not just political but also economic, and on this point too no one was ready to conclude that Hong Kong's strategy for success might be in need of major adjustment. Thus Hong Kong has been able to take the prospect of 1997 in stride partly because of the strong local economy. During the decade 1984 to 1994, the economy's official growth rate (before terms-of-trade adjustment) had continued to average 5.5 percent per year, down from 8.5 percent during the preceding decade but respectable nonetheless. Respectable, too, was Hong Kong's 1995 per capita gross domestic product of about US$23,000. The territory was able to achieve such growth, however, only because of the new opportunities for trade and investment in China. Accordingly, confidence was

37. E.g., General Chamber of Commerce economist Ian Perkins's weekly column, in *SCMP*, March 10, 1996, April 28, 1996, May 5, 1996, May 26, 1996, June 2, 1996, and August 4, 1996.

maintained as the integration of the two economies proceeded with each having become the other's main trading partner and investor by the mid-1990s.

The business community's political alliance with China is rooted in these economic realities. But the costs of Hong Kong's past lifestyle are now coming due as grassroots politicians turn the old rhetoric on its head to ask who has been given a free ride. Most provocative in mid-1995 was the unemployment rate, which rose suddenly from an average of only 2 percent for the entire preceding decade through 1994, to 3 percent in mid-1995, and 3.6 percent by October 1995. According to government statistics, about 113,500 people were out of work and another 77,000 underemployed.[38] Inflationary pressures were easing somewhat due to the economic slowdown, but remained high at an 8.7 percent average for the whole year.[39]

Although not high by international standards, the sudden rise in unemployment provided fertile ground for campaign orators several of whom, as social activists, had been campaigning for years against the government's bare-bones social security assistance programs. Such arguments were now strengthened by the structural changes resulting from Hong Kong's economic integration with China. This had meant about half a million manufacturing jobs lost within less than a decade as enterprises moved their factories across the border to escape Hong Kong's astronomical rents and rising wages. Until the downturn of 1995, growth in Hong Kong's service sector and property development had created a comparable number of new jobs—so long as one did not calculate too carefully, or consider the female component of the former factory work force and employers' endemic discrimination against middle-aged women. Adding insult to injury in 1995 was the labor-import scheme whereby the government allowed employers to bring in lower-cost foreign workers to fill gaps in the local labor supply. Tolerated under conditions of full employment, the practice became a major target for election-year polemics in 1995.

Consequently, candidate platforms at both ends of the politi-

38. *SCMP*, April 30, 1995, May 31, 1995, June 4, 1995, and September 10, 1995. *Hong Kong Standard*, October 17, 1995, and November 17, 1995.

39. *SCMP*, January 28, 1996.

cal spectrum contained planks demanding protection for workers and across the board improvements in social security. Afterward, during the first heady months of Hong Kong's first fully elected legislature, councillors bent on easing economic pain and curbing inflation began putting together majorities that challenged some hallowed colonial priorities. The labor-import scheme was slashed. A public retirement program was finally approved, after three decades of dithering and obstruction. Routine government requests to increase charges for certain public services were voted down. Even the Liberal and Democratic parties joined forces to pass a motion calling for cuts in profit and income taxes, while a host of labor-led initiatives began moving through the legislative pipeline.

The rush of social legislation naturally placed Patten in an awkward position between the government's new democratic and old business allies. He reminded everyone at the start of the 1995 legislative year that his constitutional reforms aimed to enhance Legco's oversight role, not transform it into an alternative power base. The government, he said, would remain executive-led and he would not hesitate to block initiatives he deemed detrimental to the public interest.[40] But his executive powers were easier stated than exercised as he tried to balance his political reform agenda with the demands of local democrats, Hong Kong's economic realities, and China's opposition overall.

During his early years as governor, when pressures were less intense, Patten had used his powers and skills to enforce compromises that seemed more favorable to conservatives and business than to democratic reformers. At no time were these skills more fully exercised than during the marathon effort in 1994 and 1995 to parry Anna Wu's (Hu Hongyu) equal opportunities legislation. Ms. Wu was among the last appointed legislators, and Patten had used his power to good partisan advantage by appointing her and another lawyer, Christine Loh (Lu Gonghui), to help push through his electoral reforms. But both soon demonstrated that they had agendas of their own, provoking local conservative interests with whom the Hong Kong government had always compromised to obstruct reform.

40. "Policy Address, 1995," *SCMP*, October 12, 1995.

Anna Wu's Human Rights and Equal Opportunities Commission Bill, designed to give legal credence to provisions of Hong Kong's 1991 Bill of Rights, would have established autonomous enforcement mechanisms. Comprehensive in scope, the aim was to ban discrimination on many grounds ranging from physical disability to political beliefs. The Chinese promised to dismantle any such enforcement bodies that might be set up before 1997, and employers dismissed the job-related provisions as unenforceable. Citing budgetary considerations, Patten exercised his prerogative to prevent the bill from even being put to a vote. The government then also blocked, through means both fair and foul, all subsequent moves to introduce equivalent legislation and ultimately secured passage of its own limited set of measures to protect women and the disabled.

By 1996, however, Patten seemed far less inclined to curb the new legislature despite its costly "class-based" initiatives. On the contrary, with his electoral reform task completed and the need for compromise diminishing, he appeared to have thrown caution to the wind. He ventured forth fearlessly in Legco's defense against all comers, proclaiming both at home and abroad his refusal to compromise or cooperate in any way with the preparations for its provisional post-1997 successor. He also openly criticized those who did not do likewise. Hence, if Patten did not actually tell *Newsweek* that Hong Kong's billionaires had betrayed his cause, he surely implied as much and the headline captured his meaning perfectly.[41]

Probably, Patten had been provoked by an interview given a few days earlier wherein Liberal Party legislator James Tien (Tian Beijun) outlined his alternative vision of things to come. Tien is also chairman of the Hong Kong General Chamber of Commerce. He angrily blamed the democrats and the British for their single-minded focus on politics, declaring that "the business community has never accepted" Patten's electoral reforms. Tien was highly critical of proceedings in Legco which he blamed on the new labor representatives elected in 1995. He deplored the legislation under review on severance pay, maternity

41. The headline in the U.S. edition of *Newsweek* (reading simply, "Betrayed?") was less provocative than its Asian counterpart.

leave, gender discrimination, and disability allowances. Even the government's limited initiatives in this regard were seen as excessive. Employers, he said, were being suddenly bombarded by welfare demands that should have taken decades to implement. He consequently looked forward to working with the provisional legislature to reestablish labor-import quotas and promote policies for a better business environment.[42]

The Shape of Things to Come

With so many contradictory interests competing for attention, Hong Kong's future will likely be characterized by a protracted struggle to reach a viable compromise among them. All the visions will have to be accommodated, since all have a legitimate claim on Hong Kong's future. To outside observers, the equation is simple and seen as another instance in the ongoing struggle between dictatorship and democracy. Contributing to this vision, of course, are the two main protagonists—Britain and China—who have chosen to stake their claims on those same grounds.

One of the clearest statements for the British side came from Percy Cradock, an unlikely source, since he is also the fiercest British critic of Patten's 1992 reform initiative and agrees with the logic of China's opposition. But in explaining how Britain's aggressive approach came about, Cradock listed the arguments that compelled Britain to adopt it. They were an "ill-defined sense of guilt" among British leaders for not having done more to promote democracy in Hong Kong; worry that history would question their judgment as it did the motives of Churchill and Roosevelt for compromising with Stalin at Yalta; the "painful history" of Britain's nationality legislation, which had removed the right of Hong Kong people to settle there; regret at not resisting harder China's refusal to allow direct Hong Kong representation in the Sino-British negotiations between 1982 and 1984, which decided its future; and finally, the outrage after Tiananmen, which turned misgivings into accusations of betrayal and appeasement for handing over six million colonial subjects to Beijing.[43]

The clearest response from the Chinese side to the challenge

42. *SCMP*, April 28, 1996.

43. Cradock, *Experiences of China*, pp. 247–58.

of Western democracy came just after the March 1996 presidential election in Taiwan. This statement reflects the hard-line political front maintained by China's post-Tiananmen leadership against its opponents at home, abroad, and in between. The latter, meaning Hong Kong and Taiwan, are currently the most threatening because they have established democratic precedents within China's immediate sphere of influence via political reforms. The explicit Chinese statement on Western-style democracy appeared as the first of eight commentaries published during April and May, on the Western challenge overall. According to Hong Kong's political grapevine, this series was written under the direction of CCP propaganda chief, Ding Guan'gen, as part of Jiang Zemin's effort to consolidate his power and formulate his own political agenda. Without actually naming Hong Kong or Taiwan, the statement nevertheless reiterated China's official determination to resist all democratic trends. China's course will be to stand firm against the tide of democratization while reforming from within at a pace and on terms of Beijing's choosing. Its presenters not only developed an orthodox Marxist argument on the class-based nature of all political systems, but for emphasis revived an old Cultural Revolution slogan about "drawing a clear line" *(huaqing jiexian)* against class enemies. In this case, the specific reference was to the "clear line" that must be maintained between socialist democracy and Western parliamentary democracy together with their respective proletarian and bourgeois sponsors.

The article argued, moreover, that the institutions of China's socialist democracy are superior to their Western counterparts. In particular, the components of socialist democracy that China aims to keep are the system of indirectly elected people's congresses with their governing principle of democratic centralism and the form of multiparty cooperation and consultation under Communist Party leadership. "If we indiscriminately copy the two-party or multiparty systems of Western capitalist countries, the working class, the people, and the nation will all be divided, causing the socialist enterprise to succumb to chaos and collapse with unthinkable consequences."[44]

---

44. *Jiefangjun Bao* (Liberation Army Daily/Beijing), April 1, 1996.

This defense of Chinese socialist democracy was similar in tone to the 1995 Legco election campaign coverage in Hong Kong's pro-China press. Taken together they reflect the official political context that Hong Kong will enter on July 1, 1997. But so great is the gap between the official Chinese perspective and its British equivalent that the analogy might best be expressed in tectonic terms: two continental plates about to collide with Hong Kong at the point of first contact.

In Hong Kong itself, however, the struggle for compromise solutions between these two extremes has already become a fact of daily life as alternatives on a multitude of relevant issues are presented, choices weighed, and stands taken or evaded. For some, the first decision was to opt out altogether and many thousands have taken it. According to official government estimates, about half a million people emigrated between 1980 and 1994, with the numbers rising sharply after 1989.[45] But the great majority cannot or will not leave, and their choices will ultimately determine Hong Kong's fate. For the time being, two different alternatives have been designed for them by Britain and China, inspired by the protagonists' respective commitments to parliamentary and socialist democracy. Hong Kong citizens will not have the right to design a system of their own in the foreseeable future. But the official alternatives presented to them, in the form of Patten's 1992 agenda and the Basic Law, are still primarily blueprints and the possibilities for revision have only begun to be tapped.

The significance of Britain's 1992 reform program can be judged in this light. Doubts are often raised, even among supporters, as to whether that initiative was worth the cost given China's intransigence and the damage done to Sino-British cooperation during the final years of transition. Patten's answer, although phrased as ever in terms of Britain's interests, nevertheless points to a key intervening consideration. If Britain had kept to the pre-1992 accommodations, he said, it would have been held responsible for less freedom, less democracy, and less human rights protection. And the demonstrations would then

45. Ronald Skeldon, "Emigration from Hong Kong, 1945–1994," in *Emigration from Hong Kong*, ed. Ronald Skeldon (Hong Kong: Chinese University Press, 1995), p. 57.

have been against the British rather than the Chinese.[46] Britain was undoubtedly more concerned about its international image than the nascent forces of democracy in Hong Kong. But those forces are rooted in the territory's inherited fear of communist China, and they represented 60 percent of the direct popular vote in 1995, as well as the foundation underlying Patten's reforms.

Doubts are also raised about the validity and meaning of an election where 60 percent of all registered voters chose not to participate. Considering the enthusiastic turnouts being recorded in Taiwan, however, such lethargy should probably not be written off to Chinese custom and tradition. Reasons might be traced instead to the "simulated" nature of Hong Kong's electoral process—bequeathed almost as an afterthought by a departing colonial administration to elect representatives who have been granted little real power. Given those conditions, the significant point seems not that so few voted but that close to one million people actually did. For them, Patten's constitutional reforms have provided political resources and experience they did not possess before, to serve as a precedent against which alternatives can be compared and choices made.

If Britain's democratic bequest is tentative, however, it has at least now been clearly presented to the public concerned. China's blueprint, by contrast, is tenuous and its presentation equivocal at best. The house that Patten built will be dismantled come July 1, 1997, and reconstructed in accordance with the Basic Law—which is where uncertainty begins. The starting point of this uncertainty is the disparity between China's official hostile view of Western democracy and the variant proposed for Hong Kong under the one country–two systems formula. The Basic Law defines that formula, but the Basic Law only outlines a skeletal structure the details of which are being hammered out behind closed doors.

This skeletal political system for post-1997 Hong Kong combines the principles of consultation and consensus with the practice of decision making by Beijing-led committees. A series of these advisory bodies and groups, initially designed to include as broad a cross section of local interests as possible, has

46. *Newsweek*, May 13, 1996.

been at work since the mid-1980s. The Basic Law consultative and drafting committees were the first to be formed. But the inevitable break occurred in 1989, with consensus the casualty, when democratic leaders Martin Lee and Szeto Wah were expelled from the drafting committee for refusing to repent their "subversive" support of protesters in China. Later, as the democrats' political fortunes rose in Hong Kong, the Chinese excluded them increasingly from the consultative process.

For example, the Preliminary Working Committee, set up in 1993, was composed only of mainland and pro-China Hong Kong members and was known accordingly as a sounding board for Beijing's ideas on dismantling Patten's program. When its work was concluded in December 1995, all the PWC's Hong Kong members moved on in January 1996 to the Preparatory Committee, which is formally authorized to organize the first SAR government. The Preparatory Committee is a 150-member body with 94 Hong Kong representatives and 56 from China. But the Hong Kong contingent is dominated by business figures: virtually all 94 are from the pro-China/pro-business alignment, only 14 are current legislative councillors, and the democratic camp is represented by just two ADPL members. This committee created a 400-member Selection Committee which then chose, in late 1996, the chief executive and members of the provisional legislature. The latter body will serve in a caretaker capacity for about one year from July 1997, to formalize whatever PWC proposals are carried forward and to place a stamp of authoritative approval on government measures.

The Basic Law constitutes China's agenda for Hong Kong, but it only indicates that certain tasks must be performed and structures erected; how this is to be done is currently the subject of intense debate, albeit based on principles of confidentiality and collective responsibility among the new pro-China authorities. The main contradiction running throughout the exercise is already evident, however. Under the one country–two systems formula, Hong Kong people are supposed to rule Hong Kong. But the Chinese have set about systematically excluding the democrats, who represent a major segment of Hong Kong public opinion. Banned from the Preparatory Committee, the democrats were excluded from the Selection Committee as well, because they refused to recognize or participate in the work of the provisional legislature. Zhou Nan, who heads the local branch of the Xinhua Agency and is therefore China's chief representative in Hong Kong, even reiterated recently Deng Xiaoping's preference from long ago. According to Zhou, under the "Hong Kong people ruling Hong Kong" principle, "patriots" will be the main force running Hong Kong after 1997.[47]

Obviously, the Chinese side is trying to apply Beijing logic to Hong Kong realities. Since Patten's agenda must be dismantled, the Chinese reason, its main beneficiaries must be disempowered as well—with the counterrevolutionary, subversive charge threatening overall as a reminder for those who might presume to carry their democratic demands too far. The parallels are implicit but clear: just as the pro-China community was excluded from power under British rule, so Chinese authorities seem to hope the democrats can be excluded under theirs.

Yet Chinese officials are also as yet undecided about the degree to which they should try to force Hong Kong into the Chinese political mold. After each point of conflict, someone from the Chinese side hastens forth to attempt damage control, thereby revealing further areas for maneuver. Lu Ping himself thus went on record to promise that the democrats would be allowed to contest the 1998 Legco election (even though they are likely to be excluded from all the formative steps in between).[48] He also backpedaled furiously under a barrage of criticism after trying to establish parameters for press freedom by making a distinction between (acceptable) reporting and (unacceptable) advocating in news stories deemed controversial by China.[49]

Equally significant as indicators of a middle ground and areas for maneuver are the pro-China candidates who participated in Patten's elections. The importance of these candidates, whether or not they actually won, is suggested by the contrast between their even-toned campaign oratory and the hard-line rhetoric of the pro-China press. Their platform even recom-

47. Quoted in *SCMP*, April 13, 1996.

48. Lu's promise was made in an interview with Jim Laurie, ABC television news (interview text in *SCMP*, May 30, 1996).

49. The distinction was made by Lu in a CNN television interview on May 31 (*SCMP*, June 1, 1996).

mended that all members elected to Legco in 1995 automatically become candidates for the provisional legislature. Moreover, DAB leaders continued to advocate some similar solution in order to prevent the democrats' exclusion from that body. Obviously sensitive to Hong Kong realities, local pro-China politicians straddle the Hong Kong dividing line between Chinese socialism and Western democracy as they seek viable compromises between the two.

Conclusion

Beijing may have won the next-to-last prize in its quest to reunify all of China, but the conditions surrounding Hong Kong's return in 1997 are otherwise fraught with uncertainty. As of 1996, even after years of preparation, the contest being waged over the substance of Hong Kong's future political order seemed to be intensifying with no end in sight. In the 1984 Sino-British Joint Declaration, China promised to preserve Hong Kong's way of life for 50 years after 1997. The promise was welcomed in Hong Kong at the time; it calmed fears aroused by the prospect of living under communist rule. A dozen years later, the promise is seen by many to contain threats almost as great as the danger it was designed to keep at bay. A favorite phrase of these critics is "frozen in colonial time," and they do not want to see Hong Kong emerge after 1997 in some reincarnation of its colonial state, as if transferred from one form of authoritarian rule to another.

The changed perspectives are of course a function of the changing times. In 1984, no one could have anticipated the demise of international communism and its many ramifications. But neither did anyone seem to anticipate the diverse interpretations that would intervene as general promises were translated into the specific policies, laws, and institutions necessary to govern Hong Kong's post-1997 future. Whether anticipated or not, however, the changing international power balance and imminent return to Chinese rule have provided Hong Kong with the equivalent of a crash course in political development.

China blames Britain and Governor Patten for Hong Kong's

politicization in the 1990s. In fact, Patten's 1992 reform agenda only gave sharper focus to the choices that were already being forcefully debated by Britain and China on the one hand, and by Hong Kong partisans on the other. The Chinese also picked up the gauntlet that Patten threw down in 1992, and galloped into the fray with an enthusiasm that belied their proclaimed longing for a return to the tranquil days when Hong Kong was an "economic city" with little political life of its own.

By 1996, in any case, the differing British and Chinese alternatives for Hong Kong's future were clear, as were their respective motives for championing them and the relative strength of their Hong Kong supporters. The contending forces were also evenly matched. Britain's belated effort to root government firmly in the people of Hong Kong is backed by the full force of Western public opinion which sees Hong Kong as the point of first direct contact between Western democracy and Chinese communism. In the opposing corner, the mammoth weight and bureaucratic inertia of the CCP have so far enabled it to defy the rush of dominant world trends. Similarly, in Hong Kong the 1995 Legislative Council lineup accurately reflects the relative power of the two coalitions. The dominant voice is that of the democrats, and Hong Kong's voting majority prefers leaders who are willing to articulate the public's inherited fear of communism in forthright demands for autonomy, human rights protection, and democratic development.

But pro-China forces also are rooted in the people of Hong Kong, including both its patriotic minority and the business community. The latter, moreover, sees itself not just as the architect of Hong Kong's prosperity but also as its builder and guarantor. Hong Kong entrepreneurs do not credit Britain for their success and certainly not British-style politics, which is why they did not welcome Patten's agenda for Hong Kong. Accordingly, they no longer even bother to be circumspect in voicing their disdain for his reforms and the new legislative majorities that are threatening Hong Kong's established ways of doing business. These leaders will not hesitate to work with China and the provisional legislature to dilute the benefits of Legco's new social conscience.

Perhaps more important in consolidating the China-business alliance, however, is the already well-advanced integration of the Chinese and Hong Kong economies which tends to equalize the dependency ratio between them. Increasingly, what is good for China will be good for Hong Kong and not just the other way around. Hence where contradictions occur, Hong Kong's interests may well be compromised for the greater Chinese good. But a more immediate concern is the likely upsurge of mainland-style corruption and influence peddling. In recent years, the Hong Kong government has waged a relatively successful battle against these economic evils and their politically demoralizing consequences, in an ongoing effort which the China-business alliance may be unwilling or unable to continue after 1997.

The challenge for these diverse conflicting interests is clear. The task is to work toward a middle ground and negotiate viable compromise solutions. These solutions must be able to bridge the distance between Britain's 1992 design for accelerated but still limited self-government and the Basic Law's promise of half a directly elected legislature by 2003 plus eventual universal suffrage. The outcome defies prediction because the conflicting interests are so great and because there is no precedent for an autonomous enclave, capitalist and self-governing, within the communist-led Chinese state.

Patten aims to go out with a flourish and challenges democratic supporters to "fight like hell" every step of the way in defense of the legacy he has tried to bequeath. China, meanwhile, denounces the governor for "fomenting rebellion" and is determined to dismantle as much of his program as possible. It therefore follows that the first years after 1997 will be difficult as Hong Kong partisans take the measure of their new sovereign, probe the limits of Beijing's resolve, and determine how best to promote their interests. A few democrats like Szeto Wah have already indicated their willingness to risk prison terms if necessary in defense of their cause. But most would probably stop short of so radical a course. And China does remain committed to the Basic Law's promise of gradual evolutionary development toward democratic governance for Hong Kong. Hence, however turbulent the first years of contact may be, Hong Kong will probably succeed in designing some viable working model for local self-government under Chinese sovereignty, and the model may well be able to serve in turn as a precedent for future reform within the Chinese state itself.

Taiwan in the 1990s: Moving Ahead or Back to the Future?

Cal Clark

As the decade of the 1990s passes its midpoint, Taiwan's position can be interpreted from two different perspectives. On the one hand, it appears to be moving ahead at a rapid rate. Its dynamic economy continues to grow at about 6 percent a year, despite a substantial movement of light industry offshore to countries with lower labor costs. Its gross national product (GNP) per capita of $13,000 in early 1996 (roughly comparable to Spain's or Ireland's) suggests that it may have already entered the developed world. While democratization and political development on Taiwan had long lagged behind the island's economic miracle, the 1990s witnessed a transition to electoral democracy culminating in the direct election of the Legislative Yuan (Taiwan's national legislature) in December 1992 and the president in March 1996. Finally, Taiwan's much circumscribed role in world affairs, stemming from its unfinished civil war with the People's Republic of China (PRC), appeared to be growing as well, at least until the PRC's extremely strong reaction to Taiwan president Lee Teng-hui's visit to the United States in June 1995.

Such a rosy scenario is far from totally justified, however, since ghosts from the past appear poised to drag Taiwan back to a future that would be debilitating and dangerous. Most spectacularly, the contretemps across the Taiwan Strait in 1995–96 suggested the possible reemergence of the cold war in Asia. China's suspicion of and hostility toward Taiwan, in turn, was at least partially, if not largely, caused by the growing saliency of the national identity question unleashed by democratization—that is, resentment of long-time residents against the mainlanders who fled to the island with Chiang Kai-shek in the late 1940s. In addition to the resuscitation of such old political hostilities, Taiwan's transition from a labor-intensive manufacturing economy to a high-tech and service-oriented economy has caused a significant upturn in income inequality after decades of growth that had been relatively equitably distributed.

This briefing on Taiwan at mid-decade, therefore, considers the conflicting implications of the political, diplomatic, and economic trends affecting the island. It begins with a brief synopsis of ghosts from the past that structure and seemingly threaten current events and accomplishments. Individual sections then sketch the major economic, domestic political, and international dynamics during the 1990s. Finally, the conclusion tries to assess what these various factors may portend for the evolution of Taiwan.

Ghosts from the Past

The missile tests and war games that China conducted near Taiwan during 1995–96 demonstrate the continuing potency of the unresolved civil war between Mao Zedong's Chinese Communist Party (CCP) and Chiang Kai-shek's Nationalist Party or Kuomintang (KMT) which seemingly ended when the CCP drove the KMT from the mainland to Taiwan in 1949. This shadow from the past is intertwined, moreover, with the strained relations between the long-time Han Chinese residents of Taiwan ("islanders") and the mainlanders who came with Chiang in the late 1940s. From Beijing's vantage point, islander opposition calls for independence became serious enough to threaten the integrity of China, thereby turning their old mainlander KMT enemies (who also agree that there is only one China) into tacit allies.

Taiwan is a large island (about 250 miles long and 100 miles wide) that lies 100 miles off the coast of Fujian Province, halfway between Shanghai and Hong Kong. Although the first people in Taiwan were Malay-Polynesian aborigines, the island has been overwhelmingly settled by Han Chinese, primarily from Fujian. Taiwanese of Fujianese descent now constitute about two-thirds of the population, with another 15 percent each being Hakka (primarily from Guangdong Province) and mainlanders. The initial major Chinese settlement occurred in the late 16th century as the result of growing commerce along China's Pacific coast. After a brief interlude of Dutch colonial control (1624–62), Chinese ruled Taiwan, albeit as something of a "wild west" frontier, until the island was ceded to Japan in 1895 at the end of the Sino-Japanese War. Japan developed Taiwan as a rice basket during the 50 years of colonial administration, although much of the Japanese infrastructure and nascent industry was destroyed by heavy U.S. bombing at the end of World War II. Despite the fact that Taiwanese welcomed Nationalist troops as liberators when the island reverted to China at the end of World War II, relations between islanders and mainlanders soon became tense. The Kuomintang tended to view the Taiwanese as collaborators with the hated Japanese and the island as a resource base for financing the civil war with the communists. Such reasoning justified the corrupt, brutal, and exploitive policies of the KMT military commander, Chen Yi, who administered Taiwan. Chen's repression finally sparked an uprising on February 28, 1947. A compromise between Chen and Taiwanese leaders seemed to settle the crisis. However, KMT troops invaded the island in mid-March, killing thousands of Taiwanese and evidently singling out the intelligentsia and local leaders for slaughter. While Chen was quickly replaced by a more conciliatory administrator and later publicly executed, the trauma and hatred remained; a longstanding legacy of distrust had been created. When Chiang Kai-shek and his Kuomintang-led government moved to Taiwan in 1949, political officials were primarily mainlanders who were viewed with some suspicion by much of the islander population.[1]

While Taiwan appeared close to an economic and political basket case in the early 1950s, the country soon embarked on

1. For a good summary of Taiwan's early development, see Thomas B. Gold, *State and Society in the Taiwan Miracle* (Armonk, N.Y.: M.E. Sharpe, 1986).

Table 6.1

Indicators of Taiwan's Economic Development

	1952	1962	1973	1983	1989
Population (million)	8	12	16	19	20
GNP per capita ($US)	153	162	695	2,843	7,512
Manufacturing (% GDP)	13	20	36	36	36
Agriculture (% GDP)	32	25	12	7	4
Exports (% GNP)	9	11	42	49	44
Industrial goods (% exports)	8	50	85	93	95
Trade balance (billion $US)	0	0	1	3	14
Foreign reserves (billion $US)	—	—	1	11	73
Inflation rate (%)	19*	2	8	1	4
Savings (% GNP)	9	12	35	32	31
Investment (% GNP)	15	18	29	24	23
Unemployment rate (%)	4.6	4.3	1.3	1.7	1.6

Sources: Steve Chan and Cal Clark, *Flexibility, Foresight, and Fortuna in Taiwan's Development* (London: Routledge, 1992), Appendices. *Taiwan Statistical Data Book, 1991* (Taipei: Council for Economic Planning and Development, 1991).

*1953.

extremely rapid growth that is often referred to as an economic miracle. The initial ingredients were a radical but nonviolent land reform which spurred agricultural production and a short period of import-substitution industrialization that got light industry off the ground. In the early 1960s Taiwan made the fateful switch in economic strategy to promoting light industrial exports which set off a decade of double-digit growth. By the late 1970s growing prosperity was beginning to price the island out of low-cost labor production, but it began to make another successful transition to high-tech electronics and some heavy industry. Tables 6.1 and 6.2 provide a summary set of economic and social indicators charting this economic miracle. Overall, Taiwan averaged almost 9 percent real growth per year over these four decades, a remarkable feat of sustained growth, as its GNP per capita skyrocketed fiftyfold from $150 to $8,000 in 1990. Moreover, the standard of living rose rapidly; by the mid-1970s income inequality had dropped to one of the lowest levels in the world.

Political development lagged behind the economic miracle by a considerable margin, however, as the Kuomintang maintained an authoritarian and fairly repressive regime under Chiang Kai-shek through the 1960s. Martial law provisions from the late 1940s were

Table 6.2

Indicators of Taiwan's Social Development

	1952	1962	1973	1983	1989
Income ratio**	20.47	11.56*	4.49*	4.36	4.94
Literacy rate (%)	58	75	86	91	94
% Population with secondary education	10	16	32	48	54
Infant mortality (per 1,000 live births)	45	31	14	8	5
Life expectancy (years)	60	66	70	72	74
Food (% household spending)	62	58	49	39	34
% Population with electricity	—	77	98	99	99
% Population with tap water	29	31	46	75	83

Sources: Steve Chan and Cal Clark, *Flexibility, Foresight, and Fortuna in Taiwan's Development* (London: Routledge, 1992), Appendices. *Taiwan Statistical Data Book, 1991* (Taipei: Council for Economic Planning and Development, 1991).

*1961 and 1972.

**Ratio of the income of the richest fifth of the population to that of the poorest fifth.

used to prohibit the formation of new political parties (although opposition figures could run as independents) and to stifle political debate by prohibiting advocacy of communism or Taiwan's independence as sedition. Large majorities of the members of both the Legislative Yuan and the National Assembly (the electoral college for the president) continued in office without election; both of these bodies were considered to represent not just Taiwan but all of China, so their incumbents could not be replaced until the Nationalists retook the mainland. In the early 1970s, Chiang Kai-shek's son and successor, Chiang Ching-kuo, began a gradual liberalization, bringing islander technocrats into increasingly higher levels of the regime and expanding the role of elections, which inevitably increased the power of islanders. In the two years before his death in January 1988, Chiang Ching-kuo pushed through major democratizing reforms that ended martial law, legalized opposition parties, and greatly expanded freedom of speech and political activity.[2]

From the 1950s through the 1970s, the hostility and conflict

2. For discussions of Taiwan's political and economic development, see Steve Chan and Cal Clark, *Flexibility, Foresight, and Fortuna in Taiwan's Development: Navigating Between Scylla and Charybdis* (London: Routledge, 1992); Edwin A. Winckler and Susan Greenhalgh, eds., *Contending Approaches to the Political Economy of Taiwan* (Armonk, N.Y.: M.E. Sharpe, 1988).

over international status between the Nationalists' Republic of China on Taiwan and the PRC on the mainland represented a Manichaean cold war divide, since both regimes adhered to a one-China policy—that is, that Taiwan was part of a unified China with each regime regarding itself as the legitimate ruler of China. With the military stalemate that resulted from the offshore island crises during the 1950s, the two sides turned to the diplomatic realm as the prime arena for their competition, using international recognition to validate their conflicting claims concerning national legitimacy. Consequently, each also followed a policy of breaking relations with any country or international organization that established formal ties with its rival. The turning point in this contest occurred when the PRC was finally successful in replacing Taiwan as the occupant of China's seat in the United Nations in 1971. The other shoe dropped in 1979 when the United States switched its diplomatic recognition from Taipei to Beijing and officially acknowledged the one-China doctrine. However, the U.S. Congress quickly passed the Taiwan Relations Act, which allowed for continuing informal yet substantive relations that, in reality, differed from official ones in name only but were sufficiently opaque to save face in Beijing, Taipei, and Washington.

This revolution in the world of official diplomacy had some perhaps surprising consequences in both Beijing and Taipei. First, the PRC appeared to be a gracious winner. For example, after the early 1970s, China did allow Taiwan a chance to save some face in world affairs by insisting only that official relations between Taipei and other countries be broken, while not looking too hard at informal ones that the PRC did not see as challenging its legitimacy and sovereignty. Second, Taiwan's reaction to its loss of international status was generally passive. The Kuomintang was self-deterred from changing its firm one-China policy, thus tacitly accepting Beijing's diplomatic gains, by the fear that any such shift would contradict the legitimacy of its international and domestic political claims. Externally, the acceptance of any sort of "two-Chinas" or "one China–one Taiwan" principle would have implied the ceding of the bulk of China's population and territory to the communists. Internally, it would have fueled challenges to the claim by a national government dominated by mainlanders of its right to rule over the large majority of islanders.[3]

Continuing Economic Dynamism as a Bridge Across the Taiwan Strait

Taiwan's economic performance during the 1990s has continued to be strong, as indicated by Table 6.3 which provides data for the 1990s, plus for 1987 as a comparison to highlight several important trends. While the island's growth rate has decelerated somewhat from the 9 percent of the previous four decades to just over 6 percent a year during the 1990s, such slower growth is a universal pattern once a nation reaches the peak of its industrial expansion and the rapid productivity gains associated with manufacturing. This steady aggregate growth, moreover, has not overheated the economy. Inflation held steady at 4–5 percent annually which, while significantly higher than for most of the 1980s, is good by international standards. Money supply (unlike in the late 1980s) has been expanding by a moderate rate as well.

This continued vitality and strong performance in terms of aggregate economic indicators is all the more impressive because Taiwan is in the middle of fundamental structural change in the economy which for many countries is often destabilizing. Rapid growth during the 1960s and 1970s brought prosperity and nearly full employment (see Table 6.1) which, naturally, were ultimately transferred into rising real wages. Consequently, by the 1980s Taiwan was beginning to price itself out of the niche of labor-intensive manufacturing and assembling that it had found in the global economy. These pressures were greatly exacerbated when Taiwan appreciated the New Taiwan (NT) dollar 40 percent against the U.S. dollar during 1986–87 in response to strong U.S. pressure to reduce the island's huge trade surplus with the United States (which ranked second in absolute size in the late 1980s after Japan's). This pressure was greatest on Taiwan's myriad small businesses in sectors such as textiles, footwear, toys, sporting goods, and low-tech electronics assembly, which faced

3. Nancy Bernkopf Tucker, *Taiwan, Hong Kong, and the United States, 1945–1992: Uncertain Friendships* (New York: Twayne, 1994).

Table 6.3

Taiwan's Economic Performance During the 1990s

	1987	1990	1991	1992	1993	1994
Real GNP growth (%)	12.7	5.4	7.6	6.8	6.3	6.5
Real industrial growth (%)	14.0	–0.2	7.5	4.5	3.7	6.7
GNP per capita ($US)	5,298	8,111	8,982	10,470	10,852	11,604
Manufacturing (% GDP)	39	34	33	32	31	29
Services (% GDP)	48	55	55	57	57	59
Exports (% GNP)	52	41	41	38	38	38
Trade balance (billion $US)	19	13	13	10	8	8
Trade balance with U.S. (billion $US)	16	9	8	8	7	6
Foreign reserves (billion $US)	77	72	82	82	84	92
Money supply growth (%)	38	–1	12	12	15	12
Inflation rate (%)	1	4	4	5	3	4
Savings (% GNP)	39	29	29	28	28	27
Investment (% GNP)	20	23	23	24	25	24
Unemployment rate (%)	2.0	1.7	1.5	1.5	1.5	1.6
Income ratio*	4.69	5.18	4.97	5.24	5.42	—
Food (% household spending)	36	32	31	30	28	—
Exports to China (billion $US)	1.2	3.2	4.7	6.3	7.6	8.5
Imports from China (billion $US)	0.3	0.8	1.1	1.1	1.1	1.3
% Exports to U.S.	48	32	29	29	28	26
% Exports to Hong Kong	8	13	16	19	22	23
Budget deficit (% GNP)	0.4	2	8	8	8	7

Source: *Taiwan Statistical Data Book, 1995* (Taipei: Council for Economic Planning and Development, 1995).

*Ratio of the income of the richest fifth of the population to that of the poorest fifth.

the unappetizing choice of either upgrading into high-tech or skill-intensive production, moving production facilities offshore to low-wage locations, or going out of business.

The data in Table 6.3 indicate that this choice has set off a significant transformation in Taiwan's economy. Clearly, many of Taiwan's low-end, labor-intensive operations have moved to lower-wage countries. The outflow of capital for investment in foreign countries, for example, can be seen in the fact that the domestic investment rate averaged four percentage points lower than the savings rate during the 1990s (24 percent of gross domestic product [GDP] versus 28 percent) following a huge capital outflow during the late 1980s when a surge in offshore investment occurred. Initially, Southeast Asia was the favorite target of such industrial relocation, but in the 1990s southern coastal China has dominated the offshore investment from Taiwan (see below). The loss of this industry, in turn, pushed Taiwan away from a manufacturing-based economy toward a service-oriented one. Between 1987 and 1994 manufacturing's proportion of GDP fell from 39 percent to 29 percent, while the share of services (e.g., banking, information processing, communications) increased correspondingly from 48 percent to 59 percent, another indicator of the maturing of Taiwan's economy. The offshore migration of many of its previous export leaders also resulted in a substantial drop of the export-to-GNP ratio from 52 percent to 38 percent in just the seven years covered by Table 6.3, although this decline leveled off in the early 1990s.

Such transformation often produces devastating results for an economy, but Table 6.3 also suggests that Taiwan has weathered this structural change fairly well, at least thus far. Obviously, as noted above, the declines in manufacturing and exports did not prevent robust growth of over 6 percent a year. In fact, investment in Taiwan remained at the healthy rate of nearly a quarter of GNP; the declining ratios of manufacturing production and exports to GDP had leveled off by the mid-1990s; a healthy trade balance was maintained; and Taiwan's foreign exchange reserves actually grew from $72 billion in 1990 to $92 billion in 1994 (second in the world in absolute amount to Japan). Thus, many of Taiwan's businesses clearly were able to upgrade their production as, for example, Taiwan became one of the few countries in the world to be internationally competitive in semiconductors and high-tech electronics. Consequently, the unemployment rate remained low (a significant inflow of unskilled labor from abroad actually occurred, mainly from the Philippines, Thailand, and, illegally, mainland China), and the percentage of household income spent on food continued to decline, indicating the growth of disposable income.[4]

The economic picture for Taiwan is not entirely unblemished,

4. Gustav Ranis, ed., *Taiwan: From Developing Nation to Mature Economy* (Boulder, Colo.: Westview Press, 1992); N.T. Wang, ed., *Taiwan's Enterprises in Global Perspective* (Armonk, N.Y.: M.E. Sharpe, 1992).

however. One worrisome trend is the growing amount of income inequality. For example, in 1980 the ratio of the income of the richest fifth of the population to that of the poorest was 4.2:1, one of the lowest in the world, which made Taiwan a model of growth with equity. By 1993, this ratio had risen fairly dramatically to 5.4:1, a level equal to that of the late 1960s. Two factors appeared to be at work. First, the decline of labor-intensive manufacturing hurt the wages of unskilled and semiskilled workers. Second, in the late 1980s a bubble economy arose in Taiwan as first the burgeoning trade surplus and then the inflow of speculative hot money with the rapid appreciation of the NT dollar led to skyrocketing stock and land prices, similar to the situation in Japan. Since business executives and speculators were the primary beneficiaries of this bubble, it helped to widen the income gap as well. Thus, while there was no economic implosion when the bubble burst as occurred in Japan in the early 1990s, Taiwan clearly did suffer from a similar squeeze on the middle class.

More broadly, Taiwan's rapid growth has certainly not exempted it from the side effects of industrialization and modernization; rather just the reverse appears to be the case. Industrialization brought extremely serious pollution problems to the once "beautiful island" or "Ilha Formosa" (as the Portuguese named it in the 16th century), and a combination of commitment to rapid growth and the clout of business interests has prevented an efficacious attack on pollution despite a universal recognition of the growing health and aesthetic problems. The breakdown of traditional family and community ties is also generating social problems in terms of crime, alienation, and social conflict. Thus, as in many other societies, modernization in Taiwan threatens to create almost as many problems as it solves.[5]

This latest structural transformation in Taiwan's economy also proved to be profoundly important for cross-strait relations with China. Up through the mid-1980s, there were almost no direct contacts between the citizens of the two areas, although some indirect trade, primarily conducted through Hong Kong, was

5. Murray A. Rubinstein, ed., *The Other Taiwan: 1945 to the Present* (Armonk, N.Y.: M.E. Sharpe, 1994).

permitted and some residents of Taiwan were able to make short surreptitious visits to China (Chinese authorities did not stamp their passports). President Chiang Ching-kuo of Taiwan then announced in late 1987 that people would be allowed to visit relatives on the mainland for humanitarian purposes. Over the next few years the Taiwan government greatly expanded the scope of legal contacts, providing for indirect trade with and investment in the Chinese mainland. For their part, the island's residents and business people happily stretched the legal limits.

Consequently, a tremendous growth in trade and investment across the Taiwan Strait occurred in the late 1980s and early 1990s, as illustrated by the data in Table 6.3. Investment in China by Taiwan's entrepreneurs was negligible until 1987 but then took off, reaching an estimated $30 billion in cumulative investment in early 1996. The nature of this investment became more permanent as well. Taiwan investors moved from joint ventures to solely owned enterprises and began to build their own factories. The nature of these ventures was also upgraded from simple assembly to upstream heavy and capital-intensive or high-tech production. This investment, in turn, stimulated a near explosion in indirect trade through Hong Kong—Taiwan's exports to China rose two-and-a-half times between 1987 and 1990 and another two-and-a-half times between 1990 and 1994.

In fact, by the early 1990s, there even appeared to be something of a movement toward economic integration between Taiwan and southern coastal China, especially Fujian Province which many Taiwanese islanders, who dominate the small-business sector, regard as their homeland. Thus, trade and especially investment across the Taiwan Strait reflect a complementarity between the two economies. China needs investment and entrepreneurial know-how, while Taiwan's labor-intensive industries need to find cheap workers in order to remain internationally competitive. The Chinese mainland is an enticing target for Taiwan's commercial expansion for several reasons. China has unlimited low-cost labor, strong language and cultural ties with Taiwan, and pragmatic provincial leaders who offer substantial incentives to invest in export industries. The result has been a triangular set of trade relations among Taiwan, China, and the United States which are reflected in the trade statistics in Table 6.3. First, Taiwan businesses export sophisticated intermediate products to China for assembly, along with machinery for their new factories on the mainland, resulting in a large surplus in trade with China. The final products are then exported *from China* to the United States, thereby explaining how Taiwan was able to cut its surplus with the United States in half between 1987 and 1992.[6]

The growth of an integrated economy in "Greater China" (as the Guangdong, Fujian, Hong Kong, and Taiwan area has been called) is fraught with political irony. In terms of ideology, Taiwanese (and Hong Kong) capitalists have fueled communist China's economic dynamism; in terms of ethnic politics in Taiwan, it is islander business executives, not mainlander political leaders, who are building bridges across the Taiwan Strait and (at least before June 1995) defusing the cold war rivalry between Taipei and Beijing. Such relationships, in turn, create an interdependent destiny in cross-strait relations that gives both sides an ongoing stake in strengthening the ties between them.

Democracy and Domestic Politics: Victory Is Not Always Bountiful

During the 1970s and especially the 1980s, political liberalization and democratization were probably the most central issues in Taiwan's domestic politics. An increasingly middle-class society pushed for greater political freedom and organized social movements around emerging issues (e.g., pollution and women's rights); the electoral politicians within the KMT pushed to expand their own power; and the opposition sought to increase the political space allowed by what had become a soft-authoritarian regime. The unexpectedly rapid transition to democracy in the late 1980s and early 1990s was thus almost universally welcome, and most Taiwanese citizens are justly proud of Taiwan's claim to be the first democracy in a Chinese society. However, the victory of democracy brought problems as well. The ruling party stole much of the opposition's thunder in the area of political reform, thereby pushing the opposition toward using Tai-

---

6. Ralph N. Clough, *Reaching Across the Taiwan Strait: People-to-People Diplomacy* (Boulder, Colo.: Westview Press, 1993).

wanese nationalism as its primary mobilizing appeal which, in turn, called into question the national identity of both society and polity. Moreover, more open and democratic government produced raucous politics (e.g., frequent fisticuffs in legislative assemblies) and policy gridlock, and the growing importance of elections was also associated with burgeoning corruption and money politics.

The two key events in Taiwan's democratization were the end of martial law in 1986 and the legalization of opposition parties in 1987 and the dramatic 1990 decision of Taiwan's Council of Grand Justices (the nation's highest judicial organ, which rules on constitutional questions) that forced the retirement of the senior legislators elected on the mainland in the late 1940s in the Legislative Yuan and National Assembly. An important subsequent development was the decision to allow the direct election of Taiwan's provincial governor (who had previously been appointed) and president (who had previously been indirectly elected by the National Assembly). Thus, with elections for the full National Assembly (1991 and 1996) and Legislative Yuan (1992 and 1995) and for the provincial governor (1994) and president (1996), Taiwan could credibly lay claim to the title of a functioning democracy using the normal criteria that the citizenry choose their governmental leaders in competitive and fair elections. This is not to say that further reform in some areas is not warranted. For example, the government's control of the major television networks clearly provides the KMT a significant advantage. Still, it would be hard to claim that the current composition of Taiwan's government does not represent the people's choice.[7]

Perhaps the most threatening side effect of democracy has been the explosion of corruption and money politics brought on by the transformation of government-business relations in the early 1990s. Up through the late 1980s, relations between government and business had not been particularly close. The Kuomintang's ideology (Sun Yat-sen's "Three Principles of the

7. Peter R. Moody, Jr., *Political Change on Taiwan: A Study of Ruling Party Adaptability* (New York: Praeger, 1992); Linda Chao and Ramon H. Myers, "The First Chinese Democracy: Political Development of the Republic of China on Taiwan, 1986–1994," *Asian Survey*, Vol. 34, no. 3 (March 1994), pp. 213–30; Alan M. Wachman, *Taiwan: National Identity and Democratization* (Armonk, N.Y.: M.E. Sharpe, 1994).

People") was somewhat suspicious of capitalists; and, probably far more importantly, following the export boom of the 1960s, Taiwan's business community came to be dominated by islanders who had little *guanxi* (personal relations) with the mainlanders at the top of the KMT regime.

This changed radically with democratization, reflecting an unfortunate confluence of demand-side and supply-side relationships between business executives and politicians, especially legislators. The demand side of the equation is easy to understand. A key feature of democratization was the growing importance of elections and legislators in Taiwan's politics. This, in turn, set off the dynamics of money politics and corruption. Competitive elections soon became very expensive ones. Thus, many candidates became dependent upon rich business people, as well as upon the local political factions that had traditionally been efficacious in turning out the vote.

The principal reason that many people in business were willing to make these political investments almost certainly was that democratization had greatly changed the supply as well as the demand side of the government-business nexus. Giving legislative bodies more power meant that they could hold up executive actions and demand bribes for their own or their patrons' business ventures, while prosperity created lots of potential resources that could be grabbed through the public sector. For example, complaints were raised that legislators set up their own companies and used their new power of the purse to influence bidding on government contracts, as well as using connections with organized crime to intimidate legitimate competitors from bidding. In several instances, major government deals with foreign corporations fell through because legislators demanded a prohibitively high piece of the action. Government officials have also tried to use their power and leverage to take over state corporations that are being privatized.[8] These problems were exacerbated by the $300 billion Six-Year National Development Plan approved in 1991 to upgrade Taiwan's infrastructure

8. Karl J. Fields, *Enterprise and the State in Korea and Taiwan* (Ithaca, N.Y.: Cornell University Press, 1995); Cheng-tian Kuo, *Global Competitiveness and Industrial Growth in Taiwan and the Philippines* (Pittsburgh: University of Pittsburgh Press, 1995); interviews with Taiwan government officials, Taipei, July 1993 and June 1995.

which also created myriad opportunities for money politics, as well as generating the large budget deficits shown in Table 6.3.

The process of democratization brought considerable change to the nature of political competition in Taiwan, both between the major parties and within the parties themselves. Such change can be seen in the evolution of the Democratic Progressive Party (DPP), which was formed in 1986 by opposition leaders who had previously constituted the *tangwai* (literally, those "outside the [Nationalist] party"). Throughout the 1980s, the *tangwai* and the DPP couched their explicit appeals primarily in terms of political reform and democratization, while implicitly evoking feelings of islander or Taiwanese nationalism, which could bring arrest for sedition if openly espoused. Such a strategy was fairly popular; in fact, more than a few KMT members who opposed Taiwan's independence voted for DPP candidates on occasion in the hope of pressuring the Nationalists to speed up reform.

By the early 1990s such a strategy became less viable. On the one hand, the KMT now supported substantial political reform; on the other, the opposition's success in easing limits on freedom of speech and political activities eroded the need to differentiate the DPP's explicit and implicit messages. The DPP resolved these pressures, at least temporarily, when its radical New Tide faction forced the reformist Formosa faction to include an explicit commitment to the goal of Taiwan's independence in the party's charter in 1991. This kept the party from splitting but also raised problems for its electoral appeal, since less than one-fifth of Taiwan's citizens favored an independent Taiwan at that time. However, while the association with independence probably did very little to increase electoral support for the DPP, the increased salience of this issue proved to be an inspired wedge issue that helped drive factions within the Kuomintang asunder; many mainlanders and islanders within the ruling party differed strongly on the emotional issue of what Taiwan's national identity should be.[9]

When Chiang Ching-kuo died in January 1988, he was suc-

---

9. This line of argument is developed by Tun-jen Cheng and Yung-min Hsu, "Issue Structure, the DPP's Factionalism, and Party Realignment," in *Taiwan's Electoral Politics and Democratic Transition: Riding the Third Wave*, ed. Hung-mao Tien (Armonk, N.Y.: M.E. Sharpe, 1996), pp. 137–73.

ceeded by his handpicked vice president, Dr. Lee Teng-hui, an islander technocrat, as both president of Taiwan and chairman of the KMT. President Lee had few strong ties with either the traditional top mainlander factions in the party-state or with islander electoral politicians and thus was initially viewed as not having a particularly strong political base. However, he proved extremely adept at both consolidating his power and pushing Chiang Ching-kuo's democratization reforms to their logical conclusion (e.g., forcing the retirement of senior legislators). As a result, he became extremely popular (some DPP candidates even used pictures of themselves with Lee on campaign posters), which certainly contributed to his consolidation of power within the KMT.

Lee Teng-hui's success rearranged factional relations in the KMT into pro-Lee and anti-Lee factions which came to be called the Mainstream and Anti-Mainstream factions respectively. While this division reflected ideology and personal power considerations to some extent, the core of the Anti-Mainstream group were older mainlanders in top government, party, and military positions who put strong emphasis on the one-China heritage of Taiwan and were suspicious that President Lee might have ambitions to become the father of his country by covertly promoting Taiwan's independence. After Lee was elected to a full six-year term by the National Assembly in 1990, he appointed General Hau Pei-tsun, a mainlander and leader of the Anti-Mainstream faction, as premier. At least according to rumor, Lee and Hau then divided Hau's cabinet among their respective followers. However, such a patronage approach to party unity was undermined by the ability of the DPP to increase the salience of the national identity question. In fact, the Lee-Hau alliance proved to be short-lived; the rivalry between them was soon manifest, and Lee replaced Hau as premier with his ally, islander Lien Chan, following the 1992 elections for the Legislative Yuan.

These growing strains within the KMT led in 1993 to the defection of a group of younger legislators, primarily mainlanders, who formed the New Party, which became the third party to have significant electoral success in Taiwan's politics. The New Party (NP) represented a somewhat strange combination of policies and appeals. On the one hand, the New Party was seen as strongly supporting unification with China, which greatly limited its appeal to Taiwan's 85 percent islander majority, although its leaders also differentiated themselves from the conservative old mainlanders. On the other hand, several of its leaders were former cabinet officials who had an image of promoting efficient administration and honest government, popular positions in Taiwan's increasingly middle-class society.[10]

In the mid-1990s, then, Taiwan's polity seemed to have evolved into a system with three significant parties, as indicated by the data on election returns in the 1980s and 1990s in Table 6.4. Although its potency at the polls has declined fairly steadily over the last decade and a half, the KMT retains the status of a ruling party with majority/plurality support in the 45–55 percent range. The Democratic Progressive Party has become a fairly strong competitor, garnering 30–40 percent of the vote and winning a significant number of local elections (e.g., the mayor of Taipei and the magistrate or chief executive of Taipei County), while the New Party has won close to 15 percent in the most recent elections.

This seeming stability of Taiwan's democratic system might appear somewhat surprising and fragile given the growing centrality of the national identity question in political debates; after all, the legitimacy of the polity would seem to be at risk if the three major parties cannot even agree on who "the people" really are. Yet the destabilizing effects of the national identity issue are offset because, in reality, it is a loser at the polls. Thus, while the DPP and the NP get the strongest emotional response from their ostensibly core constituencies by making appeals to, respectively, independence and reunification, such campaign strategies are probably counterproductive.

Table 6.4 suggests that the DPP's electoral support drops by almost one-third when it becomes too closely associated with advocacy of independence, as it did in the 1991 National Assembly and 1996 presidential elections. The 1994 elections provide a good illustration. In the race for provincial governor, James

10. Tien, ed., *Taiwan's Electoral Politics.*

Table 6.4

Electoral Support of Major Parties in Taiwan* (Percent)

	KMT	DPP/*tangwai*	NP
1980 Legislative Yuan	72	13	—
1980 National Assembly	66	—	—
1981 Magistrates/mayors	57	23	—
1983 Legislative Yuan	69	19	—
1985 Magistrates/mayors	61	13	—
1986 Legislative Yuan	67	25	—
1986 National Assembly	64	24	—
1989 Legislative Yuan	59	29	—
1989 Magistrates/mayors	56	30	—
1991 National Assembly	71	24	—
1992 Legislative Yuan	53	31	—
1993 Magistrates/mayors	47	41	3
1994 Provincial governor	56	39	4
1995 Legislative Yuan	46	33	13
1996 President	54	21	15**
1996 National Assembly	50	30	14

Sources: Peter Ferdinand, ed., *Take-Off for Taiwan?* (London: Pinter, 1996), p. 21; Hung-mao Tien, ed., *Taiwan's Electoral Politics and Democratic Transition* (Armonk, N.Y.: M.E. Sharpe, 1996), pp. 16–17 and 109.

*Because different sources allocate votes for independent candidates and party mavericks differently, it is hard to construct a completely consistent series. These data do, however, represent fairly clear overall trends.

**Votes for Lin Yang-kang who was an Independent closely associated with the New Party.

Soong, a mainlander mainstream KMT official who had not held elective office before, trounced an islander DPP advocate of independence, while Ch'en Shui-pien won the mayorship of Taipei for the DPP handily by stressing a pragmatic and reformist agenda. Thus, despite the uncertain and bizarre nature of Taiwan's mid-1990s limbo in terms of international status, large majorities of its citizens prefer the status quo to either reunification or independence, which are seen as threatening Taiwan's accomplishments.

In fact, two Taiwan scholars have recently argued that the countervailing implications of the national identity question have created a much more competitive party system in which victory has become somewhat problematic, thereby spawning new issues that cut across both the national identity and traditional party cleavages.[11] For example, the Mainstream faction of the KMT gains popularity for its role in promoting democratic reforms but loses it from its association with money politics; the DPP benefits from its support for expanding the social welfare state to ameliorate growing inequality; and the New Party's association with clean government is extremely popular. Consequently, the major parties and factions can win enough in elections to give themselves a stake in the system; and day-to-day politics in legislative bodies has evolved (despite the well-publicized fist fights) into bargaining relationships in which some very odd couples emerge periodically. For example, the DPP tacitly supported the Mainstream Kuomintang in pushing Premier Hau out of office in 1993, but after his retirement ended the presence of mainlander conservatives in the top leadership, the DPP and Mainstream KMT became strong rivals for islander support.

More recently, the KMT's razor-thin majority (85 of 184 seats) in the Legislative Yuan after the 1995 elections pushed the DPP and the NP into a legislative alliance on organizational issues despite their polar opposition on the national identity question, although this may well exacerbate gridlock rather than promote consensus and negotiation. The tenuousness of KMT control was soon demonstrated, for example, by the battle over reconfirming the premier following President Lee's reelection. Lee had nominated Premier Lien Chan as his vice presidential candidate. Considerable partisan battling followed in getting the Legislative Yuan to approve an interim Lien cabinet after the December 1995 elections. Lien then submitted his resignation as premier following the Lee-Lien victory. On June 5, however, President Lee announced that he would retain Lien as premier and tried to circumvent a second round of Legislative Yuan approval by claiming that he had never accepted Lien's resignation. This enraged the DPP and the New Party, as well as many Anti-Mainstream rivals; Lien's cabinet choices, moreover, slighted rival James Soong, the provincial governor, within the

11. Yun-han Chu and Tse-min Lin, "The Process of Democratic Consolidation in Taiwan: Social Cleavage, Electoral Competition, and the Emerging Party System," in *Taiwan's Electoral Politics*, ed. Tien, pp. 79–104.

Mainstream faction. Consequently, the Legislative Yuan passed a request that a new premier be appointed subject to its confirmation by an 80 to 65 margin, giving the president a considerable black eye.[12]

The much-heralded direct election of the president in March 1996 well illustrates the evolving nature of Taiwan's party system. Given President Lee's popularity and control over the KMT, he easily secured the KMT nomination. This did not sit well with the Anti-Mainstream faction, though, and Lin Yang-kang, an islander electoral politician whose rivalry with Lee appeared more personal than ideological, declared his candidacy as an independent and chose former premier Hau as his running mate. In retaliation, the KMT expelled Lin and Hau, who at the time were vice-chairmen of the party. The DPP held a long series of debates and primary voting before selecting Peng Ming-min, a longtime advocate of independence who had suffered both imprisonment and exile for his beliefs. The New Party nominated a candidate for president as well, but he withdrew after Lin and Hau began campaigning for NP candidates in the December 1995 Legislative Yuan elections. Finally, another Anti-Mainstream KMT leader, Ch'en Li-an, also ran as an independent.[13]

Lee's victory was never seriously in doubt; the major question was whether Lee could attain a majority of votes (there was no provision for a runoff). His final total of 54 percent was slightly more than expected and considered a strong victory. For the other contenders, Peng's 21 percent was seen as a setback for the DPP, and the Lin-Hau ticket failed in its hopes for finishing ahead of Peng. In contrast, the results of the 1996 National Assembly elections (in which the KMT won just under half the vote and about 55 percent of the seats, slightly better than in the Legislative Yuan contest three months earlier) showed that the DPP and the New Party continue to appeal to significant and fairly stable constituencies. Despite Lee's strong personal victory and

12. Virginia Sheng, "President Says He Will Keep Lien as Taiwan Premier," *Free China Journal* (Taipei), June 7, 1996, p. 1.

13. *Far Eastern Economic Review* (Hong Kong), March 14, 1996, pp. 14–20; Hung-mao Tien, "Taiwan in 1995: Electoral Politics and Cross-Strait Relations," *Asian Survey*, Vol. 36, no. 1 (January 1996), pp. 33–40.

some indications of growing factional tension within the DPP over Taiwan's independence, the KMT certainly cannot be sanguine about the fact that two of its leading officials ran for president against the party's designated nominee. The implication of all this is that each of the major parties will likely have an important impact on Taiwan's future.

Taiwan's dramatic democratization in the late 1980s and early 1990s, therefore, has produced some mixed results. First, the undoubted development of democracy has been associated with several negative side effects, such as growing corruption and governmental deadlock. Second, greater democracy has threatened to unleash the national identity issue. However, Lee Teng-hui's widespread appeal and the punishment inflicted by the electorate upon parties that push the national identity question too strongly have kept the divisive and destabilizing potential of this debate in check. Thus, there is at least some reason to believe that democratization on Taiwan may be creating a common destiny sufficient to give the island's major social and political forces a stake in the system.

Cross-Strait Relations: The Contradiction Between External and Internal Pragmatic Diplomacy

The cold war rivalry between the CCP and the KMT constitutes a potentially powerful ghost from the past. Even after the threat of direct military confrontation waned following the 1958 offshore islands crisis, the regimes in the PRC and Taiwan refused to recognize each other's legitimacy, and, with a few minor exceptions, each demanded that the rest of the world respect its interpretation of one China, creating a bizarre set of official relations with one and unofficial with the other. In the 1980s and early 1990s, it appeared that cross-strait relations might have stabilized. The PRC, appearing satisfied with its diplomatic preeminence, initiated a peace offensive and in 1984 proposed a one country–two systems reunification in which Taiwan would trade recognition of Beijing's sovereignty for substantial local autonomy, including the retention of its armed services. Taipei for its part remained skeptical about how real such local autonomy would be, but did little to challenge the international status of the People's Republic. Thus, the governments on both sides of the Taiwan Strait appeared to have muddled into a tacit post–cold war agreement to live and let live even before the cold war ended elsewhere. Yet the inability of the two governments to reach an explicit agreement or even talk to each other meant that the Chinese civil war might come back to haunt the present; in 1995 it did.

When Lee Teng-hui assumed the presidency in 1988, he moved almost immediately to take a more aggressive initiative toward Taiwan's greater participation in the international community by announcing a new policy of "pragmatic" or "flexible" diplomacy. In many ways, pragmatic diplomacy was simply the continuation of existing policies, but at the theoretical level it constituted a dramatic break from Taiwan's previous stance on international affairs because of its more relaxed position on the sovereignty issue. For example, Taiwan clearly broke with its past policy by establishing diplomatic relations with several countries that still recognized the PRC, beginning with Grenada in 1989. However, China then broke relations with these countries, creating an almost comical situation in 1992 when Niger jumped back and forth several times on the question of which China to recognize.

The actual results of pragmatic diplomacy appear ironic. There have been only minor gains in Taiwan's official status. However, in terms of Taiwan's substantive or informal position in world affairs, pragmatic diplomacy appears effective. Relations with many developed nations have improved to the point that their cabinet officials are making trips to Taiwan (e.g., U.S. trade representative Carla Hills in 1992 and U.S. secretary of transportation Federico Pena in 1994), which might be taken as an implicit recognition of sovereignty. Taiwan's participation in international economic organizations has expanded considerably. In fact, Taiwan's success in this regard might well be indicated by Beijing's growing protests in the early 1990s about Taipei's "creeping officiality."[14]

Yet pragmatic diplomacy was not totally directed against the

14. John F. Copper, *China Diplomacy: The Washington-Taipei-Beijing Triangle* (Boulder, Colo.: Westview Press, 1992); Martin L. Lasater, *U.S. Interests in the New Taiwan* (Boulder, Colo.: Westview Press, 1993); Robert G. Sutter and William R. Johnson, eds., *Taiwan in World Affairs* (Boulder, Colo.: Westview Press, 1994).

PRC. As noted above, Beijing even seemed to believe that it was benefiting from the part of pragmatic diplomacy that permitted the emergence of Greater China from growing social and economic links across the Taiwan Strait. Thus, Taipei has also tried to find a modus vivendi with Beijing within the framework of a one-China policy. Probably most dramatically, President Lee ended the legal proclamation of a civil war with the communists under Taiwan law and proposed government-to-government contacts between the two political entities in Beijing and Taipei in May 1991. While this did little to promote official contacts between the PRC and Taiwan, Beijing and Taipei created ostensibly private organizations (the Association for Relations Across the Taiwan Strait or ARATS and the Strait Exchange Foundation or SEF, respectively) to deal with each other. This process resulted in the Koo-Wang (the SEF and ARATS chairmen) talks and several technical agreements in Singapore in April 1993 which were seen as a major breakthrough in cross-strait relations.[15]

The domestic roots of Lee's two-pronged foreign policy—upgrading Taiwan's international position while expanding informal ties with the mainland—are easy to discern. By the early 1990s, the DPP and the Anti-Mainstream KMT were in sharp opposition over the national identity of Taiwan. At the extreme, each side accused the other of treason (that the DPP would proclaim independence or that the Anti-Mainstream group would sell out Taiwan to Beijing). This dichotomy might have left President Lee and the dominant Mainstream faction in a quandary. On the one hand, their party was associated with an argument that, if pushed to its logical extreme, could have alienated much of the domestic population and dragged Taiwan down to self-imposed diplomatic isolation. On the other hand, rejecting the one-China doctrine would have split the KMT and risked a war with the People's Republic. Lee's response, though, can be seen as pragmatic diplomacy in the domestic realm, which increased Taiwan's confidence in its de facto autonomy. Yet the movement toward Greater China was facilitated as well. The presi-

15. Tun-jen Cheng, Chi Huang, and Samuel S.G. Wu, eds., *Inherited Rivalry: Conflict Across the Taiwan Straits* (Boulder, Colo.: Lynne Rienner, 1995).

dent pledged his support for ultimate reunification, created a sophisticated set of Guidelines for National Unification that envisioned a long-term three-step process that would prevent the danger of communist domination, and began suggesting formulas that might permit negotiations as equals between Taiwan and the PRC, such as "one country, two governments."

In sum, President Lee's policies in the early 1990s appeared to link pragmatic diplomacy in both domestic and foreign affairs. David Lampton, for one, argued:

> I believe that the Taiwanese government is using the increased cultural, economic, and political interaction in Greater China (particularly between Taiwan and the mainland) to create a web of positive incentives for, and constraints on, Beijing that will induce the PRC to accept Taiwan's drive for more international breathing space, identity, dignity, and autonomy. . . . This obviously is a sophisticated strategy in which one reassures Beijing of presumed long-term intentions to reunify at the same time one reassures Taiwan's populace that this is not going to happen in any foreseeable future.[16]

In the early 1990s, therefore, President Lee Teng-hui appeared to be pursuing a sophisticated and successful pragmatic diplomacy whose domestic and international components were intricately counterbalanced. However, Taiwan's campaign for membership in the United Nations soon threatened this delicate balance. The UN campaign, which President Lee announced in April 1993, might appear to be simply an extension of pragmatic diplomacy in the sense that the UN is just another international institution to which Taiwan has sought (re)admission. From Taipei's perspective, the current situation, which excludes Taiwan's 21 million citizens from UN representation, appears a gross violation of international law and international rights that cannot even be justified by China's status as a divided nation, since both East and West Germany and North and South Korea have been simultaneously represented in the UN. However, rather than being part of a carefully balanced initiative,

16. David M. Lampton, "Commentary," in *Taiwan in World Affairs,* ed. Sutter and Johnson, pp. 266–67.

Taiwan's UN campaign almost certainly reflected a domestic logic that was followed at the risk of threatening the precarious balance in relations with the PRC.

Initially, the call for Taiwan's admission to the UN came from the opposition DPP, both to embarrass the ruling KMT over Taiwan's diplomatic isolation and to raise questions about the legitimacy of the mainlander-dominated government. At first the regime resisted such proposals, relying upon reference to its one-China policy and to the pragmatic consideration that the PRC's veto power in the Security Council made any such efforts fruitless; but several trends in Taiwan's politics soon brought this fringe issue to the center during the early 1990s. First, the island's prosperity created a well-educated middle class that responded to appeals to end the slighting of their country by the international community. Second, as political liberalization proceeded apace and then culminated in the major democratization reforms of the late 1980s and early 1990s, public opinion became more important in domestic politics, and the policy proposals of the opposition were accorded greater legitimacy.

In this situation, President Lee's announcement of support for Taiwan's readmission to the United Nations in the spring of 1993 was inspired in terms of its domestic implications. Premier Hau had led the KMT's opposition to the UN issue, so that Lee's championing of it after Hau's removal as premier allowed him to steal one of the DPP's most popular issues while rallying popular support against the Anti-Mainstream faction. Thus, the UN initiative allowed the president to overcome the zero-sum conflict between the advocates of independence and reunification by proposing a compromise that could appeal to at least some of the deeply felt beliefs of both constituencies.

Yet, the pragmatism of Taiwan's UN bid also involved Beijing's reaction, especially since the People's Republic holds a permanent seat on the Security Council with veto power over most types of UN membership and associate status. It could well have been expected that Taiwan's attempt to join the UN would raise fears in Beijing that an unacceptable threshold of "creeping officiality" that threatened to institutionalize a two-China status was being crossed. If this proved to be the case, there was certainly a danger that domestic pragmatic diplomacy might threaten external pragmatic diplomacy by reigniting the cold war battle over national identity and sovereignty with the PRC.

Probably unfortunately for both sides, this perception of a fundamental challenge to the PRC's concept of sovereignty indeed appears to have been the case. Beijing quickly responded to the request of several of Taiwan's allies to have the General Assembly form an ad hoc committee to consider Taiwan's membership during the 1993 session with an uncompromising white paper in which the PRC used its sovereignty and national identity claims to justify the exclusion of Taiwan from the normal diplomatic community. Beijing's strong opposition proved sufficient to prevent the question of Taiwan's admission to the United Nations from even being formally considered. Taiwan quickly retaliated against this stonewalling in September 1993, when, according to informed speculation, it unexpectedly cast the deciding vote in the Olympic Committee that sent the 2000 Olympics to Sydney, Australia, instead of Beijing. After this display of mutual ill will, the two sides backed off for a year and a half, combining their stalemate over the UN issue with the gradual increased economic and social integration of Greater China.[17]

In fact, 1995 commenced with what appeared to be a renewed movement toward amity and compromise in cross-strait relations. In January, PRC president Jiang Zemin issued an "Eight Points" declaration on China-Taiwan relations, and Lee Tenghui responded with his own "Six Points" in April. While neither set of points made any concessions on the fundamental sovereignty question, both reaffirmed a commitment to peaceful reunification and strongly supported increased interactions across the Taiwan Strait. Based on these conciliatory policy statements, another ARATS-SEF summit (Koo-Wang II) was scheduled for the summer.

Domestic politics on both sides of the strait, however, produced foreign policy shifts that turned détente into confrontation. In Taiwan, the government's UN initiative gradually lost its luster because of Beijing's ability to thwart it, thereby causing President Lee something of a loss of face in international affairs.

17. This analysis of Taiwan's UN bid is presented in much more detail in Cal Clark, "Taiwan's Pragmatic Diplomacy and Campaign for UN Membership," *American Asian Review*, Vol. 14, no. 1 (Spring 1996), pp. 37–61.

The central objective of Taiwan's pragmatic diplomacy then turned to arranging an unofficial visit for Lee to the United States. The PRC objected, and the Clinton administration assured Beijing that Lee would not be granted a visa. However, after Congress passed a nearly unanimous resolution supporting a Lee visit, Clinton changed his mind and granted permission for Lee to attend a reunion at his alma mater, Cornell University, in June 1995.

China reacted extremely strongly to Lee's visit. The PRC argued that it represented a major change in the U.S. policy that prohibited visits to the United States by Taiwan officials. Such a change, Beijing claimed, supported Lee's concerted effort to turn "creeping officiality" into Taiwan independence. This turn to a hard line on Taiwan probably reflected criticism of and pressure on Jiang Zemin by the PRC military for his soft policy on cross-strait relations. Consequently, China canceled the next ARATS-SEF meeting, along with cutting off a variety of other contacts, and in August 1995 began a series of war games and missile tests in the Taiwan Strait area that were clearly aimed at intimidating Taiwan voters in the December legislative elections. Indeed, the New Party, which favors steps toward reunification with the mainland, tripled its representation in the Legislative Yuan from 7 to 21 members. This evidently reinforced the PRC's hard-line policy, although the impact of cross-strait relations on the election is unclear, since domestic factors such as popular revulsion against corruption and the campaign clout of Lin and Hau could also account for New Party gains.[18] The irony in this situation is striking: the more conservative wing of the KMT (the Anti-Mainstream faction) and the CCP, once implacable enemies, are now implicit allies against the DPP and, more ambiguously perhaps, President Lee's Mainstream KMT.

In any event, Beijing stepped up the pressure with even more threatening tests in February and March 1996 in the hope of turning Taiwan's voters against President Lee in the March 23 elections. The efficacy of this intimidation was somewhat questionable, however. First, the election returns probably gave the

18. Julian Baum, "Politics Is Local," *Far Eastern Economic Review*, December 14, 1995, pp. 14–15; Tien, "Taiwan in 1995."

PRC some pause, since 75 percent of Taiwan's voters supported candidates that Beijing claimed were pro-independence. Second, the threat to Taiwan drew a strong reaction from the United States, which deployed two aircraft carrier battle groups near Taiwan. Before the election, there were some fears that both Lee Teng-hui and Jiang Zemin had committed so much face to their dispute that they could not back down. However, both sides sounded conciliatory after the election; in particular, Lee reaffirmed his commitment to the reunification of China and in his inauguration speech on May 20 expressed an interest in meeting with PRC leaders.[19]

Moving Ahead or Back to the Future?

Thus, Taiwan in the mid-1990s appears at a crossroads. Along one route lurk ghosts grasping to pull the island's future back to a less auspicious past. Externally, specters of the Chinese civil war and the cold war could easily be reawakened: in early 1996 Tokyo's *Sankei Shimbun* rated the Taiwan Strait as the "riskiest region in the world." Internally, continued corruption and political gridlock require extensive reforms. Yet a positive future can also be envisioned: the growth of Greater China, the common stake that Taiwan's major parties and factions have in the island's democracy, the continuing dynamism of many domestic businesses, and the signs of renewed amity between Beijing and Taipei. How these various processes will work out and interact is impossible to chart. Still, it is hard not to be at least cautiously optimistic that Taiwan will continue moving ahead.

19. Christie Su, "Taiwan Renews Appeal to Resume Strait Talks," *Free China Journal*, April 19, 1996, p. 1.

The United States and China: Managing a Stormy Relationship

Steven I. Levine

The relationship between the United States and China appears to be drifting toward disaster. Over the past several years, the two countries have become increasingly impatient with and suspicious of each other, more used to engaging in mutual accusations than to bending to the hard task of reconciling conflicting interests. Beijing sees the United States as a meddlesome and arrogant superpower that is contemptuous of Chinese sovereignty and determined to obstruct China's pursuit of vital national interests, including reunification with Taiwan. Washington sees the People's Republic of China (PRC) as a troublesome upstart in global politics, reluctant to abide by the norms of international conduct and constantly testing the limits of agreements it has entered into to see how much it can get away with. U.S. media are filled with reports of Sino-American disagreements over Taiwan, trade, intellectual property rights, Tibet, human rights, nuclear technology transfer, and arms sales. In the capitals of both countries, advocates of Sino-American accommodation have lost ground to hard-liners who equate compromise with appeasement.

The turbulence of the U.S.-China relationship reflects the fragmentation in the mid-1990s of the contemporary international system, which lacks both a well-defined nucleus and a central focus. During the cold war, the issue of security, understood largely in military terms, dominated international political discourse, providing a simplifying if deceptive clarity which facilitated alignment of Sino-American interests. In the late 1960s, Chinese and U.S. leaders perceived a common cause in responding to what they both considered a Soviet security threat. On this basis they negotiated a series of agreements, beginning with the 1972 Shanghai Communiqué, which constituted the foundation of U.S.-China relations for the next dozen years. As Robert Ross has persuasively demonstrated, even in the heyday of Sino-American security cooperation numerous conflicts of interest persisted between Beijing and Washington. Negotiating cooperation was never easy.[1] It required an exertion of authority by top policymakers willing to take political risks, as well as considerable diplomatic skill to craft mutually acceptable formulas concerning issues on which Chinese and U.S. interests differed, such as Taiwan.

Such political will and diplomatic craftsmanship have recently been in short supply in both the United States and China. The machinery of Sino-American cooperation has broken down in the mid-1990s, and the mechanics on duty seem at a loss how to fix it. In both countries an adversarial assumption has replaced the postulate of cooperation. A prolonged period of Sino-American estrangement, to say nothing of conflict, would have extremely serious consequences for the peace, stability, and prosperity of Asia and the world. Unless leaders on both sides can relearn how to manage the manifold issues that comprise the agenda of contemporary U.S.-China relations, the prospects for the near- to midterm will continue to look grim.

Such a prognosis may appear excessively pessimistic. Over the past quarter century, U.S.-China relations have often exhibited a resilience that belied their apparent fragility.[2] Webs of individual, institutional, corporate, and other relationships directly linking Chinese with Americans helped to buffer political disagreements between the two governments. Vivid memories of the cost to both sides of the bitter Sino-American cold war of the 1950s and 1960s served as a warning against the repetition of old errors. Unfortunately, these factors can no longer be counted on to check the powerful negative tendencies in contemporary Sino-American relations that were set in motion by the June 4, 1989, Tiananmen massacre.

1. Robert S. Ross, *Negotiating Cooperation: The United States and China, 1969–1989* (Stanford: Stanford University Press, 1995).

2. See Harry Harding, *A Fragile Relationship: The United States and China Since 1972* (Washington, D.C.: Brookings Institution, 1992).

Tiananmen punctured American illusions about the democratic possibilities of Deng Xiaoping's reform movement and refocused public attention on the repressive aspects of China's communist regime, including human rights abuses and the suppression of political dissent. It also darkened U.S. views of China's revitalized economic takeoff after 1992 and has made the United States wary of the PRC's more assertive pursuit of its national interests in East Asia within international organizations and elsewhere on the global scene. Normal trade disputes, for example, were elevated to the status of national tests of will. In addition, for the first time since the 1950s China policy became the object of partisan politics in the United States as well as an arena in which Congress asserted its foreign policy prerogatives vis-à-vis the White House. Meanwhile, in Beijing standing up to Washington has become a popular exercise for political leaders who give voice to China's national mood of disenchantment with U.S. policy.

A hopeful sign is that neither the United States nor China is satisfied with the present state of Sino-American relations. While each blames the other for the downward slide, both claim they want a more positive relationship. Meeting with Chinese foreign minister Qian Qichen in April 1996, U.S. secretary of state Warren Christopher asserted that the United States seeks "a constructive relationship with a strong, stable, open, and prosperous China."[3] China's president Jiang Zemin told then U.S. national security adviser Anthony Lake in July 1996 that despite recent changes in the world, the United States and China continue to share extensive interests and should work toward building healthy, good, and stable relations.[4] In order to translate these fine sentiments into positive changes in Sino-American relations, leaders on both sides must devote more sustained attention than they have in recent years to addressing a range of contentious issues, including political, economic, and security issues as well as the question of Taiwan which has haunted Sino-American relations for nearly half a century.

3. *New York Times* (national edition), April 20, 1996, p. 6.
4. *Renmin Ribao* (People's Daily/Beijing), July 10, 1996, p. 1.

Political Relations

U.S.-China relations have still not recovered from the shock of Tiananmen. The Bush administration (1989–93) exposed itself to domestic political criticism in the aftermath of Tiananmen when it tried to shield the Sino-American relationship from critics wishing to avenge the victims of the massacre. Although hardly a China expert, President George Bush had a special interest in China dating from his tour of duty as chief of the U.S. Liaison Office in Beijing in 1974–75. Bill Clinton, a neophyte in foreign affairs, criticized Bush during the 1992 campaign for "coddling" China, but his own administration has failed to develop a well-defined and consistent policy toward Beijing. Clinton himself has barely focused on China, and Secretary of State Warren Christopher did little to help the administration come up with a coherent set of policy objectives for U.S. ties with China or a strategy for attaining them. Washington's management of its relationship with Beijing in the past few years has been marked by neglect, indecision, policy reversals, and confusion. The absence of a clear and steady vision at the top has fragmented China policy into a number of apparently unrelated issues.

The economic, political, and cultural integration of China into the world community is a process of historic significance, certainly no less significant than Russia's transition from communism. Its importance far exceeds that of the international issues (Haiti, Cuba, North Korea, even the Middle East and Bosnia) on which Washington has chosen to concentrate in recent years. The fundamental foreign policy failing of the Clinton administration has been its unwillingness to treat China with the seriousness and respect due a great power. This is symbolized by President Clinton's steady refusal until late 1996 to agree to a formal summit meeting with his Chinese counterpart Jiang Zemin. Unwilling to risk domestic political criticism, Clinton rejected Chinese requests for an official state visit to Washington by Jiang. Instead, he tacked three brief meetings with the Chinese leader onto the annual Asia-Pacific Economic Cooperation (APEC) forum leadership conferences (in Seattle, Bogor, and Manila). Despite its growing importance in moving the region toward a free trade regime, the APEC forum receives minimal attention in the U.S. media. Clinton also met briefly with Jiang in New York on the occasion of the United Nations' 50th Anniversary celebrations in October 1995. None of these perfunctory meetings has contributed more than marginally to easing Sino-American tension.[5] Secretary Christopher had more than a dozen meetings with Chinese foreign minister Qian Qichen, but visited Beijing only twice. The meetings between the two men were more in the nature of crisis management exercises than attempts to rebuild cooperative relations. In May 1996, Christopher proposed that regular summit meetings be held between Chinese and U.S. leaders and that Cabinet-level exchanges, which were a fixture of U.S.-China relations in the past, be resumed. The July 1996 visit to Beijing of Anthony Lake signaled Washington's interest in resuming high-level official contacts with Beijing. Finally, after Clinton's easy reelection victory in November, the U.S. president met with Jiang Zemin at the Manila APEC meeting, and the two leaders announced they would exchange summit visits in 1997 and 1998. Regular high-level meetings in which substantive issues are seriously engaged would help redress the problem of neglect.

Since the opening of diplomatic relations between China and the United States in 1979, both countries have been represented in each other's capitals by distinguished senior diplomats with decades of foreign affairs, language, and area experience. On the Chinese side the list includes the likes of Zhang Wenjin, Huang Zhen, and the current ambassador Li Daoyu; on the U.S. side are senior China specialists Arthur Hummel, Winston Lord, James Lilley, and J. Stapleton Roy. The Clinton administration abandoned this tradition of foreign service professionalism by nominating ex-senator James Sasser, a political appointee, as its ambassador to China. A Tennessee Democrat who had failed to win reelection in 1994, Sasser clearly lacked the impressive credentials of his predecessors. His appointment represented an inexplicable downgrading of the Beijing ambassadorship precisely at a time when the unsettled state of U.S.-China relations

5. See *Far Eastern Economic Review* (Hong Kong), November 2, 1995, pp. 14–15. See also *Washington Post*, October 1, 1995.

underlined the need for another experienced professional in command of the embassy. By contrast, the U.S. ambassador to Japan is former vice president Walter Mondale, a respected Democratic elder statesman, who was preceded in his position by the illustrious Mike Mansfield, who taught East Asian history at the University of Montana before beginning a political career that eventually led him to become the Senate majority leader. Ambassador-Designate Sasser's nomination hearing was delayed for months as a result of efforts by Senator Jesse Helms (R-N.C.), chairman of the Senate Foreign Relations Committee, to force a reorganization of the State Department. While Sasser was cooling his heels in Washington, he was able to bone up on his new assignment.

Fortunately, Winston Lord, the assistant secretary of state for Asian and Pacific affairs, is a man of broader vision and long China experience.

The Clinton administration has tended to treat China as the source of a series of irritating but mostly unrelated problems that can be dealt with piecemeal. The U.S. media, by contrast, presents a more holistic but almost entirely critical picture of China that reinforces negative public stereotypes by focusing on topics such as China's highly restrictive population policy or highlighting "exposés" of alleged abuses in the country's state-run orphanages.[6] Positive developments in China, including greater openness, rising standards of living, greater access to international information, the implementation of competitive local elections, and examples of Sino-American cooperation, receive less attention. The result is that the educated American public's understanding of China, the foundation on which an effective China policy must rest, is badly distorted.

One of the most contentious issues in U.S.-China relations since 1989 has been China's appalling record of human rights

6. E.g., an article criticizing President Clinton's China policy by Don Feder, a syndicated columnist, begins, "The men who rule mainland China are every bit as evil as Nazi concentration-camp guards. They are as much a threat to our national security as Iraq's Saddam Hussein," and concludes by challenging Clinton to explain "how abetting a regime that deliberately starves orphans to death keeps America strong and prosperous." *Daily Oklahoman*, June 11, 1996, p. 4.

abuses. Because this issue is partly rooted in the fundamentally different value structures of the two countries, it is inherently less amenable to compromise than commercial or economic issues. For many years nongovernmental organizations such as Amnesty International, Human Rights Watch, and Human Rights in China have carefully documented numerous cases of China's abuse of prisoners' rights, including the routine use of torture, repression of minority nationality culture and religious rights in Tibet and Xinjiang, the continuing suppression of political dissent, indiscriminate application of the death penalty, and various kinds of abuses against women including the sale of some rural women into virtual sexual slavery. The U.S. State Department's annual surveys of global human rights practices confirm that Beijing has done little in recent years to improve China's human rights situation.[7]

China has responded to U.S. and other foreign criticism of its human rights practices in two ways. Its initial, almost reflexive, response was to dismiss such criticism as unacceptable interference in Chinese domestic affairs by invoking the principle of national sovereignty as a barrier against foreign judgments of Chinese practices. More recently, China has responded in a more complex and sophisticated fashion, accepting the concept of universal human rights but arguing that the particular circumstances in each country, including such factors as the level of development and social well-being, must be considered in judging a country's human rights record. China argues that at its current stage of development, it is appropriate to emphasize social and economic rights rather than the civil and political rights that are the main target of foreign critics. From this perspective, China claims that its own human rights record is superior to that of the United States with its large homeless and unemployed population as well as other citizens who do not enjoy the fundamental social guarantees included in the UN's Universal Dec-

7. See *Annual Country Reports on Human Rights Practices* (Washington, D.C.: U.S. Government Printing Office, 1996); also John Shattuck, "Human Rights and Democracy in Asia," statement before the House Subcommittees on Asia and the Pacific and International Operations and Human Rights, March 16, 1995, *U.S. Department of State Dispatch*, Vol. 6, no. 14 (April 3, 1995), pp. 273–78.

laration of Human Rights adopted in 1948. Whatever their merit, such arguments have had little if any effect on U.S. opinion concerning China's human rights record.

The Clinton administration entered office in January 1993 talking a tougher line on Chinese human rights abuses than its predecessor. Beginning in 1990, the year after Tiananmen, Democratic and Republican critics of President Bush's China policy tried to link human rights issues with the question of China's access to the U.S. market as a means of applying pressure on Beijing. To facilitate the expansion of U.S.-China economic relations, in 1980 the United States granted China most favored nation (MFN) trade status, a status routinely accorded almost all countries, which applies the lowest schedule of tariffs on imported goods to the United States. MFN was the foundation on which U.S.-China trade boomed in the 1980s. But for political reasons MFN was granted on an annual basis that required a presidential executive order and congressional approval. After Tiananmen, congressional critics of China's human rights policy tried either to revoke MFN outright or make its extension conditional on significant improvements in China's human rights practices. Revocation of MFN would have led to sharply increased tariffs on Chinese goods, pricing many of them out of the U.S. market. By threatening to exercise his veto, President Bush managed to protect MFN but not without incurring significant political costs.

When President Clinton first faced the MFN issue in the spring of 1993, a familiar array of interests lined up on both sides of the question. Business groups lobbied hard to protect MFN; most human rights groups opposed it. Not wanting to alienate either side, Clinton characteristically split the difference. He extended MFN, but stipulated that China must make "consistent overall progress" in several specified areas of human rights during the coming year or face the loss of MFN when the issue next came up for decision. In temporarily satisfying both business and human rights constituencies, the president merely deferred making the tough choice on MFN. Moreover, he wedged himself into a corner from which only the Chinese could extricate him if they responded positively to his threat to revoke MFN.

Not surprisingly China rejected the notion of attaching conditions to MFN, and during the next 12 months did virtually nothing to help Clinton out on the human rights front despite wheedling and cajoling by Secretary Christopher and other administration officials. Try as it might, the administration was unable to certify "consistent overall progress" in China's human rights practice. While business and human rights groups joined the battle for public opinion, the administration publicly agonized over its decision for weeks. Finally, on May 26, 1994, President Clinton announced that he was delinking human rights from MFN once and for all.[8] Doubtfully claiming that the policy of conditionality had served its purpose, Clinton asserted that it was no longer a useful policy tool. Henceforth Washington would pursue its commitment to human rights in China through other means. Beijing and the U.S. business community applauded the president's decision. Major human rights groups charged Clinton with betraying both his promise as well as the cause of human rights. Since 1994 the annual extension of MFN has again become the mere formality it was prior to Tiananmen, although it is an occasion for Congress to vent its displeasure with China.[9]

Clinton, meanwhile, has largely failed to honor his pledge to promote human rights in China through alternate channels. For example, the brief voluntary code of conduct that the administration drafted for U.S. companies doing business in China merely asked them to ensure workplace safety, be environmentally responsible, and not engage in bribery or discrimination. It avoided sensitive political issues entirely, contained no specific enforceable provisions, and was so bland that businessman John Kamm, a leading critic of China's human rights record, dismissed the code as "a bowl of warm mush."[10]

President Clinton's decision to delink human rights from

---

8. See *U.S. Department of State Dispatch*, Vol. 5, no. 22 (May 30, 1994), pp. 345–46.

9. In June 1996 House Minority Leader Richard A. Gephardt (D-Mo.) split with President Clinton and called for revocation of China's MFN status; see *Los Angeles Times*, June 15, 1996, p. A5. Like other calls to revoke or attach conditions to the extension of MFN, Gephardt's stance had no effect, except perhaps in his congressional district.

10. *Washington Post National Weekly Edition*, April 17–23, 1995, pp. 22–23.

MFN was a decisive moment in the evolution of his administration's China policy. It demonstrated the enormous political impact of China's dynamic economic growth in the 1990s on thinking about China in foreign capitals, including Washington. Given the high stakes, no country could afford to shut itself off from the trade, investment, manufacturing, and other opportunities that China's rapidly expanding economy presented. Conservative Chinese leaders, whether Confucians or communists, have long warned that the more enmeshed China became in the world economy the more vulnerable it would become to hostile international influences. This classic argument in favor of autarky and self-reliance posited a weak China facing stronger economic rivals. Under present circumstances, however, economic interdependence works largely in China's favor. Able to choose among competing groups of foreign investors, Chinese leaders can award or withhold contracts on the basis of whether they consider particular foreign governments friendly or hostile. For example in April 1996, China awarded a lucrative $2.5 billion commercial aircraft contract to a consortium of European and Singaporean companies rather than to Boeing or McDonnell Douglas.[11] Beijing can often count on foreign firms that want to do business in China to support the Chinese point of view when they try to influence their home country's policies toward the People's Republic.[12]

Just over a year after Clinton delinked human rights from MFN, China's arrest and trial of Chinese American human rights activist Harry Wu returned the issue of human rights to the front pages and created another problem for Washington. Wu, who had served 19 years in Chinese prison camps in the 1950s and 1960s on trumped-up charges, had already earned Beijing's ire by his expo-

11. *International Herald Tribune,* July 11, 1996, pp. 13, 15. Earlier, Chinese premier Li Peng praised Europeans and Japanese for not attaching conditions to commercial transactions, "unlike the Americans who arbitrarily resort to the threat of sanctions or the use of sanctions"; see *New York Times,* June 12, 1996, pp. A1, A5.

12. See *Washington Post National Weekly Edition,* April 17–23, 1995, pp. 22–23. See also David E. Sanger, "Two Roads to China: Nice, and Not So Nice," *New York Times,* June 9, 1996, section 3, pp. 1, 11. Sanger's article compares the efforts of Boeing, for whom China is a vital customer, to act on the PRC's behalf in Washington with the "get tough" approach of Microsoft, which is miffed by Chinese pirating of its software.

sure of Chinese prison labor exports to the United States and China's sale of human organs harvested from executed prisoners.[13] Arrested at the China-Kazakstan border crossing in June 1995 on charges of espionage, Wu was smeared in the Chinese press, convicted in a travesty of a trial, and handed a long prison sentence before being summarily expelled from China in August in response to intensive pressure from Washington.

China's expulsion of Wu cleared the way for First Lady Hillary Rodham Clinton's participation in the United Nations Fourth World Conference on Women held in Beijing. In her conference speech, Mrs. Clinton, known for speaking her mind, criticized China for manipulating the gathering by denying visas to women it deemed controversial and censoring the Chinese public's access to accurate information about the proceedings. Cataloging a long list of abuses of women's rights around the world, Mrs. Clinton asserted that "human rights are women's rights and women's rights are human rights, once and for all."[14] These fine words were also withheld from the Chinese public.

For several years, the United States in partnership with the European Union has attempted without success to get the United Nations Commission on Human Rights to examine China's human rights record. In March 1995 a resolution critical of China came to a vote in the Commission for the first time but was defeated. After China sentenced its most famous dissident, Wei Jingsheng, to a 14-year prison term in December 1995, the United States renewed its attempt. This time Beijing mobilized a coalition of third world countries in April 1996 to prevent the resolution from even coming up for debate, appealing to anti-American sentiment and reportedly bribing several African countries with offers of development aid to get them to support China's position.[15]

In sum, the experience of the past several years suggests that

13. Wu's monograph *Laogai: The Chinese Gulag* (Boulder, Colo.: Westview Press, 1992) maps and analyzes the Chinese prison camp system, and *Bitter Winds* (New York: Wiley, 1994), his autobiography, vividly describes his personal ordeal in that system.

14. *New York Times* (national edition), September 6, 1995, pp. A1, A4.

15. *New York Times* (national edition), April 24, 1996, p. A7.

Washington has very little leverage over Beijing with respect to Chinese human rights practices. At most, China has released a few well-known dissidents to bleed off U.S. pressure, particularly when the renewal of MFN was still at stake. But Beijing has learned that for the most part it can safely ignore Washington's sporadic criticism of China's human rights abuses. Within China, slow progress toward respect for the rule of law, improved judicial procedures, the emergence of a Chinese human rights constituency, and greater contact with the international community may over a period of years effect the results that external pressure, no matter how well intentioned, unfortunately can do relatively little to achieve. Meanwhile, nongovernmental human rights organizations in the United States and elsewhere will continue to expose the worst abuses of a country whose rapid economic progress has far outstripped the growth in its consciousness of, and respect for, universal human rights.

Economic Relations

Conflict over intellectual property rights, China's growing trade surplus with the United States, and the conditions of China's admission to the World Trade Organization (WTO) dominates the news but often obscures the fundamental reality of Sino-American economic relations. The United States and China are now important economic partners, and each country's stake in the economic relationship with the other is too vital to put lightly at risk. China's development through export-led growth follows the pattern of Japan, Taiwan, and South Korea during their economic takeoffs. Imports and exports combined now account for more than one-third of China's GDP, and the United States is China's largest export market. China is likewise of growing economic importance to the United States. In 1994 it was America's 14th largest export market, absorbing $9.3 billion of U.S. goods, an increase of 5.9 percent over the previous year.[16] Beijing and Washington agree that China runs an annual trade surplus with the United States, but differ sharply on its

16. Office of the U.S. Trade Representative, *National Trade Estimate Report on Foreign Trade Barriers* (Washington, D.C.: U.S. Government Printing Office, 1995), p. 47.

size because of very different accounting methods. U.S. statistics recorded a $34 billion Chinese surplus in 1995, whereas China's figures indicated only $7.4 billion.[17] The main difference is in whether to include Chinese goods reexported to the United States from Hong Kong as well as goods manufactured in China by Taiwanese enterprises. Most economists believe that a fairer estimate would be somewhere in between the U.S. and Chinese figures.

The U.S. trade deficit with China is politically important because it has become one of the main items on the U.S. bill of particulars charging China with unfair trade practices. In fact, China has replaced Japan as America's favorite foreign trade scapegoat. As with Japan, Americans grumble about unfair Chinese competition even as they continue to buy large quantities of Chinese textiles, footwear, toys, sporting goods, and numerous other consumer products.

Over the past decade or so, U.S. and Chinese trade negotiators have perfected a kind of commercial brinkmanship or "chicken" diplomacy in which high-impact collisions are averted by last-minute compromises. Here, too, Sino-American trade negotiations have come to resemble the tense but theatrical confrontations of earlier U.S.-Japanese trade negotiations. The stock scenario is roughly as follows.

In Act I the U.S. side makes a series of demands upon China for greater market access, an end to Chinese commodity dumping (that is, selling at below production prices to gain market share), or implementation of previously agreed upon measures that the Chinese are accused of circumventing. These demands are accompanied by threats to impose quotas, assess higher tariffs, or exclude certain categories of Chinese goods from the U.S. market. In Act II China indignantly denies the accusations and threatens retaliation against U.S. exports if Washington dares to follow through on its threats. In the next (optional) act, top officials of both countries amplify the threats of their subordinates, adding to the dramatic tension. In Act IV, as a U.S.-imposed deadline for compromise rapidly

---

17. Economist Intelligence Unit, *Country Report: China, Mongolia*, 1st quarter 1996, pp. 3–35.

approaches, both sides enter into marathon negotiations in an atmosphere darkened by the imminent prospect of economic warfare. Finally, in Act V, at or even beyond the expiration of the deadline, a compromise is somehow found that satisfies the minimum needs of both sides. A trade war is averted and both sides reassure each other and themselves that harmony has been restored, if only temporarily.

In recent years the issue of copyright infringements (or "intellectual property rights") has replaced textile quotas as the main subject of contention in Sino-American economic relations.[18] By U.S. estimates, illegal Chinese copying of American computer software, movies, videos, CDs, CD-ROMs, and audiocassettes costs U.S. industry between $2 to $3 billion annually. These pirated goods are then either sold domestically in China or in neighboring areas (including Hong Kong) at lower than bargain-basement prices; for example, music CDs featuring popular American singers may sell for about a dollar, and one reporter found a CD-ROM of Windows 95, OS/2, and other software selling for only $2.50 in the southern city of Shenzhen.[19] In February 1995, after protracted negotiations along the pattern outlined above, the United States and China signed a far-reaching agreement according to which Beijing promised to crack down hard on factories producing pirated goods, destroy the pirated goods themselves, disseminate information about protecting intellectual property rights, and open China's market to U.S. audiovisual products.[20] Within months of this accord, however, U.S. companies were complaining that Beijing was not properly enforcing the provisions of the agreement. Illegal factories that were raided and padlocked soon reopened under new names, and corrupt Chinese officials turned a blind eye toward the sale of pirated goods.

In April 1996, the Clinton administration formally designated China as the prime international violator of intellectual property

18. For an historical understanding of the broader Chinese context, see William P. Alford, *To Steal a Book Is an Elegant Offense: Intellectual Property Law in Chinese Civilization* (Stanford: Stanford University Press, 1995).

19. Seth Faison, "Copyright Pirates Prosper in China Despite Promises," *New York Times*, February 20, 1996, pp. A1, A6.

20. *New York Times* (national edition), February 27, 1995, pp. A1, C3; see also *Far Eastern Economic Review*, March 9, 1995, p. 16.

rights, and shortly thereafter threatened to impose 100 percent tariffs on $2 billion of Chinese imports. China responded immediately by threatening to impose tariffs on selected American goods and to place a moratorium on new U.S. investments in China.[21] Once more intense negotiations resulted in a last-minute agreement that averted a U.S.-China trade war, but it remains to be seen as of mid-1996 whether Beijing will be more successful in enforcing this new accord than it was the previous one.[22]

A more worrisome prospect for the United States is that China may be unwilling much longer to play its assigned role in these trade dramas. As suggested above, China can also retaliate against U.S. economic interests in areas other than trade, such as investment. Already U.S. industry is divided on the wisdom of playing "chicken" diplomacy with the Chinese over trade matters. Given the complaisance of their governments vis-à-vis Beijing, European, Japanese, Korean, and even Taiwanese investors have far fewer political burdens to contend with than do Americans. As noted above, the Chinese, who separate politics from economics (e.g., on the issue of human rights) when they wish to, also do not hesitate to insist upon the indivisibility of economics and politics when it suits their interests to do so. China also holds the United States chiefly responsible for blocking the PRC's entry into the World Trade Organization with Beijing balking at meeting the various criteria for market access and transparency that WTO rules require.[23]

U.S.-China Security Affairs

The peace of Asia depends, in many ways, upon stable, nonhostile relations between China and the United States. Such relations must now be worked out in the absence of a common threat that both countries believed came from the Soviet Union during the cold war. Both Chinese and U.S. leaders assert that they seek positive engagement with each other, but in recent

21. *New York Times*, May 16, 1996, pp. A1, C6; see also *Washington Post National Weekly Edition*, May 27–June 2, 1996, p. 5.

22. For a Chinese statement of their determination to stop illegal copying, see "Progress in Protection of Intellectual Property," *Beijing Review*, April 22–28, 1996, pp. 11–13.

23. For more on this issue, see the chapter in this volume by Penelope Prime.

years they have had a hard time finding common ground. Disagreements over China's military buildup, its claims in the South China Sea, its international arms sales policies, and particularly its escalating threat to Taiwan have contributed to an atmosphere of mutual suspicion and mistrust between Beijing and Washington.

Over the past several years U.S. and Chinese officials have repeatedly locked horns over a number of arms control issues. From Washington's perspective, China's behavior suggests a pattern of deliberate disregard for international arms control agreements that Beijing has pledged to respect. The United States has taken upon itself the burden of calling China to task for circumventing its commitments. Most troublesome, because of its effect on the volatile South Asian balance of power, is China's continuing export of nuclear-capable intermediate-range M-11 missiles, missile parts, and missile technology to Pakistan despite its promise in 1992 to respect the provisions of the Missile Technology Control Regime (MTCR), an informal international accord that is meant to deny nonnuclear states advanced missile technology in order to curb nuclear proliferation. Beijing has angrily denied that it has contravened its pledge to abide by the MTCR. Although Washington insists that the PRC has violated the MTCR, the Clinton administration has bent over backward to avoid imposing the sanctions against China required by U.S. law in order not to jeopardize U.S. business interests in China. Beijing has also sold missile technology to Iran as well as chemicals for producing chemical weapons such as poison gas, which is obviously very troubling to the U.S. government.[24] Nevertheless, the White House has chosen to confront China only over issues involving trade, which suggests that President Clinton gives a higher priority to U.S. business interests than to arms control and international security. The effect of the president's policy has been to encourage Chinese disregard of its international obligations.

Before a comprehensive nuclear test ban was to go into effect, in July 1996 China continued underground testing of nuclear

---

24. See Greg Milhollin and Meg Dennison, "China's Cynical Calculation," *New York Times* (national edition), April 24, 1995, p. A17; see also *New York Times*, November 10, 1995, p. A4.

weapons, brushing aside international protests, including direct appeals from the United States. China has developed a multi-warhead intercontinental ballistic missile (the Dongfeng-31) capable of striking the continental United States and has acquired an extensive inventory of modern weapons from Russia. Beijing's deployment of advanced Russian jet fighters extends China's reach in the South China Sea; the PRC has been pursuing a policy of backing up its sweeping territorial claims in this oil-rich area with expanded naval patrolling and the construction of facilities on disputed islands and reefs. Beijing's military buildup in the South China Sea is very worrisome to the other governments in the region, particularly Taiwan, Vietnam, the Philippines, and Malaysia.

These trends also do not sit well in Washington, which is concerned about their impact on stability in East Asia. Chinese leaders argue that by expanding China's military capabilities (and devoting a growing percentage of the national budget to defense) they are doing no more than other rising powers have done before them. They also dismiss Washington's criticism of Chinese arms sales as hypocritical in light of America's status as the world's leading arms exporter. These are good debating points, but they sidestep the real issue of the destabilizing effect of the growth of Chinese military power on potential conflict situations in Asia. Particularly troubling to the United States because of its interest in the security of Taiwan are Beijing's recent attempts to intimidate Taipei through displays of military force.

Taiwan president Lee Teng-hui's "private visit" to the United States in June 1995 to attend and address an alumni reunion at his alma mater, Cornell University, precipitated a crisis in U.S.-China relations. It also exposed a fundamental rift in American and Chinese ways of thinking. Few Americans could understand why the Chinese made such a fuss about an apparently innocuous visit. Many Chinese, however, read the Clinton administration's reversal of its earlier decision to deny President Lee a visa as proof of Washington's duplicity and of its support for Taiwan's policy of "creeping independence." They believed that the integrity of the three core U.S.-China agreements negotiated between 1972 and 1982 had been violated. Together these agreements precariously balanced Beijing's assertion that Taiwan is a part of China with Washington's determination to supply defensive weapons to the island within the context of what since January 1979 has been nominally an unofficial relationship between the United States and Taiwan. The formulas embodied in these agreements combined strength with elasticity, like garments that hold their shape even when stretched. But Lee Teng-hui's visit threatened to stretch them out of shape.

From Beijing's perspective, Taiwan was and remains the most critical issue between China and the United States. When the United States severed diplomatic ties with Taiwan in 1979 in order to normalize relations with the PRC, Deng Xiaoping gambled that growing international isolation would eventually force Taiwan to accept integration into the PRC on Beijing's terms. This has not happened. As Cal Clark's chapter in this volume indicates, Taiwan has refused to play the role assigned it in Beijing's script. Political and economic developments on the island have confounded Beijing's expectations. Taiwan's claims on U.S. sympathies, originating in cold war anti-communism, have been reinvigorated by the democratic transformation of the island's political system over the past ten years culminating in Lee Teng-hui's impressive victory in Taiwan's first popular presidential election in March 1996. Paradoxically, at a time when China's international power and prestige is rapidly growing, Beijing's ability to move Taiwan along the road to reunification is diminishing. Chinese leaders hold the United States largely responsible for this state of affairs.

The essence of U.S. policy toward Taiwan is spelled out in the Taiwan Relations Act (TRA) of 1979. This act renewed in different language the security guarantee Washington had first extended to Taipei in the 1954 U.S.–Republic of China Mutual Security Treaty, which was abrogated in 1980 at Beijing's insistence. In addition to pledging to supply Taiwan with such defensive weapons as are deemed necessary to provide for its security, the TRA authorizes the president to take appropriate measures to deal with military and other threats to Taiwan's security. Beijing's attempts in July and August 1995 and again in February and March 1996 to pressure Lee Teng-hui and intimidate Taiwanese voters by conducting large-scale offensive military exercises, including firing ballistic missiles into Taiwan's offshore waters, tested Washington's commitment under the TRA. Washington responded by dispatching two powerful aircraft carrier battle groups to the waters off Taiwan, sending an unmistakable signal to Beijing that the U.S. commitment to Taiwan remained firm. This action, which echoed President Dwight Eisenhower's deployment of the Seventh Fleet in the 1954 and 1958 Taiwan Strait crises, signaled to Chinese leaders that they faced extremely serious risks in challenging U.S. power. China objected to what it called "gross interference in China's internal affairs," and Foreign Minister Qian Qichen said that the United States "must not forget that Taiwan is a part of China's territory and is not a protectorate of the United States."[25] A pro-China Hong Kong newspaper blustered that the People's Liberation Army could "bury an enemy intruder in a sea of fire."[26]

The United States has refrained from playing an active role either in promoting or blocking China's reunification. It can, however, help ensure that reunification, when and if it occurs, comes about through mutual agreement, not as a result of Taipei succumbing to Beijing's coercive pressure. Unfortunately, the actions China has undertaken over the past year indicate that Beijing may already have opted for a strategy of coercion unless Lee Teng-hui reverses his policy of trying to enhance Taiwan's international standing.[27] Such a strategy is more likely to strengthen than to neutralize the U.S. commitment to Taiwan's security. A Chinese reaffirmation of the policy of peaceful reunification put forth by President Jiang Zemin in early 1995 and abstention from further missile rattling or other threatening acts would be a more effective way to influence U.S. policy in the direction of gradual disengagement from Taiwan. In China's present mood such restraint is unlikely. While China gradually enhances its power projection capabilities, it is likely to continue to test both the U.S. commitment to Taiwan's security and the political nerve of Taiwan's leadership. Even in the best of circumstances, it may prove extremely difficult to restore

25. *New York Times* (national edition), March 12, 1996, p. A7.

26. Quoted in *New York Times* (national edition), March 22, 1996, p. A7.

27. See Andrew J. Nathan, "China's Phobias Drive Strategy," *Asian Wall Street Journal* (Hong Kong), March 22–23, 1996, p. 6.

the tenuous equilibrium that prevailed until recently in the Beijing-Washington-Taipei triangle.

Building a New Sino-American Security Relationship

Broadly speaking, three structural features condition the U.S.-China security relationship. First is China's growing power vis-à-vis its Asian neighbors as well as the United States. China's modern history is the story of a weak nation coping with powerful adversaries. Most Chinese believe that over the past century and a half, the United States, like other foreign countries, used its superior power to extract concessions from China, diminish Chinese sovereignty, and seek to remake China in its own image by forcefully propagating alien values. Although the disparity of power between the United States and China is still considerable, the gap is gradually closing. As China's international prestige and economic and military power grow, Chinese leaders increasingly resent U.S. attempts to police China's international behavior no matter whether the issue is Chinese adherence to arms control agreements, sales of Chinese weapons abroad, China's compliance with international human rights standards, or any number of other issues. Like other rising powers before it, China inevitably challenges the superior position of the dominant great power.[28]

Second, Sino-American security relations are shaped by the trend toward global interdependence which has rendered obsolete earlier notions of unlimited national sovereignty. Just when China finally acquired the wherewithal to assert and defend its sovereignty, the West proclaimed that sovereignty was going out of style. No wonder many Chinese leaders tend to view interdependence as simply another method of entrapment devised by China's historic adversaries, including the United States, to limit Chinese sovereignty, frustrate its aspirations for national reunification, and interfere in China's internal affairs.

28. For more on this point, see Michael Oksenberg, "What Kind of China Do We Want?" *Newsweek*, April 1, 1996, p. 53. This issue has a special section entitled "China on the Move" that examines recent changes in China and their impact on U.S.–China relations.

Of course, other Chinese leaders are well aware of the considerable economic and security benefits China derives from an interdependent world. An improvement in the overall atmosphere of U.S.-China relations would make it easier for their voices to be heard above those of the skeptics.

Third, the end of the cold war has brought about a shift in the focus of U.S.-China security relations from the global strategic balance of power to regional issues, particularly issues concerning Asia. The issues discussed above, including China's military buildup, its territorial claims in the South China Sea, its sale of nuclear technology to Pakistan and, above all, its recent bellicose behavior toward Taiwan, feed anxieties not only in Washington but in Asian capitals as well concerning Beijing's long-term intentions in the region. Beijing's ambivalence toward the presence of U.S. forces in Asia has deepened in recent years. Washington's role in helping to maintain stability on the Korean peninsula and restraining Japanese military development is still appreciated by the Chinese, but Beijing has warned Washington and Tokyo not to turn the U.S.-Japan security alliance into an anti-Chinese vehicle.[29] Beijing's ambivalence deepens when U.S. power inhibits China's ability to threaten the use of military force, as in the case of Taiwan.

For almost a century, the United States has employed a combination of diplomacy and military power to prevent any other country from achieving a position of regional dominance in Asia. During this same period, China has struggled to reassert itself as a great power in the region. These two objectives are potentially contradictory. Over the long term, the best way to avoid a clash between them may be through the creation of a multilateral regional security system or an arrangement of interlocking subregional systems which China, the United States, Japan, Korea, Russia, and the ASEAN states all take part in creating. Such a system must emerge organically through a process of dialogue and mutual consultation that has just barely begun. The obstacles to its realization are formidable, including the questions of a divided Korea and how to deal with Taiwan.

An institutionalized U.S.-China security dialogue should be

29. *New York Times* (national edition), April 19, 1996, p. A3.

an important component of what at best will be a long-term process. A security dialogue was a vital part of the U.S.-China relationship from 1971 to 1989. But Washington suspended such talks with Beijing in response to Tiananmen and did not resume them until November 1993. Secretary of Defense William Perry held high-level meetings with his Chinese counterparts in October 1994, and lower-level military exchanges resumed as well around the same time. Beijing suspended the dialogue in June 1995 in retaliation for Taiwan president Lee Teng-hui's visit to the United States but allowed it to resume again five months later when Assistant Secretary of Defense Joseph Nye paid a visit to China. During his July 1996 trip to Beijing, National Security Adviser Anthony Lake told Jiang Zemin that one of the main purposes of his trip was to develop a strategic dialogue with the PRC. This echoes Jiang's call on the United States to consider Sino-American relations from a lofty strategic perspective and with an eye toward the 21st century.[30] Apparently, both sides now recognize that making the U.S.-China security dialogue hostage to transient issues makes little sense in an era of rising Chinese nationalism and growing Chinese power.

A recent Council on Foreign Relations (CFR) report contains what could be a protoagenda for a U.S.-China security dialogue.[31] Its authors advocate a U.S. policy of "conditional engagement" with China in place of the Clinton administration's policy of "comprehensive engagement." The latter policy emerged from an administration review of China policy in the autumn of 1993 and was an effort to reengage China on a broad spectrum of issues in order to achieve balance among the several major components of U.S.-China relations, including security, trade and investment, and human rights. Comprehensive engagement aimed at moving U.S. China policy away from the post-Tiananmen tendency to restrict and punish China for its human rights and other transgressions without returning to the lopsided preoccupation with security

30. *Renmin Ribao,* July 10, 1996, p. 1.

31. James Shinn, ed., *Weaving the Net: Conditional Engagement with China* (New York: Council on Foreign Relations Press, 1996).

issues that characterized Sino-American relations during the Nixon-Kissinger era.[32]

Conditional engagement is advocated as a middle course between laissez-faire optimism which assumes economic rationality will ensure China's smooth integration into the global system and neocontainment pessimism which views China as an ambitious and disruptive state. The CFR study group proposes "Ten Principles of Conditional Engagement" as a set of broad benchmarks against which to gauge China's international behavior and guide U.S.-China relations, the first six of which directly pertain to security affairs:

- No unilateral use of offensive military force.
- Peaceful resolution of territorial disputes.
- Freedom of navigation.
- Moderation in military force buildup.
- Transparency of military forces.
- Nonproliferation of weapons of mass destruction.
- Respect for national sovereignty.
- Market access for trade and investment.
- Cooperative solutions for transnational problems.
- Respect for basic human rights.

The concept of conditional engagement reflects a growing suspicion in the United States that China may be unwilling to abide by the evolving system of international norms and practices that limits national sovereignty in the interest of security and other global goods. If China's international behavior is deemed unsatisfactory, Washington could cite Chinese contravention of the Ten Principles, or any similar set of principles, to justify an attempt to mobilize a U.S.-led coalition of states to hold China in check. In this sense, despite the CFR study group's formal disavowal of containment, conditional engagement could be a step on the road toward precisely such a policy.

---

32. For one of the more articulate presentations of the logic of constructive engagement, see the address to the Trilateral Commission by James B. Steinberg, director of the State Department's Policy Planning Staff, in *U.S. Department of State Dispatch*, Vol. 6, no. 19 (May 8, 1995), pp. 392–95; see also Secretary of State Christopher's remarks, "Comprehensive Engagement in U.S.–China Relations" (April 17, 1995), in *U.S. Department of State Dispatch*, Vol. 6, no. 17 (April 24, 1995), pp. 354–55.

Conditional engagement unconsciously echoes an historic Western paternalism toward China that has long since been discredited in Chinese eyes. China scholar Jianwei Wang notes that the Chinese will naturally be suspicious of a strategy of conditional engagement, and he warns that such a strategy "should not be based on an anti-Chinese Asian coalition. Unless China turns to an alliance strategy first, the United States should not be responsible for once again plunging Asia into an era of pro- and anti-Chinese blocs."[33] This is sage advice. Nevertheless, at a minimum the Ten Principles could serve as a platform for a U.S.-China security dialogue that looks beyond specific areas of conflict to the principles underlying a stable Asian-Pacific security system.

Conclusion

Neither summit diplomacy nor mere expressions of goodwill can repair what is wrong with the U.S.-China relationship. The series of contentious issues that comprises the contemporary agenda of Sino-American ties derives from the structural position of both countries in the international system, their competing value systems, and their divergent interests with respect to various regional and global issues. This chapter has focused on areas of disagreement and political problems on both sides that have impeded the effective management of U.S.-China relations in recent years. Over the past 20 years, however, Chinese and Americans have often been able to find common ground and common interests. The two countries have often found it much easier to cooperate in scientific and technical endeavors, educational exchanges, cultural diffusion, and other forms of grassroots cooperation between individuals and institutions than in matters of high-level international politics.

Even the contemplation of a new cold war between China and the United States casts a chill over Asia because it would force new divisions at a time when multilateral cooperation is imperative in addressing security, environmental, developmental, and other problems. It is a hopeful sign that despite mutual

33. Shinn, *Weaving the Net*, p. 139, quote on p. 149.

wariness and even suspicion, neither China nor the United States wants a new cold war. Summing up his study of U.S.-China relations, Robert Ross wrote, "In the post–cold war era, there will be persistent conflict and only limited and tentative cooperation in U.S.-PRC relations."[34] Unfortunately, given recent trends, this somber forecast has the ring of truth to it. Nevertheless, it could prove too pessimistic if U.S. and Chinese leaders are willing to reengage in the painfully difficult but indispensable work of seeking compromises on issues where failure could spell disaster for the governments and peoples of both great nations.

34. Ross, *Negotiating Cooperation*, p. 260.

Chronology

Nancy R. Hearst

January 1994

1 In a move toward full convertibility of its currency, the yuan, China creates a market-based foreign exchange rate, thus ending the dual-rate foreign exchange system and the state-set exchange system. Foreign exchange certificates are no longer issued.

3 Washington requests resumption of textile negotiations, which broke off in December 1993 when China rejected U.S. demands for tougher controls on the transshipment of Chinese goods through other countries (notably Hong Kong) in order to circumvent import quotas.

5 Taiwan sentences mainland hijacker, former army officer Zhang Wenlong, to nine years in prison.

6 Effective January 17, the United States threatens to cut the amount of clothing and fabrics China is allowed to export to the United States by more than $1 billion in retaliation for illegal transshipments of Chinese products.

7 Ending a year-long dispute over French sales of jet fighters to Taiwan, France and China announce the restoration of friendly relations.

January 1994 ***(continued)***

15 President Jiang Zemin tells a U.S. congressional delegation led by House majority leader Richard Gephardt that China will improve its human rights record.

17 A last-minute three-year textile quota agreement, providing for joint U.S.-Chinese inspections of factories suspected of shipping mislabeled products to disguise their country of origin, freezes Chinese imports to the United States at current levels, thus averting a serious trade dispute.

19 In Beijing Treasury Secretary Lloyd Bentsen warns Premier Li Peng that President Clinton will revoke China's most favored nation (MFN) trade status in 1994 if Beijing does not improve its human rights record.

20 Victims of China's coercive population control policies become eligible for U.S. political asylum.

In Beijing, Treasury Secretary Lloyd Bentsen announces that an agreement has been reached to open Chinese prisons to U.S. customs officials to ensure that prison factories are not producing products for export to the United States.

21 Loosening foreign bank rules, China allows foreign financial institutions to conduct yuan-denominated business, and increases the number of Chinese cities in which they are allowed to operate.

24 Secretary of State Warren Christopher meets with Chinese foreign minister Qian Qichen in Paris; an agreement is reached for China to receive U.S. assistant secretary of state for human rights John Shattuck in Beijing to discuss the cases of 235 political prisoners.

25 Dissident Qin Yongmin is sentenced to two years of reeducation through labor for releasing a "peace charter" calling for political change.

The U.S. Senate votes to establish a new radio service, Radio Free Asia, to beam news and feature programs to China and other Asian countries.

The PRC's Hong Kong and Macao Affairs Office announces that the post-1997 government will not be liable for any expenditures and debts incurred in the building of the Hong Kong airport, slated for completion in April 1998.

26 Eleven dissidents sign a two-page statement calling for the release of Qin Yongmin.

27 Chinese and Russian foreign ministers sign an agreement to establish 20 border checkpoints under Moscow's control to facilitate two-way trade and to control the number of Chinese entering Russia.

30 In Taiwan local elections, the opposition Democratic Progressive Party (DPP) wins 21 mayoral or town chief seats, up from 6, and the ruling Kuomintang (KMT) loses 49 seats.

China issues a ban on new construction projects for 1994.

31 New regulations on religious activity go into effect in China, forbidding foreigners from setting up religious organizations and cultivating followers.

February 1994

1 The U.S. State Department, in its annual worldwide human rights survey, issues a mostly negative report on China's human rights record, which is said to be "falling far short of internationally accepted norms."

February 1994 *(continued)*

Under new marriage regulations, the Chinese government reserves the right to intervene if couples live together before the official marriageable age of 22 for men and 20 for women.

4 The Chinese government confirms the release of three political prisoners, including Xiao Bin, a worker who gave a foreign television interviewer estimates of the number killed in the 1989 Tiananmen crackdown.

The United States, Britain, and France appeal to China to put pressure on North Korea to open its nuclear installations to international inspection.

7 Chinese Muslims are sentenced to long prison terms for "gang fighting" in Xiji, Ningxia, in May 1993.

9 Eighty-nine-year-old Deng Xiaoping appears on Chinese TV, marking the Lunar New Year from Shanghai.

10 Security officials warn paroled dissident Wei Jingsheng that he will be rearrested if he continues to campaign for democracy and human rights.

17 The leader of an international Christian delegation to China announces that members of his group were detained and held incommunicado for four days.

24 Hong Kong legislators pass the first phase of Governor Christopher Patten's democratic reforms, despite China's threat to annul the changes when it recovers the colony in 1997.

27 U.S. assistant secretary of state for human rights John Shattuck, in a private meeting with Wei Jingsheng, agrees to carry a message to President Clinton calling for economic pressure on Beijing in order to win the release of political prisoners.

28 Pu Jie, younger brother of the last emperor of China, dies in Beijing at the age of 87.

March 1994

1 In an effort to deflect criticism, a Chinese government spokesman plays to American journalists a video showing four leading political prisoners in good health.

4 Wei Jingsheng is detained for some 30 hours, as are Wang Dan and other dissidents, a week before the visit of Secretary of State Warren Christopher to discuss China's human rights record.

10 On the eve of Secretary of State Warren Christopher's visit to Beijing, seven Chinese intellectuals and scientists, headed by historian of science Xu Liangying, appeal to President Jiang Zemin for an end to political repression.

At the opening of the annual session of the National People's Congress (NPC), Premier Li Peng outlines a series of measures to control runaway inflation.

12 In meetings with Secretary of State Warren Christopher, Foreign Minister Qian Qichen and Premier Li Peng take a hard line against U.S. threats to link human rights and trade, warning that canceling trade privileges will backfire on the United States.

March 1994 *(continued)*

15 In his speech to the annual session of the NPC, Procurator-General Zhang Siqing reports an increase in violent crime, with 574,176 people tried for criminal offenses in 1993.

31 The United States and China agree on a UN Security Council statement calling for North Korea to allow inspections of nuclear facilities.

Twenty-four Taiwanese tourists are killed in an attempted robbery aboard a tourist boat on Qiandao Lake in Zhejiang Province.

April 1994

4 Dissident Wei Jingsheng is detained for a second time when he returns to Beijing from a trip to northeast China.

11 The president of Great Wall Machinery and Electronic High-Technology Industrial Group, Shen Taifu, is executed on charges of bribery and embezzlement of $375,000.

23 Dissident Wang Juntao, who had been sentenced to 13 years in prison as the "black hand" behind the 1989 democracy movement, is released for medical reasons and sent immediately to the United States for treatment.

28 President Clinton tells the Dalai Lama that he supports the Tibetan leader's offer to meet with senior Chinese officials.

30 U.S. trade representative Mickey Kantor announces that a determination concerning China's piracy of American copyrights has been postponed.

President Clinton signs bills ending a 12-year commitment to reduce arms sales to Taiwan and authorizing the creation of Radio Free Asia to beam programs from the United States into the Chinese mainland, Burma, Cambodia, Laos, North Korea, Tibet, and Vietnam.

May 1994

2 Amnesty International reports 2,560 people had been sentenced to death in China in 1993 of whom 1,400 were executed.

3 The Chinese publication *Legal Daily* describes China's rural areas as controlled by "warlords, bandits, and feudal clans," creating chaos and a crisis in the countryside.

6 Japanese justice minister Shigeto Nagano recants his earlier statement that the Nanjing Massacre of 1937 was a fabrication.

8 The Daya Bay nuclear power plant in Guangdong Province becomes fully operational.

13 Two Chinese Americans are sentenced to prison, for 20 and 14 years each, for attempts to swindle $10 billion from a Chinese bank.

China amends its public order law to broaden the powers of the police to detain political and religious activists and restrict their activities.

Chen Ziming, the second of the two "black hands" of the 1989 democracy movement, is released on bail for medical treatment.

16 In an attempt to keep the urban jobless rate below 3 percent, new labor policies to open the employment market are announced.

May 1994 *(continued)*

17 China agrees to a visit of a team of U.S. technicians to talk about halting the jamming of Voice of America radio broadcasts.

22 Ren Jianxin, president of the Chinese Supreme People's Court, warns that "serious security problems are escalating enormously" in the rural areas.

26 President Clinton announces that he will ask Congress for unconditional renewal of MFN status for China, ending the policy of making human rights part of U.S. trade policy.

Seven leaders of the 1989 democracy demonstrations send a petition to China's leaders urging a reevaluation of the official verdict that the Tiananmen movement was a counterrevolutionary rebellion.

June 1994

4 Two human rights activists, Bao Ge and Zhang Lin, are detained on the fifth anniversary of the Tiananmen crackdown.

The text of Zhao Ziyang's June 1989 speech to the Fourth Plenary Session of the 13th Chinese Communist Party (CCP) Central Committee, defending his conciliatory position on the Tiananmen unrest, is leaked in Hong Kong.

6 A Russian-built plane crashes in Xi'an, killing all 160 passengers. A flight originating in Fujian is hijacked to Taiwan.

9 President Jiang Zemin promotes 19 army officers to the rank of general.

10 While calling for an international nuclear moratorium, China sets off its 40th nuclear explosion.

In a further curb on press freedom, China publishes a code of conduct that requires reporters to promote communism and to protect state secrets.

12 Three men, pleading guilty to murdering 24 Taiwanese and 8 mainlanders aboard a tourist boat in late March, are sentenced to death.

China assures Japan that it will play a "positive role" in the crisis over North Korea's nuclear program.

17 China protests Vietnam's efforts to prospect for oil and natural gas in the South China Sea.

21 The 29th Meeting of the Sino-British Joint Liaison Group on Hong Kong opens after a six-month lapse.

28 The Eighth Session of the Eighth NPC Standing Committee begins discussions on a draft banking law, as well as on legislation on arbitration, labor unions, real estate development, and securities regulation.

30 Britain and China conclude arrangements for the transfer of defense sites in Hong Kong.

Hong Kong legislators narrowly approve Governor Christopher Patten's democratic electoral reforms, despite pressure from Beijing.

The United States targets China for possible trade sanctions, as a result of Beijing's failure to protect U.S. patents and copyrights.

July 1994

5 China promulgates its first real estate law, to go into effect on January 1, 1995, giving authorities permission to crack down on land speculators who are blamed for fueling inflation.

10 Premier Li Peng ends a visit to Germany where he is rankled by human rights protesters; he signs business deals worth $3.5 billion.

19 Han Xu, PRC ambassador to Washington from 1985 to 1989, dies in Beijing.

20 Reports of two Chinese warships in the South China Sea blockading a Vietnamese oil rig near the contested areas leads the Foreign Ministry to accuse Vietnam of having "gravely encroached upon China's sovereignty and maritime interests."

29 China's Securities Regulatory Commission halts all new listings on the nation's two stock exchanges for the remainder of the year in an effort to check steep falls in the value of issues.

August 1994

4 A Chinese court rules in favor of the Walt Disney Company in a copyright suit accusing Chinese firms of intellectual piracy.

The highest-level talks to date between Taiwan and the People's Republic of China (PRC) begin in Taipei, with the visit of Chinese envoy Tang Shubei, vice-chairman of the Association for Relations Across the Taiwan Strait.

8 Officials from China and Taiwan sign an agreement intended to end the recent hijackings from China.

9 The U.S. House of Representatives defeats by a vote of 270 to 158 a proposal to impose steep tariffs on imports from factories owned by the Chinese military.

17 In an editorial in the *People's Daily*, the Communist Party calls for an end to the widespread false reporting of economic statistics.

22 Deng Xiaoping turns 90.

24 China's State Statistical Bureau reports increases in retail inflation; the State Council orders a new drive to end steep rises in food prices.

27 In the first high-level visit by a U.S. official since the delinking of MFN and human rights, Commerce Secretary Ron Brown, leading a business delegation, arrives in Beijing for talks on trade and economic cooperation.

Dissident Wang Dan is detained and then released.

30 Commerce Secretary Ron Brown announces a Chinese agreement to resume the high-level Sino-U.S. human rights dialogue, which had been suspended after Secretary of State Warren Christopher's trip to Beijing in March 1994 resulted in a stalemate on the issue.

September 1994

1 China issues a regulation, approved by the Standing Committee of the NPC, to abolish Hong Kong's legislature after the 1997 takeover.

September 1994 *(continued)*

2 In a move to back North Korea, China withdraws its delegate from the military commission that oversees the armistice between North and South Korea.

3 In Moscow, presidents Jiang Zemin and Boris Yeltsin sign a declaration to limit the number of troops along the Sino-Russian border, to not aim nuclear missiles at each other, and to develop economic ties.

7 The Clinton administration announces plans to expand ties with Taiwan, including support of Taiwan's entry into the General Agreement on Tariffs and Trade (GATT).

9 China angrily protests the upgrading of U.S.-Taiwan ties.

19 In Hong Kong's first fully democratic election, pro-democracy parties gain control of 5 of the 18 District Boards.

20 A Chinese soldier opens fire in rush-hour Beijing traffic, killing eight, before being killed himself by security forces, in his attempt to commandeer a jeep to Tiananmen Square.

21 China announces plans to send about $1.2 billion in aid and investment to Tibet over the next five years.

28 A CCP Central Committee meeting closes in Beijing with calls to improve party discipline and the quality of leadership; Huang Ju, mayor of Shanghai, is elected to the Politburo; Shanghai party secretary Wu Bangguo and Shandong party secretary Jiang Chunyun are named to the party Secretariat.

30 In his National Day speech in the Great Hall of the People, Premier Li Peng speaks of rampant inflation, the poor performance of state-owned enterprises, and the overall deterioration of social order.

October 1994

4 China agrees not to sell or transfer surface-to-surface missiles in exchange for the lifting of the U.S. ban on the export to China of high-technology satellites.

5 Foreign Minister Qian Qichen reports that China agrees to reopen talks with the Red Cross on access to prisoners and will invite U.S. lawyers for discussions on human rights and the "rule of law."

7 Despite an international moratorium, China explodes a nuclear device at Lop Nor, its third testing of a new generation of ballistic missile warheads this year.

16 In an effort to improve military ties, U.S. defense secretary William Perry begins talks in Beijing on arms control, defense conversion, military strategy, and human rights.

25 Forty-four people in Guangdong are executed for involvement in prostitution and drug trafficking.

November 1994

4 Ending a two-year dispute, an agreement is reached between China and Britain over construction of the new $20 billion Hong Kong airport.

12 Human rights groups report that Chinese journalist Gao Yu has been sentenced to six years in prison for "leaking state secrets."

November 1994 *(continued)*

13 President Clinton meets with President Jiang Zemin in Indonesia, during a meeting of the Asia-Pacific Economic Cooperation (APEC) forum, to discuss North Korea's nuclear policy, trade, arms proliferation, and human rights issues.

14 Top government authorities approve the construction of a $1.2 billion power plant in Guangdong Province.

At the APEC meeting in Indonesia, the United States offers to end sanctions against China if the Chinese agree to disclose their past exports of M-11 missile technology to Pakistan.

The Chinese announce a new law to prohibit sex screening of fetuses effective January 1995.

15 Taiwan acknowledges that its troops fired at least a dozen artillery shells into the village of Tatou in Fujian Province, wounding four.

25 Poet Bei Dao is held at Beijing airport, interrogated, and then deported.

December 1994

3 The KMT is defeated in the Taipei mayoral race as Ch'en Shui-pien, DPP legislator, wins; but the KMT scores a resounding victory in the governor's race.

4 As part of the upgrading of U.S. relations with Taiwan, President Lee Teng-hui meets U.S. secretary of transportation Federico Pena, the second U.S. Cabinet member to visit Taiwan since 1979.

5 Dissident Wang Dan files suit against the Beijing Public Security Bureau for invading his privacy and interfering with his freedom.

9 China orders safety inspections the day after a deadly fire killed at least 300 children and teachers watching a variety show in Xinjiang Province.

11 Former vice-premier and conservative economic planner Yao Yilin, 77, dies in Beijing.

14 Construction of the environmentally controversial Three Gorges hydroelectric project on the Yangzi River officially begins.

19 China bans luxury construction projects, such as golf courses and racetracks, in favor of infrastructure projects until 1996.

20 In Geneva, negotiations for China's bid to join the newly formed World Trade Organization (successor to the GATT) in 1995 end without agreement.

31 The United States threatens sanctions—to go into effect within 30 days—against more than $2.8 billion worth of Chinese exports to the U.S. because of China's failure to curb copyright piracy.

January 1995

1 To control economic growth and rising inflation, China raises interest rates on loans to financial institutions by an average of twenty-four–hundredths of one percent.

4 In an attempt to avoid a trade war with the United States, China orders a national boycott of pirated goods.

January 1995 *(continued)*

5 Human Rights Watch/Asia releases what is purported to be a confidential official list of names of leaders of China's exiled democratic movement who will be arrested if they attempt to return to China.

12 The first photo of Deng Xiaoping in almost a year appears on the front page of the Shanghai newspaper *Liberation Daily*.

In an interview with the *New York Times,* Xiao Rong, daughter of Deng Xiaoping, admits her father's health is failing.

14 In a radio broadcast beamed to China from Manila, Pope John Paul II offers the Vatican's acknowledgment of the officially sponsored Catholic Church in China in exchange for recognition of papal authority over China's Catholics.

26 A Chinese rocket, carrying a U.S.-made commercial satellite, explodes during a failed launch at the Xichang Satellite Launch Center in Sichuan Province.

28 U.S.-China trade negotiations break down after no agreement is reached over copyright infringements.

30 In the Great Hall of the People, President Jiang Zemin presents a speech entitled "Continue to Promote the Reunification of the Motherland" in which he outlines eight steps toward peaceful reunification with Taiwan.

February 1995

1 The U.S. State Department's annual report on human rights concludes that China made no progress in any area during 1994.

2 Philippine fishermen discover the construction of a Chinese military post atop Mischief Reef in the South China Sea, long claimed to be a part of Philippine territory.

4 U.S. trade representative Mickey Kantor announces the imposition of 100 percent tariffs on $1.08 billion worth of Chinese imports; China in turn threatens to impose 100 percent tariffs, effective February 26, on U.S.-made compact discs, cigarettes, alcoholic beverages, and other products "to protect its sovereignty and national dignity."

6 China asks U.S. negotiators to return to Beijing to resume talks on the piracy of American-made products.

7 The Clinton administration announces expansion of subsidized wheat sales to Beijing.

14 China's population reaches 1.2 billion five years earlier than planned. A new family planning program is launched to cut the annual growth rate to one percent in order to keep the population below 1.3 billion by the end of the decade.

15 Philippine president Fidel Ramos orders more troops to the Spratly Islands in the South China Sea in response to China's occupation of Mischief Reef, claimed by Manila.

At the resumption of U.S.-China trade negotiations, China says it is widening its crackdown on pirated goods from the United States.

17 Zhou Beifang, former chairman of two Hong Kong–based subsidiaries of China's Shougang (Capital Iron and Steel) Corporation and son of one of Deng Xiaoping's closest associates, Zhou Guanwu, is arrested for economic crimes.

February 1995 *(continued)*

A Chinese government spokesman says China is ready to negotiate and sign agreements with other nuclear powers to ban nuclear tests.

18 Zhou Guanwu, father of Zhou Beifang, resigns after 13 years as chairman of the state-owned Shougang Corporation.

China raids two factories that had been producing pirated laser discs.

Twelve prominent intellectuals formally petition China's NPC, calling for democratic reforms and an independent investigation into corruption in the leadership.

The United States and China reach a last-minute agreement banning piracy; sanctions are averted.

27 Two Chinese dissidents, Wang Dan and Xu Wenli, send a letter with 25 signatures to the NPC and the *People's Daily* demanding human rights safeguards and an end to one-party rule.

March 1995

1 In Beijing, Assistant Secretary of State Winston Lord says that the United States will back a UN resolution critical of China's human rights record.

2 In their second petition in less than a week, 12 intellectual dissidents call for limits on police powers.

5 In his speech to the NPC at the opening of its annual session, Premier Li Peng, citing government mistakes, pledges to rein in economic growth, control inflation, and revamp money-losing state-owned enterprises. He calls the fight against corruption "a matter of life and death for the nation."

8 In Geneva the UN Commission on Human Rights votes 21 to 20 to reject a resolution condemning China's human rights record.

10 In a statement marking the 36th anniversary of the unsuccessful Tibetan uprising, the Dalai Lama announces he is ready to talk with China and proposes a vote among exiled Tibetans on how to fight Chinese rule of Tibet.

12 China and the United States agree to press jointly for Beijing's entry into the new World Trade Organization, as China agrees to ease restrictions on U.S. farm products.

16 The NPC approves the nominations of Wu Bangguo and Jiang Chunyun as vice-premiers of industry and agriculture respectively.

18 China passes its first central bank law, placing the People's Bank of China under the leadership of the State Council.

20 In a speech carried on the front page of national newspapers, President Jiang Zemin attacks party cadres and government officials who violate the strict "one couple–one child" policy.

In an attempt to curtail the influence of the Dalai Lama, Chinese authorities announce a crackdown on temples and monks in Tibet.

22 The USS *Bunker Hill*, a guided-missile cruiser, makes a port of call in Qingdao, the first visit by a U.S. naval ship since the 1989 Tiananmen crackdown.

24 China and Britain fail to reach agreement in talks on a supreme court for Hong Kong after the 1997 takeover.

April 1995

4 After coming under investigation for corruption, Wang Baosen, vice-mayor of Beijing, commits suicide.

10 Chen Yun, architect of China's planned economy, dies in Beijing at age 90.

17 Prior to the opening session of a UN conference aimed at halting the spread of nuclear weapons, Secretary of State Warren Christopher fails to persuade Foreign Minister Qian Qichen to end China's nuclear cooperation with Iran.

20 The State Council approves a 30-year extension of land contracts for Chinese farmers.

27 Amid a growing corruption scandal, Chinese government officials report the resignation of the party leader of Beijing Municipality, Chen Xitong. He is replaced by Politburo member Wei Jianxing.

May 1995

15 In a letter to China's president and to the chair of the NPC timed to coincide with the 50th anniversary of the United Nations and the UN Year of Tolerance, 45 intellectuals protest against political oppression and call for the release of political prisoners.

China detonates a nuclear weapon in an underground test just days after backing an indefinite extension of the Nuclear Nonproliferation Treaty.

16 Chinese vessels harass Philippine naval ships carrying journalists on a tour of the disputed islands in the South China Sea.

17 China denounces the Dalai Lama for declaring that a six-year-old boy in Tibet is the reincarnation of the Panchen Lama, the second most important spiritual leader in Tibetan Buddhism.

18 Wang Mengkui replaces Yuan Mu, who had been closely linked to the Tiananmen crackdown, as head of the State Council's Research Office.

Lu Ping, director of the PRC Hong Kong and Macao Affairs Office, pledges that China will not do away with the territory's civil service, capitalist system, and freedom of travel after 1997.

20 Dissident intellectual Liu Xiaobo is arrested as he attempts to deliver to Western news organizations a copy of a petition calling for a commemoration for those who died in the 1989 Tiananmen crisis.

22 The Clinton administration reverses its previous position and issues a visa to the United States to Taiwan president Lee Teng-hui to participate in an alumni reunion at his alma mater, Cornell University.

In its first use of economic aid to protest Chinese policy, Japan announces that it will cut its grants to protest China's nuclear tests.

23 The Chinese government summons U.S. ambassador J. Stapleton Roy, demanding that the United States reverse its decision to issue a visa to Taiwan president Lee Teng-hui.

24 Despite pressure from the UN, China announces that it will hold to its decision to move the Forum of Nongovernmental Organizations on Women from Beijing to Huairou County, 30 miles outside the city, when the Fourth World Conference on Women convenes in the Chinese capital in September.

May 1995 *(continued)*

The House of Representatives votes 240 to 181 to ban $25 million from going to the UN Population Fund because of its involvement with China's population control program.

28 China halts arms talks on the control of missile technology and cooperation with the United States in protest against the forthcoming visit to the U.S. of Taiwan president Lee Teng-hui.

June 1995

1 The Maternal and Infantile Health Care Law goes into effect, requiring Chinese couples with mental illnesses and other disabilities to be sterilized or to accept long-term contraception and pressuring pregnant women with hereditary diseases to abort.

2 President Clinton extends MFN status to China for 12 months, while noting that China's human rights record is still unacceptable.

4 Two isolated protesters, who are quickly removed, mark the sixth anniversary of the Beijing crackdown by attempting to throw handfuls of yellow "funeral money" into Tiananmen Square.

8 UN sources report that organizers of the nongovernmental organizations women's forum agree to accept the decision to move the event from Beijing to Huairou in exchange for a sharp increase in the numbers of participants who will be allowed to attend.

Britain agrees to China's plan to set up a Court of Final Appeal to replace Britain's Privy Council as a guarantor of Hong Kong's separate legal system after the 1997 takeover; in exchange China promises Hong Kong "a high degree of autonomy."

9 Taiwan president Lee Teng-hui delivers an alumni reunion address at Cornell University.

15 In response to the submission of several petitions with more than 200 signatures calling for political reform, the government reportedly arrests or detains several dozen dissidents.

16 China recalls its ambassador in the United States, Li Daoyu, citing Washington's change of policy when it allowed Taiwan president Lee Teng-hui to visit the U.S. on a private visit.

17 U.S. ambassador J. Stapleton Roy leaves his post in Beijing before the confirmation of a successor.

19 Human rights activist and U.S. citizen Harry Wu is detained at the border when he tries to enter China from Kazakstan.

21 A CIA report concludes that China has recently delivered components for missile systems to Iran and Pakistan.

23 The Hong Kong government is pressured by China to announce the repeal of some colonial laws protecting press and speech freedoms.

25 Democracy activist Chen Ziming, who was released from prison for medical treatment in 1994, is rearrested and his parole is revoked for conducting a 24-hour fast on the anniversary of the Beijing crackdown and for issuing statements and organizing petitions appealing for political rights and democracy.

27 Taiwan offers the United Nations $1 billion in exchange for membership in the world body.

June 1995 *(continued)*

The U.S. State Department expresses "strong displeasure" over the detention of Harry Wu.

30 China and Britain agree on a financing plan for the new Hong Kong airport.

China announces that Vice-Premier Zhu Rongji has stepped down as governor of the People's Bank; he is replaced by Dai Xianglong, a deputy governor of the bank.

July 1995

3 The *Washington Post* reports that U.S. intelligence has strong evidence that Beijing transferred to Pakistan medium-range M-11 missiles.

4 Xinhua News Agency reports that before committing suicide Beijing vice-mayor Wang Baosen had embezzled and diverted funds, resulting in losses of more than $13 million.

8 Chinese police in Wuhan formally arrest Harry Wu and charge him with stealing state secrets.

9 U.S. House speaker Newt Gingrich announces that he supports the restoration of formal diplomatic ties with Taiwan.

11 A vote of no confidence in Hong Kong governor Christopher Patten, introduced in the colony's Legislative Council by those who felt he gave in to Chinese pressure concerning terms for the establishment of the Court of Final Appeals in 1997, is defeated (17 for, 35 against, and 4 abstentions).

12 China awards a $1 billion joint-venture contract to Mercedes-Benz of Germany.

China says that President Clinton should reaffirm that there is only one China, that Taiwan is part of China, and that Taiwan's president will not be allowed to make any more visits to the United States.

18 The Chinese army announces that it will conduct week-long military exercises in the East China Sea just north of Taiwan.

20 The House of Representatives defeats, 321 to 107, a bill to revoke China's MFN status.

21 In Geneva, China and Iran win a campaign to deny five U.S. organizations accreditation to attend the UN women's conference because of their vocal criticism of human rights abuses.

China fires four test missiles off its southern coast, about 85 miles north of Taiwan.

27 China releases a videotape showing Harry Wu being interrogated; he is reported to have confessed to falsifying information in the two documentaries he helped to prepare on China's prison system.

28 Secretary of State Warren Christopher announces that the Clinton administration will not impose economic sanctions on China for selling missile technology to Iran and Pakistan.

30 At a summit meeting of Asian foreign ministers in Brunei, China announces that it is willing to settle its disputes over the ownership of the Spratly Islands according to international law and UN conventions.

August 1995

1 In Brunei, Secretary of State Warren Christopher and Chinese foreign minister Qian Qichen agree to further high-level talks to resolve the crisis in relations between the two countries.

August 1995 *(continued)*

2 China orders the expulsion of two U.S. air force officers after accusing them of spying.

7 The State Council announces a five-year plan to boost the status of Chinese women.

15 Five Greenpeace campaigners are detained after displaying an anti-nuclear banner in Tiananmen Square.

In its second round of military exercises this summer, China begins a ten-day exercise of test firing missiles off the northern coast of Taiwan.

17 China conducts its second nuclear test of 1995 in Lop Nor.

22 Deng Xiaoping turns 91.

23 Taiwan president Lee Teng-hui announces that he will run for president for a second term in the island's first democratic presidential elections, to be held in March 1996.

24 A Chinese court sentences Harry Wu to 15 years in prison for spying but immediately expels him from China.

25 The White House announces that Hillary Rodham Clinton will accompany the U.S. delegation, as honorary chairperson, to attend the UN-sponsored conference on women in Beijing.

28 U.S. officials announce that China is sending its ambassador back to Washington, after recalling him in June over strained relations.

30 The Forum of Nongovernmental Organizations on Women opens in Huairou County outside of Beijing.

September 1995

3 The Fourth World Conference on Women opens in Beijing.

5 Hillary Rodham Clinton addresses the Fourth World Conference on Women, speaking about the abuse of women around the world and criticizing China for trying to limit free and open discussion of women's issues during the meeting in Beijing.

6 In Huairou County, Hillary Rodham Clinton addresses the Forum of Nongovernmental Organizations on Women.

13 President Clinton meets briefly with the Dalai Lama during the Tibetan leader's longer meeting with U.S. vice president Al Gore in Washington.

15 The Fourth World Conference on Women reaches agreement on a declaration to raise economic conditions of women, to protect them from violence, and to improve their status throughout the world.

17 In a vote for seats in the Legislative Council, Hong Kong voters support pro-democracy candidates and defeat pro-Beijing candidates. China declares that it will abolish the legislature after 1997.

20 China garners support for the third consecutive year to delete from the agenda of the General Assembly a proposal to consider Taiwan's representation in the UN.

22 President Clinton nominates former senator James Sasser of Tennessee to be ambassador to China after Beijing agrees to accept him.

September 1995 *(continued)*

The White House sends a memo to the Export-Import Bank advising it of the administration's opposition to aid for the Three Gorges Dam project.

24 In Taiwan, Peng Ming-min is chosen as the opposition candidate representing the DPP in the presidential elections to be held in March 1996.

27 The United States announces that Beijing has agreed to cancel a deal to sell nuclear reactor technology to Iran.

28 A communiqué issued at the closing of a CCP Central Committee meeting announces that Politburo member Chen Xitong has been stripped of his posts on charges of corruption; two military officers are promoted—Chief of the Army's General Staff Zhang Wannian and Defense Minister Chi Haotian are made vice-chairmen of the Central Military Commission.

29 Film director Zhang Yimou is asked by Chinese authorities to cancel plans to attend the opening of the New York Film Festival after the festival's organizers refuse to drop the showing of *The Gate of Heavenly Peace,* a U.S.-made documentary on the 1989 Tiananmen crisis.

October 1995

2 At the opening of the Seventh International Anti-Corruption Conference in Beijing, President Jiang Zemin calls corruption a social disease which requires ceaseless vigilance.

9 The *People's Daily* devotes its entire front page to a 10,000-word speech, "Correctly Handle Some Major Relationships in the Socialist Modernization Drive," delivered by party leader Jiang Zemin at the September 28 closing session of the Fifth Plenary Session of the 14th CCP Central Committee meeting.

21 The United States, Japan, the European Union, and Canada agree that China falls short of meeting criteria for joining the new World Trade Organization.

24 In New York, President Clinton holds a two-hour summit meeting with President Jiang Zemin as both attend ceremonies marking the UN's fiftieth anniversary.

November 1995

12 China announces that it will not accept the boy chosen by the Dalai Lama as the reincarnation of the Panchen Lama.

16 Xinhua News Agency publishes a policy document on arms control, sharply attacking the United States, Russia, Britain, and France for their continued development of nuclear weapons.

17 China and the United States resume high-level military contacts by agreeing to an exchange of top military officers in 1996.

19 At the APEC meetings in Osaka, Japan, China announces that it will cut tariffs by an average of 30 percent on more than 4,000 imports in 1996.

21 Wei Jingsheng is formally arrested and charged with trying to "overthrow the Chinese government."

28 In a letter to the NPC, 15 dissidents issue a public appeal for the release of Wei Jingsheng.

29 Cuban president Fidel Castro begins his first visit to China to learn about market reforms.

30 The United States informs China that it has 90 days to enforce the February 1995 agreement to end copyright infringements.

December 1995

2 In legislative elections in Taiwan, the KMT faces its biggest challenge from the opposition parties; its majority is narrowed as it receives only 45 percent of the popular vote.

Ending a four-day visit to Beijing, Vietnam Communist Party chief Do Muoi agrees with Chinese leaders to restore rail transportation and to boost trade and investment between the two countries.

7 A local Beijing daily reports that former Beijing mayor (1972–78) Wu De has died.

8 Russia and China sign an intergovernmental agreement on military-technical cooperation.

13 The sedition trial of Wei Jingsheng opens in Beijing. After 5 hours, he is convicted and sentenced to 14 years in prison.

20 The World Bank reports that its investigators found no evidence to support Harry Wu's allegations that bank loans for a major irrigation project had been used to provide water to operate forced labor camps.

The first draft of a bill outlining procedures for declaring and implementing martial law is submitted to the NPC Standing Committee for examination and approval.

21 The Clinton administration announces that it will support a UN resolution accusing the Chinese government of human rights violations.

27 German reporter Henrik Bork is expelled from China for his critical reporting.

The Information Office of the State Council issues a report on "The Progress of Human Rights in China."

28 China appoints the 150-person Preparatory Committee for the Hong Kong transition.

29 The Chinese government issues rules to combat corruption, banning state-enterprise officials from setting up private businesses.

January 1996

1 China imposes sharp increases in subway and bus fares.

3 The International Olympic Committee receives an official letter from the Chinese Olympic Committee stating that it will not submit a bid to host the 2004 games.

5 The State Statistical Bureau reports that growth slowed slightly in 1995, in keeping with retail inflation, which decreased to 14.8 percent.

Human Rights Watch/Asia issues a 331-page report citing Chinese government statistics showing that more than half the children admitted to state orphanages die usually in their first year of life.

6 The United States issues a transit visa to Vice President Li Yuan-zu of Taiwan to allow his plane to refuel in Los Angeles en route to Guatemala.

16 Citing national security, the State Council forbids domestic organizations from buying economic information that originates from abroad.

January 1996 *(continued)*

The U.S. State Department reports that the Chinese government has demanded the recall of an American military attaché who was detained for 19 hours on January 11. The Japanese government is also told to recall one of its military attachés.

19 China frees dissident Liu Xiaobo after holding him for more than seven months in police custody without formal charges. He had been detained while attempting to deliver a copy of a petition to Western news organizations.

22 UNICEF announces that it will train workers and help set management standards for Chinese orphanages.

23 President Jiang Zemin promotes four senior military officers to full generals.

24 In an address at a national meeting of Propaganda Department directors, party leader Jiang Zemin seeks to silence critics and attack deviations from socialist ideology, urging a new commitment to "spiritual civilization."

26 China buys 77.2 million bushels, or 2.1 million metric tons, of U.S. wheat.

Taiwan newspapers report that a U.S. aircraft carrier passed through the Taiwan Strait on December 19, 1995.

30 Premier Li Peng warns that any move toward formal independence on the part of Taiwan will trigger a military attack.

31 The U.S. warship *Fort McHenry* visits Shanghai.

February 1996

2 Li Peiyao, deputy chairman of the Standing Committee of the NPC, is killed during an attempted robbery of his home in Beijing, allegedly by one of his guards.

3 An earthquake in southwestern Yunnan Province kills over 200 and injures 14,000.

4 China issues a new set of rules to regulate Internet use, requiring that any network that offers Internet services be subject to close supervision by the Ministry of Posts and Telecommunications.

7 U.S. administration officials acknowledge a new intelligence report that China sold sensitive nuclear weapons technology to Pakistan in 1995, thus possibly facing billions of dollars in economic sanctions under U.S. law.

The *New York Times* reveals that as part of a secret deal Russia has provided the Chinese air force with 72 high-performance fighter jets.

9 The Taiwan Ministry of Defense announces that China has begun to move troops to the coastline facing Taiwan.

10 In a speech at a campaign rally, Taiwan president Lee Teng-hui emphasizes the need for peace.

James Sasser arrives in Beijing to take up the post of U.S. ambassador.

15 In anticipation of Chinese military maneuvers, Taiwan leaders visit frontline troops on Quemoy and Matsu.

February 1996 *(continued)*

In the second commercial satellite launching accident in just over a year, a Chinese rocket carrying an Intelsat satellite explodes minutes after liftoff from Xichang Satellite Launch Center in Sichuan Province.

17 Xinhua News Agency conveys Deng Xiaoping's greetings for the Lunar New Year.

26 Major General Ba Zhongtan, commander of the People's Armed Police Force and President Jiang Zemin's political ally, resigns, reportedly for negligence in the murder of Li Peiyao.

27 Clinton administration officials confirm that they have privately asked China to limit shipments of nuclear technology abroad in exchange for waivers of some of the economic sanctions being considered to punish China for such shipments in 1995.

28 The Clinton administration asks the U.S. Export-Import Bank to hold up $10 billion in loans to China for at least one month while the United States considers sanctions for Beijing's sale of nuclear technology to Pakistan.

March 1996

4 In Hong Kong, British prime minister John Major seeks to boost the morale of the colony's citizens by promising visa-free access to Britain and scrutiny of Chinese policy toward Hong Kong after the 1997 takeover.

5 China announces that it will hold missile tests at sea between March 8 and 15, in an area just off the coast of Taiwan.

In his speech to the opening of the Fourth Session of the Eighth NPC, Premier Li Peng stresses the expansion of agriculture, streamlining of industrialization, strengthening of international relations, and promotion of socialist ethics.

6 The U.S. State Department's annual report on human rights accuses China of "widespread and well-documented human rights abuses," stating that the fundamental premise of U.S. policy toward China—that economic and trade links will lead to greater individual freedoms—appears to be invalid.

8 China test fires two surface-to-surface missiles into the sea off the coast of Taiwan.

10 Secretary of State Warren Christopher announces that the United States is ordering two aircraft carriers and other warships to move closer to the island of Taiwan.

11 A Chinese spy satellite launched in October 1993 falls into the earth's atmosphere, disappearing probably into the ocean.

12 China begins naval and air force exercises with live ammunition in the Taiwan Strait.

15 China reveals plans for a new round of ground, sea, and air maneuvers northwest of Taiwan for the week of March 18–25.

17 The Fourth Session of the Eighth NPC closes with the adoption of the "Outline of the Ninth Five-Year National Economic and Social Development Plan and the Long-Term Target for 2010" and amendments to the Criminal Procedure Law of the People's Republic.

March 1996 *(continued)*

19 The United States approves an arms sale to Taiwan.

20 China ends its live military exercises and missile tests in the Taiwan Strait.

22 The United States calls off a visit to Washington by Defense Minister Chi Haotian and extends the freeze on new financing of business deals in China by the Export-Import Bank.

23 Taiwan holds its first free election for president. KMT candidate Lee Teng-hui receives 54 percent of the vote; DPP candidate Peng Ming-min receives 21.12 percent of the vote.

24 The Hong Kong Preparatory Committee votes 148 to 1 to scrap the elected legislature and install an appointed body after the 1997 takeover.

In conciliatory gestures, China calls for a meeting between Taiwan president Lee Teng-hui and PRC president Jiang Zemin and for opening direct air, shipping, and mail links.

31 On the deadline for Hong Kong residents to obtain applications for British passports, protesters in the colony, numbering in the hundreds, denounce China for its attempts to reverse democratic reforms in Hong Kong.

Chinese public security officials cancel a program to be held by foreigners in Beijing to raise funds for Chinese orphanages.

The Taiwan Ministry of Defense announces that it will conduct its own war games on the island of Matsu.

April 1996

2 Taiwan announces that it will postpone for three months the live-fire military exercises on Matsu Island.

10 In a visit to France, Premier Li Peng places a $1.5 billion order for ten Airbus jets.

14 Students in Hong Kong disrupt a stage-managed meeting to solicit public views on the establishment of the local government after 1997.

15 China announces new rules, effective immediately, to put foreign news organizations that publish economic information under tighter government control.

The Clinton administration endorses a new South Korean proposal for joint negotiations with North Korea and China to produce a formal peace treaty to mark the close of the Korean War (1950–53).

19 China rejects the U.S. plan for talks on the future of the Korean peninsula.

23 In Geneva, China succeeds in blocking a draft resolution by the UN Commission on Human Rights expressing concern over Chinese violations of human rights.

25 On the second day of his second trip to Beijing, Russian president Boris Yeltsin signs 13 trade and diplomatic agreements aimed at achieving closer ties between the two countries.

29 Student leader Liu Gang, number three on the wanted list after the 1989 crackdown, flees China and arrives in the United States.

April 1996 *(continued)*

30 China's central bank announces the first cut in interest rates since 1993, signaling success in bringing inflation under control.

In a report to Congress, the Clinton administration cites China's blatant failure to control piracy of U.S. products.

May 1996

6 A U.S. official confirms that a U.S. customs agent had been allowed to visit a prison factory in Shanghai on April 21.

7 Clinton approves a plan for sanctions on Chinese exports to the United States if Beijing does not begin closing down factories illegally copying U.S. goods.

9 Former alternate Politburo member, vice-premier of the State Council, and director of the Propaganda Department, Lu Dingyi, dies in Beijing at age 90.

10 In return for China's pledge not to sell nuclear technology to countries developing nuclear arms, the Clinton administration decides not to punish China for sales to Pakistan in 1995. The United States will proceed with the financing of pending business deals with China.

15 The United States publishes a list of Chinese goods that will be subject to trade sanctions on June 17 if Beijing does not close factories that pirate U.S. goods.

20 In his inaugural address, Taiwan president Lee Teng-hui announces his willingness to travel to China to open a top-level dialogue with Chinese communist leaders.

President Clinton announces a one-year renewal of China's MFN status.

21 China reports that nine Muslim guerrillas were killed on May 2 during religious and ethnic unrest in Xinjiang.

22 In San Francisco, federal agents arrest representatives of two Chinese state-owned companies in the United States on charges of smuggling 2,000 AK-47 rifles into the United States.

27 Bao Tong, the most senior official to be jailed for backing the 1989 democracy movement, is released from prison after serving seven years for leaking state secrets and counterrevolutionary propaganda and incitement, but he is immediately detained by the police in a government guest house.

30 The U.S. Export-Import Bank refuses to finance the Three Gorges Dam project, citing environmental concerns.

31 Separatist unrest is reported in Xinjiang and Tibet.

In an interview with CNN, Lu Ping, director of the PRC's Hong Kong and Macao Affairs Office, says that Hong Kong will face some restrictions on press freedom after 1997.

June 1996

4 In front of the Xinhua News Agency in Hong Kong, thousands of protesters join in a rally to commemorate the 1989 Beijing massacre.

June 1996 *(continued)*

6 China announces it will drop its insistence on carrying out "peaceful" nuclear explosions, thus removing a major obstacle to the signing of a comprehensive nuclear test-ban treaty.

8 Despite ongoing negotiations for a nuclear test ban, China conducts its 44th nuclear test since 1964.

9 Democracy activist Ren Wanding is released after serving seven years in prison for accusing the Chinese government of human rights abuses.

12 A classified U.S. intelligence report reaffirms that Pakistan has obtained medium-range ballistic missiles made in China.

In a crackdown on separatist movements in Xinjiang, Muslim religious activities outside of mosques are banned.

16 The Ministry of Justice approves the opening of 16 offices by foreign international law firms.

17 At a Beijing press conference U.S. trade representative Charlene Barshefsky reports that China has agreed to a new crackdown on copyright piracy of U.S. products, thus averting a trade war with the United States. The United States withdraws its threat of punitive sanctions.

26 The House of Representatives votes 286 to 141 to reject an effort to disapprove of President Clinton's decision to renew China's MFN status.

Chinese courts convict 1,725 on charges of drug trafficking and sentence 769 to death.

July 1996

1 In a speech celebrating the 75th anniversary of the founding of the Chinese Communist Party, General Secretary Jiang Zemin calls for a renewed emphasis on ideology.

In a move to overhaul its banking system, attract foreign capital, and move toward full convertibility of the yuan, China allows foreign companies to buy and sell foreign currency freely at designated banks and removes obstacles to taking profits out of the country.

5 Dissident Tibetan monk Kelsang Thutop, 49, is reported to have died in Drapchi Prison in Lhasa while serving an 18-year sentence for political subversion.

10 U.S. national security adviser Anthony Lake ends talks in Beijing, setting the stage for future reciprocal state visits for President Jiang and President Clinton.

14 Members of the Japan Youth Federation erect a lighthouse on the Diaoyu Islands in the East China Sea as a symbol of Japan's claim over the territory.

18 The U.S. Commerce Department reports that the trade deficit with China rose to $10.88 billion in May, a 13.2 percent increase over the previous month.

The Ministry of Civil Affairs reports that owing to flood waters nearly 4 million people have been cut off, 810,000 homes have collapsed, and 2.8 million homes have been damaged in eight provinces. The death toll tops 1,100.

July 1996 *(continued)*

24 Meeting in Jakarta, Secretary of State Warren Christopher and Foreign Minister Qian Qichen agree to an exchange of high-level visits. Christopher will visit Beijing in November.

29 Beijing conducts what it promises will be its last nuclear test. Later in the day, in meetings in Geneva to negotiate a global treaty to ban nuclear tests, China wants limits to treaty provisions that would allow international inspections at nuclear sites.

August 1996

7 The U.S. State Department agrees to grant a transit visa to Taiwan's vice president to stop off in New York en route to the Dominican Republic and on his return to Taipei.

In Geneva, China agrees to support the global ban on nuclear explosions.

8 In a petition letter addressed to CCP General Secretary Jiang Zemin and the Standing Committee of the Politburo, 56 leading cultural figures urge the preservation of the cultural treasures near the site of the Three Gorges Dam.

20 The U.S. Commerce Department reports a decrease in the U.S. trade gap for June, but for the first time China surpasses Japan as the largest source of the U.S. trade deficit.

22 Deng Xiaoping turns 92.

23 Despite protests from China, the U.S. Defense Department notifies Congress of plans to sell Stinger missiles and other weapons to Taiwan.

25 The U.S. government expresses renewed suspicions that China is helping Pakistan build a medium-range-missile factory.

27 Chinese Foreign Ministry officials say China will be willing to meet representatives of Hong Kong's Democratic Party if they agree to accept Hong Kong's return to Chinese sovereignty.

September 1996

6 In a move to prevent scandals, authority over the country's two stock exchanges is removed from local governments and placed under the China Securities Regulatory Commission.

9 Members of the Japan Youth Federation set out from Okinawa Prefecture to the Diaoyu Islands to rebuild the lighthouse which was tilted during a typhoon.

10 China begins censoring the Internet by blocking access to more than 100 Web sites of U.S. news media, the Taiwan government, and human rights groups.

20 For the fourth consecutive year China and its supporters block an attempt to have the General Assembly consider UN membership for Taiwan.

26 Hong Kong activist David Chan drowns after jumping into the East China Sea during a protest against Japanese claims to the Diaoyu Islands.

29 Former PRC minister of foreign trade Li Qiang dies in Beijing at the age of 91.

30 Premier Li Peng demands that Japan back off its claim to the Diaoyu Islands.

September 1996 *(continued)*

Democratic activists Liu Xiaobo and Wang Xizhe issue a statement urging freedom of religion, the press and speech, demanding that President Jiang Zemin be impeached for violating the constitution, and calling for talks on Tibet between the Chinese authorities and the Dalai Lama.

October 1996

2 In his final policy address to the Hong Kong legislature before the Chinese takeover next summer, Governor Chris Patten denounces China's efforts to change Hong Kong's political system.

7 One of the two surviving members of the Gang of Four, Yao Wenyuan, is released from prison after serving a 20-year term.

8 Dissident Liu Xiaobo is detained and ordered without trial to serve three years in a labor camp.

10 A four-day plenary session of the CCP Central Committee closes with the release of a communiqué calling on China to raise its level of "socialist spiritual civilization" and to be on guard against influences from the West.

11 After being detained for almost 17 months, student leader Wang Dan is formally charged with conspiracy to overthrow the government.

15 Dissident Wang Xizhe arrives in the United States after escaping China through Hong Kong.

PRC foreign minister Qian Qichen, in a Hong Kong interview, warns that after the transfer of sovereignty annual demonstrations commemorating the 1989 Tiananmen massacre will be illegal and that the press will not be allowed to "put forward personal attacks on Chinese leaders."

Assistant Secretary of State for East Asian Affairs Winston Lord meets with Chinese officials in Beijing to discuss deteriorating bilateral relations.

16 Health officials in Beijing report an estimated 50,000 to 100,000 people in China are infected with the HIV virus.

CIA Director John Deutch ends a three-day, supposedly secret visit to China to discuss weapons proliferation.

21 Cultural Revolution radical leader Wang Li dies in Beijing at the age of 75.

24 Chinese officials acknowledge that a common Chinese blood product produced by a military-run factory was contaminated with the AIDS virus.

25 The Chinese Foreign Ministry protests the decision of the European Parliament to award the 1996 Sakharov Freedom of Thought prize to imprisoned dissident Wei Jingsheng.

26 Chief Secretary Anson Chan, Hong Kong's top civil servant, withdraws her name as a candidate for the position of the new chief executive after Hong Kong's handover to China on July 1, 1997.

30 A Chinese court finds 27-year-old student leader Wang Dan guilty of trying to subvert the government and sentences him to 11 years in prison.

November 1996

3 Over 3,000 demonstrators march on China's Xinhua News Agency in Hong Kong to protest the sentencing of political dissident Wang Dan.

November 1996 *(continued)*

6 Dissident Chen Ziming is released on medical parole from a 13-year prison sentence for his participation in the 1989 Tiananmen protests.

10 China threatens to ban imports by December 10 of American fruit, beverages, and other goods in retaliation for a $19 million U.S. penalty levied on China in September for shipping goods through third countries to avoid quotas.

14 The First Intermediate People's Court of Beijing Municipality finds Zhou Beifang, former assistant general manager of Shougang Corporation, guilty of offering and taking bribes involving more than nine million yuan. Zhou is sentenced to death, which may be commuted to life in prison depending on his behavior and attitude during a two-year stay of execution.

19–21 U.S. secretary of state Warren Christopher visits Beijing.

24 Jiang Zemin meets President Clinton at the APEC meeting in Manila. They agree to a future exchange of presidential visits.

26 Disney executives reveal that Chinese officials have warned that the company's role in the filming of the movie *Kundun* about the life of the exiled Dalai Lama could have unspecified consequences for Disney's planned expansion in China.

27 President Nelson Mandela of South Africa shifts diplomatic ties to Beijing and downgrades relations with Taiwan.

30 During President Jiang Zemin's visit to New Delhi, India and China sign a military agreement pledging not to attack each other across a disputed stretch of border and to pull back an unspecified number of troops from the area along the Himalayas.

December 1996

9 U.S. defense secretary William Perry meets with Chinese defense minister Chi Haotian in Washington; they agree to a modest expansion of military contacts between the United States and China.

11 Pro-China businessman Tung Chee-hwa is chosen as the chief executive of Hong Kong after July 1, 1997.

22 In Shenzhen, China's 400-member Selection Committee names 60 pro-Beijing leaders to an interim legislature to take the place of the democratically elected Legislative Council of Hong Kong after the return of sovereignty to China.

25 A sophisticated bomb, detonated by remote control, explodes outside a Lhasa government office in Tibet.

26 Mao Zedong's 103rd birthday passes with little notice in Beijing.

Glossary

Anti-Rightist Campaign. A widespread purge and persecution of alleged counterrevolutionaries launched by Mao Zedong in 1957. The campaign occurred as a response to the Hundred Flowers Movement, Mao's effort in 1956 to solicit constructive criticism of the CCP that resulted instead in an unleashing of virulent condemnation of the chairman and the party. The anti-rightist campaign, which was meant to silence critics of the regime, affected millions of people in nearly every walk of life, but hit intellectuals particularly hard.

Asia-Pacific Economic Cooperation (APEC) forum. An organization, formed in 1989 as the result of an Australian initiative, that brings together the countries of the Asia-Pacific region (including the United States and Canada) to discuss economic issues of common concern. APEC has a small headquarters office in Singapore and holds annual ministerial-level meetings.

autarky. National economic self-sufficiency and minimal involvement in the global economy. To a large extent, Mao pursued a policy of autarky under the rubric of "self-reliance," which was dramatically reversed by Deng Xiaoping's efforts to open China's economy to the outside world.

Basic Law. The document, adopted by China's National People's Congress in April 1990, that will serve as the constitution for Hong Kong after it reverts to Chinese sovereignty on July 1, 1997. The Basic Law consists of a preamble, nine chapters, and several annexes and describes, among other things, the relationship between the Hong Kong Special Administrative Region (SAR) and the central government in Beijing, the rights and duties of SAR residents, and the structure of the SAR government.

cadre. Any person in a position of official authority or responsibility in the PRC. Top-ranking officials are cadres, as are local grassroots leaders. Not all cadres are party members; nor are all party members cadres.

Central Committee. The organization that directs party affairs when the National Party Congress is not in session. However, the large size (about 300) and infrequent meetings (called plenary sessions, or plenums) of the full Central Committee mean that real power is vested in smaller top-level party organizations like the Politburo and its Standing Committee. The general secretary of the Central Committee is the formal head of the party, the position of chairman having been abolished in 1982.

centrally planned economy. A type of socialist economic system in which government decisions rather than market forces, such as supply and demand, are the major determinants of production, prices, resource allocation, and other aspects of a nation's economy. Under Deng Xiaoping, China has moved since the late 1970s from a centrally planned economy to what is now called a "socialist market economy" that combines both planning and market forces, with the latter playing an increasingly large role.

Central Military Commission (CMC). There are, in theory, two separate Central Military Commissions, a state CMC and a party CMC. According to the PRC constitution, the state CMC commands the nation's armed forces and is responsible to the National People's Congress. In practice, the state CMC is firmly under CCP control. Although the precise relationship between the two CMCs is ambiguous, they have complete personnel and functional overlap.

Chen Yun (1905–1995). One of China's top political leaders for many decades. Chen was an architect of the PRC's Soviet-style First Five-Year Plan (1953–57) and was influential in restoring order to the economy after the disastrous Great Leap Forward (1958–60). Although at times a close associate of Deng Xiaoping, he became a critic of market-oriented economic reform and was considered to be a leader of the conservative faction within the CCP.

Chiang Ching-kuo (1910–1988). Late president of the Republic of China (ROC) on Taiwan and head of the Kuomintang. The son of longtime Kuomintang leader, Chiang Kai-shek (1887–1975), Chiang Ching-kuo became premier of the ROC in 1972 and president in 1978. In the last two years of his life, he initiated many domestic political reforms and conciliatory policies toward mainland China.

China International Trust and Investment Corporation (CITIC). A gigantic quasi-official conglomerate made up of numerous affiliated enterprises in China and around the world. Its holdings include banks, factories, real estate, trading companies, power stations, mines, and railways. CITIC was established in the late 1970s by Rong Yiren (b. 1916), who is known as the "red capitalist" because of his great success as a business executive and his support of government policies. Rong, who comes from a family of prominent prerevolution industrialists, is currently the vice president of the PRC, the first noncommunist to hold such a high state position.

Chinese Communist Party (CCP). The ruling party of the People's Republic of China. The CCP was founded in 1921 and won national power in 1949 after defeating the Kuomintang in a civil war that had lasted more than two decades. In the mid-1990s, the party had about 57 million members.

communes (or people's communes). The system of agricultural organization in China for much of the Maoist era. Communes were huge rural communities that were in charge of production and nearly all other aspects of life in the countryside. The commune system, which emphasized socialist values such as collectivism and equality, was dismantled in the 1980s after Deng Xiaoping came to power and replaced by the profit-driven household responsibility system.

Confucianism. A social philosophy based on the teachings of Confucius (c. 551–479 B.C.) and his disciples and interpreters. Confucianism stresses hierarchy and harmony in human relations, deference to one's superiors, benevolence to one's inferiors, and the primacy of the group (family, state, and society) over the individual. Confucianism, which still exerts a strong influence on the cultures of East Asia, was the core of the ideology that legitimized imperial China's autocratic political order and its patriarchal and highly stratified society.

Cultural Revolution. A decade of political turmoil initiated by Mao Zedong in 1966 to stop what he considered to be China's drift away from socialism and toward capitalism. The first stage of the Cultural Revolution (1966–69) was marked by the radicalism of the Red Guards, millions of high school and university students who took it as their mission to purge China of all ideologically impure influences. The latter phases of the Cultural Revolution focused mostly on intense intraparty struggle among rival CCP leaders and factions.

Dalai Lama. The title of the spiritual and temporal leader of Tibetan Buddhism. The current Dalai Lama (b. 1935)—the 14th in a line traced back to the 16th century—fled Tibet after the Chinese invasion in 1959. He lives in exile in India and was awarded the Nobel Peace Prize in 1989.

Deng Xiaoping (b. 1904). China's "paramount" leader since 1978. Deng won international respect for introducing market-oriented reforms in China after the end of the Cultural Revolution—although his reputation and popularity both at home and abroad were severely tarnished by his role in the suppression of the Tiananmen democracy movement. An old-time revolutionary, Deng was himself purged, first in 1966 and again in 1976, but returned to power shortly after Mao's death. He has never held any of the very top party or government positions, his highest posts being vice-chairman of the CCP and vice-premier of the PRC; his authority has been exercised through more informal means, including his deep personal ties to many of the country's most senior political and military leaders. In November 1989, Deng retired from his last formal post as chairman of the party's Central Military Commission. By the mid-1990s, increasing infirmity had basically removed him as a source of active influence in Chinese politics, unleashing the first stages of a power struggle among potential successors.

Great Leap Forward. A utopian campaign, begun in 1958, to promote rapid economic development and to move China from socialism into the more egalitarian stage of communism. The Great Leap was premised on a strategy of mass mobilization and ideological incentives that represented a profound break with the more conservative Soviet model of socialist development. By the time the Leap was halted in 1960, it had led to economic disaster for China and contributed to a famine that claimed millions of lives.

guanxi. A Chinese term that literally means "connections" and refers more broadly to the personal ties between individuals based on such things as a common birthplace, shared educational or military background, or mutual acquaintances. *Guanxi* play a major role in politics and economics in China, Taiwan, and other Chinese cultural areas.

Hong Kong. A British colony that borders China's Guangdong Province. Britain initially gained control of parts of Hong Kong in the mid-19th century through treaties forced upon the Chinese in the aftermath of the Opium Wars. Part of Hong Kong (the New Territories) was leased by China to Britain in 1898 for 99 years. The anticipated expiration of that lease set in motion Sino-British negotiations that culminated in the agreement to return all of Hong Kong to Chinese sovereignty on July 1, 1997. After that time, Hong Kong will become a Special Administrative Region of the PRC.

household responsibility system. The system of agricultural organization in China since the early 1980s. Decisions concerning farm production are made by individual households that contract land from their village rather than by a collective or the government. Households may keep or sell as they see fit most of what they produce and are also responsible for any losses they may incur.

Jiang Zemin (b. 1926). Former mayor and party secretary of Shanghai who replaced Zhao Ziyang as general secretary of the CCP in June 1989 in the aftermath of Tiananmen. In November 1989 he took over from Deng Xiaoping as chairman of the party's Central Military Commission and in March 1993 became president of the People's Republic of China. Deng has designated Jiang as his choice to be the core of the leadership that will run the country after his death.

Kuomintang (Nationalist Party, KMT). The governing party in Taiwan. Organized in 1912 by Sun Yat-sen, the KMT became a major political force in China during the first half of the 20th century. In 1928 Chiang Kai-shek became chairman of the KMT and head of the ROC government in Nanjing, and he remained the leader throughout the civil war. In 1949 the KMT government on the mainland collapsed; Chiang and his followers retreated to Taiwan.

Lee Teng-hui (b. 1923). The first native Taiwanese to become president of the Republic of China (ROC) on Taiwan and head of the Kuomintang. Lee is an agricultural economist with a Ph.D. (1968) from Cornell University. He was mayor of Taipei (1978–81), governor of Taiwan Province (1981–84), and vice president of the ROC (1984–88). In 1988, he succeeded to the presidency after the death of Chiang Ching-kuo. As president, Lee furthered the democratization of Taiwan's political system begun by his predecessor. He was reelected in March 1996 in the island's first free presidential election.

Li Peng (b. 1928). China's premier and member of the Standing Committee of the CCP's Politburo. Li became premier in 1988, succeeding Zhao Ziyang. He is a hydroelectric engineer by training and studied at the Moscow Power Institute in the 1950s. Considered to be among China's most conservative leaders, Li played a major role in the suppression of the Tiananmen democracy movement.

Li Ruihuan (b. 1934). One-time carpenter and former mayor of Tianjin, now a member of the Standing Committee of the Politburo and chairman of the Chinese People's Political Consultative Conference. Li is in charge of the CCP's ideological and propaganda work. He is considered a moderate reformer in the Chinese political system.

Liu Huaqing (b. 1916). The oldest and the only military member of the CCP Standing Committee. Liu joined the communist Red Army in 1930 and was one of the founders of the Chinese navy after the establishment of the PRC in 1949. He studied at a military academy in the Soviet Union in the mid-1950s. He is also a vice-chairman of the Central Military Commission and a strong supporter of the modernization of China's armed forces.

Mao Zedong (1893–1976). Paramount leader of the Chinese Communist Party for nearly four decades until his death in October 1976. Mao led the CCP to victory against the Kuomintang in the Chinese civil war that culminated in the founding of the PRC in October 1949. In addition to his position as chairman of the CCP (which he held until his death), Mao also served as president of the PRC from 1949 until 1959.

May 4th Movement. A movement for radical change in China that was sparked by a student-led protest on May 4, 1919, against the provision of the post–World War I Versailles Treaty to give Germany's possessions in China to Japan rather than return them to China. These anti-imperialist protests gave rise to much broader demands for a thorough political, social, and cultural transformation of the nation.

most favored nation (MFN). An agreement in which two countries promise to extend to each other the same trading terms that either of them grants to any other countries: that is, each nation that is party to the agreement will be treated in the same way as the nation "most favored" by the other party. The United States extended MFN status to China in 1980, which had the effect of greatly reducing the tariffs imposed on Chinese goods exported to the U.S. (especially textiles). In the aftermath of Tiananmen, the U.S. Congress and President George Bush became locked in an annual battle over whether China's MFN status should be renewed; many members of Congress believed that human rights abuses by the PRC warranted revocation, while Bush argued that change in China was best promoted by maintaining trade and other kinds of Sino-American interchange. President Bill Clinton renewed China's MFN status for one year in June 1993, but warned that future renewals would depend on improvement in China's human rights record. The following year Clinton "delinked" trade and human rights, leading to an unconditional renewal of China's MFN status in 1994, 1995, and 1996.

National People's Congress (NPC). The national legislature of the PRC, which, according to the constitution, is "the highest organ of state power" in China. The NPC consists of nearly 3,000 delegates elected for five-year terms by lower-level people's congresses; it meets annually for about two weeks. The NPC elects the president and vice president of the PRC, the State Council, the Central Military Commission, and the government's top judicial officials. When the NPC is not in session, its business is carried out by a 134–member Standing Committee. Although it still operates under the watchful eye of the Chinese Communist Party, the NPC has become increasingly active and influential as a policymaking body and forum for debate.

open policy. A development strategy adopted in 1978 by the Chinese government based on active participation in the world market. Under this policy, the government has sought to increase trade, technology transfer, and foreign direct investment, become more active in international organizations, and encourage study and training abroad.

Party Congress. According to the party constitution, the National Party Congress is the supreme authority in the CCP. But it is held only once every five years and attended by about 2,000 delegates. Thus its actual functions are largely limited to ratifying decisions taken by more elite party organizations and listening to reports by top party leaders. The First Party Congress marked the party's formal founding in 1921. The 14th Party Congress met in October 1992, and the 15th is scheduled for the fall of 1997.

Peng Zhen (b. 1902). One of the few surviving party "elders." Peng was party chief in Beijing Municipality before he was purged as a "capitalist roader" during the Cultural Revolution. He was rehabilitated in 1979 after Deng Xiaoping's consolidation of power and thereafter became head of the National People's Congress, a post that he held until 1987.

People's Armed Police (PAP). An armed component of the civilian police under the supervision of the Ministry of Public Security, with particular responsibility for guarding public buildings and officials and, when needed, quelling serious social unrest. It was created from units of the People's Liberation Army in 1983 and had more than half-a-million troops as of the mid-1990s.

people's congresses. A system of supervisory and (to a limited extent) policymaking state (not party) organs at various levels of the PRC's political system. Deputies to lower-level people's congresses (e.g., county level) are directly elected by their constituents, whereas those at higher levels (e.g., provinces and large cities) are indirectly elected by the people's congresses at the next lowest level.

***People's Daily*. See *Renmin Ribao*.**

People's Liberation Army (PLA). The armed forces of the People's Republic of China, including the army, the navy, and the air force. The size of the PLA is estimated to be over 3 million, not including reserves.

People's Republic of China (PRC). Founded by the CCP under the leadership of Mao Zedong on October 1, 1949, following the communist victory over the Kuomintang in the Chinese civil war.

Politburo. Elected by the Central Committee, the Politburo (or Political Bureau) handles the daily running of the CCP and makes the party's major policy decisions. Greatest power resides in its seven-member Standing Committee.

procurator-general. The head of the procuratorate, a nationwide system of state organizations charged with overseeing the administration of justice in the Chinese legal system. The procuratorate has a wide range of functions, including investigating criminal cases, issuing indictments, and serving in the courts as both public prosecutor and public defender. It also acts as a legal check on bureaucratic corruption and police abuse. It is guaranteed independence from outside interference in the PRC constitution, but, like all state organs, is ultimately under the control of the CCP.

Public Security Bureau (PSB). China's principal law enforcement organization, with branches throughout the country that operate under the supervision of the Ministry of Public Security. The PSB is responsible for the maintenance of law and order, the investigation of crimes, and the surveillance of Chinese citizens and foreigners in the PRC suspected of being threats to state security. The Ministry of Public Security maintains its own system of labor reform camps.

purchasing power parity (PPP). An increasingly popular method of comparing production and income levels of different nations. PPP looks at what it actually costs to buy similar goods (e.g., food, housing) in various countries to determine the real purchasing power of local currencies. Many economists feel that this gives a more accurate comparison of standards of living around the world than the more traditional method of calculating gross national product per capita in U.S. dollars based on official international exchange rates. According to the World Bank, China's exchange-rate-based per capita income in 1993 was only $490, whereas its PPP-based per capita income was $2,330.

Qiao Shi (b. 1924). Member of the Politburo Standing Committee since 1987. Qiao became chairman of the National People's Congress in March 1993. He has a history of work in security matters and rarely lets his political views be known, although he has recently become more outspoken in his support of economic reform.

renminbi (Rmb). Literally, "people's currency." The standard monetary unit in the PRC. Also called the "yuan." In mid-1996, one U.S. dollar was worth 8.7 Rmb.

Renmin Ribao (People's Daily). The official newspaper of the Central Committee of the Chinese Communist Party. It is distributed nationally and has a circulation of over 5 million. Articles in *Renmin Ribao* reflect official party policy, and editorials and commentaries are often used to publicize authoritative pronouncements of the party leadership.

Republic of China (ROC). The government established by Sun Yat-sen in 1912 after the overthrow of the Qing dynasty and the imperial system. The government of the ROC and its ruling party, the Kuomintang, moved to Taiwan in 1949 following the communist victory in the Chinese civil war. The ROC was recognized as the official government of China by the United States until January 1, 1979, when diplomatic recognition was switched to the PRC.

Secretariat. The organization responsible for administering the day-to-day affairs of the CCP and for supervising government agencies to make certain that they are working in accordance with party policy.

Shanghai Communiqué. The official statement issued by China and the United States on February 27, 1972, at the conclusion of U.S. president Richard Nixon's historic visit to the PRC. The communiqué set in motion the normalization of Sino-American relations after decades of cold war hostility and estrangement. In the communiqué, the PRC affirmed that the question of Taiwan was "China's internal affair," while the U.S. government acknowledged that "it does not challenge" the position that "there is but one China and that Taiwan is a part of China." The United States also noted its interest in a "peaceful settlement" of the Taiwan issue.

State Council. The executive arm of the PRC government, headed by the premier and composed of numerous ministries, commissions, and subordinate organizations.

Sun Yat-sen (1866–1925). A medical doctor (partly educated in Hawaii) who was the leader of the 1911 Revolution that overthrew China's last imperial dynasty. Sun was the first president of the Republic of China, a position he held for a little more than a month before being displaced by a warlord. His "Three Principles of the People" (nationalism, democracy, and people's livelihood) is the core of the ideology of the Kuomintang, which Sun founded in 1912 and is currently the ruling party on Taiwan.

Supreme People's Court. The pinnacle of China's multitiered "people's court" system. The Supreme People's Court supervises the work of lower-level courts, but hears few cases and does not exercise judicial review over government policies. The president of the Court is appointed by the National People's Congress.

Taiwan Strait Crises. In 1954 and 1958, China shelled several islands off its coast that were under the control of the KMT government on Taiwan. In both cases, Beijing's motives were probably more to signal its unhappiness with U.S. policy toward China and Taiwan and to show its resolve than to begin an effort to retake Taiwan. The United States responded to each crisis by sending a large naval task force to the area and making preparations for the use of tactical nuclear weapons to defend Taiwan and its offshore islands. Both crises were defused when China ceased its bombardment in order to avoid further escalation.

Three Gorges Dam. A project currently under construction on the Yangzi River in China's Hubei Province. When completed in the year 2009, it will be the world's largest dam and hydroelectric generating plant. The Chinese government claims that the project will provide the energy needed for the region's economic development and help control flooding along the Yangzi. Critics claim that the dam will seriously harm one of China's most beautiful and environmentally fragile areas and adversely affect the more than one million people who will have to be relocated. They also object to the government's heavy-handed censoring of opponents of the dam.

Tiananmen. Literally "Gate of Heavenly Peace," it forms the principal entry to the imperial palace (the Forbidden City) in Beijing that was home to China's emperors for more than five centuries before the fall of the imperial system in 1911. Tiananmen Square, to the south of the palace, is the largest (100 acres) public square in the world. Mao Zedong declared the founding of the People's Republic on October 1, 1949, from a rostrum on the gate. During the Cultural Revolution, millions of Red Guards gathered on the square to be greeted by Chairman Mao. In 1976 it was the site of mass protests against the radical Gang of Four and the huge memorial meeting held after Mao's death. In the spring of 1989 the square was the focal point for pro-democracy demonstrations that culminated in the bloody repression of June 4–5.

Tibet. Officially, an "autonomous region" of the People's Republic of China, but, in fact, firmly under the control of the Chinese state and the CCP. Tibet has been subject to Chinese authority for centuries, although it achieved a real degree of independence from about 1913 until 1950, when it was incorporated into the PRC. An abortive revolt against Chinese domination in 1959 led to a massive invasion and continuing military occupation by the PLA. The CCP claims to have liberated Tibet from a cruel feudal system and to have promoted economic development in the area. Tibetan nationalists accuse China of destroying the indigenous culture, and sporadic demonstrations for independence have been quashed by the Chinese authorities.

township and village enterprises (TVEs). Nonagricultural businesses, which operate largely according to market forces outside of the state plan, that are owned and run by local-level governments.

urban neighborhood committees. Quasi-official organizations staffed mostly by retired urban workers. They are under the leadership of the Chinese Communist Party branches of urban areas. Their main functions are to implement the party's directives and enforce the government's rules on public health, family planning, and public safety. Their exact legal status in the Chinese constitution is not clearly specified.

Wan Li (b. 1916). Now retired high-ranking CCP leader who has held many important government and party posts, including vice-premier in charge of agriculture and member of the party Secretariat. He also served as head of the National People's Congress from 1987 to 1993.

Wei Jingsheng (b. 1950). China's best-known and most persistent dissident. Wei was an electrician at the Beijing Zoo who rose to prominence because of a bold essay calling for extensive political reform that he wrote during the 1978–79 Democracy Wall movement. In 1979, he was sentenced to 15 years in prison for allegedly giving state secrets to foreigners. He was released in 1993 and almost immediately began criticizing the government for its human rights abuses. After being detained several times, Wei was formally arrested in November 1995 and a month later sentenced to 14 years in prison for sedition.

World Trade Organization (WTO). Established on January 1, 1995, as the successor to the General Agreement on Tariffs and Trade (GATT), the multilateral agreement based on principles of free trade and the market economy that had governed international commerce since 1947. The WTO is somewhat more expansive in scope than its predecessor, but like the GATT, its basic purpose is to promote nondiscriminatory trade and reduce import tariffs and other barriers to global commerce. It also provides a forum for the resolution of trade disputes. To join the WTO, a country must agree to abide by its free trade and free market principles, be certified as doing so by the WTO, and be approved by two-thirds of the existing members. As of mid-1996, there were 123 members of the WTO, not including China, which has applied for membership.

Xinhua (New China News Agency). The PRC's official domestic and international news agency.

Yan'an. An area of China's Shaanxi Province (in the country's northwest) that became the headquarters of the Chinese Communist Party in 1935 after its historic 6,000–mile Long March to escape annihilation by Kuomintang forces led by Chiang Kai-shek. Yan'an remained the CCP's main base throughout World War II and served as the focal point for communist-led resistance to the Japanese in northern China. It was at Yan'an that Mao Zedong fully consolidated his political and ideological dominance of the CCP.

Yao Yilin (1917–1994). One-time member of the CCP Politburo Standing Committee, vice-premier of the PRC, and head of the State Planning Commission. Yao was a critic of market reforms and a conservative gadfly within the party leadership.

yuan. See **renminbi.**

Zhao Ziyang (b. 1919). Premier of the State Council from 1980 until his appointment in 1987 as general secretary of the CCP. A trusted colleague and protégé of Deng Xiaoping, Zhao built a reputation at home and abroad as a capable technocratic leader and a chief architect of the post-Mao reform program. He fell from power during the democracy demonstrations in the spring of 1989 for being too sympathetic to the students and opposing the use of force to suppress the protests.

Zhu Rongji (b. 1928). Member of the CCP Politburo Standing Committee and vice-premier of the PRC. A former mayor and party chief of Shanghai who was trained as an electrical engineer, he has been given great credit for presiding over that city's economic revitalization in the 1980s. He is a strong proponent of market reforms and is often called China's "economic czar" because of his central role in economic policymaking.

Suggestions for Further Reading

Introduction: The Contradictions of Change

Baum, Richard. *Burying Mao: Chinese Politics in the Age of Deng Xiaoping* (Princeton: Princeton University Press, 1994).

Brugger, Bill and Stephen Reglar, *Politics, Economy, and Society in Contemporary China* (Stanford: Stanford University Press, 1994).

Dittmer, Lowell. *China Under Reform* (Boulder, Colo.: Westview Press, 1994).

Mackerras, Colin, Pradeep Taneja, and Graham Young. *China Since 1978: Reform, Modernisation, and "Socialism with Chinese Characteristics"* (New York: St. Martin's, 1993).

Meisner, Maurice. *The Deng Xiaoping Era: An Inquiry into the Fate of Chinese Socialism, 1978–1994* (New York: Hill and Wang, 1996).

Racing Against Time: Institutional Decay and Renewal in China

Goldman, Merle. *Sowing the Seeds of Democracy in China: Political Reform in the Deng Xiaoping Era* (Cambridge: Harvard University Press, 1994).

Huang, Yasheng. "Why China Will Not Collapse," *Foreign Policy*, no. 99 (Summer 1995).

Lieberthal, Kenneth. *Governing China* (New York: W.W. Norton, 1995).

Pei, Minxin. *From Reform to Revolution: The Demise of Communism in China and the Soviet Union* (Cambridge: Harvard University Press, 1994).

Sun, Yan. *The Chinese Reassessment of Socialism 1976–1992* (Princeton: Princeton University Press, 1995).

Tanner, Murray Scott. "How a Bill Becomes a Law in China: Stages and Processes in Lawmaking," *China Quarterly*, no. 141 (March 1995).

China's Economic Progress: Is It Sustainable?

Naughton, Barry. *Growing Out of the Plan: Chinese Economic Reform, 1978–1993* (Cambridge: Cambridge University Press, 1995).

Smil, Vaclav. *China's Environmental Crisis: An Inquiry into the Limits of National Development* (Armonk, N.Y.: M.E. Sharpe, 1993).

Tseng, Wanda, et al. *Economic Reform in China: A New Phase* (Washington, D.C.: International Monetary Fund, 1994).

Walder, Andrew, ed. *China's Transitional Economy* (New York: Oxford University Press, 1996).

World Bank. *China: Foreign Trade Reform* (Washington, D.C.: World Bank, 1994).

Yabuki, Susumu. *China's New Political Economy: The Giant Awakes.* Trans. Stephen M. Harner (Boulder, Colo.: Westview Press, 1995).

Gender Equality in China: Two Steps Forward, One Step Back

Croll, Elisabeth. *Changing Identities of Chinese Women* (London: Zed Books, 1995).

Greenhalgh, Susan. "Controlling Births and Bodies in Village China," *American Ethnologist,* Vol. 21, no. 1 (1994), pp. 3–30.

Greenhalgh, Susan and Jiali Li. "Engendering Reproductive Policy and Practice in Peasant China: For a Feminist Demography of Reproduction," *Signs,* Vol. 20, no. 3 (1995), pp. 601–641.

Honig, Emily and Gail Hershatter. *Personal Voices: Chinese Women in the 1980s* (Stanford: Stanford University Press, 1988).

Stacey, Judith. *Patriarchy and Socialist Revolution in China* (Berkeley: University of California Press, 1983).

Wolf, Margery. *Women and the Family in Rural Taiwan* (Stanford: Stanford University Press, 1972).

China's Popular Culture in the 1990s

Browne, Nick, Paul G. Pickowicz, Vivian Sobchack, and Esther Yau, eds. *New Chinese Cinemas: Forms, Identities, Politics* (Cambridge: Cambridge University Press, 1994).

Link, Perry. *Evening Chats in Beijing: Probing China's Predicament* (New York: W.W. Norton, 1992).

Link, Perry, Richard Madsen, and Paul G. Pickowicz, eds. *Unofficial China: Popular Culture and Thought in the People's Republic* (Boulder, Colo.: Westview Press, 1989).

Lull, James. *China Turned On: Television, Reform, and Resistance* (London: Routledge, 1991).

Schell, Orville. *Discos and Democracy* (New York: Pantheon, 1988).

Widmer, Ellen, and David Der-wei Wang, eds. *From May Fourth to June Fourth: Fiction and Film in 20th-Century China* (Cambridge: Harvard University Press, 1993).

Zha, Jianying. *China Pop: How Soap Operas, Tabloids, and Bestsellers Are Transforming a Culture* (New York: New Press, 1995).

Hong Kong on the Eve of Reunification with China

Cheng, Joseph Y.S., and Sonny S.H. Lo, eds. *From Colony to SAR: Hong Kong's Challenges Ahead* (Hong Kong: Chinese University Press, 1995).

Lau, Siu-Kai, and Kuan Hsin-chi. *The Ethos of the Hong Kong Chinese* (Hong Kong: Chinese University Press, 1988).

McGurn, William. *Perfidious Albion: The Abandonment of Hong Kong, 1997* (Washington, D. C.: Ethics and Public Policy Center, 1992).

The Other Hong Kong Report (Hong Kong: Chinese University Press, 1989–). (Academic alternative to government's official Hong Kong yearbook; published annually, with different editors and contributors.)

Scott, Ian. *Political Change and the Crisis of Legitimacy in Hong Kong* (Honolulu: University of Hawaii Press, 1989).

Taiwan in the 1990s: Moving Ahead or Back to the Future?

Copper, John F. *Taiwan: Nation-State or Province?* 2d ed. (Boulder, Colo.: Westview Press, 1996).

Klintworth, Gary. *New Taiwan, New China* (New York: St. Martin's Press, 1995).

Lasater, Martin L. *The Changing of the Guard: President Clinton and the Security of Taiwan* (Boulder, Colo.: Westview Press, 1995).

Rubinstein, Murray A., ed. *The Other Taiwan: 1945 to the Present* (Armonk, N.Y.: M.E. Sharpe, 1994).

Tien, Hung-mao, ed. *Taiwan's Electoral Politics and Democratic Transition* (Armonk, N.Y.: M.E. Sharpe, 1995).

Tucker, Nancy Bernkopf. *Taiwan, Hong Kong, and the United States, 1945–1992* (New York: Twayne, 1994).
Wachman, Alan M. *Taiwan: National Identity and Democratization* (Armonk, N.Y.: M.E. Sharpe, 1994).

The United States and China: Managing a Stormy Relationship

Harding, Harry. *A Fragile Relationship: The United States and China Since 1972* (Washington, D.C.: The Brookings Institution, 1992).
Lampton, David M. and Alfred D. Wilhelm, eds. *United States and China Relations at a Crossroads* (Lanham, Md.: University Press of America, 1995).
Madsen, Richard. *China and the American Dream: A Moral Inquiry* (Berkeley: University of California Press, 1995).
Ross, Robert. *Negotiating Cooperation: United States–China Relations, 1969–1989* (Stanford: Stanford University Press, 1995).
Shambaugh, David. *Beautiful Imperialist: China Perceives America, 1972–1990* (Princeton: Princeton University Press, 1991).

Internet Sources on China

The Internet is rapidly becoming a rich source for news and information about China, Taiwan, and Hong Kong. The Web sites listed below lead to a multitude of China-related Internet resources.

China Home Page. http://www.cernet.edu.cn/
China News Digest. http://www.cnd.org
Chinascape Chinese Web Index. http.//www.chinascape.org/
China-Time Internet Magazine. http://www.china-time.com/
Complete Reference to China-Related Web Sites. http://www.aweto.com/china
Finding News About China. http://www.hk.super.net/milesj/
Internet Guide to Asian Studies. http://coombs.anu.edu.au/WWWVL-Asian Studies.html
Internet Guide for China Studies. http://www.univie.ac.at/Sinologie/netguide.html

About the Contributors

Cal Clark is Professor of Political Science at Auburn University. His most recent publications are *Comparing Development Patterns in Asia* (1996), coauthored with Kartik C. Roy, and *The Role of the State in Asia: Beyond the Developmental State* (1997), coedited with Steve Chan and Danny Lam.

Nancy R. Hearst is Librarian at the Fairbank Center for East Asian Research, Harvard University.

William A. Joseph is Professor of Political Science and chair of the department at Wellesley College and Associate in Research at the Fairbank Center for East Asian Research at Harvard University. He is the author of *The Critique of Ultra-Leftism in China, 1958–1981* (1984), the editor of three previous *China Briefings*, and a coeditor of *New Perspectives on the Cultural Revolution* (1991), *The Oxford Companion to Politics of the World* (1993), and *Comparative Politics at the Crossroads* (1996).

Steven I. Levine is Senior Research Associate at Boulder Run Research in Hillsborough, North Carolina. In 1996 he served as director of the Duke Study in China Program. He has written widely on Chinese foreign policy with a special focus on Sino-American and Sino-Russian relations. He is currently at work on a book on U.S.-China relations.

Minxin Pei is Assistant Professor of Politics at Princeton University. He is the author of *From Reform to Revolution: The Demise of Communism in China and the Soviet Union* (1994) and has published numerous articles on democratization and economic reform in East Asia. His current research focuses on political development in East Asia and reforms in China's financial sector.

Suzanne Pepper is a Hong Kong-based American writer and currently a research fellow at the Institute of Asia-Pacific Studies, Chinese University of Hong Kong. She is the author of, among other things, *Civil War in China: The Political Struggle, 1945–1949* (1978) and *Radicalism and Education Reform in 20th-Century China: The Search for an Ideal Development Model* (1996).

Penelope B. Prime is Associate Professor of Economics in the Coles School of Business at Kennesaw State in the Georgia University System. She also works with the Eurasia Branch of the International Programs Center at the U.S. Bureau of the Census. Dr. Prime's recent research focuses on China's international trade and investment, and provincial-level analysis of China's economic development.

Nancy E. Riley is an assistant professor of sociology at Bowdoin College. Her research interests include issues involving gender, family, and population in modern China. She is currently involved in a project in Northeast China assessing the effects of working for wages outside the home on the power of women in their families and households.

Jianying Zha is the author of *China Pop: How Soap Operas, Tabloids, and Bestsellers Are Transforming a Culture* (1995), as well as articles that have appeared in the *Nation*, the *Village Voice*, and the *Utne Reader*. Now based in Houston, she writes a regular column for a Hong Kong magazine and has published two books of fiction in her native China.

Index

Abandoned Capital, The, literary controversy, 140–142
Administrative Litigation Law (PRC), 41–42
ADPL (Association for Democracy and People's Livelihood, Hong Kong)
 1995 elections and, 179, 180
 democratic platform of, 177
 Preparatory Committee members from, 190
Agricultural Bank (PRC), 70
Agricultural Development Bank (PRC), 70
Agriculture: PRC
 Agricultural Development Bank and, 70
 arable land decrease and, 54
 commune system dismantling and, 52, 299
 environmental issues and, 75
 grain production and, 4, 55–58
 gross output value and, 51, 52*t*
 household responsibility system and, 53–54, 57, 299, 301–302
 state-owned farmland and, 52, 268
 water supplies and, 55
Airports
 in Hong Kong, 251, 261, 272
 in PRC, 63–64
All-China Lawyers Association (PRC), 43
All-China Women's Federation (PRC), 85
Amnesty International, 229, 255
Anson Chan, 293
Anti-rightist campaign, of Mao Zedong, 297
APEC (Asia-Pacific Economic Cooperation) conference, 226–227, 262, 277, 294, 297
ARATS (Association for Relations Across the Taiwan Strait), 217, 220, 221, 258
Asia-Pacific Economic Cooperation (APEC) conference, 226–227, 262, 277, 294, 297
Association for Democracy and People's Livelihood (ADPL, Hong Kong)
 1995 elections and, 179, 180
 democratic platform of, 177
 Preparatory Committee members from, 190
Association for Relations Across the Taiwan Strait (ARATS), 217, 220, 221, 258
Automobile industry (PRC)
 foreign investment and, 73
 increase in, 64

Ba Zhongtan, 282
Bank of China (PRC), 70
Banking industry: PRC
 exchange rates and, 71–75, 249, 278
 foreign financial institutions and, 250
 loan nonrepayment and, 69, 70
 macroeconomic reorganization of, 5, 70–71
 state-owned enterprise and, 69, 75, 267
Bao Ge, 256
Bao Tong, 287
Barnett, Doak, 154, 155
Barshefsky, Charlene, 288
Basic Law of 1990, Hong Kong reunification and
 democratic aims of, 176
 Deng Xiaoping and, 167–168
 District Board members and, 165–166, 168–169
 Legco membership and, 165–166, 168–169
 outline vs. details of, 189–190
 purpose of, 7, 152, 158
 Selection Committee membership and, 190–191
 synopsis of, 297–298
Baum, Richard, 10*n*.5
Bei Dao, 136, 262

Beijing
  2000 Olympics and, 220
  city government corruption in, 13–14
  Internet service in, 66
  popular culture in, 133–134, 135–136
  UN Fourth World Conference on Women in, 79, 233, 269, 270, 273, 274, 275
Beijing Broadcasting Enterprise Bureau, 117
Beijing Film Academy, 143
Beijing Television Art Center (BTAC)
  No Choice in Loving You and, 123–124
  The Story of an Editorial Office and, 122–123
  Yearning and, 116–119
Beijing Youth Daily, 127
Beijinger in New York, 124
Bentsen, Lloyd, 250
Blue Kite (Tian Zhuangzhuang, PRC), 147
Bork, Henrik, 278
Brown, Lester, 55–58
Brown, Ron, 259
Budget Law (PRC), 71
Bush, George
  China's MFN status and, 230, 304
  Tiananmen incident and, 226

Cadre concept, 298
Capital Iron and Steel Corporation (PRC), 13, 265, 294
Castro, Fidel, 277
CCG (*China Culture Gazette*) (PRC), 128–129
CCP. *See* Chinese Communist Party (CCP)
CCTV (Central China Television, PRC), 114–115
Center for the Protection of the Rights of the Weak, of Wuhan University (PRC), 43
Central Bank Law (PRC), 38
Central China Television (CCTV, PRC)
  drama and, 114–115
  news and, 124–125
Central Military Commission (CMC, PRC), 298, 302, 304
Centrally planned economy concept, 298
CFR (Council on Foreign Relations) report, 244, 245
Chan, Anson, 293
Chan, David, 291
Chen Changben, 117, 121
Chen Kaige, 143, 146–147
Chen Li-an, 214
Ch'en Shui-pian, 212, 262
Chen Xilin, 131
Chen Xitong, 13, 268, 276
Chen Yi, 197
Chen Yun, 268, 298–299
Chen Ziming, 255, 271, 294
Chi Haotian, 16, 276, 284
Chiang Ching-kuo
  democratization under, 198–199, 299
  Lee Teng-hui successor to, 209–210, 302
  PRC contacts under, 204–205
Chiang Kai-shek
  Chiang Ching-kuo as successor to, 198, 299
  KMT and, 302, 311
  political repression under, 198–199
  in Taiwan, 196, 302
China Briefing, 1990 (Ching), 158
China Business Times (PRC), 128
China Culture Gazette (CCG) (PRC), 128–129
China Daily newspaper, 255
China on the Eve of Communist Takeover (Barnett), 154
China Film Import and Export Corporation (PRC), 149
China Foreign Exchange Trade Network (PRC), 71
China International Trust and Investment Corporation (CITIC, PRC), 70, 299
China Internet Corporation (PRC), 66
China Lady in Manhattan, A (PRC), 140
China Securities Regulation Commission, 291
China Youth Daily (PRC), 127, 128
Chinese Communist Party (CCP, PRC)
  anti-intellectualism of, 156
  Central Committee of, 298
  changes promoted by, 2, 4
  Chen Xitong and, 13–14, 268, 276
  Chen Yun and, 299
  corruption in, 30
  culture controlled by, 111–112, 120
  economic statistics and, 259
  organizational decay of, 12, 27–28, 44–45, 47, 260, 292
  gender equality policy of, 82
    female labor force participation and, 84–85
    marriage reform and, 83
    peasant support of, 83
    village life restructuring and, 83, 87
    women members of, 87–88

Hong Kong reunification and, 152, 155–156, 193
Hundred Flowers Movement and, 297
Jiang Zemin power consolidation within, 15–19, 187, 222, 280, 289, 302
KMT power struggle and, 2, 154–155, 196, 215, 299, 302, 311
land reform policy of, 83
legal system strengthening and, 43–44
Li Ruihuan and, 303
Liu Huaqing and, 303
Long March of, 311
Mao Zedong and, 303
mass communication controlled by, 110–111
National Party Congress of, 304–305
newspaper controlled by, 126
NPC and, 37–39
Patten's reforms and, 167–168
procurator-general and, 306
public opinion regarding, 18
rural self-government and, 4, 44–48
Secretariat of, 307
Three Gorges Dam project and, 290, 309
urban neighborhood committees and, 309–310
victory of (1949), 2
Yan'an headquarters of, 311
Yao Yilin and, 263, 311
Zhao Ziyang and, 311
Zhu Rongji and, 17, 311
See also Jiang Zemin
Chinese Communist Youth League, 128
Ching, Frank, 158
Christopher, Warren
human rights issue and, 250, 253, 259
MFN status and, 231
PRC arms sales and, 273
PRC nuclear issue and, 268
Qian Qichen meetings with, 225, 227, 268, 273, 290
Sino-American relations and, 226, 294
Taiwan protection and, 283
CITIC (China International Trust and Investment Corporation, PRC), 70, 299
Clinton, Bill
PRC and
arms sales and, 238, 273, 282, 286
Chinese ambassador appointed by, 228
human rights/MFN issue and, 15, 35, 229–234, 250, 253, 256, 270, 278, 287, 288, 304
intellectual property rights issue and, 236–237, 286
Jiang Zemin and, 226–227, 262, 277, 289, 294
Korean War peace treaty and, 285
James Sasser as ambassador and, 275
Sino-American relations and, 226–227
Taiwan and
arms sales and, 255
GATT membership and, 260
Tibetan Dalai Lama and, 254, 275
Clinton, Hillary Rodham, 233, 274, 275
Commune system. *See* Agriculture: PRC
Communism
Soviet Union collapse of, 7, 36, 157
Vietnam Communist Party and, 36, 278
See also Chinese Communist Party (CCP, PRC)
Conditional engagement concept (U.S./PRC), 244–246
Confucianism, 300
Construction Bank of China (PRC), 70
Corruption: PRC
bank embezzlement and, 255
in CCP, 30
of Chen Xitong, 13–14, 268, 276
dissident trials and, 15
in law enforcement, 29
in military, 28–29
"predatory state" concept and, 21
public opinion on, 14, 18–19
of Shen Taifu, 254
state-enterprise and, 279, 287
of Wang Baosen, 13–14, 268, 272
of Zhou Beifang, 13, 265, 294
Corruption: Taiwan, 207–209
Council on Foreign Relations (CFR) report, 244, 245
Cradock, Percy, 160, 161, 163, 186
Crime rate
in PRC, 20, 32–33, 33*t*, 254, 256, 260, 261, 288
in Taiwan, 204, 254, 257
Cui Jian, 132–134
Cultural Revolution (PRC)
female labor force participation and, 85
gender equality during, 107
lessons from, 37
of Mao Zedong, 2, 156, 300
NPC during, 37
politicized mass culture of, 112
synopsis of, 300
Wang Li and, 293
women's dress styles and, 104–105
Cultural Weekend (PRC), 128–130
Culture. *See* Popular culture, in China

DAB (Democratic Alliance for the Betterment of Hong Kong), 177, 178, 192
Dai Qing, 131
Dai Xianglong, 272
Daimler-Benz (Germany), 73
Dalian Economic and Technical Development Zone (PRC), 98
Daya Bay nuclear power plant (PRC), 255
defense sites transfer and, 257
Democracy: Hong Kong. *See* Hong Kong reunification with China, Patten's reform program
Democracy: PRC
  rural self-government and, 47–48
  socialist democracy and, 187–188
Democracy: Taiwan
  under Chiang Ching-kuo, 198–199, 299
  under Chiang Kai-shek, 198–199
  corruption and, 207–209
  direct elections and, 195, 207
  international recognition conflict and, 199–201
  under Lee Teng-hui, 210, 302
  martial law termination and, 207
  national identity issue and, 195–196, 206–207, 211, 217–218
  opposition party and, 207, 209–215, 212*t*
  social issues and, 206
  See also specific parties
Democratic Alliance for the Betterment of Hong Kong (DAB), 177, 178, 192
Democratic Party (DP, Hong Kong)
  1995 election and, 178, 179
  formation of, 174
  platform of, 176–177
  reunification and, 291
Democratic Progressive Party (DPP, Taiwan)
  1994 elections and, 212, 251, 262
  1996 elections and, 213–214, 284
  evolution of, 209
  KMT and, 209, 213
  national identity issue and, 217–218
  New Party and, 213–214
  New Tide reformist faction of, 209
  Peng Ming-min and, 214, 276
  strength of, 211–212, 212*t*
  UN membership issue and, 219
Deng Lijun, 132
Deng Xiaoping
  aging of, 252, 259, 264, 274, 282, 290, 301
  Chen Yun and, 299
  cultural policy of, 112–113, 123
  Hong Kong press and, 170
  household responsibility system and, 53–54, 57, 299, 301–302
  Jiang Zemin successor to, 3, 11, 12–19, 302
  legal system enhanced under, 40–44
  newspapers and, 127
  NPC under, 37–40
  political institutions of, 3
  rural self-government under, 44–48
  socialist market economy concept of, 1, 4, 4*n.4*, 11–12, 51–52, 297, 298, 300–301
  succession to, 9–10, 10*n.5*
  Taiwan issue and, 240
  Tiananmen incident and, 225, 300
  on Western copying, 167–168, 180
  Zhao Ziyang and, 311
  Zhou family ties with, 13, 265
Deng Zhifang, 13
Deutch, John, 293
Diaoyu Islands, 289, 291
Ding Guan'gen, 187
Dissidents: PRC
  Bao Tong, 287
  Bei Dao, 136, 262
  Chen Ziming, 255, 271, 294
  control of, 52, 270, 271
  Gang of Four, 292, 309
  Gao Yu, 261
  Guo Luoji, 43–44
  Kelsang Thutop, 289
  legal actions by, 43–44
  Liu Gang, 285
  Liu Xiaobo, 269, 280, 292
  MFN trade status and, 15
  police powers and, 255
  propaganda regarding, 253
  Qin Yongmin, 251
  Wang Dan, 253, 259, 263, 266, 292, 293
  Wang Juntao, 254
  Wang Meng, 44
  Wang Xizhe, 292
  Wei Jingsheng, 15, 233, 252, 253, 254, 277, 278, 293, 310
  Harry Wu, 232–233, 271, 272, 273, 274, 278
  Xiao Bin, 252
  Xu Wenli, 266
  Yao Wenyuan, 292
  Zhang Weiguo, 43
Do Muoi, 278
Dou Wei, 134
DP. *See* Democratic Party (DP, Hong Kong)

Drama, television, in PRC, 114–124
  See also Yearning
Drug addiction, in PRC, 33, 261, 288

Eastern Time and Space (PRC), 125
Economy: Hong Kong
  1995 elections and, 182
  1995 unemployment and, 183
  business political alliances and, 183
  China trade and, 182–183
  imported labor issue and, 183–184
  social legislation and, 184
Economy: PRC
  agriculture and, 52*t*, 53–58
  centrally planned economy concept and, 298
  contract enforcement and, 42
  exchange rates and, 71–75, 249, 278
  gender equality and, 5, 97–103
  Great Leap Forward and, 2, 156, 301
  indicators of, 51–53, 52*t*, 75–77, 76*f*, 259, 279, 286
  industry and, 58–63, 62*f*
  infrastructure and
    comparative indicators of, 64*t*
    energy, 5, 66–67
    telecommunications, 5, 65–66, 264
    transportation, 5, 63–64, 279
  institutional deepening reform phase of, 36
  liberalization reform phase of, 36–37
  macroeconomic management of, 51–52
    banking and, 5, 69–71, 267
    economic crises and, 67–68
    exchange rates and, 71–72
    public finance and, 68–69
  open policy concept and, 304
  public opinion regarding, 18
  purchasing power parity and, 306
  renminbi monetary unit and, 307
  socialist market economy changes in, 1, 2, 4, 4*n.4*, 11–12, 19–20, 36, 51–53, 297, 298, 300–301
  stock exchange regulation and, 258, 291
  township and village enterprises (TVE) and, 309
  urban unemployment and, 255
  See also Inflation: PRC; United States: PRC and, economic relations between; *specific sectors of, e.g., Agriculture, Industry, etc.*
Economy: Taiwan
  1952–1989 indicators of, 196, 198, 199*t*
  1990s indicators of, 202*t*
  agricultural growth and, 198
  export-led growth of, 234
  foreign investment in, 203
  income inequality and, 196, 198, 204
  KMT role in, 154
  light industry growth and, 198
  offshore investment and, 202–203
  pollution and, 204
  PRC trade and investment and, 205
  social problems and, 204
  transition from manufacturing and, 196, 198, 201–203
Education
  in Hong Kong, 103
  in PRC, 31–32
  in Taiwan, 103
Education Law (PRC), 38
Eight Points Taiwan policy (PRC), 13*n.2*, 220, 264
Energy needs: PRC, 5, 66–67, 73
Enterprise Bankruptcy Law (PRC), 38
Environment: PRC
  automobiles and, 64
  coal use and, 66
  Three Gorges Dam project and, 67, 263, 276, 290, 309
Export-Import Bank (U.S.), 276, 282, 284, 287

Family planning program (PRC), 6, 90*t*, 93–97, 262, 265, 267, 270
Farewell My Concubine (Chen Kaige, PRC), 143, 146–147
Feder, Don, 228*n.8*
Federation of Trade Unions (Hong Kong), 170
Feng Xiaogang, 122
Films. *See* Movies
Footbinding, 79, 82
Foreign investment: PRC
  in energy sector, 67
  exchange rates and, 71–72
  foreign law firms and, 288
  foreign loans and, 73–74
  increase in, 19–20, 72–73, 75, 250
  joint ventures and, 60–61, 73, 272
  in transportation sector, 64
  See also Trade: PRC
Foreign policy: PRC. *See* Hong Kong reunification with China; Taiwan, PRC and; United States: PRC and
Foreign policy: Taiwan pragmatic diplomacy policy of, 216–217
  See also Taiwan, *specific subject*

Forum of Nongovernmental Organizations on Women (PRC), 269, 270, 275

Gang of Four (PRC), 292, 309
Gao Yu, 261
GATT (General Agreement on Tariffs and Trade), 260, 310
Gender equality: Hong Kong, 103, 184–185
Gender equality: PRC
  birth rate decreases and, 79
  economic reform consequences and, 5
    decollectivization and, 97–98
    hiring and promotion discrimination and, 5, 100–101
    male urban migration and, 101–102
    mobility and, 100
    private employment increase and, 98–99
    rural education and, 102–103
    township and village enterprises and, 101
    Western inequality and, 99
  historical context of
    CCP policy of, 82–84
    childbearing responsibilities and, 81–82
    labor force participation and, 84–85
    marriage reform and, 83–84
    patrilocal family hierarchy and, 81–82
    peasant family crisis and, 84
    peasant support of, 83
  Maoist era ideas of, 85–86
  subordination of women and, 79
    in family life, 79
    footbinding and, 79, 82
    in politics, 79
  urban vs. rural differences and, 80, 255
  vs. Western culture, 80
  women in the 1990s and
    changing images of, 104–108, 274
    child care responsibilities and, 92
    domestic power and, 92–93
    double burden of, 91–92
    dress styles and, 5, 104–105
    economic reform consequences and, 97–104
    education levels and, 5, 89, 90*t*, 91
    family planning and, 6, 90*t*, 93–97, 262, 265, 267, 270
    indicators of, 90*t*
    labor force participation and, 5, 79, 88–91, 90*t*
    marriage customs and, 91, 252
    "missing girls" phenomenon and, 5, 90*t*, 95–96
    political activities and, 87–88, 90*t*
    public appearances and, 104
    public vs. private lives and, 86–87
    sexuality expression and, 106
General Agreement on Tariffs and Trade (GATT), 260, 310
General Press and Publishing Administration (PRC), 127
Gephardt, Richard, 250
Gingrich, Newt, 272
Golden Lotus, The, 141
Gong Li, 144, 146
Gore, Al, 175
Government: PRC
  Central Military Commission (CMC) and, 298, 302, 304
  dissident trials and, 15
  institutional decay and, 3
    anti-regime activities and, 12
    conclusions regarding, 48–49
    crime rate and, 20, 32–33, 33*t*, 254, 256, 288
    education and, 31–32
    examples of, 26–31, 27*t*
    law and order and, 32–33
    loss of authority and, 12
    public health and, 31–32
    rural infrastructure and, 33–35, 33*t*, 263
  institutional renewal and, 3–4, 35–37
    conclusions regarding, 48–49
    legal system changes and, 40–44
    NPC and, 37–40
    self-government experiments and, 4, 44–48
  people's congresses concept and, 305
  power transfer within, 11–12
  "predatory state" concept and, 3, 20–21
    arbitrary fees and, 23–25, 24*n.20*, 25*n.22*
    corruption opportunities and, 25–26, 27*t*
    expenditures of, 22–23, 23*t*
    personnel excess and, 22
    political institutions of, 19–26, 22*t*, 23*t*
    revenue of, 20, 21–22, 22*t*
  procurator-general and, 306
  public legal activism in, 4
  public opinion polls regarding, 17–19
  State Council of, 308
  succession politics in, 12–19
  Supreme People's Court system of, 308
  urban neighborhood committees and, 309–310
  See also Dissidents; Political institutions: PRC; *specific individuals, political parties, organizations*

Government: Taiwan
under Chiang Ching-kuo, 198–199, 299
under Chiang Kai-shek, 198–200
corruption and, 207–209
direct elections and, 195, 207
international recognition of, 199–201
under Lee Teng-hui, 210, 302
martial law termination and, 207
national identity issue and, 195–196, 206–207, 211, 217–218
opposition party development and, 207, 209–215, 212*t*
social issues and, 206
See also Legislative Yuan (Taiwan); *specific parties*
Great Britain, Hong Kong and
citizenship issue and, 158–159, 186
democracy and, 158–159, 186
elections and, 160
Joint Declaration of 1984 and, 7, 151–152, 159, 168–169, 192
passports and, 282, 284
synopsis and, 301
See also Hong Kong reunification with China, Patten's reform program
Great Leap Forward (PRC)
Chen Yun and, 298–299
of Mao Zedong, 2, 156, 301
Great Wall Machinery and Electronic High-Technology Industrial Group (PRC), 254
Greenpeace, 274
Guangming Daily, 130
Guanxi (connections), 301
Guidelines for National Unification (Taiwan), 218
Guo Luoji, 43–44

Han Xu, 258
Hau Pei-tsun
cross-strait relations and, 221
KMT and, 214
Lee Teng-hui and, 210
UN membership issue and, 219
Have a High, Then Die (PRC), 124
He Yong, 134
Health care: PRC
decline in, 31–32, 32*n.45*
HIV virus and, 293
Helms, Jesse, 228
Hills, Carla, 216
Hong Kong
female education trends in, 103
literature of, 137, 140
movies of, 145, 146
music of, 134, 135
newspapers of, 128, 129
PRC-Taiwan trade through, 204, 205, 249
synopsis of, 301
See also Hong Kong reunification with China; Legislative Council (Legco), of Hong Kong
Hong Kong airport, 251, 261, 272
Hong Kong Alliance in Support of the Patriotic Democratic Movement in China, 162
Hong Kong General Chamber of Commerce, 185
Hong Kong reunification with China
Anson Chan and, 293
British citizenship, passports and, 158–159, 186, 282, 284
conclusions regarding, 192–194
future directions of
Basic Law outline vs. details and, 189–190
compromise solutions and, 188–189, 191–192, 194
democratic exclusion and, 190–191
Great Britain's guilt and, 186, 282
PRC socialist democracy and, 187–188
voter turnout and, 189
historical background on
Basic Law and, 152, 158, 167–168, 297–298
CCP anti-intellectualist phase and, 156
Chinese revolution stages and, 155–156
communism fear and, 153–155
Cultural Revolution and, 156
KMT vs. CCP power struggle and, 154–155
Sino-British Joint Declaration and, 7, 151–152, 159, 168–169, 192
Tiananmen Square incident and, 7, 156–157
Legco empowerment and, 181–186
"one country–two systems concept" and, 151–152
Patten's reform program: challenge of, 161, 193
1991 election and, 162–163
democratic foundation of, 163–164, 252, 269
District Boards membership and, 164–166
electoral reforms of, 7, 164–165, 257
Legco membership and, 165–166
political parties and, 7, 162

Hong Kong reunification with China (*continued*)
Patten's reform program: China's response to, 270, 271, 275
CCP opposition to, 167, 193
copying of world trends and, 171–173
Deng Xiaoping opposition to, 167–168
negation of, 168–169, 252, 259, 267, 269, 275, 284, 287, 292
polemics of confrontation and, 169–171
political struggle and rhetoric and, 173–175, 291
Preliminary Working Committee (PWC) and, 169
Preparatory Committee for, 190, 279, 284
pro-China press and, 7, 170–171, 193
Patten's reform program: implementation of 1994, 1995, election results and, 176–180, 260
Basic Law democratic aims and, 7, 165–166, 168–169, 175–176
population emigration and, 188, 282
Sino-British Joint Liaison Group on Hong Kong and, 257
Taiwan issue and, 152
Tiananmen response and, 7, 156–157
Basic Law and, 152, 158–159
British citizenship and, 158–160
democracy development and, 158–159
Eastern European upheavals and, 157–158
elections and, 158, 160–161
See also Legislative Council (Legco), of Hong Kong
Horse Thief (Tian Zhuangzhuang, PRC), 144
Hou Dejian, 133
Howe, Geoffrey, 159
Hu Hongyu, 184–185
Huang Ju, 16, 260
Huang Zhen, 227
Human Rights, UN Commission on, 233, 266, 267, 285
Human Rights and Equal Opportunities Commission Bill (Hong Kong), 185
Human rights issue: PRC
use of, 229, 250, 251, 255, 264, 268, 279, 283, 285, 288
Clinton administration response to, 230–234, 253, 278
development, social well-being status and, 229–230
international image and, 35, 258, 266, 267, 268, 285
national sovereignty response and, 229
orphanages and, 279, 280, 284
trade status and, 15, 77, 230–234, 252
Human Rights Watch, 229
Human Rights Watch/Asia, 264, 279
Hummel, Arthur, 227
Hundred Flowers Movement, 297

In the Heat of the Sun (Jiang Wen, PRC), 148
Industrial and Commercial Bank (PRC), 70
Industry: PRC
agricultural land and, 54, 57
gross value of output and, 51, 52*t*, 61, 62*f*
nonstate enterprise development and, 52
foreign investment in, 61
vs. state-owned sector, 61, 63
state-owned enterprises and, 52
banking support of, 5, 69, 75
foreign joint venture and, 60–61, 73, 272
market reforms of, 58–59
principles of, 58
productivity decline of, 5, 60
Inflation: PRC
macroeconomic management of, 67–68
banking and, 69–71
exchange rates and, 71–72
public finance and, 68–69, 263
responses to, 263, 286
Institutions. *See* Political institutions
Intellectual property rights issue (PRC/U.S.), 234, 236–237, 254, 257, 258, 263, 264, 265, 266, 277, 286, 288
International Women's Conference, of the United Nations, 79, 233, 269, 270, 273, 274, 275
Internet, in PRC, 65–66, 281, 291

Japan
Chinese citizen war reparations by, 40
Diaoyu Islands and, 289, 291
economic growth of, 234
Japan Youth Federation and, 289, 291
Nanjing Massacre and, 255
North Korea nuclear weapons and, 257
PRC nuclear issue and, 269
PRC WTO membership and, 277
Taiwan colonial policy of, 197
U.S. trade surplus and, 234, 290
Jia Pingwa, 140
Jiang Chunyun
CCP Secretariat appointment of, 16, 260
deputy premier nomination of, 39
as industry vice-premier, 267

Jiang Wen, 144, 148
Jiang Zemin
anti-corruption campaign of, 13–14, 13n, 276
Ba Zhongtan and, 282
Clinton and, 226–227, 262, 277, 294
democracy resistance and, 187, 292
as Deng Xiaoping's successor, 3, 11, 12–19
Eight Points Taiwan policy of, 13*n.2*, 220, 264
on family planning, 267
human rights issue and, 250, 253
Jiang Chunyun and, 39
Anthony Lake and, 244, 289
Lee Teng-hui and, 284
Li Peng and, 17
military appointments of, 16, 256, 280
opposition to, 16–17
power consolidation by, 15–19, 187, 222, 280, 302
Sino-Russian agreements and, 260, 278
socialist modernization of, 276, 289
Three Gorges Dam project and, 290
trade liberalization plan of, 75
U.S. relations of, 225, 226–227, 244, 262, 277, 289, 294
Jianwei Wang, 246
Jin Yong, 140
Joint Declaration of 1984 (Sino-British, Hong Kong), 7, 151–152, 159, 168–169, 192
Ju Dou (Zhang Yimou, PRC), 143, 146

Kamm, John, 232
Kantor, Mickey, 254, 265
Kelsang Thutop, 289
KMT. *See* Kuomintang (KMT)
Koo-Wang talks (PRC, Taiwan), 217, 220, 221
Kuomintang (KMT)
1994 elections and, 212, 251, 262
1995 elections and, 278
1996 elections and, 213–215, 284
business relations with, 207–208
CCP power struggle with, 2, 154, 196, 215, 299, 302, 311
DPP candidates and, 209, 213, 221
economy and, 154
Lee Teng-hui and, 210, 214, 284
national identity conflict and, 196, 210, 217
New Party (NP) formation and, 210–211
strength of, 211–212, 212*t*
synopsis of, 302
television control by, 207
Three Principles of the People concept of, 308

Labor unrest, in PRC, 20, 34
Lake, Anthony, 225, 227, 244, 289
Lampton, David, 218
Land reform
in PRC, 83, 258
in Taiwan, 198
Lau, Emily, 163
Law enforcement: PRC
Administrative Litigation Law and, 41–42
contract enforcement and, 42
corruption in, 29
criminal code changes and, 39
dissident activities and, 43–44
enhancement of under Deng, 4, 40–44
government supported by, 52
legal community growth and, 43
Lee, Allen, 179
Lee, Martin, 162, 174, 175, 190
Lee Teng-hui, 154
1996 presidential election and, 214–215, 221–222, 284, 287, 302
as Chiang Ching-kuo successor, 209–210, 302
Guidelines for National Unification of, 218
Hau Pei-tsun and, 210
Jiang Zemin and, 284
KMT and, 210, 214–215, 302
Lien Chan and, 210, 213
"pragmatic diplomacy" policy of, 216–218, 281
Six Points policy of, 220
synopsis of, 302
UN membership and, 218–220
U.S. visit of, 13*n.2*, 195, 221, 239–240, 244, 269, 270, 271, 273
Legal Daily (PRC), 255
Legal system: PRC. *See* Law enforcement: PRC
Legco. *See* Legislative Council (Legco) of Hong Kong
Legislative Council (Legco) of Hong Kong
1991 election and, 161, 162, 177
1995 economic downturn and, 182–184
1995 election and, 170–171, 172–173, 176–180, 193, 275
after 1997 elections of, 169, 275
1998 election and, 191
empowerment of, 181–186

Legislative Council (Legco) of Hong Kong *(continued)*
election reforms and, 158, 160–161, 164
equal opportunity legislation and, 184–185
imported labor issue and, 183–184
membership reforms of, 165–166
social legislation and, 184
Legislative Yuan (Taiwan)
direct election of, 195, 207
KMT's majority in, 213–214
Lien Chan and, 213–214
mainland senior legislators retirement from, 207, 210
Li Daoyu, 227, 271
Li Lanqing, 17
Li Lianying, the Imperial Eunuch (Tian Zhuangzhuang, PRC), 147
Li Peiyao, 281
Li Peng
Diaoyu Islands and, 291
French jets and, 285
human rights/trade status and, 232*n.13*, 250, 253, 258
issues facing, 266, 283
National Day speech of, 261
political future of, 16–17
synopsis of, 302
on Taiwan, 280
Li Pengfei, 179
Li Qiang, 291
Li Ruihuan, 120, 303
Li Shaohong, 148
Li Xiaoming, 117–118
Li Yuan-zu, 279
Li Zhuming, 162
Liberal Party (LP, Hong Kong), 177, 179, 185
Lien Chan, 210, 213–214
Lilley, James, 227
Lin Yang-kang, 214, 221
Literature
of Hong Kong, 137, 140
of PRC
of early 1980s, 136
of mid-1980s, 136–137
The Abandoned Capital controversy and, 140–142
kung fu novels and, 140
publishing system changes and, 137–138
Wang Shuo and, 138–140
of Taiwan, 137, 140
Liu Gang, 285
Liu Huaqing, 16, 303
Liu Huiqing, 163
Liu Xiaobo, 269, 280, 292
Liu Xiaoqing, 129
Liu Xinwu, 130
Loh, Christine, 184
Long March, of CCP (PRC), 309
Lord, Winston, 227, 228, 266, 293
LP (Liberal Party, Hong Kong), 177, 179, 185
Lu Dingyi, 286
Lu Gonghui, 184
Lu Ping, 168, 191, 269, 287
Lu Xiaowei, 117

Major, John, 161, 282
Malaysia, PRC military buildup and, 239
Mang Ke, 136
Mansfield, Mike, 228
Mao Zedong
anti-rightist campaign of, 297
autarky of, 297
commune system and, 299
Cultural Revolution of, 2, 37, 156, 300
cultural views of, 111
gender ideas of, 85–86
Great Leap Forward program of, 2, 156, 298–299, 301
Hundred Flowers Movement of, 297
Memorial Hall of, 1
power of contradictions and, 2
synopsis of, 303
Tiananmen Square and, 309
Market Research Consultancy, of Beijing, 17
Maternal and Infantile Health Care Law, 270
May 4th Movement of 1919 (PRC), 82, 303
MFN. *See* Most favored nation (MFN) trade status
Military: PRC
buildup of, 238, 239, 257, 265, 268, 293
Central Military Commission and, 298, 302
deterioration of, 28–29
factories owned by, 259
Jiang Zemin appointments to, 16, 256, 257, 280
martial law legislation and, 278
PLA and, 16, 305
Red Guards and, 300
Taiwan threatened by, 196, 221, 222, 240–241, 273, 274, 282, 283, 284
U.S. officer exchange with, 277
Military: Taiwan, 284–285
Missile Technology Control Regime (MTCR), 238

Missing girls phenomenon (PRC), 5, 90*t*, 95–96
Mondale, Walter, 228
Most favored nation (MFN) trade status, human rights issue and, 15, 35, 229–234, 232*n.13*, 250, 256, 259, 270, 273, 283, 287, 288, 303–304
Movies
  of Hong Kong, 145, 146
  of PRC, 109, 110
    audience decline and, 145
    Chen Kaige and, 143, 146–147
    "fifth generation" filmmakers and, 143–144
    financial status and, 144–145
    foreign coproductions and, 145
    foreign film importation and, 148–149
    international awards for, 143, 146
    "sixth generation" filmmakers and, 147–148
    Zhang Yimou and, 143, 144, 146, 148, 276
MTCR (Missile Technology Control Regime), 238
Music
  of Hong Kong, 134, 135
  of PRC
    classical music and, 132
    Taiwan influence on, 132
    traditional music and, 132
    Western pop music and, 132–136
  of Taiwan, 132, 134, 135
Muslims, in PRC, 252, 287, 288

Nanjing Massacre, 255
National Party Congress, 304–305
National People's Congress (NPC, PRC)
  1994 issues of, 257
  1995 issues of, 283
  Basic Law and, 297–298
  chairman Qiao Shi of, 16, 38, 306–307
  criminal code changes by, 39, 41
  Hong Kong issues and, 259, 297–298
  Jiang Chunyun and, 16, 39, 267
  legislative actions of, 38
  local candidate endorsements and, 39, 40
  martial law legislation and, 278
  Ninth Five Year National Economic and Social Development Plan and, 283
  Organic Law of the Village Committees and, 45
  Peng Zhen and, 38, 45, 305
  Premier Li Peng and, 253, 266
  public complaints to, 19, 39–40, 266
  state Central Military Commission and, 298, 304
  strengthening of, 3–4, 37–40
  synopsis of, 304
  Wan Li and, 38, 310
  women in, 87
  Wu Bangguo and, 16, 267
Nationalist Party (Taiwan). *See* Kuomintang (KMT, Taiwan)
New China News Agency (PRC), 310
  See also Xinhua News Agency
New Party (NP, Taiwan)
  1996 presidential election and, 214
  DPP and, 213–214
  formation of, 210–211
  strength of, 211, 212*t*, 213, 221
Newspapers
  in Hong Kong, 128, 129
  in PRC
    appearance of, 110
    CCP control of, 126
    of Cultural Revolution, 112
    Cultural Weekend and, 128–130
    Deng Xiaoping reforms and, 127–128
    financial problems of, 127
    increase in, 109, 125–126
    People's Daily and, 112, 126, 130, 131, 259, 276
    political repression of, 126–127, 257, 285
    tabloids and, 128–131
  in Taiwan, 128, 129
Nixon, Richard, Shanghai Communiqué and, 224, 307
No Choice in Loving You (PRC), 123–124
North Korea
  formal peace treaty and, 285
  nuclear weapons of, 254, 257, 262
  PRC and, 260
  Radio Free Asia and, 255
North Sea Fleet (PRC Navy), 29
NP. *See* New Party (NP, Taiwan)
Nuclear Nonproliferation Treaty, 268
Nuclear weapons
  of North Korea, 254, 257, 262
  of PRC, 2, 239, 252, 257, 261, 266, 268, 269, 274, 288, 290
  PRC nuclear power plants and, 255, 262
  of U.S. and European countries, 277
Nye, Joseph, 244

Olympic Games, 220, 279
One and Eight (Zhang Junzhao, PRC), 143
Opium Wars, 301
Organic Law of the Village Committees (PRC), 45

PAP (People's Armed Police), 305
Patten, Christopher
 arrival of, 163
 equal opportunity legislation and, 184–185
 Legco legislation and, 185–186
 social legislation and, 184
 as David Wilson successor, 161
 See also Hong Kong reunification with China
Peasant riots (PRC), 34
Pena, Federico, 216
Peng Ming-min, 214, 276
Peng Zhen, 38, 45, 305
People's Armed Police (PAP), 305
People's Bank of China (PRC), 70, 72, 267, 272
People's congresses, 305
People's Daily (PRC), 112, 126, 130, 131, 259, 276, 307
People's Liberation Army (PLA, PRC), 16, 305
People's Livelihood Bank (PRC), 70
People's Republic of China (PRC), 305
 cadre concept in, 298
 Castro visit to, 277
 crime in, 20, 32–33, 33*t*, 254, 256, 260
 Diaoyu Islands and, 289, 291
 earthquake in, 281
 flooding in, 289
 Hong Kong reunification with. *See* Hong Kong reunification with China
 land speculation in, 258
 North/South Korea issues and, 257, 285
 political power in, 3
 religious activity in, 251, 252
 Sino-Russian agreements and, 260, 278, 281, 285
 socialist democracy in, 187–188
 South China Seas presence of, 238, 239, 257, 258, 265, 268
 Spratly Islands and, 273
 stock exchange of, 258, 291
 Tibet issue and, 260, 287, 292, 309
 Tibetan Dalai Lama issue and, 254, 267, 269, 277, 300
 Vietnam diplomatic relations with, 278
 See also Economy: PRC; Gender equality: PRC; Government: PRC; Hong Kong reunification with China; Political institutions: PRC; Popular culture, in China; Taiwan, PRC and; United States: PRC and; *specific individuals, political parties, organizations, subjects*
Perry, William, 244, 261
Philippines, PRC military buildup and, 239, 265, 268
Politburo
 Chen Xitong expelled from, 14, 268, 276
 Huang Ju appointed to, 16, 260
 synopsis of, 305–306
Political institutions: PRC
 decay indicators and, 3, 48
  causes of, 27
  CCP corruption, 30
  CCP organizational decay, 27–28
  crime rate increase, 20, 32–33, 33*t*, 254, 256, 261
  government revenue decrease, 20, 21–22, 22*t*
  labor disputes, 20
  law enforcement corruption, 4, 29
  military deterioration, 28–29
  peasant income decrease, 20
  public goods decline, 30
  social support decline, 30, 34–35
  urban-rural income gap, 20, 20*n.11*
 renewal indicators and, 3–4, 35–37, 48–49
  legal system enhancement, 40–44
  NPC strengthening, 3–4, 37–40
  rural self-government, 4, 44–48
 See also specific parties, organizations
Political institutions: Taiwan
 under Chiang Ching-kuo, 198–199, 299
 under Chiang Kai-shek, 198–200
 corruption and, 207–209
 direct elections and, 195, 207
 international recognition conflict and, 199–201
 under Lee Teng-hui, 210
 national identity issue and, 195–196, 206–207, 211, 217–218
 opposition party development and, 207, 209–215, 212*t*
 See also specific parties
Popular culture, in China
 conclusions regarding, 149–150
 contradictions in, 6–7
 historical background on, 110–113
  CCP control of, 110–112
  Cultural Revolution and, 112, 300
  under Deng Xiaoping, 112–113
  elite intellectualism and, 113
  Tiananmen event and, 113
 lifestyle vs. revolution interest and, 109–110
 literature and, 136–143
  of early 1980s, 136
  of mid-1980s, 136–137
  The Abandoned Capital controversy and, 140–142

kung fu novels and, 140
publishing system changes and, 137–138
Wang Shuo and, 138–140
movies and, 6–7, 109, 110
audience decline and, 145
Chen Kaige and, 143, 146–147
"fifth generation" filmmakers and, 143–144
financial status and, 144–145
foreign coproductions and, 145
foreign film importation and, 148–149
international awards for, 143, 146
"sixth generation" filmmakers and, 147–148
Zhang Yimou and, 143, 144, 146
music and, 109
classical music and, 132
Taiwan influence on, 132
traditional music and, 132
Western pop music and, 132–136
newspapers and, 109, 110
CCP control of, 126
of Cultural Revolution, 112
Cultural Weekend and, 128–130
Deng Xiaoping reforms and, 127–128
financial problems of, 127
increase in, 125–126
People's Daily and, 112, 126, 130, 131, 307
political repression of, 126–127, 257
tabloids and, 128–131
television and
drama, 109, 114–124
news, 124–125
Population
of PRC, 54–55, 75, 250, 270
See also Family planning
PRC. *See* People's Republic of China (PRC)
Predatory state concept, 20–21
Preliminary Working Committee (PWC), Hong Kong Reunification and, 169, 190
Procurator-general (PRC), 306
PSB (Public Security Bureau, PRC), 306
Pu Jie, 253
Public finance, in PRC, 68–69
Public Security Bureau (PSB, PRC), 306
Purchasing power parity concept, 306
PWC (Preliminary Working Committee), Hong Kong reunification and, 169, 190
Qian Qichen
Warren Christopher and, 225, 227, 268, 273, 290
on Hong Kong reunification, 292
human rights issue and, 250, 253, 261
nuclear weapons issue and, 268
on Taiwan issue, 241
Qiao Shi
Li Peng and, 16–17
as NPC chairman, 16, 38, 306
Qin Benli, 127
Qin Yongmin, 251
Qiong Yao, 140

Radio Free Asia, 251, 255
Radio, in PRC, 109, 110, 251, 255, 256
Railroads, in PRC, 63
Raise the Red Lantern (Zhang Yimou, PRC), 143, 146
Ramos, Fidel, 265
Red Cherry (Ye Daying, PRC), 148
Red Guards (PRC), 300
Red Sorghum (Zhang Yimou, PRC), 144
Religion
Christianity, 252, 264
Confucianism, 300
Islam, 252, 287, 288
Tibetan Dalai Lama and, 254, 267, 269, 275, 277, 292, 300
Ren Jianxin, 256
Ren Wanding, 288
Renmin Ribao (People's Daily), 112, 126, 130, 131, 259, 276, 307
Republic of China (ROC). *See* Taiwan
ROC (Republic of China). *See* Taiwan
Rock 'n' Roll Kids (Tian Zhuangzhuang, PRC), 147
Rong Yiren, 299
Ross, Robert, 224, 247
Rouge (Li Shaohong, PRC), 148
Roy, J. Stapleton, 227, 269, 271
Rural life: PRC
crime rates in, 32–33, 255, 256
family planning and, 94–95, 265, 270
female education and, 102–103
health care in, 31–32
infrastructure of, 33–35, 263
irrigation projects and, 34
male urban migration from, 101–102
marriage age and, 104, 252
peasant riots and, 34
self-government experimentation and, 4, 44–48
soil erosion and, 34
subsidies paid and, 35

Rural life: PRC *(continued)*
township and village enterprises and, 101
urban-rural income gap and, 20, 20*t*
village committee roles in, 45–47
village representative assembly and, 46
Russia
PRC fighter jets to, 281
PRC trade with, 251
Sino-Russian agreements and, 260, 278, 285

Sakharov Freedom of Thought prize, 293
Sanger, David E., 232*n.13*
SAR (Special Administrative Region), of the PRC. *See* Hong Kong reunification with China
Sasser, James, 228, 275, 281
SEF (Strait Exchange Foundation, Taiwan), 217, 220, 221
Shanghai
currency exchange markets in, 71–72
Internet service in, 66
prison factory in, 286
radio stations in, 110
Shanghai Communiqué (U.S.-PRC), 224, 307
Shanghai Film Festival, 149
Shanghai Triad (Zhang Yimou, PRC), 148
Shattuck, John, 15, 250, 253
Shehui jituan xiaofei (social group consumption), 26
Shen Taifu, 254
Shigeto Nagano, 255
Shougang (Capital Iron and Steel Corporation, PRC), 13, 265, 294
Shougang Concord Grand (PRC), 13
Shougang Concord International Enterprises (PRC), 13
Shu Rongji, 272
Shu Ting, 136
Singapore
APEC headquarters in, 297
PRC joint ventures with, 61
Sino-British Joint Declaration of, 7, 151–152, 159, 168–169, 192, 194
Sino-British Joint Liaison Group on Hong Kong and, 257
Situ Hua, 162
Soong, James, 212, 213–214
South Korea
export-led economic growth of, 234
formal peace treaty and, 285
Southern Weekend (PRC), 130
Soviet Union
communism collapse in, 7, 36, 157
PRC trade with, 251
Special Administrative Region (SAR), of the PRC. *See* Hong Kong reunification with China
Spratly Islands, 273
State Administration of Foreign Exchange (PRC), 71–72
State Development Bank (PRC), 70
State-owned enterprises (PRC). *See* Industry: PRC
Stock exchange, of PRC, 258, 291
Story of an Editorial Office, The (PRC), 122–123
Strait Exchange Foundation (SEF, Taiwan), 217, 220, 221
Su Tong, 142
Sun Yat-sen, 302, 307, 308
Szeto Wah, 162, 179, 190, 194

Taiwan, 195–196
conclusions regarding, 222
crime in, 204, 254, 257
democracy and domestic politics in
1996 presidential election in, 187, 240, 274, 276
under Chiang Ching-kuo, 198–199, 299
under Chiang Kai-shek, 198–200
corruption and, 207–209
direct elections and, 195, 207, 240
international recognition conflict and, 199–201
under Lee Teng-hui, 210
martial law termination and, 207
national identity issue and, 195–196, 206–207, 211, 217–218
opposition party development and, 207, 209–215, 212*t*
social issues and, 206
See also Lee Teng-hui; *specific parties*
economic development of
1952–1989 indicators of, 196, 198, 199*t*
1990s indicators of, 202*t*
agricultural growth and, 198
export-led growth of, 234
foreign investment in, 203
income inequality and, 196, 198, 204
light industry growth and, 198
offshore investment and, 202–203
pollution and, 204
PRC trade and investment and, 205
social problems and, 204
external vs. internal pragmatic diplomacy and, 215–222
female education trends in, 103
grain consumption of, 55

growth of, 195
historical background on
Chiang Ching-kuo democratization and, 198–199, 299
economic development and, 198, 199*t*
geographic factors and, 196–197
international recognition conflict and, 199–201
islander vs. mainlander conflict and, 196, 197
as Japanese colony, 197
KMT repression and, 197, 198–199
political development and, 198–199
social development, 199*t*
PRC and
airline hijacking and, 256, 259
Association for Relations Across the Taiwan Strait and, 258
Chiang Ching-kuo and, 204–205
Eight Points policy toward, 13*n.2*, 220, 264
French jet fighters issue and, 249
independence warning and, 280
international recognition conflict and, 199–201, 215
Lee Teng-hui pragmatic diplomacy policy and, 216–217
Lee Teng-hui U.S. visit and, 13*n.2*, 195, 221, 239–240, 244, 269, 270, 271, 273
military threat and, 196, 221, 222, 239, 240–241, 273, 274, 281, 282, 283, 284
missile tests, war games and, 196, 221, 222, 240–241, 273, 282, 283, 284
national identity issue and, 217–218
one country–two systems concept and, 215–216
preoccupation with, 152, 195–196
Taiwan Strait Crises and, 308
trade and investment with, 204, 205
UN membership issue and, 218–220, 275, 291
U.S. conflict over, 77, 260
UN membership of, 200, 218–220, 271, 275, 291
U.S. and
arms sales and, 255, 271, 272, 273, 284, 290
diplomatic relations with, 216, 272, 290
PRC recognition by, 200
PRC triangular trade with, 205–206
PRC war games response by, 222, 240–241, 283
Shanghai Communiqué and, 307
trade surplus with, 201
See also Lee Teng-hui
Taiwan Relations Act (U.S.), 200, 240–241
Tang Shubei, 258
Telecommunications: PRC, 5
Internet use and, 65–66, 281, 291
satellites and, 264, 282
telephone service, 64*t*, 65
Television: PRC
drama and, 114–124
Beijinger in New York and, 124
Central China Television (CCTV) and, 114–115
Have a High, Then Die, 124
local programming and, 115
No Choice in Loving You, 123–124
The Story of an Editorial Office and, 122–123
Yearning and, 116–122
news and, 124–125
popularity increase of, 114
Television: Taiwan, 207
Thatcher, Margaret, 151, 161
Three Gorges Dam project (PRC), 67, 263, 276, 287, 290, 309
Tian Beijun, 185–186
Tian Zhuangzhuang, 144, 147
Tiananmen Square demonstrations, 1, 14, 309
as counterrevolutionary rebellion, 256
dissident arrests and, 15
foreign capital after, 73
Hong Kong and, 156–161
music after, 133–134
public opinion regarding, 17–18
rural self-government after, 45
U.S. relations after, 224–225
Zhao Ziyang on, 256, 311
Tibet, PRC and, 260, 287, 292, 309
Tien, James, 185–186
Today (PRC), 136
Township and village enterprises (TVEs), 101, 309
Trade: PRC
currency exchange rates and, 71–72
export figures and, 51, 52*t*
Export and Import Bank and, 70
human rights/MFN issue and, 15, 35, 230–234, 232*n.13*, 250, 253, 255, 256, 259, 265, 270, 273, 287, 288, 303–304
liberalization plan of, 75
prison factories and, 250, 286
tarrifs reduction and, 277

Trade: PRC *(continued)*
third country trade and, 294
with U.S. deficit, 75–76, 289, 290
U.S. wheat sales and, 265, 280
volume increase and, 74–75, 76*f*
WTO membership and, 71, 74–75, 234, 237, 263, 267, 277, 310
Trade: Taiwan
1952–1989 figures on, 196, 198, 199*t*
1990s figures on, 202*t*
economy growth and, 234
GATT membership and, 260
PRC/U.S. triangular trade with, 205–206
U.S. surplus and, 201
Transportation: PRC
auto production and, 64
fare increases and, 279
foreign loans and, 73
rail traffic units and, 63, 64*t*
update of, 5, 63–64
Tsang Yok-sing, 179
Tu, Elsie Elliott, 179–180
TVEs (township and village enterprises), 101, 307

UDHK (United Democrats of Hong Kong), 162, 163
UN Commission on Human Rights, 233, 266, 267, 285
UNICEF, 280
United Democrats of Hong Kong (UDHK), 162–163
United Nations
Commission on Human Rights, 233, 266, 267, 285
Fourth World Conference on Women of, 79, 233, 269, 270, 273, 274, 275
Population Fund of, 270
PRC membership in, 200
Taiwan membership in, 200, 218–220, 271, 275, 291
Universal Declaration of Human Rights of, 230
Year of Tolerance of, 268
United States: PRC and
conclusions regarding, 246–247
economic relations between
export-led growth and, 234
intellectual property rights and, 234, 236–237, 254, 257, 258, 263, 264, 265, 266, 277, 286, 288
mutual importance of, 234–235
PRC tariff reductions and, 277
textile issue and, 249, 250, 303
third country shipping and, 294
Three Gorges Dam project and, 67, 263, 276
trade negotiation scenario and, 235–236
trade surplus and, 75–76, 234–235, 289, 290
U.S. grain consumption, 55
wheat sales and, 265, 280
WTO membership and, 71, 74–75, 234, 263, 267, 277, 310
issues between, 223
political relations between Clinton administration and, 226–228, 228*n.8*
human rights, MFN issue and, 15, 35, 76–77, 229–234, 232*n.13*, 250, 251, 253, 255, 256, 259, 265, 266, 270, 273, 283, 287, 288, 303–304
improvement signs of, 225, 267, 274, 280
media coverage of, 228–229, 228*n.8*
official recognition of, 200
Tiananmen incident and, 224–225, 267
Radio Free Asia and, 251, 255
security affairs between, history of, 223, 246
arms sales issue and, 238, 239
nuclear weapons issue and, 239
PRC military buildup issue and, 238, 239
Shanghai Communiqué and, 224, 305
South China Seas presence and, 238, 239
Soviet threat and, 224
Taiwan issue and, 238, 239–241, 272, 308
U.S.-Republic of China Mutual Security Treaty and, 240
security affairs between, new relationship, 246–247
arms sales issue and, 261, 271, 272, 273, 276, 281, 282, 286, 288, 291
conditional engagement concept and, 244–246
global interdependence concept and, 242–243
Lee Teng-hui visit and, 13*n.2*, 195, 221, 239–240, 244, 270, 271, 273
military attaché recall and, 280
military officers exchange and, 277
nuclear weapons issue and, 252, 261, 266, 268, 274, 276, 277, 290
objective contradictions and, 243
PRC challenge of U.S. and, 242

PRC military buildup issue and, 257, 258, 265, 268, 293
security dialogue necessity and, 243–244
South China Seas presence and, 257, 258, 265, 268
Taiwan Straits Crises and, 308
U.S. spying accusations and, 274
United States: Taiwan and
arms sales and, 255, 271, 272, 273, 284, 290
diplomatic relations with, 216, 272, 279, 290
GATT membership and, 260
Lee Teng-hui visit to, 13*n.2*, 195, 221, 239–240, 244, 269, 270, 273
PRC recognition and, 200
PRC triangular trade with, 205–206
Taiwan Relations Act and, 200, 240–241
Universal Declaration of Human Rights (United Nations), 230
Urban neighborhood committees (PRC), 309–310
U.S.-Republic of China Mutual Security Treaty, 240
USS *Bunker Hill*, 267
USS *Fort McHenry*, 280

Vietnam
communism in, 36
PRC diplomatic relations with, 278
PRC military buildup and, 239
Radio Free Asia and, 255
South China Sea oil and, 257, 258
Voice of America radio, 256

Wan Li, 38, 310
Wang Baosen, 13, 268, 272
Wang Dan, 253, 259, 263, 266, 292, 293
Wang Juntao, 254
Wang Li, 293
Wang Meng, 44, 130
Wang Mengkui, 269
Wang Shuo
literature of, 138–140
television series and, 117, 122, 123, 124
Wang Xiaoshuai, 147
Wang Xizhe, 292
Wei Jianxing, 268
Wei Jingsheng, 15, 233, 252, 253, 254, 277, 278, 293, 310
Wen Wei Po (Hong Kong), 170, 170*n.19*, 172
WHB (*Wen Wei Po*, Hong Kong), 170, 170*n.19*, 172
White Night (PRC), 142
Who Will Feed China? Wake-Up Call for a Small Planet (Brown), 55
Wilson, David, 158, 163
Women
Forum of Nongovernmental Organizations on Women (PRC) and, 269, 270, 275
missing girls phenomenon and, 5, 90*t*, 95–96
PRC family planning and, 6, 90*t*, 93–97, 262, 265, 267, 270
See also Gender equality
World Bank, 278
World Conference on Women (United Nations), 79, 233, 269, 270, 273, 274, 275
World Economic Herald (PRC), 126–127
World Trade Organization (WTO)
PRC membership in, 71, 74–75, 234, 263, 267, 277, 310
synopsis of, 310
World Watch, 55
WTO. *See* World Trade Organization (WTO)
Wu, Anna, 184–185
Wu Bangguo
CCP Secretariat appointment of, 16, 260
as vice-premier, 17, 267
Wu De, 278
Wu, Harry, 232–233, 271, 272, 273, 274, 278
Wu Mengchen, 149
Wu Wenguang, 147
Wuhan University (PRC), 43

Xiao Bin, 252
Xiao Rong, 264
Xichang Satellite Launch Center, 264, 282
Xinhua News Agency, 277, 282, 285, 287, 293, 310
Xu Liangying, 253
Xu Wenli, 266

Ye Daying, 148
Yan'an, Shaanxi Province, 311
Yang Lang, 128
Yao Wenyuan, 292
Yao Yilin, 263, 311
Ye Zhaoyan, 142
Yearning (PRC)
controversy over, 121–122
funding for, 116
political transition and, 121–122
popularity of, 109, 119–120

Yellow Earth, The (Chen Kaige, PRC), 143
Yeltsin, Boris, 260, 285
Yuan Mu, 269

Zeng Yucheng, 179
Zhang Chu, 134
Zhang Junzhao, 143
Zhang Lin, 256
Zhang Siqing, 254
Zhang Wannian, 16, 276
Zhang Weiguo, 43
Zhang Wenjin, 227
Zhang Wenlong, 249
Zhang Yimou, 143, 144, 146, 148, 276
Zhang Yiwu, 141
Zhang Yuan, 147
Zhang Zhen, 16
Zhang Zuomin, 128–129, 130
Zhao Ziyang, 256, 302, 311
Zheng Wanlong, 117–118
Zheng Xiaolong, 117–118
Zhou Beifang, 13, 265, 294
Zhou Guanwu, 13, 265
Zhou Nan, 191
Zhu Rongji, 17, 311
Zhuang Zhidie, 140
Ziao Shi, 16